After Postcolonialism

Pacific Formations
Series Editor: Arif Dirlik

What Is in a Rim? Critical Perspectives on the Pacific Region Idea, 2nd edition
edited by Arif Dirlik
Inside Out: Literature, Cultural Politics, and Identity in the New Pacific
edited by Vilsoni Hereniko and Rob Wilson
Teaching Asian America: Diversity and the Problem of Community
edited by Lane Ryo Hirabayashi
Encounters: People of Asian Descent in the Americas
edited by Roshni Rustomji-Kerns with Rajni Srikanth and Leny Mendoza
Strobel
Displacing Natives: The Rhetorical Production of Hawai'i
by Houston Wood
After Postcolonialism: Remapping Philippines–United States Confrontations
E. San Juan, Jr.

Forthcoming Titles

Pacific Rim becomes Borderless
by Xiangming Chen
Chinese on the American Frontier
edited by Arif Dirlik with the assistance of Malcolm Yeung
Voyaging through the Contemporary Pacific
edited by David L. Hanlon and Geoffrey M. White
Diversifying the State: American Grassroots Groups and Japanese Companies
by Tomoji Ishi

After Postcolonialism

Remapping Philippines–United States Confrontations

E. San Juan, Jr.

ROWMAN & LITTLEFIELD PUBLISHERS, INC.
Lanham • Boulder • New York • Oxford

ROWMAN & LITTLEFIELD PUBLISHERS, INC.

Published in the United States of America
by Rowman & Littlefield Publishers, Inc.
4720 Boston Way, Lanham, Maryland 20706
http://www.rowmanlittlefield.com

12 Hid's Copse Road, Cumnor Hill, Oxford OX2 9JJ, England

British Library Cataloguing in Publication Information Available

Library of Congress Cataloging-in-Publication Data

San Juan, E. (Epifanio), 1938–
    After postcolonialism : remapping Philippines–United States confrontations / E. San
Juan, Jr.
        p. cm.
    Includes bibliographical references (p.) and index.
    ISBN 0-8476-9860-2 (alk. paper)—ISBN 0-8476-9861-0 (pbk. : alk. paper)
        1. Filipino Americans—Ethnic identity.   2. Filipino Americans—Cultural
assimilation.   3. Asian Americans—Ethnic identity.   4. Asian Americans—Cultural
assimilation.   5. Imperialism—Social aspects—United States.   6. Postcolonialism—
United States.   7. United States—Race relations.   8. United States—Relations—
Philippines.   9. Philippines—Relations—United States.   10. American fiction—
Asian American authors.   I. Title.
E184.F4 S258 2000
305.89'921073—dc21   00-027847

Printed in the United States of America

♾ ™ The paper used in this publication meets the minimum requirements of American
National Standard for Information Sciences—Permanence of Paper for Printed Library
Materials, ANSI/NISO Z39.48-1992.

For Esther Pacheco, Karina Bolasco, and Eileen Tabios

If the Americans had never committed genocide against the Indians; if they had never incited wars of annihilation between the native peoples of the land, if there had never been a Trail of Tears; if America had never organized and commercialized the kidnapping and sale into slavery of a gentle and defenseless African people; if it had never developed the most widespread brutal, exploitative system of slavery the world has ever known; if it had never sundered and torn and ground Mexico into the dust; if it had never attacked gallant, defenseless Puerto Rico and never turned that lovely land into a cesspool to compete with the cesspool it created in Panama; if it had never bled Latin America of her wealth and had never cast her exhausted people onto the dung heap of disease and ignorance and starvation; if it had never pushed Hiroshima and Nagasaki into the jaws of hell—if America had never done any of these things— history would still create a special bar of judgment for what America did to the Philippines.

—Nelson Peery, *Black Fire*

Contents

Acknowledgments   xi

Introduction   1

1. Symbolic Trajectories of the Asian Diaspora   17

2. Historicizing the Space of Asian America   43

3. Specters of United States Imperialism   65

4. From Neocolonial Representations to National-Democratic Allegory   97

5. Displacing Borders of Misrecognition: On Jessica Hagedorn's
   Fictions   121

6. Kidlat Tahimik's Cinema of the Naïve Subaltern   143

7. Prospects and Problems of Revolutionary Transformation   163

Afterword   191

Appendix: Writing and the Asian Diaspora   213

References   223

Index   247

About the Author   253

Acknowledgments

A lthough mediated by a single author, any artifact of this kind is always the product of collaboration, alliances, and reciprocities.

Foremost among my collaborators is Delia D. Aguilar, my sharpest critic and constant adviser, who has long explored the terrain of national-liberation struggle with sensitivity and depth. My primary debt for nurturing this particular work is to Arif Dirlik (Duke University), a brilliant critic/historian of the Chinese revolution and postcolonial theory, and Sam Noumoff (McGill University), indomitable partisan of popular-democratic causes. To Eric A. San Juan and Karin Aguilar-San Juan, I owe eternal gratitude for their sagacity, good humor, and forbearance.

My intellectual debts are owed to many, and here I can only cite the following comrades who gave solidarity and generous assistance along the way: Alan Wald, Norman and Nancy Chance, Paul Wong, Evelyn Hu-DeHart, Robert Dombroski, Michael Martin, M. Keith Booker, Bruce Franklin, Donald Pease, James Bennett, Patrick Colm Hogan, Karen Gould, and my good friends here at Washington State University (WSU), among them Nelly and Cesar Zamora, Alex Tan, and all my colleagues in the Department of Comparative American Cultures. I am deeply grateful to Dean Barbara Conture of the College of Liberal Arts for her generous support. On the other shore, I want to thank the following for their sympathy and collaboration: Elmer and Nory Aguilar, Joseph Lim, Elmer and Elenita Ordoñez, Francisco and Ana Maria Nemenzo, Fe and Roger Mangahas, Roland Simbulan, Judy Taguiwalo, Cynthia Rivera, Bienvenido and Shayne Lumbera, Soledad Reyes, Lulu Torres, and Tomas Talledo. I also wish to thank my colleagues at the journals *Das Argument, Nature, Society and Thought, Weg und Ziel, Against the Current, Dialogue and Initiative,* and *Amerasia Journal* and at the Institute for Critical Research, Amsterdam.

After Postcolonialism

Introduction

As we cross the threshold of the twenty-first century, citizens of a nascent global ecumene might find lessons for what future risk-taking may bring from the centennial of three events that have linked in various ways the hemispheres of Asia and North America. We are still living in and through the impact of these nearly forgotten upheavals: the 1896 revolution of the Filipino masses against Spanish colonialism, the first of its kind in the "Far East"; the outbreak of the Spanish-American War in 1898 and the emergence of the United States as a global power with its domination of the Philippines, Cuba, Puerto Rico, Guam, and Hawaii; and the Filipino-American War (1899–1902), one of the most destructive attempts to suppress a popular struggle for national self-determination in the annals of world history. Not the victors but the victims celebrated these events with a prophetic, not nostalgic, vision; to cite one occasion, in Havana, Cuba, the Casa de las Americas organized an international forum exploring the resonance and instructive timeliness of "1898."

Meanwhile, in the Philippines, the official festivity began with the commemoration of the 1896 "cry of Balintawak" against Spanish tyranny and ended with the celebration of the founding of the first Philippine Republic in June 1898. Despite its broad grassroots support, the republic was short-lived. On 4 February 1899, the United States began a "scorched earth" campaign of destroying the Filipino revolutionary forces who were alleged to have started a "guerrilla uprising" (Famighetti 1995, 811). The U.S. military conducted a counterrevolutionary strategy of pacification climaxing in the annexation of the islands and the century-long subjugation of communities whose resistance and acts of sedition here in the metropole as well as in the neocolonial territory have persisted to this day (Francisco 1976; Ordoñez 1998).

Over half a century of U.S. colonial rule has transformed the Philippines into an American outpost, a neocolonial appendage detached from the wider Asian-

1

Pacific geopolitical arena. Although still characterized (by the Communist Party of the Philippines, for instance) as a "semifeudal and semicolonial" society, the country never had a hydraulic centralized authority that Marx and Engels considered "the foundation of Oriental despotism" (1959, 480), evinced by the stationary kingdoms of ancient China, India, and portions of the Middle East. Occupied by Spain for 400 years and for over 50 years by the United States, the Philippines witnessed a kaleidoscopic colloquy and interpellation of diverse cultures—Christianity confronted Islam, Confucianism, Buddhism, and pagan animism. Registering this confluence of incompatible and often colliding cultures, the evolving Filipino worldview, or *habitus,* has been interpreted as a hybrid, syncretic, and variegated creation from the perspective of recent postcolonial theory. Essentialist thinking, however, still conceives of the Filipino national character as distinguished by fixed traits defined by family and kinship condensed in behavioral patterns conceptualized in terms of *hiya, pakikisama, amor propio,* and so on (Friend 1965). Both accounts expunge the stigmata of colonial inscriptions and mystify the object/subject of critical inquiry.

In historical reckoning, however, Filipino society is a historical-political construction. It is a product of mercantile capitalism that happened to be inserted into the Spanish Empire in the sixteenth century and later into the domain of imperialism, a phase of finance or monopoly capitalism. Whatever was archaic or premodern became subsumed in the hierarchized totality of a peripheral formation. This latter insertion into U.S. hegemonic space converted the Philippines—already conceived as a strategic springboard for U.S. penetration of the China market—into a supplier of cheap labor power for the Hawaiian sugar plantations and the industrializing West Coast of the U.S. mainland. To accentuate this mutation as part of a larger historical phenomenon involving the diaspora of Chinese, Japanese, and Korean workers, I analyze in chapters 1 and 2 the commonality of predicaments shared by Filipinos with other Asians, a nexus of dilemmas articulated by the immigration *problematique.*

The historical trajectories of Asians and Pacific Islanders diverge and converge according to the law of motion of uneven and combined development in a commodifying world system (Löwy 1981; Wallerstein 1983). Despite these affinities, the Filipinos continue to preserve their concrete and intractable singularity, as attested to by a recent incident reported in the *Los Angeles Times* (13 July 1998): "When [John] Concordia [a high school student in California] jotted 'American' in the ethnicity box of a school emergency notification card, a counselor corrected him: " 'No, you're Filipino.' "

We should not forget the larger context of the "Pacific Idea" in which the Philippines has been inscribed by outsiders from Magellan to Admiral George Dewey and General Douglas MacArthur. Arif Dirlik has perspicaciously delineated the contradictory impulses generated by the region: the Pacific as virgin frontier for capitalist exploitation, and the Pacific as an escape from its ravages. Although the Philippines has served as a frontier for the possessive "errand into the wilderness," it now serves (like its more prosperous neighbors) to "revitalize a teleology of capitalist modernity" (Dirlik 1997, 138) at the heart of Pacific Rim discourse. A prototype of this discourse, Manifest Destiny and its guns, transported the Filipinos to the plantation factories of Hawaii and the West Coast, converting the outside into part of the inside.

A native "national" in the metropolis of the United States, but where is the locus of absence, the original habitat of his parents and grandparents? While the hegemonic "civilizing" discourse homogenized and at the same time segregated Chinese, Japanese, and Koreans, it appears that the Filipino has proved recalcitrant to such Orientalist seduction. During the violent pacification of the islands (whose repercussions I diagnose in chapter 3), U.S. invading troops stigmatized the natives as "niggers" or savages. In California and Washington in the 1930s, the vigilante attacks against Filipino workers singled them out for their menacing sexual charisma and enigmatic primitiveness. As Carlos Bulosan once summed it up, the Filipino was a dark fugitive "criminal" in America (San Juan 1998b). Unlike Chinatown, the "internal colonialism" of farm barracks where Filipinos sojourned replicated in more compressed form the actual geopolitical subjugation of the homeland. Within this framework, I chart the ethical and political vicissitudes of the Filipino odyssey in chapters 4 and 5 in the context of the U.S. machinery of knowledge-production and their myriad consequences.

Over two million Filipinos have settled in this country since the granting of Philippine independence in 1946. Although born and raised in the United States, Filipino Americans continue to be fatefully identified with their geographic origin. They are neither Americans nor Asians, but, rather, uniquely "Filipino" in one sense or another. The term "Filipino" is itself a problematic name, a question-begging tag. Whom does it really designate? The colonized "ward" from "las islas Filipinas" occupies a space between the indigenous Indian and the "inscrutable Oriental." If an alien "national," where is this nationality inscribed, in what larger metanarrative of dispossession, internment and relocation?

A historical-materialist, cognitive remapping is in order. Appraising the situation of "Asians on the Rim," Dirlik (1996) acutely poses the contradictions between the globalizing spaces of transnational capital and the local spaces of Asian American communities, contradictions that determine the identity of Asian Americans as either a new Orientalist reification or a radical panethnic force of social change. In contrast to other Asian communities whose homelands (Japan, Taiwan, Hong Kong, and South Korea) have now become key players in the global economy, the trajectory of Filipino resettlement is closely articulated with the "refeudalization" of the Philippines—about seven million Filipino overseas contract workers (OCWs) constitute the bulk of cheap domestic help around the world (Catholic Institute 1987; Beltran and de Dios 1992)—and its incipient and ongoing mass revolts. The memory of the Filipino community today gravitates no longer around the strikes of "Manongs" in the Hawaiian plantations (celebrated in Kiana Davenport's memorable *Shark Dialogues*) but around the February 1986 insurrection, the catastrophe inflicted by Mt. Pinatubo's eruption on rural folk (as well as on U.S. military bases), the violence suffered by domestics like Flor Contemplacion and Sarah Balabagan, and the collective struggle of millions of peasants and workers against the unrelenting impoverishment inflicted by global capital. Neither self-illumined by its Pacific or Asian origin, the Filipino diaspora thus unsettles the ethnic utopian conception of the Pacific Century (celebrated by McCord [1991] and others) and its assimilationist/cooptative politics of identity by returning us to the historical matrix of its bloody inception, its intensifying crisis, and possible resolution.

The intervention of the United States in Philippine affairs since the turn of the twentieth century has been the subject of voluminous scholarly research (Labor Research Association 1958). Because of alleged "special relations" between the two countries, in particular the sacrifices of millions of Filipinos to defend the Philippine Commonwealth as a U.S. possession against Japanese aggression (1942–1945), the role of its only Southeast Asian colony in shaping U.S. attitudes to the "Other" has been obscured. Except for the "February 1986" uprising against the U.S.-subsidized Marcos regime and the furor over the military bases, the Philippines has always been ignored by decision makers in government and business. Certainly Japan and China (recently eclipsed by the nuclear-capable states India and Pakistan) are the two polities today whose power and influence exceeds those of any Asian nation-state, hence the marginal and subaltern status of Philippine area studies.

Revisionist historians have suggested that the predicament of the "institutional invisibility" of Philippine studies is a result of the absence of any serious discussion of imperial American "exceptionalism" in the academy. Everyone knows that American scholars of Philippine affairs occupy a marginal or subordinate slot as a function of the low geopolitical status of the Philippines in the U.S. global profit-making horizon, a status fixed earlier by the successful hegemonic scheme of "Filipinization." This astute cooptative scheme implemented by William Howard Taft, first civil governor of the colony, may indeed be taken as the originary inspiration for the current vogue of holding the victims responsible for their plight; the most recent example is Glenn Anthony May's debunking of the Filipino "mythmakers" responsible for the cult of the Filipino revolutionary hero Andres Bonifacio in his book *Inventing a Hero* (1996). However, I do not think that this minor status of American Filipinologists involves simply the question of representation, whether political, semiotic, or ethnographic. I believe that the structural cause has something to do with this persistent failure to critique the process of U.S. hegemonic rule in the Philippines celebrated by Karnow, Fred Eggan (1991), and others because of the nature of their training and the apologetic mission of the discipline. This is compounded with the usual compensatory reward in the ascribed status of the metropolitan expert gaining mastery over "others," a normative reflex that is so integral a part of Western racist hegemony.

After the Civil War and the "taming of the Wild West," the U.S. hegemonic bloc had to wrestle with the new intrusive "Others"—mainly Chinese migrant workers—via immigration laws and extralegal violence. But it was in the Philippines that crucial U.S. imperial policy initiatives, as well as the entrepreneurial ethos of its relations with Asia, were first tried out and instituted. President Mc-Kinley's "Benevolent Assimilation" doctrine followed in the tracks of the "Open Door" policy on China, a move that confirms William Appleman Williams's argument that "the debate about Cuba and the Philippines was an argument over whether or not to adopt the pattern of imperialism developed by Britain after the Indian mutiny of 1857; and if that system were not followed, what kind of an American program of expansion was to be substituted" (1969, 77–78). The program administered in the Philippines pursued an elaborate ideological and cultural platform, with their requisite state apparatuses of surveillance, coercion, and carceral quarantine (Rafael 1993). The ordinary Filipino worship of everything American today (emblematized by the pattern of immigration, mail-order bride business, media testimonies, and other manifestations of the proverbial "colonial mentality") demonstrates the unqualified success of the program. This is the background against which I conduct my critique of both modernist U.S. critical discourse and eclectic postcolonial dogmatism whose local agents have made insidious demoralizing inroads in the petite-bourgeois mentality of the milieu.

One might mention one fact not generally appreciated by academics and whose aesthetic ramifications I investigate here and elsewhere (San Juan 1996b, 1998b): The universal crusade against communism, the containment policy mounted against China marked by the Korean War and the Vietnam War, had one of its first successful laboratories in the CIA-directed campaign against the peasant uprising of the Huks in the late 1940s and early 1950s (Smith 1976; Abaya 1984). This counterinsurgency scheme can be traced back to the "reconcentration," or hamleting, of Filipino villages during the Filipino-American War and the periodic campaigns against peasant guerrillas that characterized U.S. colonial rule from 1900 to the granting of formal independence in 1946. Its contemporary reincarnation is the "low-intensity war" (formerly known as "civic action") against the New People's Army and all progressive, nationalist sectors seeking the overthrow of the iniquitous status quo (Klare and Kornbluh 1989; for Cold War ideology, see Patterson 1997).

Despite its long and durable revolutionary tradition, the Philippines has always been an odd protagonist in the Asian Pacific drama of decolonization. Even after independence, it never occupied center-stage in scholarly and public debate in the United States as China or Japan or even gained the status of Korea, Vietnam, or Indonesia in the eyes of the business and bureaucratic elite. Scholars concentrating on the Philippines were treated as minor subaltern functionaries. The reason can be accounted for by the myth of "special relations," a trope of putative reciprocal ties and friendship between two "races" and cultures. An entire industry producing safe, acceptable knowledge of the Philippines and the

Filipino arose that was designed to keep alive, elaborate, and reinforce this myth. Chiefly for this reason, according to the experts, one cannot speak of U.S. imperialism or neocolonial hegemony.

We can demonstrate the real "underside of the collaborative empire," especially the CIA handling of the Filipino elite, by excerpts from Joseph Smith's *Portrait of a Cold Warrior* (1976). One can even venture the scandalous proposition that this book, originally written for popular consumption, affords us a survey of the character of the Filipino comprador oligarchy and its elite representatives that is more textured and cogent than tomes of statistical analysis turned out by RAND experts and researchers for congressional committees and the U.S. State Department. Even the enemy can be granted to possess a degree of realism sufficient to manipulate players that would produce results. Their realism is of course the pragmatic calculation of those in power, those determined to preserve the status quo. On the other hand, those resolved to alter that situation—one deemed unjust, painful, and inhumane by the standards of the world's conscience—would have more reason to be clear-eyed, sensitive, and cognizant of as many factors and forces in play as possible, and on guard lest illusions of success or utopia waylay them. That of course is not always the case. Nonetheless, the views of Filipino protagonists cannot be dismissed as unreliable simply because they are partisan, nationalist or egalitarian. After all, what study of social phenomena does not proceed from a certain framework of interests or set of informing assumptions?

This whole book—part of a larger project that would include a history of the socialist movement in the Philippines—attempts to anatomize this complex field of interaction between the colonizing power and its victims. It will try to elucidate the complicated transactions between Filipino civil society, American ideological state apparatuses, and the associated culture/consciousness industry. The apologists of contemporary scholarship on the Philippines (Friend, Steinberg, Stanley, May, and their numerous vulgarizers, such as Karnow) have dominated this field so far (see, e.g., Bresnan 1986), challenged only by the sporadic writings of Benedict Anderson, William Pomeroy, Jonathan Fast, and Filipino commentaries inspired by Teodoro Agoncillo (1974), Renato Constantino (1978), and Jose Maria Sison (1986; J. de Lima, 1998), among others.

In a provocative essay on U.S. interventions in the "Third World," Eqbal Ahmad (1982) underscores the tradition of bargaining, cooptation, or management in U.S. political culture for those located within the boundary of the liberal marketplace. For those defined outside this boundary (American Indians, blacks, and ethnic Others), violence and extermination are the chosen modes of maintaining the consensus. Within this authoritarian superstructure exists "a well-defined but extremely permissive infrastructure." Displaced onto a global arena, the practice of technocratic-managerial discourse (as exemplified in the archive of interventionist texts that I inventory here) underwrites the way in which American experts on the Philippines have sought to reconcile the everyday violence suffered by impoverished peasants and workers with the accumulation strategy of transnational business. Robert Stauffer (1990) has already described the reality of democracy in the Philippines as "that form of intra-elite competition for office via elections during the colonial era, and under conditions where elected officials were given a great deal of symbolic public space but were denied real power which remained firmly anchored in U.S. hands" (36).

With the rise of poststructuralist critiques of Establishment discourse now so thoroughly exposed by Noam Chomsky, Michael Parenti, Herbert Schiller, and others, the diagnosis of a "damaged culture" (popularized by James Fallows in the *Atlantic Monthly,* November 1987) based on racialized and culturalist paradigms is no longer tenable. A new school of experts addressing the "legitimation crisis" by way of reviving neo-Weberian concepts of patrimonialism, a neo-Hegelian notion of "civil society," and even a version of Marx's "Asiatic despotism" (inflected by a generation of area studies specialists for Cold War purposes) seems to be in the ascendant. But their limitations, like those of their predecessors, vitiate their sham novelty and tawdry sophistication.

One of the signal limitations of the orthodox knowledge industry is its blindness to the problems of racism and sexism, corollaries to imperial subjugation (Doty 1996). This blindness stems in part from a functionalist empiricism that takes private property, the market, and prevailing inequalities for granted. Institutions and socially constructed practices become naturalized and legitimized as the inevitable fulfillment of "Manifest Destiny," "civilizing mission," and other kindred rationalizations. This is less a symptom of Eurocentric universalism than a cynical if disingenuous reactionary stance to the challenge of socialism and other emancipatory popular movements. A classic example is David Steinberg's *The Philippines: A Singular and a Plural Place* (1982). This influential textbook propagates the idea, among others, that on present evidence Filipinos will not "surrender the individual work ethic and dream of capitalist prosperity that suffuses the society from top to bottom" (126). This neo-Weberian approach, while made plausible by references to selected circumstances and personages, still draws inspiration from the ethnocentric patronage found in earlier studies by James LeRoy (for latter-day hero-worship, see Gonzalez 1992) and other commissioned researchers. Analytically scrutinized, the epistemology and folklore of "special relations" purveyed by such academic experts turn out to be a case of individual transactions between a selected coterie of the Filipino elite and successive Washington administrations. Notably absent is the kind of insight offered by Howard Zinn (1984), for example, when he summarizes the African American response to the Filipino resistance in 1899 and foregrounds the acts of solidarity of David Fagan and other black soldiers. As for the silence on sexism, one need only cite the institutionalization of the Victorian ideology of female domesticity throughout the American colonial period to understand how this agenda rationalized the past and present subordination of women to the patriarchal commodifying dispensation (Aguilar 1988).

Introduction

With the intensification of a radical ecological consciousness in the last two decades, attention is now being given to the plight of tribal or indigenous minorities (see this book's afterword). In the past, the most brutal police action was directed toward the Moros by the early American civil governors. During the Marcos period, the Moro National Liberation Front (now incorporated into the clientelist system) waged a war of defense amid the slaughter of close to half a million inhabitants in the Mindanao and Sulu Islands (Gurr 1993). Second to the Moros (nearly six million out of seventy million Filipinos), about four million tribal peoples (Igorots, Lumads, and others) today suffer from schemes of development sanctioned by the International Monetary Fund (IMF) and the World Bank: destruction of their homes and social reproductive means by corporate mines, dams, and agribusiness (Bodley 1990). It is not possible to comprehend the sheer brutalization of these non-Christian communities without invoking a theory of racial inferiorization consonant with the dynamics of a dependent political economy that reproduces subalternity across class, gender, and ethnicity. I allude to salient facets of a neocolonial social formation in my inquiry into the modalities of cultural/literary politics and production in chapters 4 to 6.

With the collapse of the Soviet Union, the entrenchment of "state capitalism" in China, and the abandonment of the military bases in 1992, U.S. hegemonic strategy toward the Philippines—now a "weak link" between Asia and North America—is being retooled and reconstituted. The danger of communism has been replaced by the menace of popular sovereignty and the radical democratization of the public sphere (Fraser 1997). Nonetheless, the New People's Army, perhaps the only viable Communist-led insurgency throughout the planet today, is perceived to be the source of both perils (Chapman 1987). Richard Falk (1993) observes that this history has not ended for Asia or the Pacific Basin region, where most of the real fighting during the Cold War occurred: "the ideological fault-lines of the Cold War have yet to disappear in Asia . . . the Philippines continues to experience a major internal revolutionary struggle that is perceived through a Cold War optic of communism versus 'authoritarian liberalism' " (377). The Japanese activist intellectual Muto Ichiyo regards the national-democratic struggle in the Philippines as an instance of a necessary stage toward the achievement of "transborder participatory democracy" (157). Contrary to the claims of futurologists such as Alvin Toffler (1990) and his ilk, the triumph over Marcos and his generals was not the result of media/television manipulation by symbolic analysts and information technocrats. Rather, it was the fruit of years of counterhegemonic mass organizing, education, and daily acts of resistance against fascist terror, with thousands of heroic individuals sacrificing for the collective effort to redeem the nation (Davis 1989). In chapter 7 and the afterword (which rehearses key themes of my earlier, 1986 work *Crisis in the Philippines*), I sketch how this nation, which is striving to realize a multicultural and egalitarian ideal, is still in the process of being redefined and transformed by participants in both the Philippines and the United States and in the diaspora worldwide.

As everywhere else, the metamorphosis of the sociopolitical conjuncture in the Philippines is overdetermined, volatile, and highly contingent on the fierce class wars and other sectoral antagonisms sweeping the North, in particular the United States. While vestiges of the Marcos dictatorship and its autocratic institutions still litter the landscape, elite democracy—what I would call comprador or tributary neocolonialism (Amin 1994)—has been revived by Corazon Aquino and Fidel Ramos. Its fascist degeneration is now transpiring in the Estrada regime. Given the deterioration of the economy (artificially sustained by the huge volume of remittances by OCWs) and the living standards of the majority, the assumption of power by flunkeys and politicians of the Marcos entourage is bound to intensify the temporarily residual authoritarian trends and exacerbate all the contradictions destabilizing the present Bonapartist, elite populist dispensation (Instituto del Tercer Mundo 1999). The recent approval of the Visiting Forces Agreement, the censorship of mainstream mass media, and the impending revision of the 1987 Constitution, to cite only the most flagrant symptoms of the crisis afflicting the neocolonial order, all attest to the bankruptcy of the comprador ruling class and the imperative for a fundamental transformation of an unjust and historically obsolete system.

Structurally, nothing much has changed after the demise of Marcos (BAYAN 1998; Karapatan 1997). The traditional oligarchy rooted in agrarian property relations continues to collaborate with the comprador and bureaucratic elite to preserve and aggravate the inequality of power and wealth inherited from decades of corruption and patronage (McCoy 1991; Center for Women's Resources 1996). Previously indulged by the Marcos regime, the Philippine military has entrenched itself in the bureaucracy, thanks to Presidents Ramos's and now Estrada's sponsorship and U.S. complicity. Meanwhile, transnational corporations (primarily Japanese and American), with the help of the World Bank and the IMF, continue to exercise an inordinate force in shaping the domestic and foreign policies of the Philippine government through cutbacks in social services, privatization, "free trade zones," and other privileges given to investors from the North. To disguise or compensate for the neo–Social Darwinist effects of IMF conditionalities (for debt peonage, see Hoogvelt 1987), a species of neoliberal "multiculturalism" is now being deployed to refurbish the worn-out ideals of Joseph Hayden and George Taylor and enable the ruling oligarchy to cope with altered realities. This can be observed in various postmodernist cultural practices, though I think that the indigenous national-popular tradition (surveyed in chapters 4 and 5) continues to show signs of renewed vitality and relevance, especially in the cinema of Kidlat Tahimik and the oppositional repertoire as well as performance styles of regional theater groups. As long as there is oppression, there is also resistance—the adage acquires fresh life in this interregnum between the *ancien régime* and the one still convulsed and smoldering in its womb.

There are, however, new phenomena that demand further investigation. Aside from the recycling of development schemes hatched in the 1960s—export production and foreign investments are the twin slogans of peripheral capitalism (Boyce 1993)—we have regional conduits of global transnationals, such as the Asian Pacific Economic Conference (APEC) and also the proliferation of opportunistic nongovernmental organizations (NGOs). The latter is designed to coopt energies being channeled to support for the armed underground resistance (e.g., the New People's Army and the Islamic Liberation Front) and other dissident challenges to the system. With the refurbishing of the terror of the "national security state" so endemic in the Third World in the 1970s and 1980s, ideologues of free-enterprise liberalism have resurrected a quasi-Hegelian version of "civil society" made palatable by quotations from Gramsci and leaders of the "new social movements" (for a critique, see Turner 1994). One example is Isagani Serrano's *Civil Society in the Asia-Pacific Region* (1994), in which class struggle, property relations, inequality of wealth—in short, the categories of domination and subordination—are all erased in favor of putative "shared values and commitment," "voluntary action," and so on. Philanthropic metaphysics replaces the old realism of Hobbes, Locke, and Adam Smith. Democracy as merely procedural becomes fetishized, obfuscating its class content and the material specificities of oppression constituted by the rigid hierarchies of class, gender, "race," locality, and so on.

Notwithstanding all talk about democracy and sovereignty, the apotheosis of civil society by NGO evangelists ignores the basic fact of uneven development in the capitalist world system (Hymer 1972). Ironically, the idealism of the cult of civil-society coincides with the populist dogmatism of romantic nativists who glorify everything indigenous, traditional, and archaic. Tom Nairn (1982) warns against the danger of locating the individualist passion, the desire for organic wholeness and identity, in *volkish* or some such metaphysical origins: "the most notoriously subjective and ideal of historical phenomena is in fact a by-product of the most brutally and hopelessly material side of the history of the last two centuries" (432). Hence, the highly touted Marcos revival of the institution of the *barangay* and recent trends involving dilettantish spiritualism (such as the pentecostal cult of "El Shaddai" manipulated by the elite) coexist with the most shameless violations of human rights, torture of political prisoners, rape, prostitution, and so on. Although the government and the National Democratic Front (NDF) have agreed on the document entitled "Comprehensive Agreement on Respect for Human Rights and International Humanitarian Law," which enabled the release of the captured General Victor Obilla and other officers, the Estrada regime reneged on the agreement with the arrest of NDF official Vic Ladlad, the assassination of the "Mawab Four," and an accelerated military rampage everywhere (S. Ocampo 1998; KMU International Department 1999).

Uneven development may also illuminate the new reconfiguring of the Philippines as an Asian/Pacific formation occupying the borderline between the Orientalist imaginary and the Western racializing gaze. Thereby have we become the fabled sport of postcolonialism, amphibious mutants of the borderlands. But the country's geopolitical inscription in the South makes Filipinos more akin to the inhabitants of the "Fourth World," the aboriginal and indigenous peoples of the Americas as well as the Hawaiians, Maoris, Timorese, and so on. The reconfiguring of the Philippines as a terrain of contestation finds its historic validity in the transitional plight of Filipinos immigrating to the United States in the years before the establishment of the Philippine Commonwealth in 1935: They were neither aliens nor citizens but "nationals," denizens of the twilight zone, the amorphous bridge between the core and the periphery (Okamura 1997). Contrary to what postmodernists label "transmigrants," Filipinos in the United States are now beginning to grasp the fact that it is the invasion of the Philippines by the United States in 1898, the destruction of the revolutionary Philippine Republic, the annexation of the islands, and the genocidal subjugation of its people that explains why we Filipinos are somehow irreparably dislocated in this continent.

Whether we like it or not—and here I address the emergent community of "Filipinos" in the United States—Filipinos surfaced in the American public's consciousness not as museum curiosities (indeed, the "indigenous types" exhibited at the St. Louis Exposition of 1904 contributed to the fixation of a Filipino primitive stereotype, specifically "dogeaters" in popular lore) but as a nation of dissidents combating U.S. colonial aggression. We cannot go back without masochistic self-denial to the fugitives of the Spanish galleons who settled in Louisiana to reawaken us from the American dream of success. Surely, if our project is the vindication of a people's dignity and democratic empowerment, not just ethnic competition with Native Americans for precedence, we need to recover the history of popular resistance and revolution that can resolve the problem of identity—who is more Filipino or less American and vice versa, who belongs and who does not. We live in a society with a deep and long history of racist practice of which the "model minority" myth is just one revealing symptom. Whether you were born here or recently arrived, you are perceived by the dominant society as someone "alien," not quite "American," somehow a strange "other." This is the inherent racial politics of the territory that we happen to inhabit.

The transition to the twenty-first century may be the occasion to reflect again on these not-so-special relations, in fact the tortuous and disruptive connection, between the Philippines and the United States. I suggest the following thesis for discussion. The narrative of the United States as a multiracial and multinational polity is still in the process of being fought through in everyday life, in the interstices of lived collective experience. In the racializing politics of that narrative, we are all implicated as protagonists (together with other people of color) interrogating the hegemonic definition of "American" as centered in a patriarchal, white-supremacist discourse opposed to the actualization of a democratic, just, egalitarian order. The political economy of justice and collective dignity, I submit, takes precedence over individual rights governed by the market and adjudicated by an exploitative and acquisitive system.

As I have argued here and elsewhere, Filipinos cannot concentrate solely on what is happening within the physical borders of this nation-state; this border has tentacles extending to the Philippines, even though the bases are gone (U.S. access to Philippine soil, however, is guaranteed anytime now by virtue of the Visiting Forces Agreement [Paulson 1999]). For the Filipino community, such historical amnesia is impossible—even though Andrew Cunanan tried it, with tragic results. I might interject here that Cunanan's trail is littered with the remains of our own colonial history that continue to haunt all Filipinos, whether one is aware of it or not, whether you can "pass" or not. In our mediatized society governed by the mass consumption of simulacra and simulations of prestige, adventurers such as Cunanan can be catapulted into instant fame, assuming the imposed role of celebrity scapegoats that at the same time provide "cannon fodder" also for hate crimes and institutional genocide.

Continuities in history always beget ruptures and interruptions. Despite the claims that we are all decentered personas with transcultural and fluid subjectivities, we cannot ignore the power of the sovereign nation-state—passports are still needed; the U.S. military still flies the Stars and Stripes in Bosnia, Korea, Japan, Kosovo, and elsewhere; Immigration and Naturalization Service agents and border patrols still hunt for "undocumented" aliens; Germans and Japanese still consider their languages one of prestige and power; and so on (Wood 1998; for the Asian region, see Gills 1993). In this post–Cold War environment of interdependency, we are faced with a climate of reaction, the ascendancy of the neoconservative "Contract with America," the rollback of Affirmative Action, a resurgence of anti-Asian violence, and the reinforcement of the retrograde racial politics of the time before the Civil Rights offensive of the 1960s. The identity crisis of the 1960s has been transmogrified by the cutthroat identity politics of the managerial-technocratic elite. Why is the critique of "white supremacy" and institutional racism launched in the 1960s now displaced by managerial programs of cultural diversity and fundamentalist revivals of the individualist work ethic that promise to harmonize differences and make people accept their place in the normal setup? The answer here points to the general crisis of capitalist hegemony worldwide and the sharpening contention of nation-states and power blocs to preserve or transform the "New World Order," to use the Establishment idiom (Bourdieu 1998).

In this crisis, opportunities of grasping the whole scenario open up. The project of empowerment by Asian Americans, and by Filipinos in the United States in particular, cannot be advanced unless we problematize that conjunction of two fields of power, two trajectories of social formations, whose articulation has produced the Filipino as a cultural presence and immanent political force. It is easy to claim citizenship as legal identity and also to assert one's ethnicity (this is mainly construed as a matter of descent or blood lineage rather than a cultural genealogy). But mere juxtaposition devoid of historical context does not clarify anything; in fact, it begs all the fundamental questions about autonomy, social

[handwritten: citizenship and identity must be placed in historical context.]

justice, and equality of peoples in a society characterized by alienation, commodity fetishism, and mass reification (Williams 1983).

We also dare not succumb to the pathos of asserting that the question of identity is simply a state of mind or that universal values such as individualism, rationality, and so on are gained when you grow out of your inherited ethnicity. When social and political problems are reduced to a matter of ethnicity—beliefs, attitudes, and commonsensical ideas that have no grounding in the social relations of lived experience in the complex nexus of practices that produce and reproduce the lives of Filipinos in a particular geopolitical space—the fundamental racial order of society is obscured. It is then replaced by a discourse of cultural differences and plural, even indeterminate, subject positions that do not disturb the peace of the status quo. By a reduction to ethnic particularisms detached from social needs and from the historical specificity of colonial bondage, alienation and reification (features of sociopolitical conditions tied to the logic of capital accumulation and commodity exchange) are reinforced. In this process, the matter of racism, not to speak of dehumanization by gender, class, and nationality, disappears *tout court* when it is sublimated into the normalizing disciplinary process of reconciliation and pacification of subject populations.

We confront here the contentious politics of transculturation and translation. This is then also the moment to reiterate the antithesis to neoliberal multiculturalism underlying the new trends in scholarship, a "negation of the negation," which I have tried to enunciate in the difference between Hagedorn's postmodernist style and Kidlat Tahimik's endeavor to forge a vernacular idiom from the modernism of Western cinema. This antithesis is none other than a regrounding of thought in historical specificity, in the "thickness" of worldly changes in the social relations of production/reproduction. At this juncture, I would like to recapitulate a central theme of this work, affirming the historical specificity of the Philippine conjuncture.

It is now axiomatic to hold that identity is constituted by the total ensemble of social relations articulated in any given historic formation. Premised on that principle, I offer the following theses: The chief distinction of Filipinos from other Asians residing in the United States is that their country of origin was the object of violent colonization and unmitigated subjugation by U.S. monopoly capital. It is this foundational circumstance, not the settling of Filipino fugitives in Louisiana or anywhere else, that establishes the limit and potential of the Filipino life world here. Without understanding the complex process of colonial subjugation and the internalization of dependency, Filipinos will not be able to define their own specific existential trajectory here as a dynamic bifurcated formation—one based on the continuing struggle of Filipinos for national liberation and popular democracy in the Philippines and the other based on the exploitation and resistance of immigrants here (from the "Manongs" in Hawaii and the West Coast to the post-1965 "brain drain" and the present diaspora worldwide). These two distinct histories, while geographically separate, flow into each other and converge into a single multilayered and mutually determining narrative—or constellation of episodes, if you like—that needs to be articulated around the principles of national-democratic sovereignty, social justice, and equality.

So far this has not been done because, as I argue at length in chapters 3, 4, and 7 and the afterword, the mainstream textbook approaches distort both histories across the realms of lived experience characterized by class, gender, race, national-ity, and so on. In the wake of the poststructuralist trend among intellectuals, a theory of Filipinos as transnational migrants has been introduced to befog the atmosphere already mired in the insistence on contingency, aporia, ambivalence, indeterminacy, disjunction, liminality, and so on (San Juan 1998a). Symptomatic of over four hundred years of oppression and resistance, this valorization of the fissured and sedimented identity of the "Filipino"—of any survivor of imperial "tutelage," for that matter—may be read as the trademark of anomic intellectuals uprooted from the popular-democratic struggles of the working masses whose as-piration for freedom and dignity demand the prior satisfaction of basic needs as a fundamental human right. In the era of flexible capitalism, we Filipinos as parti-cipants in a process of nationalitarian reconstruction seem to be still lingering at the threshold of late-capitalist modernity. We are still inventing allegories of the birth of *Pilipinas,* a process of collective imagining and praxis, a project begun at the time when a local tribal chief killed Magellan (shortly after his "discovery" of the islands in 1521) but later on aborted by Admiral Dewey's incursion into Ma-nila Bay. Complex historical reality always defies "postcolonial" wish-fulfillments.

To avoid the "nihilism of despair or Utopia of progress," we are told to be transnational or transcultural, or else. But the notion of Filipinos as transnational subjects assumes that all nation-states are equal in power, status, and so on. Like assimilationism, this theory of transmigrants obfuscates imperial domination and the imperative of rebellion. It reinforces the marginalization and dependency of "Third World" peoples. It erases what David Harvey (1996) calls historical "permanences" (347) and aggravates the Othering of people of color into racial-ized minorities—serf labor (e.g., OCWs) for global corporations and autocratic households. Last but not least, it rejects their history of resistance and their agency for emancipating themselves from the laws of the market and its opera-tional ideology of white supremacy mixed with neo–Social Darwinism blandish-ments.

Let me conclude by submitting this proposition for further inquiry and evalu-ation: Filipinos in the United States possess their own historical trajectory, one with its own singular profile but always intertwined in a thousand ways with what is going on in the Philippines. To capture the contours of this trajectory, we need to avoid two pitfalls. first, we should guard against the nostalgic essen-tializing nativism that surfaces in the fetishism of folk festivals and other com-modified cultural products that accompany tourist spectacles and official rituals. To avoid this trap, we need to connect folklore and other cultural practices to the conflicted lives of the Igorots, Moros, women, and masses of peasants and workers. Second, and perhaps more dangerous, we should guard against minstrelsy, self-denial by mimicry, the anxiety of not becoming truly "Americanized," that is, defined by white-supremacist norms. My view is that we do not want to be classified as schizoid or ambidextrous performers forever, in the fashion of Bienvenido Santos's "you lovely people." This drive to assume a hybrid "postcolonial" performativity, with all its self-ingratiating exoticism and aura of originality, only reinforces the pluralist/liberal consensus of "rational choice theory" (the utilitarian model of means and ends that promotes alienation and fosters atomistic individualism) and its apologia for institutional racism. On the other hand, the submerging of one's history into a panethnic Asian American movement or any other ethnic absolutism violates the integrity of the Filipino people's tradition of revolutionary struggle for autonomy, our outstanding contribution to humankind's narrative of the struggle for freedom from the violence of Othering and all modes of oppression.

Becoming Filipino, then, is a process of dialectical struggle, not a matter of wish-fulfillment or mental conjuring. For Filipinos to grasp who they are, more precisely what they are capable of, and more important what they can become—for humans, as Antonio Gramsci once said, can be defined only in terms of what they can become, in terms of possibilities that can be actualized—we need to examine again the historical circumstances that fatefully joined the trajectory of the Philippines and the United States, of Americans and Filipinos, constituting in the process the dialectical configuration that we know as Filipino American in its collective interactive dimension. The Filipino in the United States is thus a concrete historical phenomenon understandable neither as Filipino alone nor as American alone but as an articulation of the political, social, economic, and cultural forces of the two societies with their distinct colliding, if amalgamative, histories. We need to grasp the dialectics of imperial conquest and anticolonial revolution, the dynamics and totality of that interaction, as the key to how, and for what ends, the Philippines and its diasporic citizenry is being reconfigured for better or worse in the next millennium.

1

~~~~~

Symbolic Trajectories of
the Asian Diaspora

She says to herself if she were able to write she could continue to live. . . . If
she could display it before her and become its voyeur.

—Theresa Hak Kyung Cha

The human body, then, is nothing but a certain proportion of motion and
rest.

—Benedict de Spinoza

It is therefore a source of great virtue for the practiced mind to learn, bit by
bit, first to change about invisible and transitory things, so that afterwards it
may be able to leave them behind altogether. The person who finds his
homeland sweet is still a tender beginner; he to whom every soil is as his
native one is already strong; but he is perfect to whom the entire world is as
a foreign place.

—Hugh of St. Victor

A fter about four centuries of the worldwide circulation of commodities—
including the hugely profitable trade in slaves from Africa that inaugurated,
for Marx, the "rosy dawn" of capitalism—the stage was set for more intense capital accumulation based no longer on commercial exchange and the regional dis-
crepancies in the price of goods but on the process of production itself. "Place"
gave way to space; lived time divided into necessary, surplus, and "free" segments. Linked by relations of exchange governed by the logic of accumulation
centered in Europe and later in North America, the trajectories of peoples of
color, the "people without history" in Eric Wolf's reckoning, entered the global
labor market with the expansion of industrial capitalism, the commercialization

17

of agriculture, urbanization, and the concomitant dislocation and displacement
of populations from their traditional homelands.

We are still in the epoch of transnational migrations and the traffic in bodies.
The breakup of the Soviet Union and Yugoslavia, plus the exacerbated ethnic/
racial conflicts in their wake, promise mutations less tractable than the configurations of earlier boundary shifts. In the nineteenth and early twentieth centuries,
the movement of the bearers of labor power, "free" workers, at first involved
mainly peasants pushed toward the industrial centers of the European peninsula;
later, 50 million people left Europe between 1800 and 1924, 32 million of them
bound for the factories and mines of the industrializing United States. (Of the
200 million migrants between 1500 and 1980, 42 million were from the continent
of Asia.) Meanwhile, the victory of imperialism in China with the Opium War
of 1839–1842 allowed foreign entrepreneurs or brokers to establish the apparatus
for the "coolie" trade that eventually facilitated the transport of 200,000 Chinese
to the United States between 1852 and 1875 (Wolf 1982). In the 1860s, about
14,000 Chinese laborers were hired to build the transcontinental Central Pacific
Railroad. Unlike the Chinese "pariah capitalism" in other regions (Safran 1991),
the Chinese exodus to North America could only mediate between an exploitative host society and a moribund tributary formation already subjugated by
Western powers.[1]

With the Native Americans resisting the conquest of their lands and alienation
of their labor power and with the majority of Africans still bound to the slave
plantations, there was no alternative but the temporary implantation of the Asian
"alien" into the territory of the United States; when no longer needed, they were
"Driven Out"—demonized as the "Yellow Peril," then purged via the Chinese
Exclusion Act of 1882 (in force until 1943). This was reinforced by the "Gentlemen's Agreement" of 1907–1908, which interdicted laborers from Japan and
later Korea. It was supplemented by the 1917 Immigration Act, which created
the Asiatic Barred Zone (all of Asia, including Afghanistan, Arabia, and Asiatic
Russia, most Polynesian and all East Indian islands), and by other paralegal,
genocidal acts of violence (Bouvier and Gardner 1986; S. Chan 1991; Cashmore
1998).

CIRCUMNAVIGATION

The inaugural scene of any diaspora involves the uneven terrain of the world
system I have alluded to that is simultaneously differentiated and homogenized
by the logic of capital accumulation This twofold process is concretized in the
movement of peoples and nationalities at specific conjunctures where, for the
most part, the bearers of the culture of precapitalist formations are inserted into
a capitalist mode of production and forcibly undergo cataclysmic transformations. Ethnogenesis or ethnicization occurs when a consciousness of this inaugu-

ral scene is acquired by the dislocated group, a consciousness of a shared crisis signified by the terms "alienation," "uprooting," "separation," "exile," and "isolation." Such consciousness always evolves in specific historical contexts, within definite temporal-spatial parameters, in the conjunction of inner and outer concourses of events, such that whatever strategies of resolving the crisis are forged engage structures and institutions with their more or less fixed traditions and contingent modes of representations (Patterson 1983). If this shared crisis of exile and uprooting implies a removal from the time–space orientation of the homeland, the sacralized site of beginnings and endings that provides the boundaries of personal identity, in what way then (apart from the return carried out by sojourners or the mythmaking of deferred homecoming sustained by "symbiotic" ethnys) have the remembering and resolution of such a crisis been explored in the writing of Asian Americans without necessarily entailing the recovery of a literal homeland?

In essence, the crisis assumes the form of the disintegration of a way of life (its telos and its conception of a collective good) nourished in organic formations when they collide with the forces of the free market and its ethos of bureaucratic individualism. Such a collision, epitomized by the colonial subjugation of peoples of color, ultimately signifies the breakup of the intelligible meaning-producing narratives of the life of whole communities and their dispersal into monadic fragments or anomic bodies. What is lost is not only temporal-spatial continuity but, more important, the practice and vision of some collective good that informs the unity of character and life-histories of its individual members. What subtends the "liberal individualism of the market system" and its utilitarian norms is the process of reification, seriality, the instrumental rationality of means-ends, and so on, which on the whole negates history and unity of character. Commodity fetishism subverts or undermines any impulse to construct a narrative of diaspora, of dismemberment, and its overcoming. Given this trajectory, one can outline in general the responses to this crisis of collective alienation and fragmentation inscribed in several broad symbolic configurations or genres that are not mutually exclusive and that are amenable to qualification because of the discontinuities in the migration patterns and sociohistoric backgrounds of the constituent Asian groups. Far from essentializing agency, these responses inflect the energies of "cultural nationalism" toward heterogeneous geopolitical and dialogical confrontations (Hall 1998).

The first strategy is what I would call a postmodernist affirmation of heterogeneity within the thematic limits of an ideologically pluralist society. It seeks to valorize the amorphous and diverse as against the uniform (the assimilationist model of Anglo conformity), the hybrid and heteroglotic as against the predictable ethnic stereotype. One example may be found in Frank Chin's protagonist in *The Chickencoop Chinaman* (1981) who tries to exhibit the virtuosity of a bricoleur as he posits a polymorphous subject position for his syncretic genealogy: "Chinamen are made, not born, my dear. Out of junk-imports, lies, railroad scrap iron, dirty jokes, broken bottles, cigar smoke, Cosquilla Indian blood, wino spit, and lots of milk amnesia. . . . For I am a Chinaman! A miracle synthetic. . . . I speak nothing but the mother tongues bein' born to none of my own, I talk the talk of orphans" (118, 120–121). Of course, Chin's commitment is not to his group's ability to absorb or reflect the varied surface phenomena of U.S. society but to the artist's expansive and capacious spirit, a sensibility that leaps over boundaries of nation or race. This is an elective affinity, an affiliation chosen to supersede tribal filiations. As an antidote to the Chinatown mentality, Chin's parodic pastiche refunctions the seriality of commodified humans to prove somehow that U.S. society itself is as decentered as the populist architecture of Las Vegas, a mammoth bricolage, without any nationalist marker. Whether or not this strategy of selective identification captures and resolves the existential predicament of young Chinese Americans, what is certain is that this route of trying to beat the enemy at his language-game is filled with recuperative temptations. In other words, this verisimilitude may be a Pyrrhic victory over the white-supremacist Leviathan.

Despite its somewhat caustic exhibitionism, Chin's aesthetic performance, in my judgment, remains the most powerful critique of "white racist love" mounted by an antidiasporic Asian American writer, a critique ranging from the heteroglossic fiction of *The Chinaman Pacific and Frisco R.R., Donald Duk,* and *Gunga Din Highway* to the trenchant polemics of *Bulletproof Buddhists and Other Essays.* His aim is nothing less than to transform the American pidgin English of the marketplace into a "language of civility." But the idiom of his effort to combat the Pearl Buck/Charlie Chan syndrome tends to alienate the mainstream audience, mobilizing a selective logistics of demystification and a Spinozan materialism inflected with Zen Buddhist candor. Here is Chin's neopicaresque testimony offered to a captive audience in Singapore:

> "Home is a kind of childhood sickness," I say. "There's no such place, no such thing as home. I can't speak for all writers, but this writer is like Monkey. At a certain age, I am born an adult, stupid and naked to the world, and have to learn everything. Life is war; all behavior is tactics and strategy. All relationships are martial. . . . Writing is fighting. All warfare is based on deception. Sun Tzu the strategist says. . . . So the first strategy Monkey has to learn is how to make the difference between the real and the fake. So he can't be deceived." (1998, 389)

A modification of Chin's learning/teaching strategy is that of Jeffery Chan in his story "The Chinese in Haifa" (which I discuss in the section "Rehabilitation"). Not deception but, rather, forgetting or loss of memory is now the main problem. To counter the loss of historicity in the diaspora, Chan envisages a community of all the dispossessed and disinherited, delineating the paradoxes of loyalty and betrayal in the process and also questioning linkages based on custom versus ties sutured to personal preference. This response characterizes the enclave micropolitics of the intellectual who rejects ethnic collectivism and opts for spiritual marginality and exile as a permanent possibility. It is possible that both Chin's and Chan's postmodernist approach, albeit with varying idiosyncrasies, can nullify if not neutralize the two intellectual operations at work in theoretical racism pointed out by Etienne Balibar (1990), namely, the mode of hierarchic classification and the deployment of anthropological universals. At least, what they refuse is the obsession with purity (racial, cultural, or whatever) as an ideal or transcendent value, the metaphysical underpinning of all racisms.

In contrast, Maxine Hong Kingston combines both counteridentification (a reversal of the negative image of the alien) and disidentification (a taking up of antagonistic positions) (MacDonell 1986). In both *The Woman Warrior* and *China Men,* the damaged narratives of her family are reconstituted to thwart the racial categorization of bureaucratic individualism. Hers is a versatile approach to envisaging community as an ongoing collective project, one that posits the intelligibility of individual lives as premised on a new civic morality so that, in effect, the extended family or the ghetto sometimes functions as a surrogate for a polis that has been eroded by colonialism and racist violence. I am not saying that Kingston has simply rehabilitated Confucianism and the ideals of the old tributary, patriarchal regime in her articulation of a social good inherent in certain practices of resistance by her characters. Indeed, her feminism enables her to thwart the seductions of pragmatic relativism as she outlines the vicissitudes of a "group-in-fusion" (to use Sartre's term) and dramatizes the ruses of disidentifications adopted by beleaguered immigrants as they test the limits of the law.

In *Jasmine* (1989), Bharati Mukherjee (originally from India) attempts to rewrite expatriation as an allegory or montage of spiritual transmigrations. While the novel also probes the limits of patriarchal law, its strategy hinges on unfolding the narrative of a quest replete with reversals and recognitions. Mukherjee, in an interview, claims that Jyoti (reincarnated as Jase and Jane) personifies the feminist revolutionary, a love goddess or life force who gets what she wants. Unfortunately, the novel ends with Jasmine's life being embedded once again in the narrative of another person's life. Its quasi-picaresque and necessarily episodic action, while registering the crisis of modern industrial society in its architectonics, foregrounds the problematic status of an intrinsically romantic project of self-transformation (Jasmine, according to Mukherjee, "ends up being a tornado who leaves a lot of debris behind"). Paradoxically, underlying the trope of a protean form of life in motion are the doctrine and institutions of the free market—a postmodern allegory, perhaps, of a "postcolonial" writer whose vision of international solidarity seems compromised in her use of the myth of the American West as an open frontier devoid of aborigines (see Mukherjee 1990, 29).

What Mukherjee's narrative seeks to achieve but fails to do is a goal associated with this genre: the composition of a narrative of a life whose unity and intelligibility spring from its being embedded in a history of a community that, though transplanted, continues to survive with some degree of autonomy. This objective,

I think, has been masterfully attained by the Japanese-American writer Hisaye Yamamoto in her story "Las Vegas Charley." Denarrativization (emblematized by the city and its mutabilities) is countered by practices demonstrating the residual power of certain public or civic virtues that serve to connect the segments of a character's life and redeem it from victimage. Las Vegas Charley refuses the route of Stoic self-mastery or of empty moral, categorical imperatives. Yamamoto's rendering of scenes in Charley's life suggests that its unity is derived not from his psychology or a superimposed ethical substance but from certain concrete practices whose actualization embody social goods—indeed, the subtext of this story may be the almost insurmountable difficulty of conceptualizing these goods when all sense of responsibility (personal and civic) in the majority of citizens has been attenuated or dissolved altogether (see MacIntyre 1984). In that case, Matsumoto appropriately wears the mask of a whole city founded on the cash nexus that extinguishes alterity and difference, a mask whose antinomic interiority may be discerned in the central character of John Okada's novel *No-No Boy*.

In stories such as "Las Vegas Charley," the strategy is twofold: While the artist of the diaspora seeks to re-create a community in exile by a resumption of traditional practices with social goods internal to them, these practices in turn generate a utopian pathos because they can no longer satisfy the individual whose will and passions have become detached from any viable community. Pure becoming or absolute contingency displaces the unity of lives sharing pasts and futures. Alienation then becomes translated into an opportunity to enact a measure of self-determination and integrity. In place of the limited understanding of the character, the author interposes her will to reconstitute if not discover the migrant's life-destiny via the mediation of a symbolic causality that threads the otherwise gratuitous contingencies of an ordinary immigrant's wanderings.

Finally, in the works of the Filipino writer Carlos Bulosan, we find a strategy of prophetic figuration that seeks to disclose the complicities between metropolis and periphery. The image of collective labor and resistance discovered in the native tradition of anticolonial revolt as it is transposed to the present becomes a kind of "objective correlative" to resolve the crisis of isolation and exilic anguish. This organon of countermemory opposed to official history is, however, not primordial or culturalist in intent because it is anchored in anticolonialism and determined by class partisanship. (Of all Asians, the Filipinos are the only subjugated "natives" who have resisted U.S. symbolic and physical violence since their homeland was occupied in 1898 in the aftermath of the Spanish–American War.) Alternatively, Bulosan focuses on multiracial work as a social practice whose rhythm and intrinsic sociality endows it with a self-renewing *habitus*. In the struggle for recognition, the protagonists in Bulosan's fiction (see, e.g., "Be American" or certain chapters in *America Is in the Heart* [1973]) learn cooperation, mutual trust, courage, sympathy, and mobilizations of latent resources as they confront the brutality of white vigilantes and the coercive ideological apparatuses of the state. This need to belong to a group in a state of siege is not fated; it is chosen—it is a commitment to a path whose unfolding is assured but unpredictable. Its goal is clearly defined as internal to its practice: not the resurrection of the homeland but the founding of a community of producers in the territory of North America, where the basis of class exploitation (the commodification of racialized labor power) has been abolished.

In this sense, Bulosan preempts the ethnic crisis by reinscribing alienation in the matrix of class and racial antagonisms. With this perspectival shift, the resolution to the crisis of loss of home (the colony) and ethnic alienation becomes also the resistance to imperialism founded on exploitation of class and national subalterns. Although this mode of renarrativization is not without its dangers, it is preferable because it has the power of curbing the seductiveness of ethnic chauvinism for demagogues as well as for victims who all too often spontaneously react to the racialized oppression they suffer. Bulosan tries to modulate the utopianism of a desired classless society by the symbolic validation of a fertile and beautiful land owned by no one and shared by all. Such a geopolitical site, a possible home to all citizens, is still extraterritorial insofar as goods are not shared equally and hierarchization by naturalized difference still prevails. Bulosan's narratives envisage emancipation not of the human essence but of social relations; they prefigure liberations not anticipated but actualized in the struggle to break down the ethnic ghetto and root one's identity in a struggle shared with others across ethnicity, nationality, and race. Home, the primal scene of deracination, is therefore not a place but a process of unifying one's life through acts of solidarity and resistance with others dehumanized by the politically constructed criteria of race, class, gender, and nationality.

TRANSMUTATIONS

In order to dramatize the unique expressive gesture of each strategy, I focus on certain aspects of Asian diasporic texts that articulate the cultural politics of collective self-transformation in late capitalism. I begin by remarking on the forced "return" or exclusion of Asians as a racial group, which I referred to earlier as a historical event that finds an inverted simulacrum in the way their entry is represented in Kingston's *China Men* (1989).

Kingston narrates two versions of the father from China entering the fabled "Gold Mountain" (the legendary image of the United States). Of these two versions, the second is the legal way of passage through Angel Island in San Francisco Bay, where "a white demon physically examined him, poked him in the ass and genitals, looked in his mouth, pulled his eyelids with a hook," and detained him until, purified by this ordeal of commodification, he passed the "American examination." The first one is, in contrast, a violation of customs law. Midwived by smugglers, the father deposits himself in a womblike crate that is stowed in the dark belly of a ship where soon he "began to lose his bearings." Caught in this self-made prison, the speaking subject becomes dispersed in a sequence of images that dissolves memory and unbalances consciousness, affording a new sensorium for the protagonist:

> Various futures raced through his mind: walking the plank, drowning, growing old in jail, being thrown overboard in chains, flogged to tell where others were hiding, hung by the neck, returned to China—all things that happened to caught chinamen. . . .
> Because of fear, he did not eat nor did he feel hungry. . . . Rocking and dozing, he felt the ocean's variety—the peaked waves that must have looked like pines; the rolling waves, round like shrubs, the occasional icy mountains; and for stretches, lulling grasslands. . . .
> He heard voices, his family talking about gems, gold, cobbles, food. . . . The villagers had to make up words for the wonders. "Something new happens every day, not the same boring farming."
> The sea invented words too. He heard a new language, which might have been English, the water's many tongues speaking and speaking. Though he could not make out words, the whispers sounded personal, intimate, talking him over, sometimes disapproving, sometimes in praise of his bravery. (Kingston 1989, 50–51)

When finally a voice interrupts the cacophony of sounds, "It's me. It's me," an announcement that identifies the Other (the smuggler/outlaw), who then delivers the father from his self-fashioned captivity, Kingston's antihero is ready to "claim the Gold Mountain, his own country." Born from the ruse of the illicit Other, this subject (or subject position) thus thwarts the normative paranoia of self-identification.[2]

The act of problematizing boundaries coincides with the refusal of one paradigmatic narrative of migration centered on the Symbolic Order authorizing racial discrimination. We elude the repetition compulsion of ethnic historiography epitomized by Ellis Island and the state apparatus of disciplinary control. Finally landing on solid ground, the stowawayed father glimpses a statue of a woman "who carried fire and a book"—the female as mythical embodiment of the civilizing mission, not so portentous a figure as the one that greeted the fictive immigrant of Kafka's *Amerika*. " 'Is she a goddess of theirs?' the father asked. 'No,' said the smuggler, 'they don't have goddesses. She's a symbol of an idea.' He was glad to hear that the Americans saw the idea of Liberty so real that they made a statue of it" (Kingston 1989, 52–53). The prudent father in Angel Island censored this idea: "If the U.S. government found out his thoughts on freedom, it might not let him land" (56).[3] With the fetish of the recuperative mother avoided thanks to this narrative artifice, we confront an "uncanny strangeness" in the unsettled characters and tempo of Kingston's "talk-stories." We sense "a disturbing Otherness" implicit in the recognition of that "erotic, death-bearing unconscious," which Julia Kristeva (1991) considers the basis of human solidarity; the living through of this internalized difference allegorized by the primal scene of arrival on the continent is the "ultimate condition of our being with others" (192). Before this condition is reached, however, the ghetto of Chinatown must be traversed first.

In establishing the practice of alterity as the condition of possibility for the Chinese fathers, the narrative disavows the doctrinaire claim that art creates authentic identity and redeems fallen reality. Although the ostensible project of *China Men* is to dramatize the negated agency of the Chinese male immanent in the pathos and waste of their experiences, what stands out is not the foundational rite of Eurocentric Americanization—adaptation to the Puritanical conquest of the wilderness, individualism, the work ethic, and so on. Rather, it is their resistance to hegemonic corporate power and the racialized nation-state. A distinctly utopian celebration of manual work on the land aims to subvert the drive of an expansive economy toward differentiation and equalization, while a desire to reconstruct the genealogy of the "castrated" patriarchs substitutes for a promised return to the homeland the continuity of certain virtues tested in actual practice—such as the Brother's refusal to kill Vietnamese—integral to the preservation of the community. A return is deferred, then displaced; memory induces a delayed effect, making the land of origin coeval with the present. In effect, the resistance to colonial oppression is relocated to the interior of the metropolis. This does not of course disrupt the circulation and exploitation of migrant labor power. But the evocation of a territory free from the imperial plunder of the past (the socialist People's Republic of China during Mao's time) and of the resistance of the Vietnamese (whose victory ironically will provide the next reservoir of cheap labor for a deindustrializing economy), together with the suture of archaic myth and documentary testimonials in an open-ended account, suffice, I think, in neutralizing the constantly refunctioned paradigm of ethnic success (via accommodation/integration) that has so effectively underwritten the racism of the past and the injustices of the present.

In tracking the dispersal of "Asian" bodies in the United States, it is imperative to stress one elementary proposition: that the heterogeneous cultures of both ethnic and racial minorities (in Robert Blauner's terms) are not "primordial" social relationships preserved from the past but, rather, historical effects of asymmetrical power relations between uneven formations, specifically of labor market segmentation. This segmentation derives in turn from the shifting ratio of fixed capital (machinery) to variable capital or wage labor. What results is the phenomenon of uneven development of the world system—the spatial configuration of the margin and periphery, the core and the dependencies—that configures the way that Asians, among other people of color, have been marked for the calculation of their price in the global labor market (Rhodes 1970; Melotti 1977). The geography of early imperial conquest has predefined Asians when absolute space (feudal relations) was abolished through the universalization of wage labor; but simultaneously, various relative spaces (on the scale of the urban, the nation-state, and so on) were generated within which the bourgeoisie through the state organized the expansion and accumulation of capital, in particular the political control over the working class (Poulantzas 1978). As Neil Smith (1984) puts it, "The internal differentiation of national territories into identifiable regions is the geographical expression of the division of labour, both at the level of individual capitals and the particular division of labor. . . . Capital produces distinct spatial scales—absolute spaces—within which the drive toward equalization is concentrated. But it can only do this by an acute differentiation and continued redifferentiation of relative space, both within and between scales" (144, 147). This systemic process of spatial realignment underlies the allochronism of Western discourse on people of color. It also informs Eurocentric knowledge-production premised on relativism and denial of coevalness with these Others, whose existence its self-identification required (Fabian 1983).

How was this hegemonic knowledge challenged by Asian writers in the United States? Because the emergence of Third World labor and its differential incorporation into the Euro-American polity are consequences of the uneven development of the capitalist mode, of the dialectic of equalization and differentiation embodied most starkly in colonial subjugation (of the Philippines and Puerto Rico, among others), how writing represents Asians transgressing the boundaries of the U.S. racial order can suggest a framework for articulating the character of the diaspora not simply as an uprooting of peoples from their homelands but also as a process of transformative critique and self-determination. As David Palumbo-Liu (1999) acutely observes, "diaspora" retroactively names "the discursive effects of the production of knowledge about *diaspora*" (356), including its ideological investments. Deracination in retrospect precipitates the dream of autonomy. Instead of projecting a collective myth of return that constitutes the diverse libidinal economies of their peoples, Asian writers—if I may posit the hypothesis—endeavor to dramatize the vicissitudes of ethnogenesis, opposition, and self-empowerment. If capital ingests or devours the bodies of immigrant workers, how are they able to survive this "incorporation" and preserve their integrity?

Although the syndrome of "the West and the Rest" is usually deconstructed by postmodern thinkers in order to prioritize a politics of radical difference, we might use for research purposes the attempt of schizoanalysis to explain the particularity of Asian dissemination. The first move is to refuse the claim of purity. Rejecting capital's ideals of universality identified with the self-identical subject (patriarchal, ego-centered, white) and a representative Totality, Gilles Deleuze and Felix Guattari (1987) suggest that those who are able to survive the cannibalism of the Whole belong to the tribe practicing nomad thought. "Deployed in a horizonless milieu that is a smooth space, steppe, desert, or sea," this "race," necessarily bastard and mixed-blood, is defined "not by its purity but rather by the impurity conferred upon it by a system of domination." Instead of invoking a myth of return, the nomadic race dissolves the differentiated space engendered by capitalist modernity and invents a new habitat. Deleuze and Guattari offer this thesis: "In the same way that race is not something to be rediscovered, the Orient is not something to be imitated; it only exists in the construction of a smooth space, just as race only exists in the constitution of a tribe that peoples and traverses a smooth space" (380). Migration plays with and around fixed boundaries, soaking up heterogeneous influences and contriving new environments.[4] Schizoid thought, however, seems to flatten the map prematurely by conjecturing a liberated "space" not hitherto codified by previous engagements where authority or some sovereign power shows its hand. Can this space of "free play" and promise of mobility be the alibi of immigrants who have mortgaged their labor (life) time beforehand?

RE-INSCRIPTIONS

The topography of the United States, however, was not smooth (literally or figuratively) when the Chinese, Japanese, Asian Indians, and Filipinos first arrived.

On the West Coast from California up to Alaska, it was already demarcated by the seasonal routine of planting and harvesting that defined the itinerary of the Filipino migrant-workers chronicled by Carlos Bulosan in the classic testimony *America Is in the Heart.*

After more than a decade of suffering and struggle, the representative persona in Bulosan's ethnobiography sums up, "The terrible truth in America shatters the Filipinos' dream of fraternity." Prohibited from marrying white women, isolated in barracks and confined to gambling halls and cabarets, and targeted by lynch mobs and the state's coercive bureaucracy, these Filipinos reclaimed tabooed spaces and transvalued them. Circumscribed in their movements, they conducted a reconnaissance of the landscape of Euro-American ambivalence and contradiction in private letters, anecdotes, photographs, and various modes of semiotic resistance other than linear print. Like Kingston, Bulosan charts the territory from a carnivalesque perspective that combines the pastoral idealization of the farmer/artisan in the homeland with the myth of America as a site of inexhaustible opportunities and resources.

In the story "Be American," for example, Bulosan celebrates the line of flight and fluctuation, "multiplicities of escape and flux," whereby the colonized "native" tries to encompass and name his predicament. Eventually, the narrator anchors physical motion to an idealized perception of nature that functions as a reactive answer to the degradation of the environment by monopoly agribusiness:

Yes, indeed, Consorcio: You have become an American, a real American. And this land that we have known too well is not yet denuded by the rapacity of men. Rolling like a beautiful woman with an overflowing abundance of fecundity and murmurous with her eternal mystery, there she lies before us like a great mother. To her we always return from our prodigal wanderings and searchings for an anchorage in the sea of life; from her we always draw our sustenance and noble thoughts, to add to her glorious history. (Bulosan 1995, 71)

Such nostalgia for the organic community incarnate in virgin land that is fecund but not denuded, coupled with the fact that Bulosan received generous help from white women in a time of vicious racist attacks on Filipino workers, enables Bulosan to represent the Filipino experience as a transitional stage, a border zone of passage, from dispossession to emergent self-integration. Unprivatized land becomes fetishized as everyone's maternal home, refuge, and haven. The Filipino resistance to Japanese colonialism, evoking those against the Spanish and the American invaders in the past, inspires a recovery of ideals that the young Bulosan originally ascribed to a mythical America and thus redeems the fallen present. This evokes a neo-Stoic ideal of human fellowship that transcends the chauvinist register of the nation-state. In *America Is in the Heart,* the Filipino condition of exile ends when Filipinos join in the united front against world fascism to liberate the homeland and also purge their host's body of the imperial virus. But the Cold War and McCarthyism extinguished Bulosan's hope. Nearly 40 years after Bulosan's death, the Filipino nationality in the United States, now in the process of comprising the largest segment in the Asian American category, continues to inhabit an internal colony that reproduces in microcosm the dependent status of the Philippines and its castelike role as supplier of cheap labor for U.S. multinationals.

It appears that the "New World Order" inaugurated by the Persian Gulf War replicates on a different scale the uneven development of capitalism in the nineteenth century. A complicating factor is this: Demographically, the racial minorities in the United States, soon to be the majority in the next 50 years, are bound to reconstitute the racial politics of neo–Social Darwinism and alter the iniquitous hierarchy of power. The concept of minority, however, is not quantitative or numerical; it signifies the emergence of a new subject position in the global ecology of permanent crisis. What characterizes the minority are multiple connections that "constitutes a line of flight . . . a universal figure, or becoming-everybody/everything" (Deleuze and Guattari 1987, 470). In opposition to the axiomatics of the State and the logic of the market, minorities cannot be integrated or assimilated into denumerable sets or subsets with regional, federal, or statutory autonomy because their calculus proceeds "via a pure becoming," flows, events, incorporeal transformations, and "continuums of intensities or continuous variations, which go beyond constants and variables—becomings, which have neither culmination nor subject but that draw one another into zones of proximity or undecidability" (Deleuze and Guattari 1987, 507): a plane of consistency or immanence that multiplies connections. This postmodern conception of minorities may exhibit a certain excess (compare the Foucauldian approach of Arturo Escobar [1995]), but it is, I think, more faithful to their metamorphic responses to the dilemma of dispossession and dislocation than either the old functionalist race-relations cycle or the prevailing ethnicity paradigm that underpins the "model minority" myth.

So far, the Chinese in Kingston's fiction and the Filipinos in Bulosan's memoirs are represented as decolonizing flows or becomings that strive to recuperate the meaning of home in cooperative work or in their precarious residence in the United States. They problematize the polarity of inside/outside. Meanwhile, two world wars intensified uneven development, ravaging the hinterlands and preventing any return for sojourners and expatriates. In the aftermath, Chinese, Japanese, and Filipinos, victimized by assorted discriminatory laws and practices, have reterritorialized their alienation via claims to property and the rights of full citizenship. Their strategies of multiplying connections were deployed for a time in a regime of signs that valorized the depths and eccentricity of singular psyches, a sacred realm of interiority that resisted conversion to the counters of exchange value. In the age of mass consumption of spectacles and simulacra, however, even the borderlands of fantasy, sexuality, and utopian desire are now subject to the surveillance of the interventionist state, a panoptic gaze reinforced by sophisticated electronic media and computerized communication. The paranoia of subjectivity attached to the cash nexus can easily become the surrogate for ramifying connections, affiliations, and solidarities until the ghetto mentality is revitalized—this time armed with a micropolitical rhetoric to match the dispersive and atomistic logic of postmodern capital (Smith 1984; Harvey 1989).[5]

EXTRAPOLATIONS

Perhaps a telltale figuration of the postmodern mode of incorporating the Asian, specifically the Indian subject, into the crucible of flexible accumulation can be found in Mukherjee's novel *Jasmine* (1989). Mukherjee's fiction is a protracted meditation on the plight of immigrants, refugees, expatriates, and exiles in a world transfigured by the rapid consumption of localities or places as a means of production. What the narrator apprehends is the dialectic of sameness and difference, the shifting ratio of capital and labor in racial categorizations that demarcate the zones of contact and separation:

> But we are refugees and mercenaries and guest workers; you see us sleeping in airport lounges, you watch us unwrapping the last of our native foods, unrolling our prayer rugs, reading our holy books, taking out for the hundredth time an aerogram promising a job or space to sleep, a newspaper in our language, a photo of happier times, a passport, a visa, a *laissez-passer*. . . .
> We are the outcasts and deportees, strange pilgrims visiting outlandish shrines, landing at the end of tarmacs, ferried in old army trucks where we are roughly handled and taken to roped-off corners of waiting rooms where surly, barely wakened

customs guards await their bribe. We are dressed in shreds of national costumes, out
of season, the wilted plumage of intercontinental vagabondage. We ask only one
thing: to be allowed to land; to pass through; to continue. We sneak a look at the
big departure board, the one the tourists use. Our cities are there, too, our destina-
tions are so close! . . .
    What country? What continent? We pass through wars, through plagues. I am
hungry for news, but the discarded papers are in characters or languages I cannot
read. The zigzag route is straightest. (Mukherjee 1989, 90–91)

The last statement anticipates the waning of allochronism in Western epistemology and the realization of coevalness in affirming the cotemporality of speaking
subject and listener (more on this later), where the Other occupies the same
ground and the same time as ourselves. We suspect that the implied referent here
that can be only alluded to but not realistically described is the massive, ongoing
"warm-body export" of the Asian countries to Europe, the Middle East, and
North America. This summons up a horizon of trajectories and redundancies
whose passage across continents mocks the claims of market liberalism to under-
write and promote equality, modernity, and progress everywhere through the
principle of difference.
    A new speaking subject, the "I" behind the apparatus of enunciation, is initi-
ated into the discursive field of the internationalized Gothic novel where diach-
rony collapses into synchrony. In this context, time dissolves into spatial disjunc-
tions. Difference indeed relates, but from what point of view? We find that the
narrative releases an allegorical force from the woman's obedience to tradition,
a force that counterpoints the effects of the global shift of production and appropriation in the life of the Third World subaltern. Jasmine may be said to person-
ify the return of the repressed—the primal scene of deracination—so as to make
it (rootlessness) a generalized lived situation for all.
    What is striking here in the light of my remarks on Kingston's China Men is
an analogous smuggling of the Asian, this time a woman obsessed with the past
rather than with future success, into U.S. territory via a break in the unguarded
coastline of Florida. (In both China Men and this novel, the Caribbean functions
as a locus for testing the vulnerability of the nation-state's closure.) She is ferried
by The Gulf Shuttle, commanded by Half-Face, a sinister figure who "had lost an
eye and ear and most of his cheek in a paddy field in Vietnam," in what he calls
"the armpit of the universe." This deformed exemplar of the rugged individualist
is a survivor of the disastrous attempt by the United States to dominate the Pacific Rim and roll back the gains of several Asian revolutions as well as that of
Cuba. Jasmine's first sight of the New World undercuts well-known literary ana-
logues—from the Puritan evangelists to The Great Gatsby. Her recollection fore-
shadows the suicidal agonies of the Iowa farmers and registers the surface mutations of uneven development at the core still visible to the newcomer:

I smelled the unrinsed water of a distant shore. Then suddenly in the pinkening
black of pre-dawn, America caromed off the horizon.

The first thing I saw were the two cones of a nuclear plant, and smoke spreading from them in complicated but seemingly purposeful patterns, edges lit by the rising sun, like a gray, intricate map of an unexplored island continent, against the pale unscratched blue of the sky. I waded through Eden's waste: plastic bottles, floating oranges, boards, sodden boxes, white and green plastic sacks tied shut but picked open by birds and pulled apart by crabs. . . .

I wonder if Bud even sees the America I do. We pass half-built, half-deserted cinder-block structures at the edge of town, with mud-spattered deserted cars parked in an uncleared lot, and I wonder, Who's inside? What are they doing? Who's hiding? Empty swimming pools and plywood panels in the window frames grip my guts. And Bud frowns because unproductive projects give him pain. He said, "Wonder who handled their financing?"

My first night in America was spent in a motel with plywood over its windows, its pool bottomed with garbage sacks, and grass growing in its parking lot. (Mukherjee 1989, 95–97)

Retrospection insinuates the presence of Bud, the patriarch-banker, impotent before the signs of unproductivity. Raped in a room that seemed to her like a madhouse or prison, Jasmine performs a ritual of purification and then kills Half-Face, agency of the Symbolic Order of laissez-faire competition, who has transported her to the land where she has vowed to sacrifice herself according to the code of marital obedience. Allochronism gives way to coevalness. In the borderland between incompatible life worlds, "undocumented" cheap labor confronts microchip technology; the time of suttee intersects the age of predatory, booty capitalism.

One can stress here how Jasmine's violation by Half-Face, symbol of the ethos of commodification and white male supremacy, releases her from her vow and assigns her to a new mission, a cognitive and mock-naive mapping of the United States. Among the connections revealed by her experience—her sequence of becomings, if you like—is the kind of commercial circuit that links her countryman, the Professorji in Flushing, New York, with Indian women whose virgin and innocent hair, compared to the "horrible hair of American women" ruined by shampoos and permanents, is highly prized as an integral component of the defense industry and high-tech business. One wonders, Is the diaspora a pretext for recolonizing the Third World?

After a stay in New York City with a seemingly ideal couple, she ends up temporarily in Iowa with Bud Ripplemeyer, purveyor of credit and the future, whose body, paralyzed from a shot by a disgruntled farmer-customer, betokens the plight of the heartland. But it is her association with their adopted Vietnamese child Du that enables Jasmine, who has "bloomed from a diffident alien with forged documents into adventurous Jase," to recover her sense of being "rhizomatic," open to multiple transactions and intensities. She is, however, still vulnerable to the seductions of the stereotype: "Bud courts me because I am alien. I am darkness, mystery, inscrutability. The East plugs me into instant vitality and wisdom. I rejuvenate him simply by being who I am" (Mukherjee 1989, 178). Gender inequity becomes romanticized under the aegis of Orientalism, a compensatory response to the indifference of cultural relativism and the mystique of American pluralism.

In contrast, it is instructive to note how, for the Korean Younghill Kang, the West taught him "rebellion against nature and fatality"; confronted by the pithless derelicts of New York City, he invokes the Korean experience in Japanese prisons: "And yet I clutched to a new world of time, where individual disintegration was possible, as well as individual integration, where all need not perish with the social organism" (Kang 1974, 239).

In Mukherjee's novel, it is Du, however, who reconnects Jasmine to the traumatic violence of Half-Face and the whole mechanism of exchange in business society. As mysterious as her own image, Du is Jasmine's "silent ally against the bright lights, the rounded, genial landscape of Iowa." Her reading of Du's past— she has counseled herself before to "learn to read the world and everyone in it like a photographic negative of reality"—constructs a site for affirming her capacity to mobilize energies suppressed by the power of a disciplinary regime based on reification and private property. Who is this survivor of the seemingly gratuitous violence of Half-Face and the whole phallocentric machinery? Jasmine thematizes the allegory of the refugee as the typical inhabitant of the postmodern milieu:

> Considering that he has lived through five or six languages, five or six countries, two or three centuries of history; has seen his country, city, and family butchered, bargained with pirates and bureaucrats, eaten filth in order to stay alive; that he has survived every degradation known to this century, considering all those liabilities, isn't it amazing that he can read a Condensed and Simplified for Modern Students edition of *A Tale of Two Cities?*
>
> Du's doing well because he has always trained with live ammo, without a net, with no multiple choice. No guesswork: only certain knowledge or silence. Once upon a time, like me, he was someone else. We've been many selves. We've survived hideous times. I envy Bud the straight lines and smooth planes of his history. (Mukherjee 1989, 189–190)

But this hermeneutics of the refugee who eludes hegemonic power by the myth of transmigration expresses not only Jasmine's intuition of difference, the "uncanny strangeness" personified by Du. It also foregrounds the hypocrisy of pluralism and the inadequacy of evangelical anticommunism or any other "civilizing" metaphysics in helping her comprehend the geopolitics of the Vietnam War. Moreover, it reflects in general the limits of the Westernized Indian intellectual's understanding of the lived situation of other people of color: "I should have known about [Du's] friends, his sister, his community. I should have broken through, but I was afraid to test the delicate thread of the hyphenization. Vietnamese-American: don't question either half too hard" (Mukherjee 1989, 200).

The last half is scarcely interrogated—unless Half-Face, Bud, and their ilk function as synecdoches.

It is at this juncture that Mukherjee's protagonist installs the psychoanalytic figure of the lack, the absence, on which the political economy of the Symbolic Order of difference thrives—the lack premised on castration of the female, the absence that can be rectified only by Taylor rescuing her from the panic-stricken farmlands of Iowa and delivering her to a fabled haven in California. In this context, the Asian Indian diaspora refunctions the syndrome of the escape/journey to the Western frontier as a vehicle for its realization of the vicissitudes of karma. Nevertheless, we are expected to understand that the encounter between the flux of the Asian female body and the axiomatics of possessive individualism has again confirmed the perception that for capitalism both nature and women are "objects of conquest and penetration as well as idolatry and worship" (Smith 1984, 14). The fact of Indian economic success in the United States does not detract from the truth of that perception. Based on the latest census, Indians among Asian immigrants today earn the highest income and enjoy privileges denied to the Vietnamese, Cambodians, Laotians, Hmongs, and other recent arrivals. Mukherjee's novel does not address this fact but rather allegorizes the fate of the Asian woman (especially one invested with the touristic charm of Hindu mythology) who is still conceived by mainstream U.S. society as a fetishized object of pleasure, all the more seductive because behind the docility and magical fatalism lurks an inscrutable and enigmatic power that seems to resist domestication by the liberal code of individual rights, administrative rationality, consumer goods, money, and bourgeois feminism. On the other hand, Mukherjee believes that she has once again narrativized her belief that "we murder who we were so we can rebirth ourselves in the image of our dreams" (Mukherjee 1990, 8).[6]

In one sense, Jasmine is a parabolic inflection of *Madame Butterfly* and *Miss Saigon* metamorphosed into an avenging messenger of the body, of ancestral habitats, of places wrecked by the drive for capital accumulation. Emblematic of the "combined and uneven development" of two modes of production (Novack 1966), Jasmine's journey across the United States stages a reversal of the immigrant pattern of adjustment and adaptation, unfolding the paradox of the postmodern compression of time/space as the matrix for the return of the repressed: the Other as accident, chance, pure contingency.

REHABILITATION

Returning to the theme of minorities and the notion of multiple connections and deterritorializations theorized by Deleuze and Guattari, I want to comment finally on two other representations of the Asian diaspora that implicitly critique the narrative of resolved crisis exemplified by the fiction of Kingston and Bulosan

and the model of aesthetic sublimation offered by Mukherjee's novel. One de-
tects in them a primordialist retreat to a rich coherent tradition (Kingston), a
regress to the organic romanticism of an insurrectionary peasantry (Bulosan),[7]
and the reconciling catharsis of transcendental myth (Mukherjee). These may be
deemed three capitulationist tendencies immanent in the diasporic archive that
still exercise some influence today.

It is possible to demonstrate that aestheticized humanism as an essentialist
ideology lingers in the interiority of the characters portrayed by our three exem-
plars. This ideology seeks to defuse the critical-satiric force of their narratives and
recuperate their vision of self-empowerment in order to legitimize commodity
fetishism. It is appropriate now to propose extraterritorial (more exactly, spatially dialectical) alternatives to the exorbitance of aestheticized humanism practiced by celebrities such as Amy Tan, Gish Jen, and others. I have in mind two
texts, one by John Okada and the other by Jeffery Paul Chan, that explore horizons beyond the parameters of descent (*jus sanguinis*) and putative consent (*jus
solis*) that circumscribe the apologetics of academic discourse on ethnicity and
its imaginative rendering. The first exemplifies the route of negativity and the
refusal of a pluralist synthesis, and the second illustrates the route of interpellat-
ing the Asian subject position via a triangulation of the family breakup, the diasporic return, and the discovery of the stranger within (the margin brought to
the center).

Published twelve years after the end of World War II, Okada's *No-No Boy*
(1957) attempts to capture the agony of self-division in the life of Ichiro, a second-generation Japanese American who is caught in the dilemma of claiming an
identity from the nation whose government has imprisoned his parents and his
racial kin. His problem replicates that of his friend Kenji while detained in the
concentration camp during World War II: to prove that he is a Japanese who, in
spite of or because of his descent, loves America. This predicament is only a
symptom of that malaise bedeviling the *nisei* who grew up in the camps: "Was
there no answer to the bigotry and meanness and smallness and ugliness of people?" Because Ichiro refused to forswear allegiance to Japan and serve in the U.S.
armed forces, he was imprisoned; his nay-saying, however, does not affirm his
mother's fantasy of a victorious Japan or his father's pathetic resignation. His
predicament may be intractable, given the absence of any community that recon-
ciles natives and aliens as well as the ascendancy of a rhetoric of exchange devaluing wholeness into atomized fragments: "But I did not love enough, for you were
still half my mother and I was thereby still half Japanese. . . . I was not strong
enough to fight you and I was not strong enough to fight the bitterness which
made the half of me which was you bigger than the half of me which was America
and really the whole of me that I could not see or feel" (Okada 1974, 281). How
does Okada symbolize the way out of this suspended state where difference tends
to be essentialized, where an irresolvable antinomy becomes invested with libidinal affects?

The return to the "primal scene" of a repeated deracination, of life before concentration camp, adumbrates the passage beyond negativity and aporia. Okada conceives of a process of living through the contradictions and paradoxes of the whole society, a practice of negotiation associated with the chronotope of the stratified city. In the following section, the novelistic discourse intimates a mode of knowledge in which the protagonist begins to see himself in the eyes of victimized Others amid the urban decay of the Asian quarters spatially removed from, but also communicating with, the affluent district by a single street. Here class segregation qualifies the doxa of racial difference, freezing temporal motion in the landscape of a dream aborted into nightmare. In the way that Ichiro's homecoming becomes transfigured by the encroachment of what U.S. nationalism/ white supremacy has so effectively repressed, its racialized antithesis in the image of blacks performing a parodic carnival, we comprehend the illusory substance of pluralist democracy:

> Being on Jackson Street with its familiar store fronts and taverns and restaurants, which were somehow different because the war had left its mark on them, was like trying to find one's way out of a dream that seemed real most of the time but wasn't real because it was still only a dream. The war had wrought violent changes upon the people, and the people, in turn working hard and living hard and earning a lot of money and spending it on whatever was available, had distorted the profile of Jackson Street. The street had about it the air of a carnival without quite succeeding at becoming one. A shooting gallery stood where once had been a clothing store; fish and chips had replaced a jewelry shop; and a bunch of Negroes were horsing around raucously in front of a pool parlor. Everything looked older and dirtier and shabbier.
>
> He walked past the pool parlor, picking his way gingerly among the Negroes, of whom there had been only a few at one time and of whom there seemed to be nothing but now. They were smoking and shouting and cussing and carousing and the sidewalk was slimy with their spittle.
>
> "Jap!"
>
> His pace quickened automatically, but curiosity or fear or indignation or whatever it was made him glance back at the white teeth framed in a leering dark brown which was almost black.
>
> "Go back to Tokyo, boy." Persecution in the drawl of the persecuted.
>
> The white teeth and brown-black leers picked up the cue and jogged to the rhythmical chanting of "Jap-boy, To-ki-yo, Jap-boy, To-ki-yo. . . ."
>
> Friggin' niggers, he uttered savagely to himself and, from the same place deep down inside where tolerance for the Negroes and the Jews and the Mexicans and the Chinese and the too short and too fat and too ugly abided because he was Japanese and knew what it was like better than did those who were white and average and middle class and good Democrats or liberal Republicans, the hate which was unrelenting and terrifying seethed up. (Okada 1974, 270–272)

Initiated in this ritual of lostness, *ressentiment,* and self-affirmation of one's presence as the enemy, Ichiro reaches home—a passage forecasting the diaspora's true destination. So here the Asian mock-prodigal son returns not to a utopian image of a tribal hearth but to a reaffirmation of what is antithetical to exchange value, to the bureaucratic rationality of a regime founded on racial/ethnic segmentation: the virtue of the slave's labor (valorized by Hegel in *The Phenomenology of the Spirit*). In this case, virtue inheres in Ichiro's courage to refuse subjection by the racial state. But while this entails Ichiro's repudiation of his mother's fantasy (mirror-image of imperial power), it sublates personal guilt born of an irrecusable dualism (American nationalism versus Japanese) and ushers a condition of indeterminacy on which the genre of the diasporic novel turns and returns. This uneven development in the protagonist's dilemma attests to the delayed aftereffects of the phenomenon of "unprecedented transportation," which John Berger (1984) characterizes thus: "Emigration does not only involve leaving behind, crossing water, living amongst strangers, but, also, undoing the very meaning of the world and—at its most extreme—abandoning oneself to the unreal which is the absurd. . . . To emigrate is always to dismantle the center of the world, and so to move into a lost, disoriented one of fragments" (56–57). Ichiro's life may also be evaluated as a defeat, a failure of synthesis. But what is the rationale for this denouement? One answer is, "To whisper for that which has been lost. Not out of nostalgia, but because it is on the site of loss that hopes are born" (55). I suspect that what we are witnessing here is the emergence of a new subject position that interrogates what "American" signifies, just as we perceive in the absences punctuating the life of Yamamoto's protagonist a locus of agency whose condition of possibility is prefigured by the misrecognition and circumstantial heterology embedded in the name "Las Vegas Charley." Is the juxtaposition of city and stereotype a ruse to frame and contain the threat of an alien accidentally revealing the internal corruption of the host society? Is not Ichiro's bifurcated psyche symptomatic of the return of this repressed in the "political unconscious" (Jameson 1981)?[8]

We are still operating within the problematic of exile and homesickness now appropriated by postcolonial theory as the privileged zone of the "in-between," the locus of ambivalence and syncretism. Contingency determines boundaries and borderlands, according to this skeptical perspective. The home for some groups of the Asian diaspora is, as we have seen, not already predestined by the contingencies of mass dislocations; instead, it is constructed by the mundane tasks of everyday life, by enduring and learning from the ordeal of racial exclusion and the problems of separation, the disintegration of the family, the surrender to the lure of reconciliation, and the ephemeral catharsis of mass consumerism. Fantasy and hallucination attend these critical moments of the passage. If the victimization of Asians in the United States is an effect of the overarching metanarrative of Enlightenment modernization and progress, a master-plot legitimized by an epistemology founded on allochronic distancing of Others, their reduction to objects of instrumentalizing knowledge and bureaucratic manipulation, then is a praxis of coevalness and dialogism the solution?[9] J. Chan's (1997) intriguing story, "The Chinese in Haifa," problematizes this approach and stages the nuances of its implications.

Brooding on the aftereffects of his recent divorce and separation from his children, Bill Wong—the central character in Chan's story—is comforted by Mrs. Goldberg, a Jewish mother visiting her son Herb and his wife, Ethel, Bill's close friends and neighbors. In answer to the question, "What are families for?" Mrs. Goldberg replies, "So when you lose one, you have more. . . . Everybody's got a family. . . . You come from one family, you make another" (J. Chan 1991, 88). This is the filiative solution to reification. It heralds the advent of sociobiology and ethology. Bill's situation of solitary freedom and anxiety to escape it enters into an ambiguous dialogue with Mrs. Goldberg's traditional view of the family, marriage, and children as the stable, harmonizing center of society—a view that has also characterized the tributary formation of Confucian China and recent "politically correct" neoconservative programs of reinstituting U.S.-style apartheid. This mentality is then syncopated with the fragmentation of life in a world where spatiotemporal distances are compressed in order to secure a differential politics of exchange:

> Ethel winked at Bill from over her shoulder. "Maybe you can find Bill a nice Jewish girl, Mama, in Haifa."
> "Are there Chinese in Haifa?" Herb asked.
> "The Jews and the Chinese," she said, standing in the middle of the room and weaving her eyes back and forth from her son to his wife, "they're the same." She walked to the door and Herb followed. "You know there are Jews in China, there must be Chinese in Haifa. It's all the same, even in Los Angeles." (J. Chan 1991, 90)

But are the two diasporas the same? When Mrs. Goldberg flippantly suggests to Ethel, "You get him married," this concern acquires a self-fulfilling resonance when we learn later that Ethel and Bill have already begun a secret liaison, an affair that belies Herb's claim of his successful marriage as one based on "sharing and caring." But such an attempt of the narrative to establish linkages between this anguished Chinese intellectual and his Jewish friends becomes an ironic commentary on the humanist belief in the naturalness of trust and interdependency among beleaguered communities.

Given the unrelenting war for *Lebensraum* in Palestine, encountering the Chinese in Haifa is less conceivable than meeting Jews in China. Amid the trials of such dislocations both real and imaginary, Bill and Ethel offer extraterritorial compensations. Hovering over this somewhat idyllic relation between Bill and the Goldbergs is a reported event that makes the quest for the homeland (fantasized or documented) an occasion for a minor holocaust: Three Japanese terrorists, equipped with machine guns and grenades, opened fire on passengers getting on an Israeli jetliner in Rome. Herb's exclamation of perplexity foregrounds the issue of allochronism and coevalness: "And here my mother's going to Israel today. Christ on his everlovin' crutch! What in the hell do the Japs have against us?" The ironic pathos of Herb's question is symptomatic of a failure to make connections. Internationalism, the "bad faith" of narcissistic nationalism, becomes a paltry apology when Herb assures Bill Wong that he can tell he is not a Japanese. On the other hand, what is Chan's message about the adequacy of the individual Chinese male whose *ressentiment* begins to invent a chain of signifiers that binds together incongruous elements, such as the Palestinian loss of their land, the Japanese Red Army's internationalist sympathy with the Palestinians, Jewish Zionism, Israel's image as a pariah state, and Bill Wong's (and his generation's) alienation from the ancestral culture? Contrast the burden of history intimated by the opening passage, "Bill dreamed he heard the cry of starving children in Asia bundled together in a strangely familiar school yard," with the fantasy of power conjured in the last sentence, "A vague collection of swarthy Japanese in mufti crowding around Herb's station wagon at the airport grew in his mind's eye." Is this a symptom of anarchist *ressentiment* that fills up the space once occupied by Confucian virtues, or is it an index of "an extreme individualism" flawed (as Kristeva 1991 puts it) by "a weakness whose other name is our radical strangeness" (195)? This surmise prompts us to suggest that here, as in the other texts analyzed, the dynamic of collective envy and loathing articulates itself with the ethos of market liberalism to produce the expenditures of spirit witnessed in all diasporic testimonies.

In commenting on Jean Mohr's photographs of Palestinians conducting their normal lives in abnormal circumstances, Edward Said (1985) observes that his people are "presented addressing our world as a secular place, without nostalgia for a lost transcendence" (146). And even as we look at these victims of a resolved or reversed diaspora, they are also scrutinizing, assessing, and judging us. Perhaps this is what our Asian American writers have also accomplished in their staging of difference (cultural, sexual, and racial) into dialectical contradictions, in reflexively transcoding Asian difference into a historical predicament implicating the dominant group, in articulating the immigrant consciousness as sensuous practice, a body speaking and producing meaning through the materiality of language and thus constituting minds and sensibilities as cotemporal participants in the process of social interlocution. In superseding the spatial hegemony of Western culture by a temporalizing strategy of recall that disrupts the instrumental coherence of the market and the discourse of exchange, Asian American writers have been trying to express and communicate to a world audience the historical specificity of the Asian diaspora in the United States. They have sought to locate their ethnic and racial subjectivity in a semiotic domain hitherto ruled by a homogenizing, albeit multiculturalist, ideology where "Asian" still bears the stigmata (though now conjugated with its function as "model minority" defending private property against Latinos and blacks) of being inscrutable, devious, cunning, and exotic. This socially constructed Otherness, confirming the putative superior identity of the Euro-American bloc, manifests its double signification in an officially coded presence endowed with the miracle-inducing "wisdom of the Orient." This Orientalized subjectivity, a repeated ideological effect and a product of symbolic violence, is deeply compromised and has been gradually eclipsed by the fetishism of the "superminority" model.[10]

We are now able to grasp the truth of this commonsense conception of the Orientalized subject as soon as it is concretely grounded in the historical events marking the expansion of U.S. monopoly capital throughout the world. The diverse and uncoordinated narratives documenting the specificities of the Asian diaspora have to contend not only with the legacy of such received notions but also with the juridical limits established by a racial state, as attested by two unprecedented actions: the 1882 Exclusion Act and the imprisonment of 110,000 Japanese Americans during World War II.[11] The uneven development of the world system of capital after the end of the Cold War and the dissolution of various state/bureaucratic socialisms has so far evolved to a point where the systemic crisis of capital accumulation will now conflate residual, dominant, and emergent impulses, margin and center, metropolis and periphery, in spaces where Western hegemony will take on new forms and guises. With the movement of populations in Eastern Europe and elsewhere, the primal scene of deracination returns to haunt the premature celebration of civic nationalism, unity in diversity, and consumerist "common culture."

Here I want to enter a brief parenthesis that can only suggest the scope of further research into the aesthetics and politics of an emergent and genuinely international genre. The advent of a feminist praxis in Filipino writing (most notably in the novels of Lualhati Bautista) in the 1970s and 1980s may be explained by the phenomenon of millions of Filipino contract laborers, mostly women, sojourning in the Middle East, Europe, Japan, Hong Kong, Singapore, and elsewhere. When these migrant workers return home, they construct stories of their heterogeneous experiences that assume a narrative form conflating the quest motif with the seduction/ordeal motif—a plot that violates all probabilities found in the schemas of semiotic narratology. When the female subaltern returns, the mimesis of her struggle for survival almost always implicates the diegesis of the world system as a metanarrative of the global circulation of commodified bodies and phallocentric energies. Exchange of her labor power short-circuits the time/space compression of the postmodern economy. Whether as household servant in Kuwait or "hospitality girl" in Tokyo, she narrates the lived experience of victimage as a reversal of the "civilizing mission" (Beltran and Rodriguez 1996). She thus repeats the whole epic of colonization—but with a difference: Her gendered subject position or agency yields not surplus value but the hallucination of commodity fetishism when consumer goods and traumas become cargo myths for native consumption in the Philippines. In this sense, the migrant worker as "speaking subject" destabilizes the regularities of the "New World Order" and the "free market" discourse of privatized self-fulfillment. Her fabula decenters the *sjuzhet* of technocratic modernization. Overall, this new genre of migrant narrative explodes the traditional definitions of the gendered subject provided by the Symbolic Order of dependent capitalism, while its transgressive allegory destroys the conventional plots of immigrant success and postcolonial hybridity.

Meanwhile, the scenario in the United States may be said to vary only in its determinate historical particularities. New Asian immigrants will have to invent their own imaginative responses to changed class and race alignments that subtend U.S. political dynamics in the twenty-first century. However, the task on the whole remains the same: the reconstitution of the Asian subject position as an agency of resistance to racist subjugation and of emancipation from the bondage of globalized capital. In the words of Genny Lim, a distinguished Chinese American playwright, "We are living in such adverse times—ecologically, economically, morally and spiritually—that any effort made to mobilize peoples' consciousness into self-determination, self-validation, compassion, and racial, class, and sexual understanding is a step further along in the difficult journey of human survival on this planet" (quoted in Houston 1993, 153–154).

NOTES

1. For a summary of the historical background of Asian immigration, see S. Chan (1991).

2. Note the analogous rite of passage in Younghill Kang's arrival in the United States recounted in "From East Goes West": "It was in New York I felt I was destined really 'to come out from the board.' The beginning of my new existence must be founded here. In Korea to come out from the boat is an idiom meaning to be born, as the word 'pai' for 'womb' is the same as 'pai' for 'boat' " (Kang 1974, 217–218).

3. For testimonials of how Chinese lived through their ordeal at Angel Island, see Takaki (1989, 231–239).

4. This praxis of playing with boundaries and limits signifies, for Fredric Jameson (1991), the act of totalization, which he privileges as the necessary orientation for any emancipatory or revolutionary project.

5. Perhaps a revealing indication of this contradictory process may be illustrated by one urban policy in Britain to achieve racial integration by way of "ecological dispersal" (see Cashmore 1998, 80–81).

6. For a critique of Mukherjee's temporizing responses to her Canadian and U.S. milieu, see Tapping (1992).

7. I initiate a revisionist approach to Bulosan in *From Exile to Diaspora* (1998b).

8. Aside from Kristeva's speculative reflections on the function of the stranger in history, I recommend Georg Simmel's (1977) essay "The Stranger" as one of the most provocative, seminal reconnaissance of this character type and social phenomenon.

9. For some, the scenario is that of postcolonial subaltern academics at last priming themselves up to speak to Western poststructuralists. One recent instance can be cited. Elaine Kim (1993) has taken on board the postmodernist notion that identities are "fluid and migratory," that the dominant culture is "not monolithic and unitary," and this leads

her to recycle the assimilationist paradigm in a new apologetic version: New Asian immigrants, she writes, "have moved to cities and towns where few Asian Americans had lived before and are doing things to earn their livelihoods that they could not have imagined when they were in their homelands: Cambodians are making doughnuts, Koreans are making burritos, South Asians are operating motels, Filipinos are driving airport shuttle buses" (xi). Erasing the prodigious history of intervention of U.S. imperialism into the homelands of these newcomers, Kim revives the "Statue of Liberty" slogan of the United States as the home to refugees, persecuted peasants, and so on—resurrects, indeed, the ghost of Charlie Chan!

10. In his recent book, David Palumbo-Liu (1999) inquires into the instrumentalization of the "model minority" myth by the media apparatus to direct envy and loathing toward hegemonic ends.

11. Contrary to the thesis (argued by Nathan Glazer and others) that the United States was founded *inter alia* on the principle of free entry granted to everyone, the Chinese Exclusion Act of 1882 stands as a landmark decision in which members of a specific ethnic group for the first time in U.S. history were denied entry.

From 1910 to 1940, the Angel Island Immigration Station served to process Asian immigrants. For insightful analysis of recent trends in labor migration, see Ong, Bonacich, and Cheng (1994).

2

Historicizing the Space of Asian America

I intended to come to America to earn a living. . . . How was anyone to know
that my dwelling place would be a prison.

—Anonymous, graffiti from the Angel Island Detention Center

If we can see the connections of how often this [internment of Japanese
Americans in World War II] happens in history, we can stem the tide of
these things happening again by speaking out against them.

—Yuri Kochiyama

I rejoice at the changing of the guard. . . . I am glad that I am still around
not only as a participant but as a griot to pass on the story of how we got to
this place—because to paraphrase Kierkegaard, if the future is to be lived,
the past must be understood.

—Grace Lee Boggs

The catastrophic fall of the Asian financial market following the disintegration of Thailand and Korea as the miracle newly industrializing countries
(NICs), or Asian "tigers," cannot but alter the parameters of theory and representation that produce and reproduce the image/knowledge of Asians inhabiting
the continental United States. Perceptions of Filipinos fleeing the Philippines are
contaminated by the atmosphere of disaster and chaos. In a book that celebrated
the Asian economic renaissance before the collapse, *The Dawn of the Pacific Century*, by William McCord (1991), the Philippines is eclipsed by the successes of
Hong Kong, Singapore, Taiwan, and South Korea. Focusing on local corruption
and cultural inadequacies, McCord downplays U.S. colonial domination of the

Philippines and thus reinforces a prevalent racializing technology of ethnocentric developmentalism and modernization.

Given the economic depression and political turmoil in the Philippines since the demise of the Marcos dictatorship up to the present, Filipinos have comprised the largest number of immigrants from Asia since the 1970s. But the connection between the "sending" and "receiving" societies has never been satisfactorily clarified. One scholar rejected "world system" theory about dependency relationships between peripheral and core nations by claiming that Filipinos in the United States enjoy an occupational status better than native-born Americans (Cariño 1996, 297). The facts of income received, however, belies the claim (Aguirre and Turner 1998). So far, the epistemology of ethnic studies concerning Asian Americans (in my terminology, U.S. Asians) is tenaciously circumscribed by the "model minority" myth and the perennial "Yellow Peril" stereotype. Assimilationist ideology has been refurbished by multiculturalism, affording us a schizoid if pragmatic optic to circumscribe the enigma of successful pariahs while capital's global axiomatic continues to function as "a decentered system with manifold apparatuses of capture—symbolic, economic, and political" (Escobar 1995, 99) able to exploit while claiming to foster heterogeneous social forms and cultural practices in the "third world."

Notwithstanding the accelerating crisis of global capital witnessed recently in Kosovo, Mexico, Colombia, and East Timor, one recent textbook complacently registers the double inscription of Asians in a fissured cartography: "The history of Asian Americans combines the immigrant's quest for the American dream and the racial minority's confrontation with discriminating laws and attitudes" (Dudley 1997, 14; see also Kitano and Daniels 1995). Antinomies and paradox are inscribed in the logic of commodity exchange, the chief commodity here being labor power and its differential/sexual embodiment. In addition, the chief mode of ensuring hegemony by the dialectic of assimilation and segregation answers the need of the regulatory state to adjust its immigration and citizenship policies according to the changing economic and political conditions (Gran 1996; Hing and Lee 1996). In an acute analysis of Judge Karlin's sentencing colloquy in the 1992 trial of Du Soon Ja (accused killer of Natasha Harlins), Neil Gotanda (1995) found that old stereotypes are alive and well, fruitfully cohabiting with the new multiculturalist doxa: that is, Asians are both hardworking and wily, intelligent and obsequious, adaptable and inscrutable. Amid the thoroughgoing reconfiguration of the planet's political/economic map, why this persistence of a racializing agenda with respect to U.S. Asians?[1]

THE SINGULARITY OF THE PLURAL

A review of demographic trends can situate the predicament of Asians as intractable "foreigners" despite the incorporation of a few. By the year 2020, the population labeled "Asian Americans" in this country will number 20.2 million. The Asian Pacific population increased from 1.5 million in 1970 to 8.8 million in 1994, with the Filipinos becoming the largest component (more than two million, up from 1,406,770 in the 1990 census report [Gonzales 1993, 181]). In the year 2000, Asians and Pacific Islanders will total 12.1 million, about 4 percent of the total population (Kitano 1997, 307). In California, the projection is that the number of Asians will grow from 2.9 million to 8.5 million in 2020. Articulated with manifold interethnic conflicts amid large-scale social crises, this change is bound to complicate and intensify the multiplication of differences enough to confound taxonomists and the high priests of a normative "common culture."

Given the heterogeneity of the histories, economic stratification, and cultural composition of the post-1965 immigrants and refugees, all talk of Asian panethnicity should now be abandoned as useless speculation. Class, gender, locality, generational, and other conflicts all militate against panethnicity as a tactical form of coalitional politics. Not so long ago, Professor Roger Daniels (1993) stated the obvious: "The conglomerate image of Asian Americans is an illusion." This is even truer today. No longer sharing the common pre–World War II experience of being victimized by exclusion acts, antimiscegenation laws, and other disciplinary apparatuses of racialization, Vietnamese, Kampucheans, and Hmongs have now diverged from the once dominant pattern of settlement, occupation, education, family structure, and other modes of ethnic identification. After 1965, one can no longer postulate a homogeneous "Asian American" bloc without reservations. Fragmentation now characterizes this bloc even as new forms of racism totalize the incompatible subject positions of each nationality. To use current jargon, the bureaucratic category "Asian American" (not even including "Pacific Islander") has been decentered by systemic contingencies. The putatively homogeneous inhabitants of the Asiatic "Barred Zone" (ascribed by the immigration laws of 1917 and 1924; see Reimers 1992) have been deconstructed beyond repair to the point where today, among "postality" scholars, a cult of multiple and indeterminate subject positions is flourishing. Evelyn Hu-DeHart (1999) reports sightings of Asian American "transnationals and bridge builders on the Pacific Rim" (9). However, we have yet to meet a cyborg or borderland denizen of confirmed U.S. Asian genealogy.

Despite such empirical grounding, versions of the "melting pot" theory are still recycled to homogenize variegated multitudes. Let me cite examples. A monograph of the Population Reference Bureau, *Asian Americans: America's Fastest Growing Minority Group,* by William O'Hare and Judy Felt (1991), while acknowledging disparities, lumps its subjects indiscriminately: "While Asian Americans have slightly higher average family incomes than non-Hispanic whites, they also have much higher poverty rates" (15). A more recent book, *Asian Americans,* edited by Pyong Gap Min (1995), has no hesitation predicting that Asians will be easily assimilated in time. While admitting the fact that language barriers still exist and the old stereotypes of disloyal or enemy aliens still affect mainstream perception, Min relies on three factors that will promote rapid assimilation: (1) the presence of well-assimilated native-born Asian Americans will eliminate the image of the "stranger," (2) multiculturalism or cultural pluralism will promote the toleration of "subcultural differences," and (3) the economic and political power of Asian nation-states will create a positive image in general. These factors are supposed to displace the immigrant-centered argument with the neo-Weberian paradigm of situational ethnicity, a simple affair of marking social boundaries. The problem with this is obvious: It ignores power imbalances, "the absolute centrality of power relationships" (Jenkins 1986, 178), and thus leads to blaming the victims for their cultural deficit and the poverty of their cultural orientations, values, and goals.

The factor of Asian nation-states creating a positive image of U.S. Asians has now been canceled by a recent turn of events. Recession in Japan competes with Chinese human-rights violations to resurrect an image of the culpable Asian. It is also nullified by what I call the Vincent Chin syndrome: Political demagoguery in times of economic crisis can shift the target of scapegoating onto the Japanese, the Korean, or any Asian and thus reactivate the sedimented persona of the recalcitrant, non-English-speaking, shifty-eyed foreigner in our midst. The second reason pertaining to multiculturalism is fallacious since "cultural pluralism" has been around since the attenuation of the Anglo-Saxon supremacy/nativist movement; multiculturalism is now, in fact, the enshrined cooptative formula for peacefully managing differences among the subalterns (San Juan 1995). And finally, the process of acculturation of second- or third-generation U.S. Asians has been qualified (by Min himself) as valid only for the cultural and not for the social dimension. In fact, the sociological data lead to this seemingly paradoxical conclusion: "Although the vast majority of second-generation Asian Americans will lose their native language and cultural tradition, they are likely to maintain a strong ethnic identity and to interact mainly with coethnics" (Min 1995, 279). Acculturation, then, heightens ethnic difference and even fosters separatism.

Given this persistence of the ethnicity paradigm criticized in the 1980s by Michael Omi and Howard Winant (1986) in *Racial Formations in the United States,* commentators on the Asian scene still toe the party line of Glazer and Moynihan (1975). As their colleague Werner Sollors (1986) put it, ethnicity is not a matter of descent or lineage but "of the importance that individuals ascribe to it." Form determines content. In his pathbreaking book *Racial Oppression in America,* Robert Blauner (1972) repudiated the fallacy of subsuming the diverse experiences of subjugation of people of color under the ethnic immigrant model that privileges the teleology of Eurocentric assimilation in defining the U.S. nation-state. But obviously the lessons have not been learned (Takaki 1987; Steinberg 1995), or else the specter of "American exceptionalism" has a way of being resurrected, especially in periods of economic crisis and nativist resurgence. But it is not immigration as such or its statist subsumption that generates the racialized exclusion and oppression of U.S. Asians; rather, it is the totality of social relations and its juridical materializations explored by Critical Race Theory (Crenshaw et al. 1995; Delgado 1995).

I submit that racism is a salient ideological symptom of the general logic of capitalist rule that Georg Lukács (1971) described as "reification," the effect of commodity fetishism pervading all of social life (including the cultural realm). This does not reduce racism to a matter of class struggle or an economistic triviality but rather locates it within the political economy of social practices and ideological–cultural moments in a specific nation-state formation within which it acquires its efficacy and concrete (in the sense of multiply determined) historicity. Etienne Balibar (1999) asserts that "class and race constitute the two antinomic poles of a permanent dialectic, which is at the heart of modern representations of history" (204). Overdetermined by class antagonisms, racism cannot be conflated with ethnocentrism or caste prejudice, particularly in the complex genealogy of the U.S. racial order.

THE VICISSITUDES OF PANETHNICITY

Panethnicity is one specimen of the ideological recuperation of what I would call the Myrdal complex (the presumed ambivalent nature of U.S. democracy preaching equality but institutionalizing discrimination) that plagues all pluralist liberal thought, including its radical and pragmatic variants.[2]

Asian American panethnicity has been promoted by some scholars as a historical product of the unity and solidarity of "internally colonized" U.S. Asian minorities during the 1960s. The pan-Asian framework arose from the common experience of oppression of Chinese, Japanese, and Filipino workers, students, and middle strata, underpinned by the ideological conception of "Orientals" in the majoritarian consciousness and institutions (Hamamoto 1994). Yen Le Espiritu (1996) explains the origin of the change: "To define their own image and to claim an American identity, college students of Asian ancestry coined the term Asian American to stand for all of us Americans of Asian descent. . . . While Oriental suggests passivity and acquiescence, Asian American connotes political activism because an Asian American gives a damn about his life, his work, his beliefs, and is willing to do almost anything to help Orientals become Asian Americans" (57). The first pan-Asian political organization founded in Berkeley in 1969, the Asian American Political Alliance, was composed mainly of students, mostly third- and fourth-generation Asian activists. In the 1970s, pan-Asian organizations among social workers, media, public health, and other fields, mushroomed, but—as Espiritu herself acknowledges—pan-Asianism "barely touched the Asian ethnic enclaves" (1996, 58). In fact, pan-Asianism concealed the ethnic chauvinisms and class cleavages, hierarchy, and conflicts generated by the operation of U.S. racializing politics or inherited from imperial divide-and-rule policies. (One recent instance is the Filipino American protest at the award given by the Association of Asian American Studies to Lois Yamanaka's novel *Blu's Hanging* allegedly satirizing Filipinos in Hawaii.) The "cultural entrepreneurs" of pan-Asianism turned out to be agents for opportunist electoral politics, lobbyists for transnational corporations, and brokers for the bureaucratic utilitarian ethos. They served as the progenitors of the post-1980s Asian neoconservatives who glorify the "model minority" stereotype while opposing Affirmative Action and social programs for the disadvantaged.

The more profound motivation for pan-Asianism is the historically specific racism of white supremacy toward Asians. Sucheng Chan (1991) formulated the consensus in her interpretive history, "In their relationship to the host society, well-to-do merchants and poor servants, landowning farmers and propertyless farm workers, exploitative labor contractors and exploited laborers alike were considered inferior to all Euro-Americans, regardless of the internal ethnic and socio-economic divisions among the latter" (187). Instead of valorizing ethnicity or cultural difference per se, we need to concentrate on what Robert Miles (1989) and Colette Guillaumin (1995) calls the "racialization" process, its ideological and institutional articulations.[3] This process embraces not just immigrant cultures and rituals of citizenship but also labor markets, sexual subordination, diplomacy, and in particular colonial domination of territories and peoples (Hawaii, the Philippines, Puerto Rico, and the "internal colonies" within the imperial metropole). There is still no gainsaying the cogency of Edna Bonacich's observation that racism, racial inequality, is inextricably tied to capitalism as a political–economic system that produces and reproduces inequality, utilizing modalities of winning consensus—assimilationism, liberal reforms, and so on—to displace its ineluctable crises and prolong its life.

We need to contextualize the plight of Asian Americans as a racialized, not just ethnic, group in the all-encompassing narrative of globalization. In a provocative essay using a historical-materialist framework, "The Construction of Peoplehood," Immanuel Wallerstein (1991) argued that the varying usages of people, race, nation, and ethnicity stem from their function in expressing political claims whose legitimacy depends on the historical structure of the capitalist world economy. While "race" concerns the axial division of labor in the world economy (the core–periphery antinomy), "nation" refers to the political superstructure of this historical system (sovereign states in the interstate system). Wallerstein explains that "ethnic group" is the concept designating "household structures that permit the maintenance of large components of non-waged labour in the accumulation of capital" (79). Given the differential costs of production in the core–periphery system, we have differing internal political structures that serve as the "major sustaining bulwark of the inegalitarian state system that manages and maintains the axial division of labor" today. Race and racism "is the expression, the promoter and the consequence of the geographical concentration associated with the axial division of labour" (179–180). While race/racism and nation/nationalism function as categories that register competing claims for advantage in the capitalist world economy, it is ethnicization conceived as the distinctive cultural socialization of the workforce that enables the complex occupational hierarchy of labor (marked by differential allocation of surplus value, class/status antagonisms, and so on) to be legitimized without contradicting the formal equality of citizens before the law in liberal-democratic polities. Further, Wallerstein (1991) points out that capitalism gains flexibility in restructuring itself to preserve its legitimacy: "Ethnicization, or peoplehood, resolves one of the basic contradictions of historical capitalism—its simultaneous thrust for theoretical equality and practical inequality"—by exploiting the mentalities of the segmented working populace. In this way, people-based political activity, or the new social movements premised on authentic identities and autonomy of communities, arises because of the contradictions of the system.

Ethnicity, then, is not a primordial category that testifies to the virtue of a liberal pluralist market-centered system but, rather, a means utilized to legitimate the contradictions. This is not to imply that we should return to the orthodox Marxist view that dividing workers according to race or ethnicity is a conspiratorial tool by capital to destroy class unity. What I would stress is precisely the need to analyze the racialization of ethnicities into class/gendered identities (see chapters 6 and 7 of Hutchinson and Smith 1996). In the United States, "whiteness" mediates individual/group conceptions of self, gender, community, and class interest, so that the traditional cost–benefit calculations of economists cannot be valid unless linked "to the self-understanding of workers creating and consenting to whiteness as a culture and political economy of domination" (Williams 1995, 307). John Hope Franklin (1989) has delineated the trajectory of ethnic exclusion in the United States as coinciding with the racializing drives of finance capitalism. Surveying the "images of the outsider" in American law and culture, Richard Delgado and Jean Stefancic (1997) have noted the metamorphosis of Charlie Chan to the "Yellow Menace" and the "master Oriental criminal" in synchrony with U.S. imperial strategy toward China and Japan.

WHITENESS BECOMES VISIBLE

In the context of our inquiry, the term "whiteness" alludes to the sociopolitical constitution of the various European cohorts as a hegemonic collectivity coinciding with the history of the formation of the U.S. nation-state as a "settler society." To avoid the trap of multiculturalism as a discourse of formalistically reconciling ethnic differences, we need to recall how the founders of the U.S. nation-state "legitimated and perpetuated . . . the plural society of a racially bifurcated colonist America regulated by the normative code of a racial creed" (Ringer 1983, quoted in Janiewski 1995). The "settler society" paradigm (instead of the immigrant model), which sanctioned racially based subordination of nonwhite groups and communities (indigenous, enslaved, conquered), entails the corollary notion of "internal colonialism." The notion of "internal colonialism" involves juridical and state apparatuses that legitimized the exploitation of minorities in segmented labor markets, hierarchical wage scales, residential segregation, and other effects of numerous discriminatory practices by employers and state apparatuses (Stasiulis and Yuval-Davis 1995). Implicitly subscribing to the doctrine of "American exceptionalism" and its associated ethos of laissez-faire multiculturalism, postmodernist racial-formation theory fails to grasp the fundamental fact of institutional racism in the United States as well as the reality of North–South contradictions and its replication within the metropoles of North America and Europe—the division between rich white nations and poor nations comprised of people of color—that exemplifies today the most insidiously dehumanizing form of racism (Rex 1982) sustaining worldwide capital accumulation. It also fails to comprehend the reality of the U.S. neocolonial subjugation of the Philippines and many Caribbean and Central American nations, including Mexico. As Hugh Tinker (1993) reminds us, "To the Third World, white racism is a continuing legacy of white imperialism and an aspect of the still pervasive force of neocolonialism" (135).

Recent scholarship on the ideological construction of "whiteness" in U.S. history should illuminate also the invention of the "Asian American" as a monolithic, standardizing rubric. It is clear that the diverse collectivities classified by official bureaucracy as "Asian American" manifest more discordant features than affinities and commonalities. The argument that they share similar values (e.g., Confucian ethics), ascribed "racial" characteristics, and kindred interests in politics, education, social services, and so on cannot be justified by the historical experiences of the peoples involved, especially those who came after World War II. This does not mean that U.S. Asians did not and do not now engage in coalitions and alliances to support certain causes or cooperate for mutual benefit; examples are numerous. In fact, the insistence on pan-Asianism can only obscure if not obfuscate the patent problems of underemployment and unequal reward (the "glass ceiling"), occupational segregation, underrepresentation, and class polarization. One need only cite the high rates of poverty among Asian refugees: 26 percent for Vietnamese, 35 percent for Laotians, 43 percent for Cambodians, and 64 percent for the Hmongs (Kitano and Daniels 1997, 179). All studies also show that most Filipinos today find themselves condemned to the secondary labor market—low-wage jobs in the private sector—despite higher educational attainment (Nee and Sanders 1985; Cabezas and Kawaguchi 1989; for a general survey, see Ong, Bonacich, and Cheng 1994). These structural realities escape the culturalist articulation theory propagated by Laclau and Mouffe and the elite-centered populism of social-movement advocates.

BEWARE THE "MODEL MINORITY" TRAP

At this point, some conscientious readers might already be ruminating about "model minority," the contemporary version of the "yellow peril" that used to haunt white-supremacist America. Lest we be overwhelmed by all the optimistic predictions of impending assimilation/acculturation of U.S. Asians into the larger body politic, I offer as a reminder this concluding observation by the U.S. Commission on Civil Rights (1992): "The root causes of bigotry and violence against Asian Americans are complex. Racial prejudice; misplaced anger caused by wars or economic competition with Asian countries; resentment of the real or perceived success of Asian Americans; and a lack of understanding of the histories, customs, and religions of Asian Americans all play a role in triggering incidents of bigotry and violence" (191; see also National Asian Pacific American Legal Consortium 1999). Faced with the racial politics of the 1980s and 1990s, all talk about fashioning or searching for an "authentic Asian American identity" and "reclaiming" our history can sound only fatuous. More culpable is the view that in order to transcend the Frank Chin–Maxine Hong Kingston misrecognition of each other, U.S. Asian artists should utilize their "ethnic sensibility to describe aspects of the Asian American experience that appeal to a common humanity" (Wei 1996, 357)—a plea for commodifying the exotic into plain American pie. To conceive of the "Asian American Movement," including its oppositional or contestatory cultural production, in terms of its place in the hegemonic scheme of things is to submit to the rules of the game contrived and manipulated by the very forces that any self-respecting egalitarian movement is supposed to overthrow.

A study conducted in 1991 concluded that the economic success story of U.S. Asians is undermined by two facts: that their reward is not commensurate with their educational attainment and that they have higher poverty rates than non-Hispanic whites (for an earlier survey, see Woo 1989). The myth of the "model minority" persists in obscuring these facts. Because of this, U.S. Asians are collectively perceived as a threat by other minority groups, especially blacks in New York, Washington, D.C., and Los Angeles, and whites who fear the competitive power of Pacific Rim countries. Asian Americans are thus caught between two antithetical pressures: "On the one hand, Asian Americans are lauded as a 'model minority' that is fulfilling the American dream and confirming the image of America as a 'melting pot.' On the other hand, they seem hampered by invisible barriers—a so-called glass ceiling—that keep them from climbing to the top rungs of power" (O'Hare and Felt 1991, 15). What is clearly configuring the dilemma is not the regime of immigration laws or procedures of naturalization but the contradiction between ideology—the imaginary mode of connecting subjects to reality—and the limits of a racialized political economy, the constraints of transnational, late capitalism.

On the face of these developments, postmodernism enters the scene and proclaims the ontological imperatives of hybridity, multiplicity, and fragmentation as a more viable optic for analyzing the situation. Keith Osajima (1995), for example, proposes a synthetic postmodernism that will combine the virtues of panethnic generalizing with "the multiplicitous nature of our constructed identities." Ethnic absolutism translates into "identity politics." In general, postmodernists uphold antiessentialist, fluctuating, or ambiguous subject positions premised on the rejection of "grand metanarratives," rationally constituted agency, and the normative discourse of justice and equality (Stabile 1995). A typical enunciation of this theoretical standpoint may be discerned in Lisa Lowe's (1995) thesis: "A multiplicity of social contradictions with different origins converge at different sites within any social formation—the family, education, religion, communications media, sites of capitalist production—and each is uneven and incommensurable, with certain contradictions taking priority over others in response to the material conditions of a given historical moment" (46). Contingency thus overrides the hegemonic imperative polarizing social blocs.

Following the poststructuralist semiotics of Ernesto Laclau and Chantal Mouffe (1985) (see the critiques of Hunter 1988; Eagleton 1996; Amin 1998), postmodernists celebrate the alleged dispersal of power into shifting and arbitrary sites of the social field. This move, I submit, effectively disables any long-range collective project of discovering a possible Archimedean point at which the whole system can be dismantled. This is because it does not address the key aspects of the legitimation crisis subtending the production-and-reproduction dynamics of the U.S. formation inter alia: the racializing agencies of "whiteness" in a settler society, the political economy of "internal colonialism" and its neo-colonial extensions, and the continuing injustices and reproduction of oppression fomented by institutional racism.

Postmodernists repudiate politics (critique of political economy) in favor of cultural studies (modes of representation). In doing so, they miss the key to understanding the legitimation crisis of the capitalist state (Jessop 1982). I want to indicate briefly what abdication from politics implies, namely, ignoring those crucial institutions determining racial ideological practices, partly surveyed in works such as *The New Asian Immigration in Los Angeles and Global Restructuring* (Ong, Bonacich, and Cheng 1994), *Race, Ethnicity, and Nationality in the United States* (Wong 1999), and others. The sexploitation of Asian American women, the linchpin of the racializing machine, detailed by Teresa Amott and Julie Matthaei (1991), deploy state and bureaucratic machinery well outside the realm of cultural production, encompassing the "gender-role stratification" that Esther Ngan-Ling Chow (1994) alludes to in charting the barriers to an Asian American feminist movement.

Critical Race Theory has also reminded us of the imbrication of state and civil society in the hegemonic process. Official racial policy in the United States is generally conservative and tradition bound despite the recent vogue of consensual multiculturalism (Potter and Knepper 1998). The development of an Asian American legal scholarship traced by Robert Chang (1995) demonstrates succinctly the mediation of state institutions and bureaucratic policies in defining citizenship and other kindred juridical categories that made possible the 1942 Presidential Executive Order 9066, which affected over 110,000 Japanese Americans. Aside from these obvious cases, one can cite the central role played by Asians as "buffer" races that replaced the darker-skinned Europeans already segregated by the U.S. Census Bureau (Patterson 1997), allowing federal programs such as the GI Bill to operate selectively. State and civil society comprise the symbiotic nexus of practices and institutions that cannot be artificially separated in any critical analysis of racism toward U.S. Asians. I think the clearest example of how Gramsci's injunction to analyze the alignment of political forces can be applied is found in Michael Goldfield's (1997) historical summation of how the anti-Chinese movement was a means used by factions of the ruling class to rally the white populace behind their platforms, divide the working people, and maintain their continued exploitation of all.

PITFALLS OF POSTMODERNISM

Incalculable damage has been inflicted by a postmodernist skepticism that claims to be more revolutionary than the radical guidelines of research into internal colonialism or dual labor market within the horizon of a historical-materialist methodology. This does not mean we do not have the traditional individualistic, aestheticizing trends regurgitated by assorted self-performers (see Hongo 1995). The ubiquitous troupe of Lotus Blossoms and Gunga Dins, now of course sporting more fashionable trappings, still dominate the traveling road shows of "Asian American" cultural production today. Probably the most provocative application of Foucauldian and deconstructive tools in analyzing U.S. racial politics remains Omi and Winant's (1986) *Racial Formation in the United States*. But its inadequacy demonstrated itself in being unable to anticipate the 1992 Los Angeles interethnic conflict between blacks and Korean Americans, nor could it foresee the rise of neoconservatives among Asian Americans (San Juan 1992a). By devaluing the role of ideological state apparatuses and the political economy of labor in globalized capitalism, postmodernist thinking remains trapped in a metaphysics of textualism and an ontology of pragmatic "language games" that only reinforce the unequal division of labor and the unjust hierarchy of power in U.S. society and in the domain of international relations.[4]

One example of postmodernist speculation in which a notion of transnational subjectivity is substituted for the now obsolete idea of panethnicity may be cited here. It does not require Superman's X-ray vision for us to tell that the paragon of the diasporic subject as a postcolonial "hybrid" often masks the working of a dominant "common culture" premised on differences, not contradictions. Heterogeneity can then be a ruse for recuperative patriotism. The latest version is the theory of "multiple identities" and "fluid" positions of immigrants straddling two nation-states assumed to be of equal status and ranking in the world system; such identities are unique because they allegedly participate in the political economies of both worlds. This is obviously a paradigm based on the dynamics of market exchange value whereby a third abstract entity emerges and circulates between two incommensurable objects or domains, supposedly partaking of both but identical with neither. The artifactual entity, however, hitherto remains parasitic on the superior nation-state (the United States), belying its claim to inclusiveness and transcultural catholicity.

Postmodern valorization of identity as a self-reflexive project has become the easy, fashionable cure for the "unhooking" of human relations in alienated/reified bourgeois society. Because of the seductive potential of this postmodern stance, I would like to comment on Yen Le Espiritu's (1995) study *Filipino American Lives*, in which she applies the new conceptual model of transnationalism. When post-1965 second- and third-generation Filipinos (mostly professionals) devise strategies to construct multiple and overlapping identities, thus presumably altering their rank in U.S. society, they succeed (for Espiritu) in resisting the dominant ideology of subordination by race, class, gender, nationality, and so on. While the self-interpretation of Espiritu's informants does contain indices of flux rather than continuity, multilinear lines of narrative rather than one monologic strand, I think that this is not due to their overall success in elevating their country and culture of origin to equal status with the United States and its hegemonic prerogatives. This is the fatal mistake of the transnational model despite its gesture of acknowledging it: It assumes the parity of colonized/dominated peoples and the U.S. nation-state in contemporary global capitalism.

All kinds of fallacious judgments stem from the error of marginalizing the colonial subjugation of the Filipino people by the United States, directly from 1898 to 1946 and indirectly from 1946 to the present (San Juan 1996b). As Audrey Smedley (1993) recounts, the racial worldview attached to Jim Crow laws framed the conquest of the Philippines: "With the start of the Spanish–American War in 1898, a conflict permeated with racial elements, America entered into the colonial world and took upon itself some of the 'white man's destiny' and 'burden' in the form of the 'little brown peoples' of the Philippines" (270). Those "brown peoples" acquired a menacing look when an American congressman in 1900 opposed the suggestion that they be given citizenship because of his picture of Filipinos as "physical weaklings of low stature with black skin, closely curling hair, flat noses, thick lips and large clumsy feet . . . mongrels of the East . . . with harem habits" (Okihiro 1997, 205). Coercively fabricated inequality becomes naturalized in this anatomy of physical appearance. Western superordinate gaze could not exercise surveillance on this horde of captive subjects without resubjectifying it by techniques of Orientalization and feminization and by extralegal taboos and threats that convert the spectacularized Others into a pathologized caste. Ultimately, the Filipino had to be quarantined, hence Commonwealth status was granted in 1935 to stop the flow of immigrants—until the dam was opened again after 1965. Evoking the image of Filipinos as quiet proto-Puritans in Morro Bay, California, in the sixteenth century or resourceful fugitives in Louisiana in the next century—a species of desperate if pathetic self-exoticizing by alleged community leaders—will not expunge the record of racist violence inflicted on the "Manongs" and their more inspiring narratives of revolt described by Carlos Bulosan and Philip Vera Cruz in their autobiographical writings. These narratives have yet to be read and appreciated by the young newly arrived generation of Filipinos who are just beginning to experience the subtle impact of new racisms amid the resurgence of the national democratic revolution in the homeland.

The inroads of "manifest destiny" cannot be dismissed so easily by the sporadic tokens of success. The resourceful cunning and prudence of Filipino immigrants in trying to survive and flourish in a generally inhospitable environment (San Diego, California, is implicitly assumed to be representative of the whole country) should not be unilaterally construed as a sign of postmodern playfulness and inventiveness. Veteran union organizer Philip Vera Cruz (1992) discerned the proverbial duplicity or borderline amphibiousness of Filipinos as a strategy of defense, calculating the oscillating lines of force triangulating their lives: "It was as if many of us Filipinos were living behind hidden identities for fear of associating with the realities of our lives, our real names, and therefore our real identities" (123). But that way of "speaking truth to power" belies the claim of postmodern hybridity that borders are permeable anytime anywhere. Unlike the self-serving "community leaders" who boasted of their "Americanization" (e.g., Cordova 1983; Root 1997), Filipinos in the front line of the anti-imperialist struggle mapped the contours of boundaries and borders that demarcated their collective odyssey. Adaptation or assimilation spelled more than death—it negated their dignity as individuals and as a people.

The current scholarship on immigration, with its equalizing apparatus of push/pull concepts, not only distorts history but replaces it with a market-centered model. Not only is the burden of adaptation placed on the colonized subject but, more reprehensible, his cultural baggage is made to account for his victimage. Consider this somewhat incredible explanation of one scholar who attempts to exonerate the racial discrimination found in the host society by shifting our attention to the "human resource" characteristics of the victims:

> For Filipinos, however, a subordinate status is a familiar experience. Filipino immigrants come from a country that is beset by severe social and economic problems. They have also suffered under centuries of colonial domination and from the development of an oligarchical leadership composed mostly of the social and economic elite of the country. This may help explain the apparent vulnerability of Filipino Americans to structural discrimination and subordination. (Cariño 1996, 300)

In short, the Filipinos' familiarity with "structural discrimination" at home allows them to withstand if not survive an analogous form of discrimination abroad. But the transparent tautological "wisdom" of this discovery cannot explain the reason for the collective resistance of Filipinos who organized multiethnic workers in the Hawaiian plantations and fought the vigilantes on the West Coast throughout the first half of the twentieth century, culminating in their founding of the United Farm Workers of America and their leadership of militant unions in Seattle, Washington, and elsewhere. Nor can it shed light on the revolutionary mass insurgency raging today against the moribund class of compradors, landlords, and bureaucrat capitalists—dutiful clients of U.S. neocolonialism in the Philippines.

Decolonization of the Filipino began right in the midst of entrapment in "the belly of the beast," the empire's metropolis. Mindful of the historical relationship between subaltern people and colonizing state, one should interpret Filipino ethnic strategies as symptoms of the colonial trauma and the ordeal of enduring its revival in new forms, this time in the heartland of the imperial power. Because of this, most Filipinos seek assimilation and welcome acculturation; but experiences of racist insult, discrimination, ostracism, and violence disrupt their modes of adaptation and suspend their psyches in a limbo of symbolic ethnicity if not political indeterminacy. This is not a bipolar state oscillating between nostalgic nativism and coercive Europeanization; it is a diasporic predicament born of the division of labor in the world system and the racialization of people of color by capital accumulation (Wolf 1982; Miles 1986). Concerning the fallacy of the "dual" or schizoid personality that was deployed to rationalize immigrant poverty and maladjustment, David Palumbo-Liu (1999) demystifies this diagnosis: "Rather than assuming simply a free-floating land of neurosis and schizophrenia, we should see that the separation of 'Asia,' 'America,' and "Asian America' is *itself* a psychic rationalization that, in seeking to simplify complex forms of identification and disidentification, blinds us both to the precise politics of separation, and, concomitantly, to their grounds for interpenetration" (308).

Without disavowing other limitations of an eclectic theoretical apparatus and its neglect of contemporary social problems (poverty, teen pregnancy, gang violence, AIDS, drug abuse, and so on) for most Filipinos, I take issue with the positivistic reading of the narrative of Americanization that ignores the symptoms I have alluded to. It is a truism that for colonized, subaltern subjects in the conjuncture of the post-1965 United States, the process of survival involves constant renegotiation of cultural spaces, revision of inherited folkways, reappropriation of dominant practices, and invention of new patterns of adjustment. All these embody the cultural practice of a people attempting to transcend subalternity (see Theo Gonzalves's [1995] testing of this hypothesis in his analysis of Pilipino Cultural Night in California). What is crucial is how and why this set of practices is enabled by the structures of society and the conditioned disposition of the agents themselves. When Filipinos therefore construct the meaning of their lives (whether you label this meaning Filipino American, U.S. Filipino, or Americanized Pinoys, the content determines the form), they do not—contrary to Espiritu's claim—simultaneously conform to and resist the hegemonic racializing ideology. This implies a reservoir of free choices that does not exist for most colonized subjects. Indeed, the construction of a subjugated Filipino identity as a dynamic, complex phenomenon defies both assimilationist and pluralist models when it affirms its antiracist, counterhegemonic antecedent: the revolutionary opposition of the Filipino people to U.S. imperial domination.[5] Molecular micropolitics favored by acolytes of "new social movements" cannot hide the salience of the overarching narrative of the anti-U.S. imperialist struggle that continues today to unfix all academic perversions and bureaucratic stereotypes of the Filipino people.

Certain recent developments, particularly the emergence of U.S. Asian neoconservatives (described by Glenn Omatsu 1994) and the tension between Korean Americans and black communities, direct our focus to the fierce class war waged by the U.S. corporate elite against both the U.S. working masses and their international rivals (Japan, the European bloc, and recently China). Meanwhile, the value produced by unpaid labor continues to be expropriated from thousands of Asian and Latino women in the sweatshops of the metropolis and "Third World" borderlands called "free trade zones." I would like to mention here the presence of seven million Filipino "contract workers" engaged in domestic and low-paid, demeaning work in the Middle East, Hong Kong, Singapore, Japan, and many European countries.[6] This new diaspora of domestic slaves defies the theory of transcultural ethnoscapes and carnivalesque border crossings applied to icons such as Salman Rushdie, Gayatri Spivak, Homi Bhabha, and others. What can postcolonial "delirium within" and "strategic essentialism" scrupulously chosen offer to Flor Contemplacion, Jocelyn Guanezo, Maricris Sioson, and thousands of victims of free trade and unrestrained commodity exchange?

THE RETURN OF THE REPRESSED

New post–Cold War realignments compel us to return to a historical materialist analysis of political economy and its multilateral determinations in order to grasp the new racial politics of transnationality and multiculturalism (Bruin 1996). Obviously, I am not advocating a vulgar Marxist (or economistic or mechanical deterministic) approach in understanding race/ethnic relations. What may prove revitalizing for the post-1965 generation is a creative return to the "basics," perhaps a counterfundamentalism that Richard Appelbaum (1996) rehearses in these terms:

> Capitalism has always reinforced class divisions with divisions based on race, ethnicity, gender, and other forms of ascription. In any system based to a large degree on the exploitation of one group of people by another, such distinctions provide a useful basis for justifying inequality. Not only does this foster a "divide-and-conquer" ideology among those who otherwise might find common cause, but it also helps to foster a standard of exploitation based on what is accorded the least common denominator—whichever group finds itself at the bottom of the economic heap. (313)

Together with Appelbaum's elucidation of global capitalism's flexibility instanced by the subcontracting modes of manipulating the commodity chains, we can learn from Edna Bonacich's (1996) analysis of how the Los Angeles garment industry deploys multiculturalism to cut production costs and increase surplus value (see also Yamato et al. 1993, 135). Studying the phenomenon of "cultural citizenship as subject making," Aihwa Ong (1999) describes the disparate cultural performance and subjectification of two groups—the Cambodian refugees and the wealthy Chinese immigrants from Hong Kong and Taiwan—to show the "different modalities of precarious belonging" under the aegis of pluralist or multiculturalist accumulation in late capitalism.

In the light of these reconfigurations, we do not need an ethnic politics for moderating the private expropriation of the social surplus but a counterhegemonic strategy that articulates the imperatives of ethnicity, gender, sexuality, place, and so on—the major coordinates of cultural identity that David Harvey (1996) has inventoried for us—with class-based resistance and other oppositional trends charted within the political economy of racist exploitation and oppression. This transposes differences into a unified constellation of opposites. Such a united-front politics can be viable only within a larger framework of a wide-ranging program targeting the material foundation of iniquitous power and reification in the commodity logic of unequal exchange.

With respect to the Asian/Pacific Rim countries whose destinies now seem more closely tied to the vicissitudes of the U.S. market, the reconfiguring of corporate capital's strategy in dealing with this area requires more careful analysis of the flow of migrant labor, capital investments, media manipulation, tourism, and so on. There are over a million Filipinos (chiefly women) employed as domestics and low-skilled workers in Hong Kong, Singapore, Japan, Taiwan, Korea, and Malaysia. A total of seven million Filipino Overseas Contract Workers remit billions of dollars, enough to keep the Philippine neocolonial system afloat and buttress economic and political dependency. Their exploitation is worsened by the racializing process of inferiorization imposed by the Asian nation-states, the Asian "tigers," competing for their share in the realignment of the international division of labor. The Western press then reconfigures the Asian as neo–Social Darwinist denizen of booty capitalism in the ethnoscapes of a revanchist "New World Order."

Most of these Filipina domestics are virtual slaves of patriarchal households. They congregate in front of Rome's railway stations, in Philippine Embassy precincts of Arab sheikdoms, in London parks, in city squares in Hong Kong and Singapore, and in other stigmatized or quarantined spaces. Marginality of migrant labor defines the identity of the master citizens while the metropole, the "space of flows," resists these foreigners carving a habitat or locale for their trammeled sociality. For migrant workers in general, their nationality signifies their subaltern status within the interstate hierarchy of nations, while money (chiefly petrodollars and yen) gives them cosmopolitan rank. Meanwhile, the globalized city of Metro Manila exudes a mirage of consumerist affluence, sporting the "postcolonial aura" of megamalls and *ersatz* Disneylands amid the ruin of fragmented families, criminality, and alienation from traditional neighborhoods—the suppressed public sphere of bourgeois life. Articulated with this transnational flux of labor, the urban experience of the inhabitants of Metro Manila (population over 12 million) replicates and also parodies that of residents in Los Angeles, New York, London, Paris, and other cities: segregation, fissured communities, ethnic tensions, and so on. Like other "third world" conurbations, Manila becomes a conduit for commodified bodies, an ideological and disciplinary apparatus that converts the place of rest and dealienation into carceral sites for "killing time." In the duration between escape to the United States and imprisonment in Asia, these enclaves of Filipinos are plotting mischief: disruptions and mayhem, sporadic rebellions, even protracted mass revolts.

All these recent developments inevitably resonate in the image of the Asian—its foreignness, malleability, affinities with the West, and so on—that in turn determines a complex of contradictory and variable attitudes toward U.S.-domiciled Asians. Such attitudes can be read from the drift of the following questions: Is Japan always going to be portrayed as the scapegoat for the loss of U.S. jobs? Is China obdurately refusing to conform to Western standards in upholding human rights and opening the country to the seductions of market individualism? What is going to happen to Taiwan? What about mail-order brides from the Philippines and Thailand as possible carriers of the AIDS virus? Are the Singaporeans that barbaric? How is the Hawaiian sovereignty movement going to affect the majoritarian perception of the "natives"? And despite the end of history in this post–Cold War milieu, will the North Koreans continue to be the paragons of communist barbarism, hopelessly atavistic and irredeemable? Rumblings from Indonesia, East Timor, Myanmar, Malaysia, and so on threaten to disturb our enchantment at the beauty of the arias in Puccini's *Madame Butterfly*.

NOT ONE, BUT MULTITUDES

Before focusing on the Philippines, I might recapitulate themes already rehearsed here and in my other works. Based on the historical construction of the U.S. racial formation, the immigrant paradigm has functioned as an essentializing and perpetually revitalized ideological ingredient for ethnic identity making. Hegemony requires ethnic identity to maintain consensual rule. The deployment of ethnicity as a means of categorizing minority groups has reproduced the very problem it is trying to displace: a racializing taxonomy. While presumably highlighting cultural particularities, ethnicity foregrounds surface differences as a sign of liberal pluralist tolerance. Difference, then, translates into a plurality of ethnic constituencies assumed to enjoy parity. This mystification is periodically disrupted by national or international political crisis. In specific historical contexts, those marked racially "Asian" have expressed a panethnic reaction to the prevailing discriminatory ideology and practice of white supremacy—only to dissolve when the economic cycle turns around for the trickling down of benefits even without a welfare state machinery.

Ethnicity also occludes class inequality via the fable of the "model minority." The Filipino segment of Asian America as well as globalizing trends have succeeded in decentering the panethnicity model. Multiculturalism and other postmodern schemes of neutralizing or naturalizing class antagonisms fail to hide the multifaceted layers of contradictions and injustices that afflict the multiethnic social body in which national identity, or the definition of citizenship, persists in being centered on a Euro-American memory or symbolic capital that is reproduced whenever the issue of immigration occupies the stage of public debate.

Meanwhile, the immigration paradigm continues to obscure the reality of racial exclusion, segregation, and marginalization of people of color whose labor power continues to be devalued. At the same time, their presence in the social and political domain continues to serve as the Other against which the ideal of success is measured. Recognition of this Other is permitted occasionally to divide the ruled. The neoliberal ideology of Asian Americans as the model of successful adaptation and its postmodernist articulation should be opposed by a counterhegemonic politics of a "historic bloc" that would transcend the instrumentalization of ethnicity and the neoliberal self-aggrandizement of individual rights. The emergence of powerful Asian Pacific economies as well as the anti-imperialist struggle in the Philippines and elsewhere suggest trends that can initiate a paradigm shift enough to foreground a popular-democratic program centered on political movements demanding not just recognition but just redistribution of the social wealth, a goal without which multiculturalism would be only a circus spectacle for the angry millions massing at the gates.

The historic conjuncture of the turn of the century presages new initiatives in cultural production and political mobilization of U.S. Asians. This can be gleaned, for instance, from Frank Chin's (1998) strategic enunciation of principle delivered at a convocation in Singapore:

> The Chinese Americans are a lovingly despised minority in America. I have been despised all my life in the country of my birth. Fear of white racism is a childhood disease. I am no longer a child. I don't write for white acceptance. I don't write to get along with anybody. I write to tell the truth. Writing is fighting. Nations come and go. It's a good day to die. Let the good times roll. (392)

Periodic revaluation punctuates the conversation of intellectuals and artists in the field. In a review of Asian American cinema, Renee Tajima (1991) borrows the term "culture of necessity" from Mexican artists and applies it to the three decades of cultural practice by committed Asian American activists. A quote from Friedrich Engels (1935) comes to mind: "Freedom is the recognition/appreciation of necessity" (130).

The agenda surely calls for organization and mobilization of constituencies across the geopolitical terrain of class, gender, ethnicity, and so on. Given the demographic and sociopolitical rearticulation of both dispersed as well as aggregated collectivities, we have not even begun to address what Nancy Fraser (1995) calls the redistribution–recognition dilemma, that is, how politicoeconomic justice and cultural parity can be realized together by transformative and deconstructive means instead of refurbishing liberal nostrums so popular among people of color in the mainstream academy. In short, the challenge of transformative critique still needs to be taken up as we confront the disintegration of pan-Asian metaphysics and discourse amid the post–Cold War realignments of nation-states and transnational power blocs.

One example of this new emerging trend in historical-materialist scholarship is illustrated by Nancy Ablemann and John Lie's (1995) book on Korean Americans and the Los Angeles riots, *Blue Dreams*. In their chapter "American Ideologies on Trial," Ablemann and Lie dismantle the mainstream paradigm of inter-ethnic conflict by dissecting the practical effects of the individualist "American Dream" within the economic order of laissez-faire capitalism. They show the contradictory articulation of the "American Dream" in both model minority urban and underclass syndromes whose concrete dialectics they unravel. Unlike pseudo-Gramscians, Ablemann and Lie do not disjoin the intricate linkage between civil society and state but precisely focus on it in charting the tensions between solidarity and racism, conflict and cooperation, among various communities caught in a conjunctural crisis. They conclude that "an attempt to understand Korean American responses to the riots and the "black–Korean conflict" requires us to consider their transnational context and their heterogeneity" (1995, 180).

But the dominant trend in U.S. Asian scholarship remains apologetic and celebratory of neoliberal pluralism broadcast by celebrities such as Richard Rorty, as noted by Wald (1992), Palumbo-Liu (1995), and Dirlik (1997). Despite the avant-garde triumphalist voice of its postmodernist faction, it has not been able to grapple successfully with the old but continually revitalized episteme of market individualism. I am afraid that even George Lipsitz's (1998) perspicaciously argued thesis on "the possessive investment of whiteness" cannot convince the majority unless their privileges are shown to be directly dependent on the exploitation and oppression of "third world peoples" in the global South committed daily by U.S.-based transnational corporate power. An obsession with a populist "cultural studies" approach fails to expose that parasitism. This failure vitiates all conversation about revising invidious immigrant or national paradigms since the ghosts of the past, unless we settle accounts with it, will forever continue to haunt us in our future peregrinations and sabotage all attempts at liberation, no matter our versatile border crossings and nuanced, flexible syncretic evasions. Perhaps we can encounter new possibilities germinating elsewhere, in the re-imagined borders of the empire across the Pacific Ocean.

NOTES

1. In a fit of exasperation, Russell Leong, editor of *AmerAsia Journal*, sent this e-mail circular to all his colleagues concerning the "current rap about redefining, throwing away, or retheorizing the term Asian American into diasporic this or that":

"Asian American" is a tenacious word, born out of struggle, fire, darkness and color. It means that America is not white, particularly, but that Asians, as well as Native Americans, Latinos and African Americans are politically, culturally, and economically of the United States. For even as we are disenfranchised, separated, and discriminated against, at the same time our bodies, our labor and our intelligence are exploited, as our cultures and communities are appropriated. Thus the strength of the term, "Asian American," lies in its power to point out the contradictions that characterize America at the end of the 20th century—a society whose popular rhetoric is one of inclusion, but whose primary history has been one of continued exclusion.

We applaud this reiteration of self-evident truths, but the signification of the term "American" and its supererogatory claim to exclude all others in the continent, not just within the U.S. nation-state, is not so easily amenable to arbitrary definition or periodic negotiation. It drags with it a whole massive history of what we want to reject: exploitation, racist violence, exclusion, and oppression.

As a footnote to recent interethnic dissension, consider the kind of ethnocentric arrogance in David Mura's (1993, 189) discounting of the Philippines as deficient in authentic culture compared to Japan, the homeland of his parents.

2. Enamored by the fashionable Foucauldian view of multiple power/discourse formations, Howard Winant (1994, 107) endorses a "radicalized pluralism" as the antidote to the virulent institutional racism of the 1990s. Meanwhile, U.S. Filipinos continue to repeat the mistake (see Jacinto and Syquia 1995) of blaming the victim's culture while subscribing to the Glazer/Moynihan thesis that it is the immigrant's normative values, not the freedom and opportunities of market society, that perpetuate marginality and even the "underclass" status.

3. For this, a world-systems analysis (see Balibar and Wallerstein 1991) may prove heuristic and catalyzing. In line with the assault against Eurocentrism and following the model of Afrocentrism, its mirror opposite, Paul Wong and colleagues (1995) have suggested "Asiacentrism" as an alternative paradigm in academic studies. The attempt is bold and pathbreaking but open to objections. One objection is that it valorizes selected commonalities and downplays substantive differences, sidetracking historical specificity for a project of reversing the past. This trend is immanent also in the indiscriminate "culturalism" that, for example, reduces the Korean–black conflict to a matter of cultural differences (Karnow and Yoshihara 1992).

4. I think the most positive offshoot of the postmodern trend is Critical Race Theory (CRT), which intends to expose the political and ideological function of law and legal rules. By applying hermeneutic methodology to specific legal cases, Neil Gotanda (1995), for example, demonstrates the historical contingency of court rulings. He also shows how legal judgments embed racializing narratives that conjoin national–state boundaries, immigration practices, and colonial/imperialist patterns of domination. At best, he discloses the contradiction and instability that are the conditions of possibility for liberal law's efficacy. For his part, Robert Chang (1995) believes that CRT will be revitalized by going

through its "Asian American Moment," in which the violence and disenfranchisement of Asian Americans (through law, model minority myth, and so on) can become paradigmatic cases for deconstructing the positivistic neutrality of liberal law and evince its irreconcilability with any program of realizing participatory democracy and social justice.

5. Filipino Americans still muse over the vexed topic of U.S.–Philippines relations, a "dark romance" sprung from the problematic results of the Philippine revolution of 1896–1898 and the "insurrection" against U.S. rule. I take this as a symptom of the Myrdal disease. A little review of history should cure if not alleviate the symptom. After and before the anti-Filipino riot of Watsonville in January 1930, Filipinos carried weapons with them, even while they told their folks back home, "Everyone treated me good" (see Johnson 1989, 14). Racial and national discrimination of Filipinos as wards or "nationals" (neither citizens nor aliens) is distilled in the antimiscegenation laws against them (declared unconstitutional in 1948 but not revoked until 1967). In 1926, Filipinos were declared "not Mongolians" but Malays predisposed to running amuck! Still they were "persons of mixed blood" and covered by the California Civil Code as subjects prohibited from marrying white persons (Quinsaat et al. 1976).

6. About seven million Filipinos comprise the Overseas Contract Workers diaspora consisting mainly of Filipina women recruited by labor agencies in the Middle East and in Europe, making the Philippines a remittance economy based on the dollars sent by these workers to their families back home. Given the scattering of the Filipino nationality around the world—particles of "brain drained" but also the flesh of "hospitality" entertainers in Japan and elsewhere—the neo- (not post-) colonial plight of the people has worsened. This demands a new materialist analysis. The "identity politics" of Commonwealth postcoloniality needs the categories of peoplehood—a historicized concept of nation, class struggle, sexuality, and gender—in order to make sense of the Filipino predicament in the United States. To avoid the postcolonial "blackmail," Filipinos need to redefine their communities and their trajectories in the ongoing social transformation as a force either for preserving the status quo or for accelerating the movements for popular democracy.

7. A strategy of pacification is being mounted to contain dissidence and disruption from unruly sectors of the U.S. Asian populace as world recession deepens. One indication is the multiculturalist approach deployed by Stanley Karnow and Nancy Yoshihara (1992) in a monograph published by the Asia Society. I juxtapose two passages, the first from the introduction where the "model minority myth" and a naive Orientalism find renewed life:

But despite their dissimilarities, Asian Americans share common characteristics. Whether their backgrounds are Confucian, Buddhist, Hindi, Muslim, Christian or animist, they tend to adhere to the concept of filial piety, and see achievement as a way to honor their families. Hence their devotion to classic American virtues—hard work, discipline and a willingness to defer instant fulfillment for the sake of future goals. Above all, they make enormous sacrifices to educate their children—a commitment that reflects their esteem for scholarship, supposedly assures success and also raises their own social status.

By national standards, the aggregate accomplishments of Asian Americans are spectacular. [Here follows a listing of statistics whose veracity and implications are at best questionable.] Forever seeking to enshrine the American dream, the news media constantly extol Asian Americans as Horatio Alger heroes. Professor William Petersen, a sociologist at Berkeley, called them the "model minority"—a term, wrote Louis Winnick in *Commentary* recently, that is yesterday's coinage: "By now, Asian Americans have vaulted to a more exalted station—America's trophy population." (6)

Next consider this observation from the section on "Politics":

Apart from Japanese Americans, most Asian Americans are immigrants. Many though not all come from countries with despotic and corrupt regimes, and are either unacquainted with the democratic process or distrust government. Many are riveted more on news from their homelands than on events in America. (51)

The fissure between the patronizing endorsement of the "model minority" archetype and the factual errors compounded with a self-righteous paternalism betrayed by the second quotation is not as wide as it seems. For both are symptomatic of the doctrine that Asian immigrants, like all aliens, should be measured against a white-supremacist standard, a measure that precisely guarantees the hegemony of capital's "civilizing mission" that is now being challenged by its unruly subalterns in core and periphery.

3

Specters of United States Imperialism

I hope the Americans will understand that the present state of culture of the
Filipino people shall not put up with subjugation by force as a permanent
condition. The Filipinos may be vanquished now and again, but as long as
they are denied every kind of right, there will not be lasting peace.

—Apolinario Mabini

The terrible truth in America shatters the Filipinos' dream of fraternity.

—Carlos Bulosan

In his magisterial study of the bond between the colonizing West and the
speech-deprived subalterns, the distinguished scholar Edward Said, in *Culture
and Imperialism* (1994), reminds us that "imperialism did not end, did not suddenly become 'past,' once decolonization had set in motion the dismantling of
the classical empires" (282). Recapitulating what his illustrious predecessors
(Frantz Fanon, Walter Rodney, C. L. R. James, and Kwame Nkrumah) had already observed, Said quotes two authorities, Michael Barratt-Brown and Noam
Chomsky, to ground his thesis (Vizmanos 1989; see also Francisco, in Schirmer
and Shalom 1987). In 1970, Barratt-Brown noted that "imperialism is still without question a most powerful force in the economic, political and military relations by which the less economically developed lands are subjected to the more
economically developed" (1982, 8). In 1982, Chomsky concluded his commentary: "[T]he 'North-South' conflict will not subside, and new forms of domination will have to be devised to ensure that privileged segments of Western industrial society maintain substantial control over global resources, human and
material, and benefit disproportionately from this control. Thus it comes as no
surprise that the reconstitution of ideology in the United States finds echoes

65

throughout the industrial world" (84–85). These trends have been substantially confirmed by recent developments in the Philippines, once reputed to be a model "showcase of U.S. democracy" in Asia but now its rigorous and unforgiving crucible.

Not yet a decade since the U.S. military bases were forced to withdraw in 1991 by nationalist demand, the passage of the Visiting Forces Agreement (VFA) between the Republic of the Philippines and the United States in February 1998 marks the return of imperial power in a more total repudiation of Filipino sovereignty (Nemenzo 1998). Pushed through by both the Ramos and the Estrada administrations, both inheritors of President Aquino's ingratiating submission to transnational capital, the VFA grants the ex-colonizer extraterritorial rights and privileges exceeding the privileges that the United States once enjoyed in the heyday of the Laurel–Langley Agreement and parity rights. Ostensibly for the sake of national security, the U.S. military will return with nuclear and other genocidal weapons. What is at stake is really control over the natural resources and labor power of the Filipino people via the destruction of their national sovereignty and territorial integrity.

The trend toward a refurbished populist authoritarianism is clear. Corrupt and extremely brutal in its treatment of the New People's Army combatants, the Estrada administration is now gearing the state machinery for drastic changes in the 1987 Constitution that will allow foreign monopoly firms unrestricted rights to own land, exploit the natural resources, operate public utilities, and amass superprofits, all sanctioned by the slogans of liberalization, privatization, and deregulation. Rapacious globalization has the backing of the International Monetary Fund (IMF), World Bank, and World Trade Organization, whose policies of "structural adjustment" and "conditionalities" have now been publicly exposed as favorable to the local reactionary compradors, landlords, bureaucrat capitalists, and their military henchmen. Claiming to be defending the impoverished workers and peasants, the successor to an entourage of U.S. clients (from Quezon and Osmeña to Magsaysay and Marcos), the Estrada regime cannot conceal its subservience to transnational or globalized capital, the latest incarnation of U.S. imperial hegemony.

In both academy and public common sense, however, "U.S. imperialism" does not exist—even as an aberration, like the Vietnam War, or as a fit of mindlessness. According to Microsoft's *Encarta Encyclopedia* (1993–1997), Filipino cooperation with a benevolent United States became "the keynote of the postwar policy." Even the liberal *New Basic History of the United States,* by Charles Beard and Mary Beard (1968), assumed that the United States had now departed from "the 'imperialist' doctrines of the old school of American expansionists" in order to allow the Philippines to become, on 4 July 1946, "a free and independent nation" (459). Other non-American observers apply a Eurocentric standard when they bewail the inadequate Westernization of the Filipinos, who suffer from "dualism in outlook and a longing for a national identity" (Nelson 1968, 117). Modernization theory, exemplified by Vera Micheles Dean's *The Nature of the Non-Western World* (1966), has been refurbished by conceding limited agency to those under unconscionable tutelage. Pundits from the mass media recycled official platitudes about "special relations," postulating equality between subalterns and neocolonizer. Sandra Burton (1989), a former correspondent for *Time* magazine, rehashes a question-begging scenario: "In order to cope with the acute sensitivities of Filipinos, who both craved the attention of their superpower ally and chafed at its counsel, the officials responsible for fulfilling America's commitments to the Philippine government had had to adopt a Filipino-like attitude of fatalism" (239). Racist patronage is mixed with naive celebration of elite personalities in such accounts as Bryan Johnson's *The Four Days of Courage* (1987), Fred Poole and Max Vanzi's earlier *Revolution in the Philippines* (1984), and the self-serving commentaries of Monina Mercado's *People Power: An Eyewitness History* (1986). Exceptions, such as Raymond Bonner's *Waltzing with a Dictator* (1987), William Chapman's *Inside the Philippine Revolution* (1987), and Leonard Davis's *Revolutionary Struggle in the Philippines* (1989), are few and not widely circulated. Only when dissident intellectuals such as Gore Vidal or Noam Chomsky cite from the historical record of U.S. interventions does the colonial experience of Filipinos impinge on the American public consciousness. Otherwise, "politics and ideology are largely bounded by the consensus of the business community" (Chomsky 1992, 59), and thus the norms of the "free market," of consensus management and violent intervention (Ahmad 1982), screen out conflicts arising from popular resistance to oppression and exploitation.

To remedy this amnesia, we need to problematize the received consensus of U.S. history and its representation of the Philippines in the archive. At the same time, we need to appraise and critique the position of mercantile, postmodernizing nativism purveyed by the parasitic comprador elite. What may be instructive and heuristic for this occasion is a selective review of how the disciplinary regime of Western civilization and its peculiar mode of articulating racial/cultural difference in the Philippines—an instance of academic hubris predicated on the inferiorization of the cultures of "Others" for its own self-validation—have been "produced" and circulated by liberal discourse with "postcolonial" pretensions. Its recent postmodernist reincarnation calls for urgent critique if we need to rectify a centenary of liberal-democratic mystification and racist violence.[1]

AFTER THE FEBRUARY STORM

For the first time since the outbreak of the Spanish–American War in 1898 and the fall of Bataan and Corregidor to the Japanese invaders in 1942, the Philippines seized the world's attention for a few days in February 1986: An urban mass insurrection of over a million people overthrew the long-entrenched Marcos dictatorship without too much bloodshed, in the face of tanks and soldiers

armed to the teeth (Davis 1989). Scenes of this uprising were televised throughout the world, images exuding an aura of the miraculous. Few know that the
restoration of neocolonial democracy—rule of globalized capital through the
comprador/oligarchic elite—after that event ushered in a new stage for the revival of neocolonial apparatuses of domination, agencies of hegemonic rule designed to protract the nation's subservience to transnational corporations and
the IMF/World Bank (Tujan 1998).

Less publicized is one epochal achievement of the nationalist resurgence that
began with the student revolts called the "First Quarter Storm" in 1970 and persists up to this day: In 1992, the U.S. government finally yielded to Filipino resolve and abandoned its two huge military installations (Clark Air Field and
Subic Naval Base), symbols of colonial suzerainty and possibly (as springboard
for intervention in the China market and the Asian–Pacific geopolitical theater)
the main reason for U.S. territorial annexation of the islands (Tujan 1998). Despite some attenuation, the Philippines today has the only viable communist-led
guerrilla insurgency in the whole world.

But like most "Third World" societies plagued by vestiges of colonial bondage,
the Philippines today suffers the negativity, not the dynamic fruitfulness, of contradictions. Although nominally independent, its economy is controlled by the
draconian "conditionalities" of the IMF/World Bank; its politics by semifeudal
warlords, bureaucrats, and military officials beholden to Washington; its culture
by U.S. ideological apparatuses and its consciousness industry—in general, by
the Western information/knowledge production monopoly (Constantino 1970).[2]
Although direct colonial rule was finally terminated in 1946, the cultural and
political hegemony of the United States persists to this day. When the Reagan
administration intervened in 1986 to shore up the ruins of empire by rescuing
its client despot from the wrath of Filipinos and to install a new set of overseers
(namely, Corazon Aquino and her successor, General Fidel Ramos, former "im-
presario" of Marcos's martial law), it was less nostalgia than a tactical defensive
retreat. Desperate maneuvers to salvage the military bases confirmed a long-
range strategy of retrenchment (see Kerkvliet and Mojares 1991; Parenti 1995;
Schirmer 1997). There was definitely no retreat in the realm of politics, ideology,
and culture, given the claim of academic pundits (e.g., Claude Buss 1987; Richard Kessler 1989) that such intervention demonstrated U.S. goodwill to preserve
its investment in its long-revered "showcase of democracy" in Asia after its deba-
cle in Vietnam (for a recent apologia, see Kirk 1998).

Whatever the fixations of U.S. civic memory, the public is now about to celebrate the centennial anniversary of Admiral George Dewey's defeat of the Spanish fleet in Manila Bay on 1 May 1898—a farce turned into a heroic milestone.[3]
Perhaps the commemoration will not be accompanied by the usual jingoistic
fanfare of yore despite the nostalgic reassertion of proprietary rights over the
Balangiga souvenirs. We are, after all, inhabiting today a "New World Order"

characterized by U.S. triumphalist incursions in the Middle East and its post–Cold War refurbishing of humanitarianism and "free market" nostrums.[4]

Contrary to the claim that the first U.S.–Philippines contact began when Filipino recruits jumped off the Spanish galleons in the seventeenth century and settled near what is now New Orleans, Louisiana, I would contend that the inaugural scene points to the intrusion of Dewey into Manila Bay in 1898. That was immediately followed by the Filipino–American War (1899–1902), an event charged with antinomies: While suppressing the revolutionary forces, it laid the groundwork for proletarian unionism and the rise of organic intellectuals of the nation-people born from "uneven and combined development." American hegemonic power continues today in covert, mediated or sublimated forms—proof that what Mark Twain called the Philippine "temptation" persists amid profound mutations in the physiognomy of transnational, post-Fordist capital.

But for the moment I want to cite here Twain's comment on the U.S. (mis)adventure that (in Carey McWilliams' s view) prompted the government to "guide the natives in ways of our own choosing," especially when the "lesser breeds" or "little brown brothers occupied a potentially rich land" (McWilliams 1964, 232). The ironic resonance of this self-proclaimed "civilizing mission" is registered in Twain's inimitable idiom:

> We have pacified some thousands of the islanders and buried them; destroyed their fields, burned their villages, and turned their widows and orphans out-of-doors; furnished heartbreak by exile to some dozens of disagreeable patriots; subjugated the remaining ten millions by Benevolent Assimilation, which is the pious new name of the musket; we have acquired property in the three hundred concubines and other slaves of our business partner, the Sultan of Sulu, and hoisted our protecting flag over that swag. And so, by these Providences of God—and the phrase is the government's, not mine—we are a World Power. (quoted in Zinn 1984, 20)

In his nuanced satire, Twain marveled at the report that 30,000 American soldiers killed a million Filipinos: "Thirty thousand killed a million. It seems a pity that the historian let that get out; it is really a most embarrassing circumstance" (Twain 1992, 62).[5] In February 1899, the month in which the Filipino–American War began and the U.S. Senate ratified the treaty formalizing the annexation of Spain's former colonies, Rudyard Kipling's poem "The White Man's Burden" appeared. In it the poet echoed U.S. Senator Albert Beveridge's (1987) claim of "the mission of our race, trustee under God, of the civilization of the world."[6]

This inaugural event in the chronicle of U.S. territorial expansionism is not without precedent, a fact thoroughly documented and argued by Gareth Stedman Jones (1973), William Appleman Williams (1962), Michael Hunt (1987), and Jack Woddis (1967). From the Monroe Doctrine to the Tonkin Gulf Resolution, a narrative of intervention gives intelligibility and telos to U.S. foreign policy. The historian Geoffrey Barraclough (1967) reminds us that 1898 "signalized the involvement of the United States in the dialectic of imperialism" (63) from which there was no turning back. In his perspicacious commentary on the U.S. war machine, *War Stars,* H. Bruce Franklin (1988) remarks, "The warfare waged against the Cuban and Philippine nationalists, for whose ostensible benefit we had defeated Spain, was an export of the genocidal campaigns against the 'savages' and 'redskins' who had inhabited North America" (92). This cognitive/contextual mapping is performed by Richard Hofstadter (1967) in his essay "Cuba, the Philippines, and Manifest Destiny," in which he delineated the configuration of "psychic crisis" that intertwined several elements: the chauvinist self-aggrandizement of the 1890s, the imperialist ethos of duty and populist self-assertion, the disappearance of the frontier, and the bureaucratization of business amid cyclical economic depression. We can place within those parameters the logic of intervention announced by President McKinley as one of emancipating and redeeming the Filipinos's "fatherland" and setting the Filipinos "in the pathway of the world's best civilization" (Leech 1959, 362). In a masterly synoptic reappraisal, Gabriel Kolko (1976) returns us to Twain's insight and supplies an optic through which U.S. *Realpolitik* (euphemistically labeled "sentimental" and "benevolent") acquires its undeniable genealogy:

In Asia the framework in which United States efforts proceeded was far more complicated and, ultimately, was to fail to preserve both peace and American power in an environment in which the balance-of-power diplomacy was eventually to become increasingly irrelevant before the tides of nationalism and revolution germinating throughout Asia. But the first American entry—and the most ignored—was the bloody acquisition of the Philippines and the long repression, eventually costing at least 200,000 Filipino lives, which was required when the Americans found that in order really to take the islands they had first to retrieve it by force and chicanery from a Filipino independence movement largely in control at the end of the war with Spain. Americans, with few exceptions, refused to reflect on the enormity of this crime, which it later repeated again in a yet more brutal form in Vietnam. But it was from this island base, held firmly in hand with terrible force, and then also co-option and cultural imperialism, that the United States was to embark on its Asian role, a role that eventually became the most demanding and troublesome in America's long history. (42)

Violence in America antedated industrialism and urban life, and it was initially a product of an expansive rural-commercial economy that in the context of vast distance and a hastily improvised and often changing social structure saw barbarism, violence, and their toleration ritualized into a way of life. Slavery consisted of institutionalized inhumanity and an attack on the very fiber of the black's personal identity and integrity. . . . Against the Indians, who owned and occupied much coveted land, wholesale slaughter was widely sanctioned as a virtue. That terribly bloody, sordid history, involving countless tens of thousands of lives that neither victims nor executioners can ever enumerate, made violence endemic to the process of continental expansion. Violence reached a crescendo against the Indian after the Civil War and found a yet bloodier manifestation during the protracted conquest of the

Philippines from 1898 until well into the next decade, when anywhere from 200,000 to 600,000 Filipinos were killed in an orgy of racist slaughter that evoked much congratulation and approval from the eminent journals and men of the era who were also much concerned about progress and stability at home. From their inception, the great acts of violence and attempted genocide America launched against outsiders seemed socially tolerated, even celebrated. Long before Vietnam, that perverse acceptance of horror helped make possible the dominating experiences of our own epoch. (286–287)

This synthesizing historiographic stance, an intellectual orientation enabled not by Nietzsche and deconstructive postcolonialists but by the now much maligned "national liberation" struggles, has been expunged from approved textbooks and from civic memory (Loewen 1999). But despite the prevalent neoconservative atmosphere with its cynical bureaucratic pragmatism, it is now being slowly grasped and applied in the canon-revising program of progressive scholars throughout the country (on "Filipinization," see Paredes 1988). The present work is an index of its salutary influence.

ANTICIPATING PARADIGM SHIFTS

The major obstacle to any rigorous exploration of U.S. imperialist hegemony in the Philippines inheres in the controlling paradigm of philosophical idealism (instanced in methodological individualism and empiricist functionalism) that ushered in academic disciplines addressing U.S. "exceptionalism" and legitimized their regimes of truth. Mainstream social theory hinges on at least three doctrinal assumptions that operate as enabling research paradigms: "[T]he market depends on the subjective values of commodities; social action depends on the value-orientation of the actor; society is constituted by its collective conscience or central value-system" (Shaw 1975, 84). I suggest that the dominant epistemological approach hinges on a positivistic, evolutionary theory of culture—traditional patterns of conduct, norms, beliefs, and attitudes, together with their corresponding practices of symbolic translation and signification—as the explanatory key to the subaltern condition of the Filipino.

That constellation of action, meaning, and *habitus* (in Pierre Bourdieu's construal) also explains the production/reproduction of dependency relations now assuming more covert and deceptive disguises.[7] Reduced to a few pivotal notions such as *hiya*, internal debt (*utang na loob*), "mutuality of power dynamics," and so on, culture, with its complex symbolic economy, is divorced from its constellation of determining sociopolitical forces, from the circumstantial network of power. It becomes a generalizing formula utilized to unravel affairs of extreme "thickness" and intricacy, with weighty ethical and moral resonance. The functionalism of deploying the patron–client dyad is not totally without value in shedding light on specific empirical phenomena.[8] But the effects of neocolonial exploitation, racism, and gender oppression are absent, marginalized, or concealed. The notion of "the politics of combined and uneven development," so perspicaciously demonstrated by Michael Löwy (1981) and others, is absent in functionalist discourse. Lacking the historical world system dynamics involving "asymmetrical relations" between exploitative occupier and subjugated indigenes, devoid of any sensorium for registering the unequal power relations between contending subjects who necessarily impinge on each other's physiognomies, what we have in such accounts is nothing but a banal exercise in apologetics.

A recent example of this revisionist genre is Stanley Karnow's *In Our Image: America's Empire in the Philippines* (1989). Its thesis of U.S. nonculpability for its subjugation of the Philippines hinges on the notion that the Filipinos "submitted voluntarily to their own exploitation." In context, Karnow's performance is symptomatic of an entire reactionary backlash trying to settle accounts with the liberal conscience of the 1960s and the skepticism of "third world" multitudes in the 1970s. But despite rehashing tired opinions and attempting to vindicate the Anglo-Saxon "civilizing mission" for the *n*th time, Karnow fails to balance debits and credits. Why, after nine decades of trying to instill American values of "integrity, civic responsibility, and respect for impersonal institutions," did the United States fail to remold the natives into their own idealized self-image, producing instead the horrible Marcos episode and a fertile breeding ground for communist insurgents?

Karnow's retort is naively evasive: "History is responsible . . ." By acceding to the Filipino aspirations for sovereignty soon after the conquest, Karnow counsels us, the United States deflated the nationalist elan in the course of tutelage; this left the Filipinos confused, ambivalent, duplicitous. To win hearts and minds, U.S. officials accommodated to Filipino traditions, "customs and social life," the inertia of opportunistic alliances and "coils of mutual loyalties" that characterize the "tribal texture" of Filipino life. Karnow's argument is plain: The durable and seemingly impervious *compadrazgo* system, with its familial dyadic ties that imposed the patron–client grid on political relations, frustrated any intent to duplicate the ethos and productivity of the American system. Clientelism in fact brought out the worst in the fallible American administrators (including General Douglas MacArthur). Thus, it is not U.S. colonial subjugation but the quasifeudal ordering of Filipino society and its immutable hierarchy of values that account for the underdevelopment, corruption, and tragedies of the Philippines. What we observe here in this indictment of local mores and folkways is really "the insertion of colonial bodies into a metropolitan discourse [that] provides sanction for the politics of colonialism at the same time as it reproduces them" (W. Anderson 1995, 86).

In his perceptive review of *In Our Image*, Peter Tarr (1989) refutes Karnow's spurious claim to ethical neutrality and high-mindedness. Tarr shows how the journalist has resurrected myths about the destructive dynamics of U.S.–

Philippines relations, in particular how the brutal conquest of the Philippines has been more than atoned for by the benefits given to the losers: sanitation, health care, roads, schools, "honest judiciary," and an ostensible democratic political system (what Benedict Anderson calls "cacique democracy"; see B. Anderson 1995)[9]—reforms that, it is implied, Filipinos would not have attained by themselves. "A model of enlightenment" is Karnow's phrase for the Philippine Commission's advice to Washington to use the *ilustrado* elite as "transmission belts" in governing the masses, to win over the *mestizo principales,* whose precarious and endangered position was eventually normalized by the tactical ploy of Taft's slogan "Philippines for the Filipinos" and then entrenched as the ruling bloc in the stratified dispensation. The fable that underpins Karnow's recuperation of imperialism with a smiling face is what Tarr calls the "Immaculate Conception myth," which mystifies the origins and motivations of U.S. foreign policy so perspicuously described by Kolko, Williams, and others.

Tarr's review sharply exposes the vacuity of Karnow's claim to an impartial reading and evaluation of the imperial record. What Tarr judiciously points out is that the so-called atonement that Karnow recites with great zeal did not really benefit the majority of Filipinos. On the contrary, it perpetuated oppression and injustice, sharpening class and ethnic divisions through the entrenchment of oligarchic rule, from Osmeña and Quezon to Roxas, Marcos, and Aquino, all of them invariably supported to one degree or another by a succession of U.S. policies and administrations. This unremitting patronage culminated in the Cold War involvement of the CIA with Magsaysay's anti-Huk campaign. And it persisted throughout the years of intervention in Indochina, Central America, Africa, and the Middle East.[10] It goes without saying that Karnow is a shrewd popularizer, a bricoleur of hackneyed notions and received doxa culled from the researches of mainstream scholars such as David Joel Steinberg, Peter Stanley, Theodore Friend, Glenn May, and other "gatekeepers" who guard the parameters of acceptable, safe thinking on the problematic of U.S.–Philippines encounters.[11]

INTERROGATING THE ARCHIVE

From a more theoretical vantage point, Karnow's apologia tries to define the American Self via representing the Other from the Self's ethnocentric, racializing gaze. In this process of othering, the "Filipino" becomes both an empirical referent and a construct of cross-hatched narratives, approximating the hybrid, amphibious creatures encountered in postcolonial terrain. Genealogically, Karnow's text belongs to a still entrenched tradition of U.S. colonial discourse purporting to supply the veracious, objectively "scientific" knowledge of the Filipino—his thoughts, feelings, behavior, even his "unconscious." This knowledge is inscribed in the ideological apparatuses (schools, media, philanthropic organizations, sports, and so on) necessary to maintain sustainable hegemony in the Philippines and justify the prophylaxis of periodic intervention to the tax-paying public.

Of about a dozen texts that have invented and disseminated the received "truths" about the Philippines and Filipinos, texts central to the constitution of the disciplinary field called "Philippine Studies" (a residual legacy of Cold War "area studies"), one may cite three that are acknowledged to be influential in crafting state policies and fabricating mass consensus: W. Cameron Forbes's *The Philippine Islands* (1945), Joseph Hayden's *The Philippines: A Study in National Development* (1942), and George Taylor's *The Philippines and the United States: Problems of Partnership* (1964), the latter serving as the Cold War primer and baedeker. These canonical texts were preceded by James A. LeRoy's *Philippine Life in Town and Country* (1905) and Dean C. Worcester's *The Philippines Past and Present* (1914). Aside from accumulating, tabulating, and systematizing a vast amount of statistics and raw data, these texts (in particular Hayden and Taylor) are foundational reference points for a corps of specialists I call "Filipinologists." They endeavor to organize and integrate a large body of information and ideas by using the accepted Eurocentric theories of culture and society found in mainstream social sciences. When applied by appointed functionaries and instrumentalized by the ideological apparatuses of the state, this official body of knowledge and its corresponding administrative translation serves to legitimate the logic and efficacy of U.S. rule. The key idea of "tutelage," a signal marker of evolutionistic positivism invested in this archive, is captured in this succinct formulation of David Joel Steinberg (1982): "[T]he U.S. policy of self-liquidating colonialism, in which the 'little brown brother' was permitted to achieve independence when he grew up, a maturation process that took forty-five years" (50)[12]

Together with other institutional mechanisms, these texts of legitimation constructed the object of knowledge and exercised mastery over it. They were in turn authorized by a whole panoply of regulations (economic, political, and cultural), at once hortatory and conciliating, governing the relations between the United States as a colonizing sovereignty and the subjugated inhabitants of the territory once administered by the Bureau of Indian Affairs. What is more insidious is that this archive has also profoundly conditioned the configuration of people-to-people relations in everyday life, sanctioning patterns of deliberation and decision making that reproduced stereotypes and hegemonic "common sense." It also reinforced a worldview that tended to repress critical thinking and deny creative autonomy by circumscribing if not proscribing possibilities of change within certain fixed boundaries of the public sphere that are always under surveillance by an elaborate network of policing (internal and external) mechanisms. "Philippine Studies" is the rubric for the ideological machine that facilitated the shaping of Karnow's text and other discursive themes fulfilling the managerial tasks dictated by the drive for safeguarding U.S. global hegemony.

Notwithstanding their authors' claims to objectivity, all these texts have now

Set up U.S. image as benevolent, democratic + civilising.

been compromised by the reality of seemingly ineradicable social injustice, un-mitigated poverty of millions, rampant atrocities by the military, exploitation of women and children, and widespread violation of human rights by business and government. Aspects of this reality have been exposed by concerned Filipinos (see, e.g., Hernando Abaya's 1984 exposé of the shady deals of General Douglas MacArthur and Paul McNutt in his autobiography)—proof that subalterns can speak if not fully represent themselves (see also de la Torre 1986b; Aguilar 1988; Lindio-McGovern 1997).[13]

Now the theme of "imperial collaboration" between the Filipino elite and U.S. bureaucrats has been a recurrent leitmotif in the archive of U.S. diplomacy since Forbes's two-volume inventory of U.S. achievements. Hayden schematized the replication of subalternity by the time of the Commonwealth period (1935–1940), while Taylor streamlined its analytic of expediency to fit Cold War geopolitics. With the influence of Taylor's book at the height of the Korean War and the anti-Huk campaigns of Lansdale–Magsaysay, the official routine of knowledge production about the Filipino began that applied a more systematic culturalist grid on laboratory specimens labeled "Filipino character and social practices."

The procedure of truth making is simple. The culture of one sector, the domi-nant landlord–merchant class, is taken as the normative consensus model for understanding the whole formation. Functionalism in its empiricist and positiv-ist version was thoroughly mobilized for hegemonic purposes (a good illustration is Jean Grossholtz's *Politics in the Philippines* [1964]). The structural-functional-ist deployment of notions such as *hiya, utang na loob,* and *pakikisama,* or "smooth interpersonal relations," propagated by Frank Lynch, George Guthrie, John Carroll, Mary Hollnsteiner, Chester Hunt, and their disciples became the approved operational paradigm for explaining any event or relationship, say, Quezon's duplicity, Marcos's tactics toward Benigno Aquino, President Corazon Aquino's incapacity to reform or discipline her kins, the psychology of disaf-fected members of the New People's Army, and practically all aspects of Philip-pine politics and society. The imperative is to maintain and buttress social equi-librium. One recent example is Claude Buss's *Cory Aquino and the People of the Philippines* (1987), whose refrain echoes a now predictable reflex of scapegoating: "[T]he Filipinos found it hard to break the habit of special dependence on the United States" (143)[14] This may be a slight improvement over the old rhetoric of conceiving the whole country as "a penal reformatory," an enlarged Iwahig underpinning the "logic of the carcereal continuum" (Salman 1995, 122) that has structured the peculiar symbiosis between the two countries since 1898.

Reason yields to the exigencies of governance, universality to historical contin-gency. Given the renewed threat of Filipino nationalism to expunge once and for all the myth of U.S.–Philippines "special relations," the desideratum of contem-porary U.S. knowledge production about the Philippines (as demonstrated by the works of David Steinberg, Theodore Friend, and Peter Stanley, among oth-ers) is to reconceptualize the fact of U.S. domination as a transaction of equal partnership between Filipinos and Americans. It is essentially an interpretive strategy to revise the canonical emplotment of a Saxonified *mission civilizatrice* into a universal mission of spreading American-style democracy and individual progress worldwide (Tenbruck 1990). This project of revaluation, what I would call a post hoc–ergo rationalization to underscore its retrograde instrumentalism, would center on a refurbishing of the patron–client paradigm; the notion of reciprocal obligations entailed by it would arguably serve as the theoretical framework within which one can then exorcise the burden of U.S. responsibility for what happened in the Philippines from 1898 on by ascribing the cause of the failure of American tutelage to the putative shrewdness of Filipinos in "manipulating" their masters.

We tried to do our best, but. . . . This is the basic thesis of Peter Stanley's *A Nation in the Making: The Philippines and the United States, 1899–1921* (1974), an updated sequel to the family of metanarratives cited earlier. It is an argument recycled by Karnow and other commentaries before and after the February 1986 insurrection. A dialectical twist of historical sensibility seems to have occurred. The sharp contrast between these reconstructive texts and previous works critical of U.S. imperialism—to cite only the most accessible, James Blount's *The American Occupation of the Philippines* (1973), Leon Wolff's *Little Brown Brother* (1961), William Pomeroy's *American Neo-colonialism* (1970), Stephen Shalom's *The United States and the Philippines: A Study of Neocolonialism* (1986), and Stuart Creighton Miller's *"Benevolent Assimilation": The American Conquest of the Philippines 1899–1903* (1982)—may be read as symptomatic of a cleavage in hegemonic governance. This requires a change of tactics attuned to recent realignments of political agencies and the reactionary climate now ascendant since the mid-1970s. It can also be conceived as a defensive mechanism set into play to counter a resurgent anti-U.S. hegemonism around the world in the wake of the Vietnam defeat and the revolutionary ruptures in Central America, South Africa, the Middle East, and elsewhere. This mutation needs to be clarified because of its impact on contemporary cultural studies and the conduct of intellectuals in both metropolis and periphery.

The agenda of the present neoconservative trend in Philippine studies in the U.S. academy is geared chiefly to the task of redefining U.S.–Philippines putative "special relations" by downplaying the power of American imperial governance. In the process, scholars enlarge the role of the Filipino elite in order to convert "empire" into an evolutionary experiment in "tutelage," shifting the onus of accountability to the victims.

In reviewing a volume edited by Peter Stanley titled *Reappraising an Empire: New Perspectives on Philippine-American History* (1984), Robert Stauffer (1987) acutely points to the dogmatic ideological framework of the new apologetics, a variant of neo-Weberian Parsonian sociology. He isolates the theoretical basis of this trend in the inflation of the concept of patron–client dyad based on reciprocal obligations. This conceptual framework ignores a more amply calibrated

[handwritten annotations in top margin: "given shift against U.S. post-Vietnam lits. / changes to blame Filipino elite made .. fails / to explore aspects of prior classes in Philippines - therefore / no agency attributed to them"]

world-systems approach (developed and refined in the last two decades) that predicates dependency on unequal exchange. Why? Because such a cogent alternative theory would rule out the patron–client schema of explanation since dependency excludes reciprocity. Stauffer contends that Stanley and like-minded Filipinologists romanticize the relation of "collaborative elites" and colonizers; they give "a Victorian legitimacy to past conquests and in so doing justify—[by demonstrating how satisfactory are the relations between Filipinos and Americans, e.g. Lansdale and Magsaysay]—future imperial ventures" (Stauffer 1987, 103). Further, by reducing all relations to that of patron–client over and above the context of sharpening class and other sectoral divisions, the proponents of the "collaborative empire" give the impression that such relations are permanent.

It is clear that the revisionary thrust of scholars employing the patron–client model aims to recast the exploitative relationship of dependency into a reciprocal one where responsibility is equalized if not dispersed. By downplaying any serious U.S. influence on Philippine social structures and inflating the ingenious duplicity of the colonized, Stauffer argues that Stanley and his colleagues make "empire" into a romantic ideology.

From this angle, one can understand Stanley's partisanship in openly espousing a program of exoneration: "[I]t is a hubristic illusion for Americans to imagine that, in the colonial era, they liberalized, modernized, or, for that matter, exploited the Philippines in any large, systemic, or lasting way."[15] That is of course disingenuous. Since a seemingly immutable patron–client pattern of relationship determined political life during U.S. ascendancy, Filipino nationalism is relegated to the "manipulative underside of the collaborative empire," with the oxymoron of "collaborative empire" recuperating McKinley's "benevolent assimilation" proclamation, the tropological matrix of U.S. rule over the island colony. In retrospect, one can describe this new "civilizing mission"—a phrase evoking the period of a socioeconomic transition from European mercantilism to a new international division of labor subtending capital's strategy of "counterrevolution," to use Arno Mayer's (1971) term[16]—as the ideological impetus behind the march of Anglo-Saxon progress over the conquered territories and subjugated bodies of African slaves, American Indians, Mexicans, Chinese workers, and so on from the erection of the pilgrim settlements to the closing of the western frontier at the end of the nineteenth century. As Walter Rodney (1982) remarked with reference to the plunder of the African continent, "The U.S.A. was a worthy successor to Britain as the leading force and policeman of the imperialist/colonialist world from 1945 onwards" (194).

THE EXCEPTION AND THE RULE

The United States as a political formation is "exceptional," according to Establishment historians, because it did not follow the European path to colonial expansion. The discourse and practice of "American exceptionalism" as part of Cold War strategy has been criticized acutely in the 1960s as an outgrowth of technocratic modernization and developmentalist thought. Aside from purveying statistical information for official policy, social scientists and various academics have tried to legitimize the existence of the national-security, authoritarian state in peripheral societies (Thomas 1984). Commenting on U.S. scholarly trends concerning China at that time, Leigh and Richard Kagan (1971) noted the privileging of cultural values and the sociocultural system as the key to shaping an economic–political environment "conducive to the dominance of middle-class American values . . . American culturalism denotes the intent to rule the world by the imposition of her values, safeguarding them when necessary by military occupation and colonization" (31)[17] This neo-Weberian one-sided emphasis on value orientation informs and vitiates such anthologies as David Rosenberg's *Marcos and Martial Law in the Philippines* (1979), John Bresnan's *Crisis in the Philippines* (1986), and Patricio Abinales's *The Revolution Falters: The Left in Philippine Politics after 1986* (1996).

Despite its weakness and for lack of any substitute, this culturalist functionalist paradigm still exercises authority among Filipinologists and their followers. It has now been thoroughly exposed for the following inadequacies, among others: its one-sided attribution of rationality and normative equilibrium to a particular social arrangement, its dismissal of the complex intentionality of individual's (agent's) conduct, and its circular mode of explaining social activity as meaningful insofar as it fulfills a temporally limited normative need, such as the reinforcement of a code of values required for social coherence. In sum, structural functionalism pivots around a subjectivist concern with values divorced from the social relations of production, from the historical matrix of social actors in a specific milieu. It posits a static, ahistorical view of society removed from its interdependency in a dynamic world system and its ceaseless transformations.

Anthony Giddens (1984) has argued that identifying a functional need of a system has no explanatory value at all (see also Shaw 1975). Aside from ascribing a teleological quality to a social system whose parts perform functional roles, it attributes to a given political setup a higher degree of cohesion and stability than what the facts warrant; indeed, it occludes dissonant and disintegrative factors at work. Because it cannot really provide a comprehensive explanation for the intentional activity of agents and for the unintended consequences that result from purposive actions, functionalism of the kind employed by Karnow and his sources distorts and reifies Filipino character, society, and history. It can only prejudge the actions of the Sakdals and the Huks as factional deviations from the oligarchic norm even if it concedes to them a modicum of moral credence. It dismisses the ideas of Filipino nationalists (always labeled "extreme" or "ultra" if not demonized altogether) in general as inexplicable in terms of the homeostatic imperatives of the status quo or simply the "manipulative underside of the collaborative empire."

We can now grasp the rationale for Karnow's deployment of the patron–client formula to give a semblance of intelligibility to imperial "aberrations." By focusing not just on Filipinos as equal participants but on their ability to "manipulate" their masters, Karnow, together with Stanley and other progenitors, endorse the putative evangelizing mission of the colonizers and their definition of a conflict taking place on conquered soil, effectively obscuring if not erasing U.S. responsibility for the ravages of capital accumulation. Karnow's montage of close-up scenes of action begets the illusion of valorizing personal intentions, but, in actual fact, the technique subordinates agency to structural constraints dictated by systemic inertia. The result seems paradoxical: Values supposedly drive human agents, but ultimately "fate" supervenes. That "fate" is what our experts want to ignore: the political economy of the market, racialization, the conflict of labor and capital. Trapped by the theoretical näiveté and internal incoherence of their approach, Karnow and his colleagues cannot remedy the legitimation crisis of American interventionism. What they have contrived so far, a containment strategy for Filipino nationalism, survives today in the ruins of the welfare state and the *Pax Americana* that once reigned over the anticommunist "free world" (Giddens 1984).

Karnow's book should then be appraised within its specific sociopolitical, historic conjuncture. His tendentious summary of over 80 years of diligent archival labor to understand the dynamics of U.S. involvement in the Philippines has yielded only what the aforementioned classics of "Philippine Studies" have repeatedly posited: The effort to Americanize the Filipinos partly succeeded in terms of introducing the forms of institutions such as electoral democracy, mass public education, and so on, but it completely failed in altering traditional "Filipino" values, in particular those sanctioning the patron–client tributary relationship and its effects. (Except perhaps in the case of Filipina women in which the Victorian ethos of domesticity enforced by the capitalist division of labor herded women back from the public sphere to housekeeping and reproductive chores.) In brief, as Roxanne Lynn Doty (1996) argues, the Philippines continued to be represented by imperial ideological practice (U.S. State Department reports, U.S. official pronouncements, and their academic counterparts) as a realm of irrational passion, chaos, internal disorder, corruption, and inefficiency to which only the "disciplinary technology" of counterinsurgency (if the surveillance of legal apparatuses for securing consent fails) can be the appropriate remedy. Lacking agency, the "uncivilized" Filipinos far from the gaze of U.S. administrators cannot enjoy full, positive sovereignty (Doty 1996, 80–82).[18]

In the light of the traumatic Marcos interregnum and the persistence of national-democratic resistance, this legitimation crisis of U.S. hegemony may be said to frame all inquiries into U.S.–Philippines relations. It is a condition of possibility for constructing the object of knowledge called "Philippine Studies." From the end of World War II up to the 1990s, "Philippine Studies" has evolved as part of the worldwide strategy of containing the Soviet Union and its "satellites." Two commentators, Howard Zinn and Noam Chomsky, inscribe the role of U.S. historians and experts on the "third world" in the instrumentalization of the humanities and social science research; among others, "Philippine Studies" during the Cold War assumed U.S. foreign policy as "identical with peace and freedom." This follows from what William Appleman Williams (1971) noted some time ago: how the U.S. ruling class tended to equate imperial expansion, the marketplace, and the belief in propagating freedom right from the beginning of the social crisis of the 1870s. From another angle, the seeming paradox can be explained by Giovanni Arrighi's (1993) comment that "global 'decolonization' has been the most significant correlate of U.S. hegemony" and its accommodation of certain nationalisms within "free trade imperialism" (181; see also Zinn 1967; Chomsky 1982, 1992).

Karnow's tendentious chronicle forms part of this Cold War arsenal to sanitize the zones of contention between the "Evil Empire" and the "free world" under U.S. patronage. Conceived as one ideological weapon mobilized for the post-Marcos era of mending "fences" and "bridges," it is symptomatic not only of the U.S. Establishment's need to redefine periodically its global mission in the context of international rivalries, especially in the light of its economic decline, but also of the urge to rewrite the past—precisely to represent many "other" wills and events purged from the official records—in order to define the "American Self" anew. Since the dogma of white supremacy is deeply embedded in all Western discourse, this act of U.S. self-definition operates within that episteme and seeks mainly to recover lost ground. Theodore Friend (1989), for example, shifts the blame to the "Hispanic tradition" for all the social ills afflicting the Philippines.[19] Neo-Weberian culturalism and residual anticommunism underpin such remarks. The functionalist approach of most U.S. area experts betrays its instrumentalism when the data that it surveys serve to constitute the norms of its own legitimacy. In other words, the epistemology of "abstracted empiricism" reinforces imperial cultural norms by judging the behavior of the colonized subjects as deviant, perverse, irrational. Meanwhile, rehashing the cliché of an exotic and "uncivilized" territory, Alan Berlow's (1996) investigative reporting of killings in Negros, *Dead Season*, "captures the dynamics of an entire culture: one mired in atavistic rules and the tangled legacy of colonialism," according to the publisher's blurb. Like Karnow and many other "instant" experts on the Philippines, Berlow was assigned in the late 1980s by National Public Radio to report on the Philippines. Karnow's discourse can be perceived as the latest in a long series of recuperative strategies to represent the Filipino people as a reflection of Anglo-American "manifest destiny" in its ongoing metamorphosis, particularly urgent at this conjuncture when U.S. ascendancy has eroded and the threat of other capitalist blocs opens up the possibility of a reactionary if not fascist and decadent solution.

A TIMELY DIGRESSION

A recent example of ideological intervention may be cited here. Postmodern thinkers influenced by poststructuralist and neopragmatic trends contend that objective truth in historical writing is impossible. History is not a body of incontrovertible, retrievable solid facts (in Mr. Gradgrind's sense) but, rather, a text that is open to various, disparate interpretations. Michel Foucault's lesson for us is that historical accounts are problematic representations of life because they are constituted by heterogeneous cultural codes and complex social networks entailing shifting power differentials. Knowledge, in short, is always complicit with power. Ultimately, questions of truth reflect conflicting ideologies and political interests associated with unstable agencies. Not that reality is a mere invention or fiction; rather, its meanings and significances are, to use the current phrase, "social constructions" that need to be contextualized and estimated for their historically contingent validity. Such constructions are open to critique and change. From this angle, texts by dissident figures such as Rigoberta Menchu or the survivors of various holocausts are riddled with ambiguities and undecidables that cannot be resolved by mere arbitration over facts—such arbitration and facts are themselves texts or discourses that need to be accounted for and so on. In the end, it is all a question of power and hegemony. Do the victors then always have the last word when they write the history of their coming to victory?

The excesses of postmodernist reductionism are now being acknowledged even by its practitioners. What discipline or method of inquiry can claim to be justified by a thoroughgoing skepticism and relativism? While I do not subscribe to an overvalorized notion of power, whether decentered or negotiated through an "infinite chain of signifiers," a power not embedded in concrete sociopolitical formations, I think the stress on historical grounding and its determinate contingencies is salutary. This is perhaps a commonplace. But I mention it nevertheless to foreground the need to be more critical about the contemporary resonance of what is involved in historical representation of non-Western groups, collectivities, and peoples by intellectuals of the economically powerful North—in this case, by Americans pontificating on Filipino identity and dignity. Self-awareness of the limits of one's mode of knowing Others is now a precondition for any engagement with subjects that once were defined or constituted by ethnocentric, preemptive, and often exploitative worldviews and their coercive apparatuses.

We confront here an enactment of the subtle politics of Othering, not the now banal identity politics when Indian postcolonial intellectuals subject Macaulay and his successors to endless interrogation. When "first world" producers of knowledge of indigenous peoples claim to offer the "truth" or the credible representation of people of color inhabiting colonized or neocolonial regions and internal dependencies, should we not stop and ask what is going on, what is the context of the dialogue, who is speaking to whom and for what purpose? In any communication event, there are no pure languages of inquiry where traces or resonances of the intonation, words, idioms, and tones of the Others cannot be found. This holds true for the intertextual investigation of Philippine history by American experts whose claims to objectivity and pedagogical supremacy replay the maneuvers and stakes of the Filipino–American War of 1899–1902.

That war actually lasted for at least a decade. A lingering dispute exists as to how many Filipinos actually died in this "first Vietnam." Karnow cites 200,000 Filipinos, while the Filipino historian Renato Constantino puts it at 600,000, the number of casualties in Luzon alone, given by General Bell, one of the military planners of the "pacification" campaigns. Another scholar, Luzviminda Francisco (in Schirmer and Shalom 1987), concludes that if we take into account the other campaigns in Batangas, Panay, Albay, and Mindanao, the total could easily be a million. Do we count the victims of "collateral damage," civilians not involved in direct fighting? The U.S. strategy in fighting a guerrilla war then was to force all the natives into concentration camps in which many died of starvation, disease, and brutal treatment. What is the truth, and who has recognized and comprehended it? Where are the reliable informants who can provide authentic narratives? Whom are we to believe?

In the Balangiga, Samar, incident of 28 September 1901, exactly 45 American soldiers were killed by Filipino guerrilla partisans. The Filipinos suffered 250 casualties during the attack and another 20 soon after. In retaliation, General Jacob Smith ordered the killing of all Filipinos above the age of 10; in a few months, the whole of Samar was reduced to a "howling wilderness." No exact figures of total Filipino deaths are given by Karnow and other American historians. Exactly what happened in the numerous cases of American military atrocities against Filipinos investigated by the U.S. Congress is still a matter of contention. But there is general agreement that the war was characterized by, in the words of Filipino historian Teodoro Agoncillo, "extreme barbarity." Exactly how many died in the Samar campaign or during the entire war is again a matter of who is doing the counting and what criteria are employed and for what purpose. Historiographic methodology by itself cannot answer our demand for a sense of the whole, a cognitive grasp or mapping of the total situation and its complex ramifications.

Of more immediate relevance here is the recent controversy over the stature of the Filipino revolutionary hero Andres Bonifacio (1863–1897). An area studies expert, Glenn May, acquired instant notoriety when his book *Inventing a Hero: The Posthumous Re-Creation of Andres Bonifacio* came out in 1996. May questioned the veracity of certain documents attributed to Bonifacio by Filipino intellectuals and political leaders. Without any actual examination of the documents in question, May, hedging with many cases of "maybe" and "perhaps," accused Filipino historians—from Agoncillo to Reynaldo Ileto—of either forging documents or fraudulently assigning to Bonifacio certain texts responsible for his heroic aura and reputation. The plaintiff and witness also performed the role of judge.

Except for evincing the customary and pedestrian rationale for the academic profession, this exercise in debunking an anticolonial hero lends itself to being construed as a cautionary tale. It can be interpreted as a more systematic attempt by a member of the superior group to discredit certain Filipino nationalist historians who are judged guilty of fraud and other underhanded practices unworthy of civilized intellectuals. Ileto's (1998) defense tries to refute the prejudgment. He accuses May of privileging "colonial archives" over oral testimonies, of deploying the patron–client/tutelage paradigm that prejudices all of May's views of Filipinos, and of one-sidedly discounting any evidence that contradicted May's thesis that the Philippine revolution was really a revolt of the elites, not of the masses. In short, May's version of the "truth" cannot be trusted because he functions as an apologist of U.S. imperial policy, a role that has a venerable genealogy of scholars from the anthropologist Dean Worcester to academic bureaucrats such as David Steinberg, Theodore Friend, and Peter Stanley. Their scholarly authority cannot be divorced from the continuing involvement of the U.S. government in asserting its control, however indirect or covert, over Philippine political, cultural, and economic affairs. I suppose that joining this group of luminaries is enough compensation for May and other "disinterested" seekers of facts and truth.

In retrospect, May's outright condemnation of at least four generations of Filipino scholars and intellectuals is revealing in many ways. The following heuristic questions may be offered for reflection: Should we still insist on the axiomatic dualism of objective truth and subjective interpretation in accounts of fraught events? Should we not consider the exigencies of the dialogic communication: Who are the parties involved? In what historical moments? In what arena or set of circumstances can a citizen of a dominant global power question the veracity of a citizen/subject of a subordinated country without this act being considered an imperial intrusion and imposition? Can the investigation of individual facts or events in these dependent polities be considered legitimate as sources of "objective" knowledge without taking into account the hierarchical ordering of nation-state relations? What attitude should researchers from these powerful centers of learning adopt that will dispel the suspicion of "third world" peoples that they are partisans of a neocolonizing program, if not unwitting instruments of their government? Obviously, the more immediate stakes in the ongoing "culture wars" are social policies and programs within the United States, with secondary implications in terms of foreign policy and academic priorities. Still, we cannot ignore how the attacks on indigenous *testimonios,* such as that of Rigoberta Menchu, or on heroic figures of nation-states that claim to be sovereign and independent (including scholars and intellectuals of these nation-states) are both allegories of internal political antagonisms/class warfare and the literal battlefields for

Question of method.

recuperating the now attenuated imperial glory of *Pax Americana* of the Cold War days.

Contrary to some pundits of deconstruction, I believe that the subaltern, whether Menchu or Agoncillo (now deceased), can perform the role of witnesses and "speak truth to power." For indigenous, oppressed peoples anywhere, the purpose of speech is not just for universally accepted cultural reasons—affirming their identities and their right of self-determination—but, more crucially, for their physical survival. Such speech entails responsibility, hence the need to respond to criticisms or questions about "truth" and its grounding. A warning by Walter Benjamin (1968) may be useful to clarify the notion of "truth" in lived situations where "facts" intermesh with feeling and conviction. In his famous "Theses on the Philosophy of History," Benjamin expressed reservations about orthodox historians such as Leopold von Ranke, whom Marx considered "a little root-grubber" who reduced history to "facile anecdote-mongering and the attribution of all great events to petty and mean causes." Benjamin speculated that the "truth" of the past can be seized only as an image, as a memory "as it flashes up at a moment of danger." I believe that this moment of danger is always with us when, in a time of settling accounts in the name of justice, we see the Mays and their ilk suddenly come up with their credentials and entitlements in order to put the "upstart" natives in their proper place.

GLOBALIZATION AND ITS POSTMODERNIST AURA

Let us return to the dynamic force field of geopolitics and the trajectory of historical contradictions. What seems imperative now is to insist on a more dialectical comprehension of the global process that subsumes both the United States and the Philippines in the context of a world system crisscrossed by chronic breakdowns, schisms, and contradictions. While U.S. hegemony since 1980 has been reconstituted by the deployment of military force and diplomatic fraud, we should not forget the astute and strategic use of international civil society to push through anti-Keynesian laissez-faire *diktat* over "third world" societies (Augelli and Murphy 1993). Civil-society NGO (nongovernmental organization) programs have been pushed by multilateral international agencies (including the United Nations) to displace politics as the arena of social activism. Social pacification through ideological education supplements violence to restore post–Cold War *Pax Americana*.

Mindful of this long-term target of ideology critique, the impasse reached by the apologists for empire seems inconsequential. Cultural representations are always being constructed and deconstructed along race, class, gender, and ethnic lines relative to the heterogeneous struggles going on, a situation that seems to defy the codes and assumptions of the traditional disciplines. Such struggles are occurring in both state structures and the sphere of civil society. Against such a background, it is necessary not only to demystify neocolonial myths but also to expose the insidious working of the entire commodity system that we have inherited and continue to inhabit often without our knowing it. Such a system includes the whole network of mass-media production and distribution of signs and spectacles. The agenda needs to elucidate the material practices and structures that perpetuate reification.

Central to this is the circuit of exchange involving tourism and leisure industries (mass-media events, sports, and so on), the fabrication of tokens and images repackaging "the Philippines" or parts of it for quotidian mass consumption. Voyeurism substitutes for actual financial investments and complements the export-oriented economy of the "free trade zones," mail-order brides, and Overseas Contract Workers (OCWs). Here global commodity fetishism converts locality and indigenes into exchange value, salable goods. Extraterritorial pleasures are offered with panoptic versatility. While one travel writer bewailed the price the Philippines paid for its "mutual intoxication with the West" (thus lacking the magic of Thailand or Indonesia because it is Asia sanitized; *The Guardian*, 20 September 1982), another hymned the country as "a paradise waiting for those [Western businessmen] who wish to avoid cityscape and . . . sit amidst Mother Nature's ethereal beauty" (*The Daily Yomiuri*, 20 September 1989).

Commodification reaches its apogee in a media event of some consequence. In the last days of the Marcos dictatorship, the Philippine countryside was suddenly transformed into a stage prop for Francis Ford Coppola's $35 million extravaganza *Apocalypse Now* (ostensibly based on Joseph Conrad's novella *Heart of Darkness*), which reprised the Vietnam War as both spectacle and therapy, utopian dream and technological nightmare. In this context, the carnage at Balangiga, Samar, or the massacre at Bud Dajo, Mindanao, at the turn of the twentieth century are eclipsed by My Lai and displaced in the vertigo of cinematic illusion.

One might suspect that historical reality finally succumbed to seductive "simulation" and the hyperreal pastiche in this film. On the surface, yes, but the reality-effects are unforgettable. Shot in Baler, Quezon province, Philippines, Coppola's blockbuster production featured a cast of hundreds of Vietnamese "boat people," Filipino extras, and specimens of the immortal "water buffalo" (*carabao*) that colonial governor William Howard Taft once honored with his buttocks. Initially hyped as a criticism of U.S. aggression in Vietnam, the film actually collaborated with Washington in endorsing the Pentagon's version of the "foreign invasion" of South Vietnam. It also aided the U.S.-backed Marcos dictatorship in fighting the New People's Army combatants led by Marxist–Leninist cadres. Beyond that, Coppola's "conspicuous consumption" poisoned the local environment with prostitution, discriminatory treatment of Vietnamese and Filipino participants, and other con games that usually gravitate around Hollywood big-time spending (Sussman 1992).[20] Coppola's vision of the "heart of darkness" flickered and dissolved in the terrorized milieu of the national-security state, stirring up memories of the past violence and fantasies of Western conquistadors, missionaries, and hustlers who have produced the received "truths" about the "Philippines" and "Filipinos" for everyone's profit and delight except for the Filipinos themselves.

In the global process of commodification, the gurus of postcoloniality have contributed not a little to the cause of reification and fetish worship. I do not know whether to laugh or be outraged when Jean Baudrillard (1984), in his notorious essay "The Precession of Simulacra," uses a group of aboriginal Filipinos known as "Tasaday" (which the Marcos dictatorship fabricated for its commercial and publicity needs) for his virtuoso ruminations. When the Marcos regime supposedly returned the Tasadays to "their primitive state," this withdrawal (according to Baudrillard) afforded ethnology "a simulated sacrifice of its object in order to save its reality principle." The French shaman performs his own magical number here in updating the myth of the "noble savage": "The Indian thereby driven back into the ghetto, into the glass coffin of virgin forest, becomes the simulation model for all conceivable Indians before ethnology. . . . Thus ethnology, now freed from its object, will no longer be circumscribed as an objective science but is applied to all living things and becomes invisible, like an omnipresent fourth dimension, that of the simulacrum. We are all Tasaday" (Baudrillard 1984, 257–258). A trope indeed to end all rhetoric, all discourse dealing with truth, reality, and other unrelenting life-and-death issues.

What escapes this postmodern sage but not the victims of his ludic legerdemain is the quite ordinary staple of bourgeois politics: publicity utilized for speculation and profit making. We are confronted by the hoax perpetrated by the Marcos regime, by elite bureaucrats and the military (not by ethnologists), who stand to gain by driving the Manobos (members of whom were forced to pose as a Stone Age tribe) from their mineral-rich homeland. This fabrication was then processed into commodity form by the National Geographic Society and other Western media mills, reinforced by a gallery of spectators, including Gina Lollobrigida, relatives of General Francisco Franco invited by Minister Manda Elizalde, and Imelda Marcos, and other celebrities to which Baudrillard ascribes a tremendous mana power of transforming all reality into simulation. But this item is not a simulation: One of those who testified in an international conference in 1986 to expose this hoax, Elizir Bon, was killed in September 1987 by paramilitary agents near the Marcos-declared Tasaday reservation, while the rest of the "Tasaday" have been silenced by a machinery of terror that Baudrillard would rather ignore (Berreman 1990).

The duplicities of neocolonial life thus interrogate the ethics of postmodern theory and expose the inconsistencies of postcolonial thought. In complicity with Western rationality, Baudrillard punishes the "Indians" (the Manobos are indiscriminately dissolved into this erroneous generic classification) by depriving them of their history, their embeddedness in a specific sociocultural setting—in short, their integrity as humans. This is the textualizing revenge of imperial power on a world that dares claim precedence over it. How can one recognize the Other as more than a distorted projection of all the negativity and lack in one's Self? Is this case of unconscionable fraud entangled in the wake of dead bodies reducible to a disposable pastiche of information, simulacra, and language games, to the *jouissance* of hyperreal bricolage? What is really at stake here?

A crisis of the logic of representationalism—the "Orientalist" mode of representing "others" already encountered in the archive of "Philippine Studies"—has furnished the pretext for prematurely drawing up a "postal" balance sheet. But I submit that we have not yet transcended or overcome the material limits of global capitalism, much less its residual stages. What may be scandalous to the pundits of the "free market" are part of what millions witness, suffer through, and engage with everyday: the anticolonial struggles in Puerto Rico, East Timor, Colombia, Hawaii, Kurdistan, Myanmar; popular rebellions (e.g., the Zapatistas in Chiapas, Mexico) in states ruled by the comprador bourgeoisie, as well as the resistance of subjugated aboriginal peoples on all continents. Amid the turbulence of global realignment, Haiti, the country of "marvelous realism," is still struggling to escape the stranglehold of U.S. neocolonial intervention under the guise of democratic reform and humanitarian assistance. Not yet postcolonial, we, "hewers of wood and drawers of water," still languish in the hinterlands of the empire's outposts that overlook armadas of nuclear gunboats—spectral reincarnations of Dewey's fleet encroaching into Philippine shores in 1898.

In the world system of historical capitalism, the relations between peoples and nation-states have been characterized by inequalities at all levels. Contradictions between oppressor and oppressed overdetermine cultural/ideological, political, and economic exchanges. What needs more conscientious application is the axiom of "uneven and combined development" that should orient all knowledge of metropolis–periphery transactions so as to avoid a one-sided fetishism of cultural trends.[21] Any given social formation is constituted by the nonsynchronous conjunction of various modes of production; this differential articulation of residual, emergent, and dominant modes of production enables us to exercise a "hermeneutic relationship to the past which is able to grasp its own present as history only on condition it manages to keep the idea of the future, and of radical and Utopian transformation, alive" (Jameson 1988, 177). By applying materialist dialectics, we can also avoid the narrow focus on either market exchange or its obverse, local power relations. If one rejects (as postcolonialists would) this metanarrative of "uneven development," then how is comparatist study feasible? If the serial instances of the local become incommensurable and we are prohibited from distinguishing one from the other, forbidden to grasp determinate qualities and discriminate among *differends* in the field of antagonisms and antinomy-laden processes, how can we make judgments about the direction of historical change? How is the production of transformative knowledge even possible?

WHAT IS TO BE UNDONE?

In 1947, the great historical-materialist philosopher Karl Korsch turned his attention to the new form of imperialist control being set up in the Philippines based on puppets, Quislings, and variegated collaborators, with the concession of political independence being used to increase economic and social dependence. In general, Korsch (1990) observed that Western colonization violently disrupted "all the traditional living habits in the indigenous community," but the mounting of the anticommunist crusade led by the U.S. ruling bloc after World War II resurrected the nineteenth-century slogan of "tutelage" (if somewhat more coercive and treacherous) for benighted natives in order to camouflage the neocolonial stratagem. Aside from repudiating the spurious rationale of "tutelage," Korsch points to the degeneration of ideology (white supremacy and apartheid) into fascist barbarism when it "loses practical validity." Korsch's insight needs quoting in full:

> It would be false, however, to expect that the old fine-sounding justifications of Western colonial policies would perish with the historical preconditions on which they are based. It is in the nature of an ideology to gain severity as it loses practical validity. And thus it is by no means paradoxical that the most obstinate support for the theory of evolution and education by capitalist colonization is found today in the public opinion of the one country [United States] which cannot even furnish a real basis in experience for the theory in its history. (Korsch 1990, 40–42)[22]

Korsch's thesis has been doubly validated by a renewed influx of latter-day "Thomasites" who preach postmodernist nostrums and stale anti-Marxist propaganda. Counterinsurgency measures by the CIA and the United States, diluted with the offerings of the Agency for International Development (U.S. AID), the Peace Corps, the U.S. Information Agency (USIA), and assorted NGOs, confirm the veracity of this insight from the Magsaysay administration to those of Marcos, Aquino, and Ramos (BAYAN International 1994).[23]

From the beginning, as I have suggested earlier, the entire disciplinary apparatus of U.S. knowledge production has been organized to provide an explanation for such an eventuality. Challenged by mounting popular resistance from the late 1960s on, the rationale for U.S. support of the Marcos dictatorship—from Nixon to Ford, Carter, and Reagan—for almost three decades has drawn its logic and rhetoric from the scholarship of American historians, political scientists, sociologists, and functionaries in various disciplines. Complicit with state policies since the advent of empire in the late nineteenth century, this archive of U.S. ideological self-validation is now being reconceived as a postcolonial phenomenon, with Filipino agency being discovered in the gaps and silences of intertextual discourse and practices. After 100 years of producing knowledge of the "Filipino" (in the generic sense), is the postcolonial fiction of the hybrid, ambivalent, syncretic subject all there is to celebrate? Is the Filipino intellectual's position one of hybridity, "part of the colonized by ancestry while aligning with the colonizer by franchise," and therefore complicitous? Is the Filipino from this angle simultaneously an artifice of subjugation and resistance? Is she a transcultural freak amalgamating Asia and the West, the reflexive Self and the others, and other ontological polarities?[24]

Proposed by postmodernist critics, this strategic positionality or nexus of subject positions is tied to the larger problematic of utilitarian pluralism. It is entailed by the logic of pragmatic individualism whereby a stratified and hierarchically ordered polity is legitimized whenever the terms "freedom" and "democracy" are brandished. Multiculturalism is the name of the official language game acceptable to the state. "Difference" in the asymmetrical marketplace, after all, is what constitutes the dominant mode of U.S. self-identification, a disciplinary mode of agency formation whose reifying power seems infinite until it encounters the refusal of the outcast, the pariah, the "lazy native," the "terrorist" and communist—enemies of the "American Way of Life." Toleration of those who differ, the strangers or aliens, is allowed so long as they stay within bounds.[25] "Hybridity" is a term that one can choose or reject. But the central issue is this: What is the actual balance of power relations and access to resources in which we find ourselves imbricated? This is the crucial question that remains bracketed and "unspoken" even while postmodern deconstructionists claim to challenge, disrupt, and unsettle everything.

Given the predominance of elite careerism and other varieties of petite-bourgeois opportunism among postcolonials, I am afraid that the inventory of ourselves that Antonio Gramsci (1971) once prescribed as a preliminary heuristic imperative might take some time to accomplish.[26] Meanwhile, what I think can be reaffirmed is the attitude of being conscious and critical of one's framework as a point of departure, predisposed to analyzing events in terms of their multiple determinants and extrapolating the network of internal relations that comprise their differentiated and overdetermined unity. I would urge here a critical orientation geared to historicizing and cognitively demarcating the limits of theory (vis-á-vis social practices and forms of life) and assigning responsibility. In this way, the praxis of producing knowledge—one inevitably asks for what purpose and for whom—recognizes its multiple determinants, its condition of possibility, in the terrain of popular struggles and synergistic *praxis* across class, gender, "race," nationality, and so on. Thus we come to understand the process whereby the knower becomes an integral part of the known; the educator is educated, to rehearse the adage, when reading/writing ceases to be an end in itself and coincides with the act of transforming and transvaluing the world.

The acquisition of such a critical sensibility, transgressive and radically utopian at the same time, is an arduous task for the excolonized sensibility. What any subject of neocolonial bondage faces in this attempt to liberate her psyche from the temptations of servility has been intimated by the great Caribbean revolutionary thinker C. L. R. James (1993) when he discerned how the myth of white/Western supremacy, now become an organic part of postcolonial doctrine, is so difficult to disgorge: "It is not that the myth is not challenged. It is, but almost always on premises that it has itself created, premises that (as with all myths) rest on very deep foundations within the society that has created them" (109)[27] Demystification of idols and their dethronement then becomes the first order of the day.

Historical experience teaches us that some idols may last as long as finance capitalism (now mediated through the IMF/World Bank and their military agencies) survives its periodic and ineluctable crisis. In the spectrum of reactions to the terror of white supremacy, the most common one (in the Philippines) seems to be the nativist glorification of traditional pieties, archaic customs, and tributary rituals, often labeled by well-intentioned educators as "Filipino values." These values are then privileged to be what distinguishes the organic community of the rural countryside, a locus of affection refigured as the authentic homeland counterposed to the alienating, diabolic, and strife-torn postindustrial cities. This type of "nationalism" is understandable but scarcely defensible. Of late, that essentialism has given way to the cult of the hybrid and aleatory, the indeterminate and in-between—in short, the decentered subject.[28] In this disaggregated milieu, should we Filipinos then make a virtue of the neocolonial predicament, celebrating our fractured identities and disintegrated histories as our avant-garde sublime? Disavowing the perils of essentialism and the proverbial "grand narratives," we sometimes succumb to the sirens of anomie and *jouissance* in our endeavor to affirm our dignity, our autochtonous tradition, our right to self-determination. There is something intriguing in the characteristic gesture of "postcolonized" intellectuals embracing their schizoid fate as a virtue, at best a springboard for future nomadic quests. On the other hand, the transnational corporate system invariably proves clever enough to utilize this posture of sophistication to promote self-commodifying ventures and the reifying aura of spectacles (San Juan 1998b; Harvey 1996).

Before examining more closely the dynamics of the Philippine cultural formation, I want to interpose a necessary digression here, a hiatus that seeks to resolve the dilemma of Filipinos who have settled in the United States and the predicament of their brothers/sisters at home. It is a transition from the preceding chapter on the emergent Filipino diaspora to a prospective reconnaissance of "native ground" taken up in the next chapter.

What makes for the singularity of the Filipino presence in the United States? The chief distinction of Filipinos from other Asians domiciled here is that their country of origin was the object of violent colonization by U.S. finance capital. It is this foundational event, not the fabled presence in Louisiana of Filipino fugitives from the Spanish galleons, that establishes the limit and potential of the Filipino life world. Without understanding the complex process of colonial subjugation and the internalization of dependency, Filipinos will not be able to define their own specific historical trajectory here as a bifurcated formation—one based on the continuing struggle of Filipinos for national liberation and popular democracy in the Philippines and the other based on the exploitation and resistance of immigrants here (from the "Manongs" in Hawaii and the West Coast to the post-1965 "brain drain" and the present diaspora worldwide). These two distinct but syncopated histories, while geographically separate, flow into each other and converge into a single multilayered narrative that needs to be articulated around the principles of national sovereignty, social justice, and equality (see San Juan 1998b). So far this narrative has not been fully grasped and enunciated; mainstream sociologists have distorted it to suit the assimilationist dogma, while poststructuralists have conjured the image of the Filipino as transmigrant to muddle the atmosphere already mired by free-floating signifiers, contingency, aporia, ambivalence, indeterminacy, liminality, and so on. What could be more muddled than the notion that all nation-states are equal in power and status, making the newly arrived Filipina "transmigrant" indistinguishable from the white American middle-class suburbanite?

To avoid the "nihilism of despair or Utopia of progress," we are advised to be transnational, or else. What this means is to perform nonstop minstrelsy to gratify the nostalgic essentialism of those in power born long after the glorious days of empire, to assume the role of schizoid or ambidextrous entertainers—a parodic pastiche of Bienvenido Santos's "you lovely people." This program of trying to assume a hybrid "postcolonial" visage, with all its fetishized exoticism and auratic magic, only reinforces the liberal consensus of utlitarianism and entrepreneurial rationality. Like ludic multiculturalism, this notion of transmigrancy obfuscates imperial oppression and the imperative of revolution. It sustains the New World Order by glamorizing the marginalization and dependency of neo-colonized peoples. It erases what David Harvey (1996, 347) calls historical "permanences" and their dialectical supersession (see also San Juan 1998b). It aggravates the invidious Othering of people of color into racialized minorities—cheap labor for transnational business, mail-order brides, domestics, and so on. It rejects their histories of resistance and their agency for emancipating themselves from the laws of the market and its operational ideology of patriarchal white supremacy. So much then for transmigrancy, and back to the real world.

The legacy of classic colonialism and its delayed effects—300 years under Spain, almost a century under the United States (compounded by the disastrous Japanese Occupation of World War II)—has proved devastating, exorbitant, even incommensurable from the standard Enlightenment criteria. In the twilight days of the Marcos dictatorship, Filipino Senator Jose W. Diokno remarked that almost a century of U.S. (neo)colonialism "failed to understand the need to change our economic and social structure to produce a viable Filipino independent nation." What resulted was a subaltern state without sovereignty, with an authoritarian government pretending to be democratic, a missing or absent nation "in a rich land filled with poor people" (Diokno 1987, 94, 101). Approximating the nightmare of the Filipino–American War, the Filipino postcolonial sublime may be said to crystallize in the banality of daily humiliation, suffering, and injustice suffered by the majority of 70 million citizens today. Not surprisingly, U.S. Filipinologists are unable to generate knowledge of this everyday "trivial" phenomenon, much less keep track of its vicissitudes in the rise and fall of inflation, exchange rates, unemployment, and so on.

Aside from widespread poverty—in the 1980s, the Philippines was often lumped with Bangladesh as the poorest country in the world—Filipinos are the second most malnourished people in the whole world despite the country being a top producer and exporter of food, minerals, and labor power, one of the most vital resources for transnational capital: about seven million Filipino OCWs satisfy the needs of the world for cheap semiskilled nonunionized labor with destructive implications for the health of women, families, and entire communities (Ofreneo and Ofreneo 1995; see also Ofreneo 1995).[29] Given the rising unemployment, inflation and high prices for basic foods, lack of capital goods industries, corruption in government, and an onerous foreign debt, the immediate prospect for amelioration of the lot of the majority is practically nil. Especially in the wake of the collapse of the Asian "tigers" (South Korea and Thailand) as well as Indonesia, the IMF/World Bank schemes of deregulation and privatization pursued by the Philippine government are bound to worsen the plight of ordinary working people and deepen the destitution all around.

The major source of political and economic inequality in Filipino society, all recent studies concur, is the control of land and other resources by an oligarchic minority—the chief middlemen and "transmission belt" of U.S. neocolonial rule—who also manipulate the bureaucracy, the legislature, the courts, and the military in order to preserve their power and privileges. State power in a disarticulated formation such as the Philippines encroaches deep into the trenches and ramparts of civil society; consequently, the sphere of civil society—the interstices of private life and ego-centered interests—cannot be considered an inviolable refuge of domestic peace and liberty.[30] It is owing primarily to U.S. support of this parasitic and moribund elite since the turn of the twentieth century that millions of Filipinos, according to one human rights lawyer, "will never forget that it was U.S. tanks, guns, bullets, bombs, planes and even chemicals that the Philippine military used to kill them" (Capulong 1986)[31] United States–sponsored "low intensity" warfare (initiated by the Reagan administration and fostered by its successors) proceeds without much impediment. In the aftermath of the removal of U.S. bases, Senator Wigberto Tañada warned us recently, "Despite the demise of the Cold War, ship visits by nuclear-armed U.S. naval vessels continue to make port calls in the Philippines. [With secret official agreements we anticipate] continued U.S. military access to Philippine territory, despite the clear-cut prohibition against this kind of deployment of foreign forces by the Philippine Constitution" (Tañada 1994–1995, 5, 9). The only Asian territory annexed by the United States in 1898, with an ensemble of communities that has been undergoing profound social and political transformations for a century, the Philippines today exemplifies a disintegrated socioeconomic formation in which the major contradictions of our time—antagonistic forces embodying the pressures and impulses of class, ethnicity, gender, nationality, religion, sexuality, and so on—converge into a fissured and disjunctive panorama open for interpretation, critique, and ecumemical exchanges. The challenge is posed and made more urgent by the suffering of at least 70 million people. But can U.S. knowledge production of the traditional kind we have inventoried here, whose performance and achievement cannot be dissociated from its complicity with imperial capital, ever succeed in confronting what it has produced or comprehend the dialectic of material forces that is its condition of possibility, its raison d'être?

NOTES

1. This revisionary project has been cogently initiated by Amy Kaplan and Donald Pease (1993). Filipino contributions would include Constantino (1978), San Juan (1986, 1996b), De Dios et al. (1988), and Bauzon (1992).

2. Symptomatic of Filipino dependency is the report of Pico Iyer on the Philippines cited by Appadurai (1994).

3. For an eyewitness account of the advent of U.S. power in the Philippines, see Sheridan (1970).

4. For the post–Cold War global realignments, see Bennis and Moushabeck (1993).

5. For Twain's anti-imperialism, see the numerous works of Zwick (1992, 1995).

6. For a historical overview, see Agoncillo and Alfonso (1967), Constantino (1975), and Chapman (1987).

7. This value-centered research has been criticized by, among others, Enriquez (1992) and Weightman (1987). Despite the decades that have passed since the foundational texts of Forbes, Hayden, and Taylor, not to mention the workings of an entire range of ideological apparatuses in school and media, we find old categories and a whole repertoire of tropes and syllogisms still validated in a plethora of books on the February 1986 insurrection. These journalistic productions have tried to exploit the commercial opportunity opened by that conjuncture—another testimony to the commodifying reach of capitalist mass communication. Most of these works, however, are flawed by the naive adoption of the functionalist/empiricist paradigm that claims to represent the "truth" of the dense, multilayered experience of millions of workers and peasants victimized by U.S–Philippines "special relations."

8. Further refinements have been introduced by Benedict Kerkvliet in theorizing the everyday micropolitics of resistance in a Philippine village at the expense of erasing the historical totality of social relations; see his *Everyday Politics in the Philippines* (1990). Various writers have supplemented the normative analysis with eclectic approaches, as evinced by the contributions in Kerkvliet and Mojares (1991).

9. The inadequacy of Anderson's speculations on "imagined communities" is discussed by Rosaldo (1994). Employing a Foucauldian approach, Reynaldo Ileto (1997) argues against a developmentalist linear approach that underwrites "nationalist" historiog-

raphy (such as Anderson's) because the privileging of nationalist actors suppresses their binary opposites (bandits, millenarians, and so on). The exposure of modernization or developmentalism has been going on for a long time now; a poststructuralist example is Escobar (1995). The genealogical method is quite recent. But as Habermas (1987) and other critics of Foucault have pointed out, this antimodernist view is internally incoherent and subjectivist, caught in a dualistic metaphysics of subject–object the material-historical context of which it cannot grasp, thus reproducing all the antinomies that it originally seeks to transcend. Such a nonlinear populist history can only elaborate the pathos of victimage in pursuit of an exclusivist anarchist utopia or nihilism, as Bryan Palmer suggests in *Descent into Discourse* (1990). See also Dews (1987), Merquior (1986), and Callinicos (1989). For a response to the populist historiography of Ileto, Nemenzo, and others, see Richardson (1993).

10. For the complicity of a series of U.S. administrations with Marcos's authoritarian rule, we have to consult other works, such as Raymond Bonner's *Waltzing with a Dictator* (1987), Alfred McCoy's *Priests on Trial* (1984), Leonard Davis's *Revolutionary Struggle in the Philippines* (1989), Thomas Churchill's *Triumph over Marcos* (1995), and the periodic reports by the Lawyers' Committee for Human Rights, the Permanent People's Tribunal, and others.

11. In the vanguard of this reactionary Filipinology is Glenn May, whose aforementioned book castigates the mythmaking conspiracy of Filipino historians and scholars and in the process debunks Bonifacio as a nationalist hero. Of interest is May's (1987) own assessment of "Philippine Studies."

12. With appropriate adjustments, the canonical paradigm underwrites assessments as disparate as these two texts: Sullivan (1987) and Hutchcroft (1995).

13. Lest I be accused of chauvinism or xenophobia, I hasten to state here that I do not subscribe to the view that accounts by Filipino scholars are more authentic and trustworthy just because they are "insiders." That would be patently false because numerous Filipinos claiming nationalist credentials have openly worked for CIA/Cold War outfits such as Operation Brotherhood in Vietnam, U.S. AID, Philippine Rural Reconstruction Movement, and other fronts. Recent works by Putzel, Boyce, and others are examples of excellent critical analysis that provide a wider and deeper comprehension of what is going on than the apologetic texts I have mentioned. An earlier monograph by Robert Stauffer can be cited here as a brilliant model of concrete historical analysis: *The Marcos Regime: Failure of Transnational Developmentalism and Hegemony Building from Above and Outside* (1985).

14. Buss's intervention recalls the philanthropic mission of Agnes Newton Keith (1955) in the time of Magsaysay.

15. No more explicit whitewashing of the past and defense of the status quo can be found from an Establishment scribe than that asserted belief (Stanley 1974).

16. The real political import of the trend diagnosed here has to be calculated in the context of ongoing "low-intensity warfare" in the Philippines and in the "third world," as discussed by Klare and Kornbluh (1989). For a dissenting view of the Sakdal and Huk rebellions, see Davis (1989, 36–42, 47). Another antithesis to the mainstream reduction of the "Other" may be exemplified in Leon Wolf's reference to how General Lawton was killed by the Filipino general Licerio Geronimo in an encounter on December 18, 1899: "The nemesis of Geronimo the Apache, at the Yaqui River thirteen years before, had been

struck down (as if revengefully) by another Geronimo on the banks of another river thousands of leagues away" (see Wolf 1961, 292). McKinley's explanation of how he decided to colonize the Philippines is found in "Remarks to Methodist Delegation," in Schirmer and Shalom (1987, 22–23; also cited in Parenti 1989, 86). In diametrical opposition to the self-righteous, racist patronage of the commentaries we read today, it is an immense joy to find splendid accounts of recent cultural/political developments, such as Eugene Van Erven's *The Playful Revolution* (1992) With the current revision of Establishment canons and the emergence of "cultural studies" with radical or oppositional orientation, we hope that the parochial chauvinism of Filipinologists such as Netzorg, Eggan, and their ilk can be permanently consigned to the museum of colonial artifacts without much loss for a new generation of students.

17. The modernization theory of Walt Rostow and Clifford Geertz that informs Cold War scholarship on the Philippines is criticized by Patterson (1997).

18. The persistence of exoticization inheres in the denial of coevalness to the "Other," as explained by Fabian (1983). For the situation of Filipina women under U.S. colonial rule, see Eviota (1992, 63–76).

19. Friend may be the original source of the revisionist thesis when he claimed in 1965 that "[t]he democracy which evolved [in the Philippines] was a complex result of native tradition and aspiration, of imperial sufferance and restraint"; see his *Between Two Empires: The Ordeal of the Philippines 1929–1946* (1965, 33). The idea is further elaborated by the numerous writings of Stanley, Steinberg, and May. An ironic confirmation of the thesis may be found in Doronila (1992, 35–40).

20. This caesura of commodification and reification punctuates the vicissitudes of U.S.–Philippines relations in a way that allows us to appreciate, next to specimens of the "ugly American," Fredric Jameson's exhaustive reading of Kidlat Tahimik's *The Perfumed Nightmare* (1977). Composed in the same era as Coppola's masterpiece, Tahimik's film adopts Aesopian language and seriocomic techniques in satirizing the "colonial mentality" and foregrounding the historical linkages between the Philippine authoritarian regime and U.S. imperial dominance. The American Marxist critic Jameson, however, is fascinated with the film's aesthetics of revolt sublimated in the formal qualities of a unique innovation of the naïf film genre, an experiment that opens up, for "First World" activists," a pretext for the "constant re-functioning (Brecht's *Umfunktionierung*) of the new into the old and the old into the new." Kidlat's jeepnies, Jameson informs us, "mark the place of a properly Third-World way with production which is neither the ceaseless destruction and replacement of new and larger industrial units (together with their waste by-products and their garbage), nor a doomed and nostalgic retrenchment in traditional agriculture, but a kind of Brechtian delight with the bad new things that anybody can hammer together for their pleasure and utility if they have a mind to" (1992, 211). Overseas Filipino cultural activists have endeavored to "salvage" (a term refunctioned during the martial-law era to signify political assassination) from the wreckage of U.S. superpower hubris the invaluable lesson that "weak links" exist in the heart of the postindustrial metropolis. We do not have to eschew the political for the economic or the economic for the social—all three levels of the historical-materialist hermeneutic crystallized in specific crisis points are addressed here as well as in the projects of seasoned national-democratic forces in Philippine cities and countryside. See San Juan (1998a).

21. On the concept of "combined and unequal development, " see Löwy (1981), Mandel (1995), and Smith (1984).

22. Ferdinand Blumentritt, Rizal's close friend, expressed opposition to U.S. annexation of the Philippines in an article published in the *Washington Sentinel* (10 March 1900) and doubted whether the Filipinos would progress under U.S. rule: "The experience of the American Indians . . . does not speak in favor of the so-called mission of civilization, which used lead, powder and muskets as means of propagation." Two works of that period resonate with Luis Taruc's *Born of the People* (1953; Andrews 1946) and Benjamin Appel's *Fortress in the Rice* (1941), one of the few novels by a progressive American writer that registers the "structure of feeling" behind the Huk rebellion and the extraordinarily durable Filipino tradition of anticolonial insurgency. See also Abaya (1967).

23. For a background survey, see Sison (1986).

24. An example of how the ideology of postmodern chic versatility is played out may be illustrated by a tourist guidebook that enacts a virtual commodification of the Filipino "essence" as one mixing Mexican, Peruvian, Argentinean, and "all the other indios of Madre Espana's former colonies" given to, among others, "the pursuit of all fads and fashions with avid enjoyment" (Mayuga and Yuson 1980). The Filipino's hard act of "sudden shifts from Utopian optimism to moody fatalism" is neither unique nor inimitable. Peoples displaced or transported across borders—slaves, refugees, émigrés, fugitives, and exiles—and forced to live by cannibalizing cultures and carnivalizing them as well may be said to exhibit this contrariness, this mirage of protean versatility. This is one contemporary version of what some Filipinos have become as a result of the struggle to endure colonial domination and still try to retain their humanity.

25. For U.S. racism, see Goldfield (1997). For a critique of liberal multiculturalism, see San Juan (1995).

26. For the dialectical approach, consult Harvey (1996).

27. Two other thinkers may be cited here as helpful in the decolonizing project: Paulo Freire, in *Pedagogy of the Oppressed* (1972), once taught us the elementary lesson of decolonization via "conscientization." In *The Wretched of the Earth* (1968), Fanon outlined the vicissitudes of this Manichaean ordeal in the native psyche (in his essay "On National Culture"), a trial of cunning, resourcefulness, and perseverance.

28. For a Foucauldian approach to the colonial experience, see Stoler (1996). For an application on U.S.–Philippines transaction, see Rafael (1993).

29. For earlier studies, see Canlas (1988), Putzel (1992), and Boyce (1993).

30. The fascination with the counterrevolutionary ideology of "civil society" as the solution to the ills of capitalist reification, poverty, and stagnation has misled some former activists into a futile double bind in which the state becomes mystified and demonized; for an example, see Serrano (1994) and the critique of Noumoff (1999). For a Gramscian application of civil society in international relations, see Augelli and Murphy (1993).

31. For a survey of the Ramos administration, see Karapatan (1997).

4

From Neocolonial Representations to National-Democratic Allegory

I repeat that the so-called anarchists, nihilists, or as they say nowadays, Bolsheviks, are the true saviours and disinterested defenders of justice and universal brotherhood. . . . I took advantage of the occasion to put into practice the good ideas I had learned from the anarchists of Barcelona who were imprisoned with me in the infamous Castle of Montjuich.

—Isabelo de los Reyes

Of all the ends to which the writer may dedicate his talents, none is more worthy than the improvement of the condition of man and the defense of his freedom.

—Salvador P. Lopez

It is not individuals who make history; it is the people who are the makers of history.

—Renato Constantino

Where are we now? Where did we come from? Where are we heading to? Postality—postcolonial, postindustrial, even postrevolutionary—seems to characterize the current impasse in modern critical thought. Inaugurated by the UN bombing of Iraq for occupying the territory of another nation (Kuwait), the post–Cold War era we inhabit today may be as far removed from the Enlightenment vision of a cosmopolitan world culture (expressed, e.g., in Goethe's notion of a *Weltliteratur*) as the years when this century opened with the Boer Wars in South Africa, the Boxer Rebellion against foreign incursions in China, and the Spanish–American War. Our postmodern conjuncture is in fact distinguished by ethnic particularisms and by the valorization of the aleatory, contingent, and heterogeneous—all symptoms of a more profound structural crisis.

Globalization is the proposed answer, an internationalism that transcends national boundaries. But, in truth, the ideal of internationalism presupposes a plurality of nation-states asymmetrically ranked in a conflict-ridden global market. It thrives on national differences since "world interdependence has diffused balance of power considerations and transformed them into a balance of terror" (Smith 1979, 196). As long as the ethnic archive persists amid the homogenizing secular ideals of modernization and liberal individualism that subtend the policies of most states, an order grounded on exchange value and the logic of capital accumulation, nationalism will remain a major if not decisive force shaping the economic, political, and ideological contours of the "New World Order." I want to stress a warning here: Nationalism is a phenomenal form whose content is part of a concrete dynamic totality that we must try to grasp if we do not want to succumb to all the excesses (e.g., fascism and ethnic cleansing) stemming from reifying or fetishizing only a part (Lefebvre 1968). Nationalism as a world phenomenon is thus a historically determinate process of group-identity formation with diverse manifestations and ramifications. In the project of constructing the national-popular (in Gramsci's sense), the form of the "nation" loses its essentialist quality (embodied in petite-bourgeois cultural nationalism or cultural populism) when it affirms its contestatory socialist content. How is national-democratic writing as a cultural practice and expressive *habitus* in the Philippines configured in this dialectic of identity and difference?

Before venturing to answer this question, I would like to illustrate how the Filipino first entered the U.S. imperial imagination as an image or figure of the Other—the ethnic alien/stranger—before his national identity could be ascertained or asserted. By comprehending the historic modalities of this representation, a production of axiomatic knowledge subtending imperial power delineated in the previous chapters, it would be possible to appreciate the Filipino struggle for seizing the space for a project of national-democratic allegory. On the rationale of this retrospective, I advert to Marx's theoretical insight concerning the problem of persistence. This concerns the "active anachronism" of past cultural formations whose material infrastructure may have disappeared but whose values and meanings continue to exercise a powerful impact on the present (Mulhern 1995).

The genealogy of this allegorical metanarrative begins from a critique of colonial and neocolonial epistemology embodied in anthropology, humanistic research, art criticism, and so on deployed in U.S. ideological state apparatuses. It proceeds toward a didactic and pragmatic articulation of ideals unfolded in "guerrilla" theater (inventoried by Doreen Gamboa Fernandez in her substantial book *Palabas: Essays on Philippine Theater History* [1996] and Eugene Van Erven in *The Playful Revolution* [1992]), in underground publications put out by armed partisans, and in recent commercial films such as *Bata, Bata, Paano Ka Ginawa?*

Bienvenido Lumbera (1997) has surveyed the emancipatory and subversive tendencies in recent popular culture and films crafted by Lino Brocka, Ishmael Bernal, and Ricardo Lee since the end of martial law. The ineluctable subtext to which they all respond is the U.S. template of the Filipino as the object of its civilizing crusade (revitalized today with the Visiting Forces Agreement), which begets its contradictory, nationalist rebellion and its unpredictable ramifications.

NIGHTMARES OF "MANIFEST DESTINY"

The closing year of the twentieth century signaled the end of the centennial celebration of the Philippine Revolution against Spain and marked the beginning of the centennial anniversary of the Filipino–American War, ironically celebrated by Mark Twain in his journalistic slogan, "Thirty thousand [American soldiers] killed a million [Filipinos]." In 1899, Rudyard Kipling wrote his poem "The White Man's Burden," subtitled "The United States and the Philippine Islands," the latter inhabited by "Your new-caught sullen peoples, / Half-devil and half-child." Although the historical matrix of the Spanish–American War and the subsequent U.S. colonial domination of the Philippines is complex, a quote from Senator Albert Beveridge's speech simplifies reality by urging English-speaking Teutonic peoples to "establish system where chaos reigns" and to govern "savage and senile peoples." The Filipinos have no right to independence because they are not a "self-governing race. . . . What alchemy will change the Oriental quality of their blood and set the self-governing currents of the American pouring through their Malay veins?" (quoted in Wilden 1987, 30). Sanguinary rhetoric of this kind heralded the flow of U.S. commodities and the concomitant transubstantiation of Filipino bodies into profane cash (surplus and exchange values).

As Audrey Smedley (1993) and other commentators have observed, the late nineteenth and early twentieth centuries witnessed the rise of eugenics, social Darwinism, and the pseudoscientific measurement of phenotypical and genetic characteristics as the ideological legitimation of "Manifest Destiny" for the Anglo-Saxon race. Bourgeois society, in contrast to feudal or tributary social formations, deploys various legitimation schemes to supplement violence and other coercive means. Given the lessons of social engineering applied on the American Indians, the U.S. colonial bureaucracy mobilized a whole corps of social scientists, primarily anthropologists, linguists, educators, and geographers, to prepare the ground for winning hegemony (which, by the way, necessarily implies concessions to the subaltern and astute patronage of protégés and underlings).

Quite exemplary is the role of Dean Worcester, professor of anthropology at the University of Michigan, who was appointed by President McKinley to the first Philippine Commission in 1899 on the basis of his knowledge of zoological specimens collected in the Philippines. Worcester later wrote a book denouncing the barbaric practices of slavery and peonage of the Muslims in the Philippines (for a critique of Worcester, see Adamkiewicz 1994). In 1914, an article appeared in the *New York Evening Post* exposing Worcester's not so impartial stance, given his employment by a corporation (the American–Philippine Company) profiting from exploiting the natural resources of the newly acquired territory:

> The earnest labors of Dean Conant Worcester, for thirteen years Secretary of the Interior in the Philippine Islands, in violent opposition to the policy of the present National Administration as regards the islands, for example, might lose somewhat of their moral force if by any chance it should be found that Mr. Worcester embodied not so much an altruistic devotion to the welfare of the Filipinos as concern for sufficiently legitimate but relatively selfish commercial interests in the Philippines, whose prosperity might seem likely to be curtailed should the Filipinos acquire control of their own government. (*New York Evening Post*, 21 January 1914)

In order to buttress the rationality of its civilizing mission, the ruling elite of the United States, like previous European colonizers, operationalized a worldview of evolutionary progress. This paradigm of development—from a lower to a higher stage—required taxonomic and other classificatory mechanisms in order to hierarchize humans into categories deemed natural. In Worcester's classification of tribes (similar to his table of birds), Filipinos were ranked from the Negritos, the lowest in mental and physical characteristics, to the highest, the Indonesians of Mindanao. Roxanne Doty (1996) comments, "This classificatory scheme, this rhetorical supplement to colonialism's divide and rule strategy, permitted the assertion that the Filipinos did not constitute 'a people' or a 'nation' " (37). The natives were portrayed as "a very peculiar mass, a heterogeneous compound of inefficient humanity," "a jumble of savage tribes" that cried for order and pacification. Like the Negro, Chinaman, and Indian, Filipinos were "alien races. . . incapable of civilized self-government (43). Mounting peaceful resistance within the United States, Sixto Lopez, a Filipino intellectual sponsored by the New England Anti-Imperialist League, countered that the Filipinos were a homogeneous people not so much because of their Malayan identity but because "they are opposed not solely to American but to any foreign rule; and they are united in the desire for independence and for the purpose of maintaining a stable, independent government" (Lopez 1900).

After the killing of a million of those "savage tribes," the U.S. civil government in the Philippines was able to transport over 100 specimens of their survivors to the 1904 St. Louis Industrial Exposition. Inspect the photographs of these exhibits of the Negrito and the Igorot in the recent volume *Confrontations, Crossings and Convergence* (de la Cruz and Baluyut 1998). With proper guidance and exposure to Western material cultures, the wild Bontoc Igorot boy can be transformed in nine years into a gentleman via sartorial alteration. The spatial juxtaposition of the photo before donning Western clothes and after syncopates the passage of time here, but it reflects also the underlying allochrony and temporal distancing—the denial of coevalness between natives and Western colonizers—that anthropology and other modes of scientific knowledge production resort to in order to generate inferior "Others" and establish disciplinary control over them (Fabian 1983).

Spectacle is an instrument of reinforcing the obvious, underlining the reality of what is given or the received status quo. Instrumentalized techno/biopolitics enters the scene. Photography or the institution of public fairs (as evidenced in the St. Louis Exposition) derives its functionality within the larger project of civil order, the class hegemony of the bourgeoisie based on capital accumulation (Fast 1973). The control of behavior so as to extract surplus value from the labor power of these bodies demanded surveillance, conceived as the "bureaucratic, managerial and disciplinary form" of spectacle (W. J. T. Mitchell, quoted in de la Cruz and Baluyut 1998, 18). Schools and prisons are the most visible forms of disciplinary technology implemented by modernizing colonial powers. The Bilibid Prison in Manila, Philippines, for example, used a manual of "Philippine Types," including Christians and Moros, to index "criminal types" in the manner of Cesar Lombroso and other taxonomic classifiers.

A film documentary titled *Savage Acts and Fairs,* produced by the American Social History Project in 1995, has detailed the mobilization of world fairs from 1893 to 1904 as a complex ideological apparatus to construct an American national identity and its civilizing mission around racial hierarchy. Others have argued that the mystique of U.S. Manifest Destiny revitalized at the turn of the twentieth century invented the supremacy of "imperial whiteness" by subjugating Filipinos, Puerto Ricans, and Hawaiians as the benighted "others" without whom order, morality, and progress would have remained empty ciphers. Since then, the alterity or "otherness" of the Filipino has functioned to guarantee the imperial authority of the American Self.

Ever since the St. Louis Exposition, when Igorots (tribal mountain groups) from the new possessions called "the Philippine Islands" were exhibited to the U.S. public, the Filipino image has always served the "civilizing mission" of the colonizer. Unlike the Chinese and Japanese stereotypes, the Filipino "enigma" as it was then perceived was interpreted within the framework of the U.S. experience with the "ferocious" and belligerent Indians of the Western frontier at the turn of the twentieth century and the Mexican "bandidos" who challenged U.S. power. The dark-skinned Filipinos also fitted the emergent apartheid system of the post-Reconstruction period. Modes of representing the colonized Other resonated with the ideological shifts in the hegemonic rule over the "internal colonies" of American Indians, slaves from Africa, and subjugated Mexicans.

At first viewed as wild savages, the Filipino "racial type" shifted from the African category to the Asian one: Filipino guerrillas in the first decades of the century resisting U.S. pacification appeared wily, devious, recalcitrant. Anthropology paved the way for the use of jurisprudence, the penal system, the annual census and surveys, and more quantifying forms of surveillance accompanying military conquest. The photographs of primitive types gathered by the colonial bureaucracy in the first three decades of U.S. rule soon gave way to the spectacle of unruly migrant workers on strike in Hawaii, California, and Washington in the 1930s (see photographs in Bock's *Pearls* [1979]). The "oversexed" Filipino depicted in the media was attacked and stigmatized, then driven out. Soon the pariahs metamorphosed. With the sacrifices of Filipinos for the U.S. empire in World War II, the Filipino image changed into the successfully Americanized native—until its latest mutation into the versatile, cunning "good" and "bad" Filipino during and after the Cold War era. The portrayal of a neocolonized subject like the Filipino is governed by what Roland Barthes (1981) calls the "studium" of a racializing apparatus with a predictable code, while the "punctum" of the Filipino image reveals a space open for articulating what is hidden or repressed: the national-popular subject on the margins of the labor market and the semifeudal countryside.

In recent years, positivist and abstract empiricist thought found in the dominant academic commentary on the Philippines has led to the now fashionable neoliberal apologia of imperialism in scholarship by American experts such as David Steinberg, Peter Stanley, and others. One flagrant example already dealt with is Karnow's *In Our Image: American Empire in the Philippines* (1989; see San Juan 1998a) alluded to earlier, an apologetic exercise that overextends itself with the egregious blaming of the natives for submitting to their own oppression. This is just a notch removed from the old habit of calling the backward natives "nigger, gook, slant, heathen, pagan" (Keen 1986)—epithets applied to Filipinos at various times. With the postmodernist trend in anthropology, we get a reflexive but subjectivist interrogation of the old functionalist approach exemplified by Worcester and others. Before the postmodernist reaction, however, critical voices have already been raised about the complicity of social science research with the classic colonial project. While noting their sympathetic recording of indigenous forms of life, Western anthropologists, according to Talal Asad (1973), have contributed "towards maintaining the structure of power represented by the colonial system. . . . Its analyses—of holistic politics most of all—were affected by a readiness to adapt to colonial ideology" (17–18). A recent example is the Tasaday hoax (Berreman 1990; San Juan 1992b) perpetrated by *National Geographic* magazine and assorted American academics and publicists in collusion with the bureaucrats and business cronies of the Marcos dictatorship.

Heedless of the continuing unequal power relationship between the "third world" and the metropole, though more cagey and cynical in other ways, postmodernists subsume everything into discourse, or discursive formations, removed from what Bakhtin would call the dialogical communicative context. Here is James Clifford's (1988) well-intentioned but somehow naively disingenuous comment on the photograph of an Igorot in his influential book *The Predicament of Culture*

Several years ago, while doing archival research on the history of ethnographic photographs, I found in a file a face that stuck like "an overly insistent friend, like a too-faithful regret, like a mute wanting to ask a question." No amount of flipping through other files—countless images of Indians, Africans, Melanesians, Eskimos—could fan this face away. Nor could I penetrate its fixed, eloquent silence.

The archive's caption records an "Igorot Man" (brought from the Philippine Highlands to be exhibited at the 1904 World's Fair in St. Louis). If we look intimately into this face, what disturbances appear behind? (Don't turn around.) (163)

The disturbances do not lurk behind but around us, implicating us. We do not have to invoke the image of the "noble savage" to compensate for the damage inflicted by the ideological machinery of capital accumulation on colonized peoples (Solomos and Back 1996). In all the territories where the present descendants of the "Igorot man" are found, there has been fierce and protracted resistance to U.S. military bases (before they were removed in 1992), airplanes, weaponry, and the attendant toxic wastes destroying the fields, forests, and rivers where millions lived. Like the writers in English and Pilipino noted here, indigenous visual artists are now representing themselves, their people, mediated by the actions of the New People's Army and the National Democratic Front's political maneuvers to develop a counterhegemonic national popular consensus. Clearly, the problem of representation has been resolved by the discourse of collective action, a pragmatics of transformative communication (Fraser 1997). As the new representatives of this "fourth world" strategy formulate the distinction without implying any exclusive binary opposition, "Ours is a struggle of existence, theirs is a more profound issue of humanity's survival" (Duhaylungsod and Hyndman 1997). In any case, contrary to what postcolonial pundits allege, the subalterns demonstrate that they can indeed speak and represent themselves with cogency and tactical astuteness.

ALTER/NATIVE GROUNDING

Let us return to the inaugural, or "primal," scene of colonial aggression at the turn of the twentieth century. When the United States occupied the Philippines by military force at the beginning of that century, a Filipino nation had already been germinating with over 200 revolts against Spanish colonialism. Filipino intellectuals of the Propaganda Movement (1872–1896) had already implanted the Enlightenment principles of rationality, civic humanism, and autonomy (sovereignty of all citizens) in the program of the revolutionary forces of the Katipunan and the first Philippine Republic. At the outset, the *Propagandistas*—Jose Rizal, Marcelo H. Del Pilar, Graciano Lopez Jaena, and so on—used the Spanish language to appeal to an enlightened local and European audience in demanding reforms. With the aim of conscientization, Rizal's novels *Noli Me Tangere* (1887) and *El Filibusterismo* (1891; published in English as *The Reign of Greed* in 1912) incorporated all the resources of irony, satire, heteroglossia (inspired by Cervantes and Rabelais), and the conventions of European realism to criticize the abuses of the Church and arouse the spirit of self-reliance and sense of dignity in the subjugated natives. For his subversive and heretical imagination, Rizal was executed—a sacrifice that serves as the foundational event for all Filipino writing.

Although a whole generation of insurrectionist writers (the most distinguished is Claro Recto) created a "minor" literature in Spanish, only Rizal registered in the minds of Spaniards such as Miguel de Unamuno. In effect, Hispanization failed. In 1985, when I visited Havana, Cuba, I found Rizal's two novels newly reprinted and avidly read—a cross-cultural recuperation, it seems, of a popular memory shared by two peoples inhabiting two distant continents but victimized by the same Western powers.

In 1898, the Philippines then became U.S. territory open for the "tutelage" of its civilizing mission. Among other ideological maneuvers, the English language and American literary texts, as well as the pedagogical agencies for propagating and teaching them, were mobilized to constitute the natives of the Philippine archipelago as subjects of the U.S. nation-state. In sum, then, American English was used by the colonial authorities when the U.S. military suppressed the Filipino revolutionary forces and its Republic while waging war against the moribund Spanish Empire. Language became an adjunct of the imperial machinery of conquest and subjugation. Bakhtin's notions of monoglossia and heteroglossia can be deployed to elucidate how language functions as the vehicle for enforcing the hegemonic rule of a social bloc over a polyglot mass of subjects. The "otherness" of Filipinos comprised of multiple speech genres and semantic worlds eventually yielded to a unitary medium of communication enforced in government, business, media, and the public sphere. American English became the language of prestige and aspiration.

Just as an independent Filipino nation was being born harnessing the vernacular speech of peasants and workers, U.S. imperial hubris intervened. Its conquest of hegemony or consensual rule was literally accomplished through the deployment of English as the official medium of business, schooling, and government. This pedagogical strategy was designed to cultivate an intelligentsia, a middle stratum divorced from its roots in the plebian masses who would service the ideological program of Anglo-Saxon supremacy. Americanization was mediated through English, sanctioned as the language of prestige and social mobility.

Meanwhile, the vernacular writers (the true organic intellectuals of an emergent *populus*), who voiced the majority will for sovereignty against U.S. "Manifest Destiny," sustained the libertarian Jacobin heritage of the Propagandists. Witness to this were Lope K. Santos, author of the first "social realist"—more precisely, anarchosyndicalist—novel *Banaag at Sikat* (1906) and Isabelo de los Reyes, founder of the first labor union and of the Philippine Independent Church, both of whom were deeply influenced by Victor Hugo, Proudhon, Bakunin, and the socialist movement inspired by Marx and Engels. As I argued in my book *Reading the West/Writing the East* (1992b), "[V]ernacular discourse articulated a process of dissolving the interiority of the coherent, unitary subject" (91) in texts that dramatized the breakdown of taboos (what Deleuze and Guattari call "territorializing" codes) and the release of Desire in the sociolibidinal economy of violence and delirium. What Santos, Reyes, and the seditious dramatists neglected is to privilege the agenda of seizing the means of artistic/cultural production, a task emphasized by Walter Benjamin (1978) in his instructive address "The Author as Producer."

While U.S. imperial power preserved the tributary order via the institutionalization of patronage in all levels of society, the use of English by apprentice writers fostered individualism through the modality of aesthetic vanguardism. Personal liberation displaced the dream of national sovereignty. The overt and subterranean influence of the "Lost Generation" (Anderson, Hemingway, and Gertrude Stein) on Jose Garcia Villa and his contemporaries shaped the content and direction of Philippine writing in English from the 1920s to the 1960s. Internationalism in this case took the form of imitation of U.S. styles of private revolt against alienation in bourgeois society. While Villa enacted the role of the native as Prometheus and achieved a measure of recognition by the U.S. New Criticism in the 1950s, he has never been included in the U.S. literary canon (Lopez 1976). In encyclopedias and directories, Villa has always been identified as a "Filipino" writer. Interred in the pantheon of formalist mannerism, his ethnic signature survives only in his name, though the lyric subjectivity of the persona that he invented and the anonymous inwardness of the avant-garde pose that he affected are thoroughly saturated with social motivations registered from, and animating, the dense textures of Villa's metropolitan milieu (San Juan 1996b).

The Philippine Commonwealth (1935–1946) epitomized the transitional, in-between zone of engagement for beleaguered nationalists. However, the victory of English over the vernacular speeches of Filipinos (a polymorphic mass of ethnic and religious communities artificially unified by Spanish and U.S. colonialism) could not be unilateral and definitive. The power of language precisely inheres in its ability to coopt, absorb, or incorporate others, in a precarious and unstable synchronic order. This is because language itself is a transitory and mutable balance of protean forces whose integrity is contingent on the shifting configuration of the political economy. Bakhtin writes in *The Dialogic Imagination* (1981), "At any given moment of its historical existence, language is heteroglot from top to bottom: it represents the co-existence of socio-ideological contradictions between the present and the past, between differing socio-ideological groups in the present, between tendencies, schools, circles and so forth" (263). Alterity then defines the nationalized usage system of English (or any language for that matter) even as it is used to constitute and instrumentalize unitary subjects for colonial administrative ends. While the Filipinos had no choice except to submit to the imposition of American English in order to survive and gain a measure of autonomy, their use of English in literary and public discourse demonstrates an ethics of utterance that challenges colonial power. The colonizer's language is then abrogated and reappropriated for the purpose of critique and transformation. I analyze examples of early and later modernist writings (prose and poetry) in English by Filipinos to illustrate the carnivalesque potential of English, the discovery of multiaccentual signifiers, what Bakhtin calls "double-voiced" words or speech acts with loopholes. In various modalities of communication, Filipino mimicry of American English sought to explode the "Ptolemaic" universe of colonial regimentation and to release the "Galilean" potential of language to articulate contradictions and incommensurable differences. Within the sign as an arena of struggle, a Filipino "English" is born.

In my book *The Philippine Temptation* (1996b), I tried to illustrate the inter-textuality of the varying practices of Filipino writers in English and their resonance with the vernacular and borrowed traditions. My purpose in doing so accords with Bakhtin's central insight that complex political, ideological, and social conflicts in any society permeate and constitute the play of language and discourse in and between societies. This locutionary dialectic offers a heuristic point of departure for a more historically informed "postcolonial" inquiry into the field of world literature written in English, or "Englishes." It has become academic consensus by now that the canonical language of Shakespeare and Milton and its literary conventions cannot be imposed as a universal standard for appraising the value of writing in ex-colonized formations (e.g., Australia, Canada, and India, among others) without resurrecting the specter of imperial domination and racial subordination. Notwithstanding the notion of "American exceptionalism," this applies also to the American English of Hawthorne, Whitman, and Henry James as the canonical standard for judging and evaluating the works of the racialized "minorities" in North America: African Americans, Latinos, Native Americans, Asian Americans, and Pacific Islanders in the United States.

The literary history of Filipino writing in English thus exhibits a more tangled and labyrinthine surface than official histories would admit. Given the complex historical background absent in most textbooks that I have sketched here, writing in English in the Philippines is no doubt an ideological practice firmly imbricated in the conflicts and ambiguities of subaltern existence. If we deploy a historical contextualization of the field of writing practices, we will see that English is only one "language game," or one choice in the means of cultural production amid a space where electronic visual communication (television, video, and cinema), together with its insidious "commodity aesthetics" (Haug 1986), predominates. In fact, Filipino English can be construed as only one kind of vernacular medium or vehicle with a fairly limited, and even shrinking, audience within a decolonizing but assuredly not yet postcolonial site of multifarious antagonisms. The sign, indeed, is one strategic arena of political struggle.

A breakthrough in the conformist practice of imperial speech acts occurred in the 1930s. It was the global crisis of capitalism and the intense peasant dissidence throughout the islands that impelled Salvador P. Lopez, Teodoro Agoncillo, and others to mount a challenge to U.S. hegemonic authority and the threat of fascism by establishing the Philippine Writers League (1939–1941). For them, nation signified the working people, the producers of social wealth, whose alignment with the antifascist insurgency in Europe and Asia invested with apocalyptic *Jetztzeit* (Walter Benjamin's term) the solidarity of all the victims of capital. For the first time, the insurrectionary legacy of 1896 was rediscovered and utilized for grassroots empowerment. We find this stance of nationalist internationalism in the fiction of Manuel Arguilla and Arturo Rotor; in the novels of Juan C. Laya; in the essays of Jose Lansang, S. P. Lopez, Angel Baking, and Renato Constantino; and in the massive testimonies of Carlos Bulosan. For the first time, writers in English rallied together with the vernacular artists (Jose Corazon de Jesus, Faustino Aguilar, and Amado V. Hernandez, among others) to affirm the diacritical interaction between spiritual creativity and radical mobilization, even though the protest against continuing U.S. domination had to be sublimated into the worldwide united front against fascism.

The praxis of Filipino national allegory was thus born in the conjuncture of what was desired and what was exigent. It was conceived in this hiatus between the project of liberating the homeland (from Japanese invaders) and the defense of popular democracy everywhere. Consequently, it sublated nineteenth-century bourgeois nationalism in the heuristic trope of what came to be known as "national democratic revolution." This allegory is not the antithesis of social realism but rather its sublation into a dialectically mediated form of communication. It combines observation and explanation, ethics and politics, expressing what Filipinos want to be and how things are, unmasking fetishisms and protesting against them, at the same time conceiving of the possibilities for change based on the plasticity of history (when read from the viewpoint of the exploited producers). Deploying this stance of materialist critique, I adapt Theodor Adorno's "determinate negation" to the unraveling of this sociopolitical conjuncture, a mode of dialectical thinking that Fredric Jameson (1990a) describes as "a consciousness of contradiction which resists the latter's solution, its dissolution either into satiric positivism and cynical empiricism on the one hand, or into utopian positivity on the other" (131).

The exemplary practitioner of this allegorical mode was Carlos Bulosan, a worker–exile in the United States from the early Depression to the beginning of the Cold War. His now classic ethnobiography *America Is in the Heart* (1973) synthesized the indigenous tradition of antifeudal revolt in the Philippines with the multiracial workers' uprising on the West Coast and Hawaii against racist exploitation. Bulosan's art expressed his partisanship for popular/radical democracy. It demonstrated his faith in the intelligence of people of color—Reason's cunning, in the old adage—rooted in cooperative labor. His sympathy with Republican Spain beleaguered by fascism coincided with his union organizing against racist violence in the United States and Japanese militarism ravaging his homeland. Because Bulosan's sensibility was deeply anchored in the proletarian antiracist struggles of his time, he was able to capture the latent transformative impulses in his milieu as well as the emancipatory potential of the realist–populist genealogy in U.S. literature: from Whitman to Twain, Dreiser to Richard Wright. In this he devised a performative typicality of characterization that fused the symbolic impetus of drama and the realist unfolding of trends in epic, a feat that Georg Lukács (1973) considers formally impossible. But the pretext here may be the popular-front politics of the 1930s and the national-democratic strategy of the Huks in the 1940s and 1950s. The prime exhibit is Bulosan's novel *The Power of the People* (1972; reissued in 1995 as *The Cry and the Dedication*), whose thematic burden was to render in concrete incidents the reciprocal dynamics between the Huk uprising in the 1950s against U.S. imperialism and its comprador allies and the farmworkers' agitation in the United States for equality and justice. Following the tradition of a feasible socialist realism, Bulosan's art transformed "psychological conflicts into historical contradictions, subject as such to the corrective power of men" (Barthes 1972, 74). In contrast, the aesthetes who emulated Villa could only gesture toward, or parody, U.S. neoconservative styles and banalities ranging from the compromised liberalism of the welfare state to the slogans of religious fundamentalism, laissez-faire utilitarianism, and packaged postmodern fads fresh from the dream factories of California and New York.

Despite Bulosan's achievement, it remains the case that the vision of a nation-in-the-making sedimented in Filipino writing in English cannot be fully assayed except in antithesis to the metropolis. Since the 1960s, however, the U.S. Establishment claim of truthfully representing the Filipino has entered a period of protracted crisis. For U.S. scholarship, Filipino writing in whatever language remains invisible, at best peripheral. Because Filipino writers challenging the realism of the center and the pathos of the status quo have not refused to abandon the theme of national/class emancipation, the now contested project of modernity given a subaltern inflection, they have not been so easily coopted by paternalistic strokes and assimilated to a sanitized multicultural canon. The neoliberal ideology of the United States may accord formal rights to Filipino cultural identity, but it does so only to deny recognition of its substantive worth.

This is then an appropriate juncture to stress the hard lesson of historical critique and political extrapolation. What we need to inculcate in the sensibilities of every generation is how the "civilizing" ethos of global capital assumes new disguises at every stage of uneven development and that oppositions and contradictions cannot be converted into a series of differences for the sake of celebrating a formalist pluralism without sacrificing the ultimate goal of justice, participatory democracy, and self-determination of peoples. An aesthetics of "postcolonial" difference or hybridity is a poor substitute for a politics of thoroughgoing popular-democratic transformation. What makes a real difference in the Philippine scene is the moment of recognition by the millions of the powerless and disenfranchised that their society can be changed if they can organize and act in order to alter iniquitous property/power relations radically. When performed by the masses, cultural criticism within the tradition of Rizal, Mabini, Crisanto Evangelista, Amado Hernandez, Salvador Lopez, Renato Constantino, and others becomes a handmaiden to the process of seizing the initiative and demanding full recognition and substantive equality.

LABOR OF THE NEGATIVE

Writing finds itself historicized, so to speak, without knowing it. Unless the production of such discourse is historically situated, one cannot grasp its power of producing effects on the body politic and also comprehend what Foucault calls the knowledge/power *combinatoire* and its dual effects of inhibiting and in the same breath mobilizing people into action. Filipino scholar Nicanor Tiongson (1992) offered a version of this historicizing strategy by stipulating five questions that critics must address: (1) What is the content or message of the artwork? (2) How is this conveyed? (3) Who is transmitting it? (4) When and where did this artwork come into existence? (5) For whom is this artwork? In a classic formulation "On Literature as an Ideological Form," Etienne Balibar and Pierre Macherey (1992) have systematized the dialectical-materialist historicizing of criticism with more precise calibrations of the relative autonomy of the political, ideological, and aesthetic levels and their interanimation. In the Philippine context, Tiongson's intervention is crucial because it rejects the reactionary poison of formalist aestheticism that American New Critics have inflicted on Filipino students and educators via Cold War channels. This imperative of contextualizing aesthetic form becomes more compelling if we accept Earl Miner's (1990) theory that Asian poetics is fundamentally affective–expressive rather than mimetic or dramatic like European poetics in general, a distinction originating from unbridgeable socioeconomic disparities, in particular the asymmetries in the mode of production (82–87). Conversely, Third World mimesis, unlike the Western kind, can be deciphered as ultimately allegorical and collective in meaning and motivation, as Fredric Jameson (1981) has so persuasively argued.

This view of a contextualized literary practice has even influenced oppositional trends. While theorists of postcolonial letters celebrate their difference as the part of Commonwealth/British literature that really matters, they have so far not claimed to appropriate Philippine writing in English as an illustration of what the Australian authors of *The Empire Writes Back* call a "hybridized" or "syncretic" phenomenon" (1989, 180, 196). The reason is not far to seek: whether in the U.S. or in the Philippines, Filipino writers cannot escape the vocation of resistance against neo- (not post-) colonial forces gravitating around the International Monetary Fund (IMF)/World Bank, guarantors of transnational hegemony, agencies of finance capital. They cannot shirk the task of reinventing the national-popular body anew in a world where the eclectic pragmatism of the transnationals seeks to impose everywhere the internationalist mandate of Eurocentric supremacy. This program of reimagining the national-popular (in Gramsci's terminology), not the state that has instrumentalized the nation, is not nationalist in the vulgar sense of seeking to preserve ethnic purity or instigate a cult of linguistic uniqueness; rather, it is "nationalist" in defense of the integrity of the work process in a specific time–place. This nationalism inheres in affirming the dignity and worth of workers and peasants that constitute the nation-people for-itself in the ultimate analysis.

Whenever U.S. experts on the Philippines pronounce judgment on our literature, the implicit standard may be seen to originate from the notion of "tutelage." In sum, U.S. knowledge production of the truth about the "Filipino" rests in part on the organic metaphors of parent–child and tributary–stream, a figural strategy whose repetition endows U.S. representational authority with sacramental aura. In the 1969 *Area Handbook for the Philippines,* an official government baedeker, we read, "For the first two decades of the American occupation the short story suffered from a stiltedness of style when written in English, but, after the authors went through a period of practice in acquiring the idiom, excellent writing began to emerge" (Chaffee 1969, 140). This is repeated in subsequent editions, together with the citation of authors (Villa, Romulo, Nick Joaquin, and N. V. M. Gonzalez) who acquired importance by being published in the United States. In addition to such marginalizing techniques, U.S. critical discourse also occluded the reality of resistance to its client regime (the Marcos dictatorship) by the tactic of omission. One evidence among others: After 1972, "themes shifted from social comment to a search for self-awareness and personal identification" (Vreeland et al. 1976, 148). What actually happened was that "social comment" faced with government censorship either stopped, turned Aesopean, or went underground. Further, the U.S. "postcolonial" will to categorize and subjugate its clients can be illustrated by the well-intentioned but patronizing comments of Donald Keene (1962) in a review of an anthology of modern Filipino short stories: "[W]e are certainly fortunate that there are now Filipinos who can speak to us beautifully in our own language . . . [this collection] is an admirable testimony to the emergence of another important branch [*sic*] of English literature" (44).

One response to this strategy of incorporation by subsumption is the privileging of contradictions inscribed in the site of what is alter/native, the other of paranoid mastery. I submit that Philippine writing is not a "branch" of American or English literature; it is *sui generis.* This is not just a matter of "differences 'within' English writing" or embedded national traditions, which Bill Ashcroft et al. (1989) consider "the first and most vital stage in the process of rejecting the claims of the centre to exclusivity" (17). Nick Joaquin (1987), the most acclaimed portrait painter of the petite-bourgeois Filipino, formulates the genealogy of his maturation as a process of awakening to the exuberant rituals of the folk and the pious gentry. After describing the itinerary of his education in the reading of American and British authors (from Dickens to Willa Cather), he finally discovers the Philippine folk-Catholic milieu of ceremonies and festivals that provide the raw materials for his imagination. While rightly denouncing the mechanical imitation of U.S. standards and styles, Joaquin seeks to locate the authenticity of Filipino creativity in a populist version of Christianity lodged in the psyche of characters resisting commodity fetishism—in *The Woman Who Had Two Navels, Portrait of the Artist as Filipino,* and *Cave and Shadows.* My provisional assessment of Joaquin's oeuvre (see San Juan 1988) applies a combination of negative and positive hermeneutics to uncover the oppositional and emancipatory tendencies in texts that generally are regarded on the surface as nostalgic and pathetically anachronistic celebrations of a romanticized Hispanic legacy.

More problematic than this essentialist quest for an indigenous *genius loci* subordinated to Eurocentric Christianity is Joaquin's idea of tradition as a cumulative inventory of the colonial past: Rizal was produced by 300 years of Spanish culture, Villa by 400 years (add about 100 years of American colonial tutelage) of Westernization, a frame of reference that includes for Joaquin "Adam and Eve, Abraham, Venus, St. Peter, Cinderella and the Doce Pares" (1982, 42). So Joaquin contends that "if Philippine writing in English is to be justified at all, it will have to assert its continuity with that particular process and development" of absorbing the Western episteme and the problematic of the Cartesian ego. Rather than a radical rupture with the past, Joaquin's empiricist näiveté legitimizes a syncretic adaptation of European forms, values, knowledge—an internationalism that replicates the less subtle conditionalities of the IMF/World Bank. Such a mimicry of colonial icons and paradigms springs from a myth of self-apprehension characterized by border crossings and hybridity, signs of "differance" so highly prized by the current theoreticians of postcolonial or minority discourse reacting to the master narratives of utilitarian freedom and progress.

But what would differentiate this axiom of syncretism from the doctrine of a modified *Herrenvolk* pluralism (either post-Keynesian or post-Fordist) under which the "New World Order" of the United States, Japan, and the European Community seeks to redivide the world into their respective spheres of influence? Is nationalism, interpreted recently as a mode of "ethnic cleansing," a genuine alternative? Is ethnocentric nativism (a return to the *pasyon,* various tribal mores, and other sectarian or autarchic practices) a viable option? How have Philippine writers succeeded in transcending the either/or dilemma of choosing between abrogation through appropriation or unilaterally privileging the indigenous? Is Samir Amin's universalist resolution of this predicament (proposed in his book *Eurocentrism* [1989]) a cogent way of breaking through the impasse?

As one response, I want to cite the example of the most celebrated Filipino writer in the United States today, Jessica Hagedorn, whose achievement I appraise in chapter 5. But one may hazard the following hypothesis. Moving from a postmodernist position of indifference to significant political and ideological contradictions, Hagedorn epitomizes a predicament shared by other "third

world" or racialized minority intellectuals in the United States. Given the neocolonial dependency of the Philippines, her country of origin, and its vicissitudes
during the Cold War, Hagedorn's imagination could not transcend the limits
of the vacillating petite-bourgeois imagination: Her fiction centers on individual
quests for identity. The reasoning behind this is furnished by Christopher Caudwell (1937): "All art is conditioned by the conception of freedom which rules in
the society that produces it. . . . In bourgeois art man is conscious of the necessity
of outer reality but not of his own, because he is unconscious of the society that
makes him what he is" (297–298). Hagedorn evinces no comprehension of the
objective necessity, the determinate conditions of possibility, of her own practice,
her own compromised subject position. She has been simultaneously domesticated and idolized as a cult figure by a neoconservative discourse centered on
rhizomatics, nomadology, archipelagic poetics, liminality, and the fetishism of
disjunctures and a libidinal sublime. Read via negative dialectics mindful of the
pressures of racism, violence against subalterns of color, and patriarchal oppression, Hagedorn's style and narrative strategy suffer a disintegration that marks
their singularity and realism. They begin to register the historical limits of the
postmodern ideology of valorizing idiosyncratic differences over and above the
determinate forces of class, race, and gender. Her novel *The Gangster of Love*
(1996) can be read as a quasi-allegory of the Filipino sensibility triangulated by
the force field of imperial subjection, racial subordination, and sexist repression.
Her work may be taken to represent the cutting edge of anti-"postcolonial" writing in the epoch of late or global capitalism in permanent crisis.

IN DREAMS BEGIN RESPONSIBILITIES

Initiatives for a renewal of national allegory (Jameson 1986), the renaissance of
the insurrectionary imagination, might be witnessed in a critique of what I might
call instrumental or culinary nationalism—the ideology and culture of the "New
Society" of the Marcos regime drawn up by progressive intellectuals just after the
February 1986 insurrection. It might be instructive to recall, in this context, how
in Africa and Asia after the 1960s, the triumph of elite nationalism led to the
catastrophic disillusionment of writers who expected the radical transformation
of society after independence. What the "passive revolution" (see Chatterjee
1986) ushered in was neocolonialism, not release from the bondage to capital.
During the Marcos dictatorship, pseudohistorical propaganda and self-serving
kitsch that manipulated symbols of the archaic tributary/feudal past tried to
project a state obsessed with "national security" and anticommunism and at the
same time purvey a simulacrum of the nation's "authentic identity." This was
allowed within the parameter of the Cold War. Nicanor Tiongson and his circle
exposed how the ethos of communal cooperation called *bayanihan* or *kapitba-
hayan* was ascribed by the state to the barangay (the pre-Spanish village govern-

ment) as its "soul." This ethnic locus would then function as the political base for the authoritarian political party, *Kilusang Bagong Lipunan* (Tiongson et al. 1986, 53). Incidentally, a variant of this nativistic and ahistorical primitivism undermines the petite-bourgeois trend of *sikolohiyang Pilipino* and its academic offshoots.

In 1969 Imelda Marcos raided the public treasury to realize her fantasy, the aristocratic and fetishized edifice called the "Cultural Center of the Philippines," which she designated as the "Sanctuary of the Filipino Soul." These icons, symbols, and rituals of Marcos's "Filipino Ideology" might have fooled his narrow circle of cronies and lackeys, but it was easily grasped by most Filipinos as mystification and apologetics for corrupt oligarchic despotism as well as marks of subservience to Western and Japanese transnational interests. Lino Brocka, the leading progressive filmmaker then, pointed out that such "nation-building means trying to give a 'beautiful' picture of the country, trying not to disturb people, not to make them angry by depicting the truth to them" (Tiongson et al. 1986, 57). This understanding was shared by most artists who sympathized with the platform and principles of the underground coalition, the National Democratic Front (NDF). The NDF's alter/native project of constructing a "democratic and scientific culture" via participation of the broad masses ensured that nationalism of the kind that disappointed many African writers, such as Chinua Achebe and Ayi Kwei Armah, would not be a substitute for the thoroughgoing transformation that would be brought about by a change in property relations and the redistribution of social wealth/power. Such a change would by necessity entail the assertion of national sovereignty against U.S. impositions. Above all, it would prioritize the democratic control of a circumscribed space or territory without which the Filipino people—the emergent polity—cannot make any contribution to the community of states claiming to represent nations.

Thus we come back to the paradox that the internationalism of Goethe, Condorcet, and Marx conjured: For "national one-sidedness and narrow-mindedness" (to quote the *Communist Manifesto*) to be eradicated, what is required is precisely nationalism conceived not just as a collective primordial sentiment but as a mode of organizing a community of participant citizens. It is not the concept of the nation-people that is problematic but the comprador or dependent state that manipulates the "nation" and the state machinery as its instrument for accumulation. Neil Larsen (1995) exposes the universalizing culturalism of postcolonial critics who insist on the irreducibility or incommensurability of difference as an inverted form of Eurocentrism (echoing Amin) and draws the apt lesson: "Those who currently protest the anachronism of the 'national' as such, reducing all to a question of the 'transcultural' and global hybridity, merely think the whole *without* the part, apparently 'solving' the problem by conceptual fiat but in fact condemning themselves to theoretical and political irrelevance" (215).

Within the Marxist tradition, one finds a rich archive of inquiries into and controversies on "the national question," from Lenin, Trotsky, Luxemburg, and

Otto Bauer to Mao Tse-tung, C. L. R. James, Che Guevara, Edward Kardelj, and Amilcar Cabral. Surveying this field, Michael Löwy (1978) concludes that the principle of self-determination centers on a given community's act of deciding consciously to constitute itself as a nation (157). But before judging one nationalism as legitimate and another as suspect if not reactionary, Löwy advises us to undertake "concrete analysis of each concrete situation" relative to the goal of defeating international capitalism. In his study of ethnonationalism in Britain, Tom Nairn (1977) counseled us about the enigmatic Janus-faced nature of historical nationalisms.

Whatever the ambiguity of this phenomenon, the idea of the nation cannot be exorcised from thought without negating the historicist temper of modernity. As noted before, nationalism and its corollary, the nation-state, are energized by a teleology of the conquest of necessity by reason, of humanity's progress toward freedom and self-fulfillment of all. This position has been questioned by postmodern thinking, as I have suggested from the beginning. It is also questioned by Regis Debray (1977), who believes that the idea (or ideal type) of the nation, which for Marxists will be rendered obsolete by the advent of communism, is permanent and irreducible. For Debray, the idea of a nation is necessary to thwart entropy and death. It performs this function by establishing boundaries and thus generating identity through difference. Claiming to be more materialist than Marx, Debray insists that the universalizing thrust of bourgeois-analytic reason (as instanced by Amin's book mentioned earlier or the messianic thrust of Frantz Fanon's Third World advocacy) ignores the reality of contemporary developments, specifically the resurgence of identity politics in the forms of ethnic separatism, nationalist or regional schisms, and so on. We are witnessing "a growing interdependence of the conditions of economic production and exchange, comporting a trend towards uniformity; yet this is dialectically accompanied by a new multiplication of cultural diversity. . . . Equality is never identity. . . . What we are seeing now is indeed a growing divergence of cultural identities, a search for specificity as the other face of emerging globalism" (Debray 1977, 31).

Such a schematic mapping of the present world system, a recapitulation of the principle of "uneven and unequal development," is enabled by the very contradictions of late capitalism. In this totalizing regime of exchange value, there are multiple overdetermined antagonisms. However, the primary contradiction from the perspective of oppressed people of color is still between the advanced industrial centers negotiating alliances and compromises on the one hand and their victims within and outside their borders on the other. And while these victims (whole groups and populations) are heterogeneous, their commonality of sharing the collective fate of domination by mainly Western capital underpins the sociolibidinal economy of their individual quests for recognition as world-historical nations.

On the terrain of an extremely uneven social formation, writing in the Philippines stages in rhetoric and narrative an emergent popular agenda or "structure of feeling." It proceeds by refunctioning residual forms (such as the *dupluhan* and *zarzuela,* folk theatrical genres) and marginalized conventions in order to subvert the aestheticist formalism authorized by U.S. disciplinary regimes as well as by the commodified imports and imitations from Japan, Europe, and elsewhere. By the logic of opposing an exploitative and alienating force, the resistance assumes the modality of revitalizing indigenous cultural practices so as to constitute an allegorical narrative of their return with new effectivities. What distinguishes this tendency is a tactically astute selectiveness demonstrated not just in the adaptation of Western genres (e.g., Brecht's epic distancing retooled in collective productions such as *Buwan at Baril*) or in the feminist abrogation of neocolonial/feudal patriarchy (as in Lualhati Bautista's *Bata, Bata, . . . Paano Ka Ginawa?* and other vernacular experiments). Nor is it fully registered in the invention of a new style of tracking the metamorphosis of the migratory sensibility, as in the works of a whole generation of women/feminist writers such as Lualhati Bautista, Marra Lanot, Soledad Reyes, Lulu Torres, Fatima Wilson-Lim, Fanny Garcia, Rosario Lucero, Joi Barrios, Marjorie Evasco, and many others. Rather, it can be discerned in the process of contriving a national-popular idiom addressed not to the *Volk* (Herder and Fichte) but to a resurgent *sambayanan* (*populus*). An allegorizing strategy of storytelling is explored to rescue the progressive heritage (in both feudal and bourgeois trappings) from neocolonial recuperation. Its point of departure is an alter/native sensibility rooted in acts of decolonizing intransigence, in a critique of the illusions propagated by the world system of transnational capital.

The Filipino praxis of alter/native writing interrogates the "post" in "postcolonial" theory. We observe this in the partisan texts of Emmanuel Lacaba, Estrella Consolacion, Levy Balgos de la Cruz, Ruth Firmeza, Jason Montana, Romulo Sandoval, and others. They all strive to actualize what Father Ed de la Torre once called "incarnation politics," a theology of liberation indivisible from the daily acts of resistance against a client state that has sacrificed the nation-people to profit making (see San Juan 1991b). This project of articulating the subject denominated as "becoming Filipino" is not nationalist in the orthodox construal of the term. For one, it rejects a state where the nation is hostage to comprador entrepreneurs ready to sell it to the highest bidder. Its nationalism is prophetic because it materializes in everyday acts of popular resistance. The nation appealed to here would then signify a "concrete universal" embodying solidarity with other oppressed communities engaged in fighting the same enemy; such unity with others is premised on the cultural differences of peoples, including those whose histories have not yet been written or those whose narratives have been either preempted or interrupted by the West's "civilizing mission," otherwise known as "the White Man's Burden." We comprehend and appreciate differences invested with identity drives to the extent that they can be translated for the recognition of others and our mutual enrichment. How is the Other fully recognized? By transposing the mimesis of the Self (the parasitic colonizer within), as contradistinguished from the Other's mimicry, into an allegory of its own constitution and self-reproduction.

What I have in mind can perhaps be suggested by Edward Said's (1990) hermeneutics of the culminating moment of the decolonization process plotted by Fanon. This is the moment of liberation—"a transformation of social consciousness beyond national consciousness"—(Said 1990, 83) enunciated, for example, in Pablo Neruda's materialist poetics and in Aimé Césaire's *Cahier d'un retour* and actualized in the life of the Filipino revolutionary intellectual Amado V. Hernandez. Because of the general reification of social life today, we cannot as yet fully understand the dynamics of these complex mutations without the mediation of allegory: Neruda evokes through Macchu Pichu the heroic resistance of the aboriginal or indigenous communities, while Césaire's Caribbean locus evokes the promise of Negritude in utopian rhythms. Allegory, however, needs to be articulated with the repertoire of generic forms and cultural practices specific to every social formation undergoing national-popular genesis, experiencing the birth pangs of decolonization. This is why I suggest that it is important to situate Filipino literary expression in the specific historical convergence of political, economic, and ideological forces—the transition from colonial dependency to the initial stages of socialist autonomy—that I have outlined previously. While everyone recognizes the axiom that the linguistic system (Saussure's *langue*) is self-contained, a differential system of signifiers structured in binary oppositions, it is also the case that, as Voloshinov/Bakhtin (1973) have shown, parole or speech is what sets the system in motion and generates meaning among interlocutors in the speech community. Speech acts or performances of enunciation are social, not individual phenomena. In other words, discourse is always intertextual and complicit; the world, the concrete historical life situation of speakers and horizon of listeners, is a necessary constitutive element of the semantic structure of any utterance. Consequently, it follows that the character of any discourse cannot be fully understood without reference to its intertextuality, its axiological embeddedness in social process, its circumstantial filiations and networks. To separate code from the context of enunciation is thus to annul discourse, to negate utterance in its modalities of communication and artistic expression. In the social text foregrounded here, namely, the conjuncture of colonial occupation, the twin aspects of U.S. hegemony and Filipino resistance are two moments or phases of the same event.

This is the reason why I would endorse the methodological criterion of the "dialectical paraphrase" of the poetic image as elaborated by Galvano della Volpe, George Thomson, and others. We may also experiment with a modified deployment of what Mary Louise Pratt (1989) calls a linguistics of contact instead of the conventional linguistics of community (or its late-capitalist variant, Habermas's "communicative action") in order to displace the "normative vision of a unified and homogeneous social world" and accentuate instead "the relationality of social differentiation" (59), provided that ethnographic performativity is qualified by attention to the political determinants of the writers/speakers of mediated testimonies. This is the moment to re-evoke Bakhtin's idea of intertextuality, the triad of speaker/theme/addressee, as constitutive of the act of communication—dialectics, then, instead of functional empiricism. This mode of linguistic comprehension would decenter a self-identical community, foregrounding instead "the operation of language across lines of social differentiation." It would focus on modes and zones of contact between dominant and dominated groups and on "how such speakers [with multiple identities] constitute each other relationally and in difference, how they enact differences in language" (Pratt 1989, 60). The theatrical experiments of PETA (Philippine Educational Theater Association) and other groups, Bienvenido Santos's fiction, and the writings collected in the anthologies *The Politics of Culture: The Philippine Experience* (Tiongson 1984) and *Bangon* (Atienza et al. 1998), to cite only a few, may thus be conceived as attempts to explore the operation of an aesthetics of contact and disjunction between U.S. hegemonic instrumentalities and the corresponding Filipino artistic responses.

Within the Filipino community in the United States, the use of American English registers the confluence of residual, dominant, and emergent oppositional trends. In the works of Hagedorn, R. Zamora Linmark, and Al Robles, to cite only the most recent authors, the power of language as hegemonic agency for constituting postcolonial subjects is parodied and subverted. Linmark's *Rolling the R's* (1995) may be cited as one example of a polyglotic or multiaccentual exercise in heteroglossia, syncopating idioms, stylistic registers, rhetorical figures, and so on to project the bewildering ethnic mix of Hawaii in a postmodern pastiche. The colonizer's "English" undergoes a grilling, an interrogation from the subalterns, from which it comes out no longer the same—no longer with a superior messianic mission. Such is the power of the language users to change the rules of the game or at least some of the moves. Aside from satiric humor, irony, and other postmodern idioms of equivocal intonation, the reinvention of the colonizer's speech into a "postcolonial" vernacular proceeds in other Asian American communities (as, e.g., in Frank Chin's novel *Gunga Din Highway* [1994]) influenced by African American, Latino, and Native American voices. In surveying this evolving multicultural canon, I suggest that we deploy Voloshinov/Bakhtin's theory of utterance and of speech genres as theoretical tools for interrogating the limits of what is now the official discourse of bureaucratic multiculturalism premised on "cultural diversity," on the "free market" of decentered and cyborg identities.

Any attempt to describe with finality the speech performance of a neocolonized people struggling for liberation in the arena of global capitalism is a hazardous enterprise. All we can do here is lay the groundwork for an exploratory mapping of the trajectory of nationalist efforts toward inventing its own idiom, its own language of self-determination. Production is "unforeseeable," as Brecht

(1977) once quipped; and it is harmful, as Mao Tse-tung (1960) wisely proposed, to implement "administrative measures" if you want writers and artists to produce the blossoming of more than a "hundred flowers." Filipino cultural workers are integrating with the masses, blending realism with creative impulses from diverse sources and through collaborative experiments synthesizing theory and practice, the central thrust of revolutionary Marxism (Baxandall and Morawski 1973). What is encouraging is the displacing of tendentious or propagandistic art with more creative expressions of serious analysis and critique of the imperatives of social reality, not programmatic obedience but conscious and polyvalent alignment of artistic will to the genuine determinations and the "hard and total specificities of commitment" (Williams 1977, 205). The radical reorientation of Filipino cultural politics coincides with the restructuring of its history, a process suffused with irony and ambiguities that can be adequately comprehended only if one bears in mind Marx's vision of revolution described by Terry Eagleton (1990) in this memorable statement: "History would be transformed by its *most* contaminated products, by those bearing the most livid marks of its brutality. In a condition in which the powerful run insanely rampant, only the powerless can provide an image of that humanity which must in its turn come to power, and in doing so transfigure the very meaning of that term" (230). From that perspective, a Filipino nation is therefore not just being imagined but constructed and shaped by the sweat, tears, and sacrifices of millions of people in myriad acts of revolt and in the process finding their autochthonous agency in the arts of revolutionary popular democracy and national liberation.

We have so far charted the discursive terrain where the salient contradictions of our time involving race, ethnicity, class, gender, sexuality, and so on are refracted in a multilayered textuality open for interpretation, critique, and ecumenical dialogue. My intervention here should be deemed a prologue to a substantial and more nuanced inventory of the historical specificities of the Philippine social formation that would determine the various modes of cultural production and appropriation pivoting around the event called "becoming Filipino." Less ethnogenesis than alter/native poiesis, the goal is to convert the "state-nation" (Smith 1971) to an evolving national-popular site of dialogue and praxis. Such a reconnaissance of a Third World people's struggle to define and validate its agency in effect is a task of reconstituting the revolutionary masses and their position in the world community. In doing so, we encounter ourselves in others. We engage in a catalyzing exchange with voices from other societies using a constantly revised lexicon of "communicative reason" or a historical-materialist cultural politics, an exchange oriented toward a fusion of counterpointing horizons where all can equally participate in the creation of meaning and value under conditions where social justice operates not just as a regulative ideal but as the founding principle of the totality of life forms.

My proposal of an alter/native poetics of prefigurative allegory as a hypothetical paradigm for Third World cultures depends of course on the peculiarities of each nation's history. One last example from the Philippines may be adduced here to illustrate the dialectic of metropolis and periphery that informs the ever-changing configuration of the nation-people in the former colonies. When Arturo Rotor (1973) wrote his essay "Our Literary Heritage" on the eve of World War II to exhort his fellow writers to respond to the needs of the working masses, he invoked as models of committed intellectuals the names of Ralph Waldo Emerson, who publicly combated slavery, and Thomas Mann, who admonished artists to seek "Right, Good and Truth not only in art but also in the politico-social sphere as well, and establish a relation between his thought and the political will of his time" (Rotor 1973, 21). Rotor ended his nationalist and by the same token internationalist manifesto vindicating literature's *raison d'être* by quoting Maxim Gorki: "[Literature] must at last embark upon its epic role, the role of an inner force which firmly welds people in the knowledge of the community of their suffering and desires, the awareness of the unity of their striving for a beautiful free life" (1973, 23). In this way, Philippine vernacular allegory transcends narrow cultural nationalism and may be said to harmonize its pitch and rhythm with others from North and South (now replacing East and West), speaking tongues whose intelligibility is guaranteed by our sharing common planetary needs, the political unconscious of all art.

5

Displacing Borders of
Misrecognition: On
Jessica Hagedorn's Fictions

On the Asiatic coast, washed by the waves of the ocean, lie the smiling Philippines [where] American rifles mowed down human lives in heaps.

—Rosa Luxemburg

The old is dying and the new cannot be born; in this interregnum there arises a great diversity of morbid symptoms.

—Antonio Gramsci

It seems almost an unavoidable if somewhat comic necessity now, at least in the academic world, for someone who appears to be from a minority enclave to be labeled a "postcolonial" scholar or expert—unless you happen to be from East Timor, Corsica, Kurdistan, or, nearer our shores, Puerto Rico, in which case your postality is in danger of evaporating. My mailing address is no longer Manila, Philippines. For about half a century a bona fide colony of the United States and once administered under the Bureau of Indian Affairs, the Philippine Islands was granted formal independence in 1946.

The year 1998 marks the centennial of the first Philippine Republic born from the fires of the 1896 revolution against Spain. In search of a springboard to the China market, the United States suppressed the Philippine Republic in the Filipino–American War of 1898–1902 by killing a million resisting Filipinos and converting the rest into what William Howard Taft called "little brown brothers." During World War II, Filipinos under the American flag died fighting against the Japanese. Independence was given soon after—but under duress: The

Philippine Constitution had to be amended to give U.S. citizens parity in exploiting the country's natural and human resources. Throughout the Cold War epoch, the Philippines remained a virtual possession, a neocolony if you will, with over a dozen U.S. military installations, dependent militarily, economically, and culturally on the rulers in Washington. Despite the removal of the bases, however, most Filipinos have been so profoundly "Americanized" that the claim of an autonomous and distinctive identity sounds like plea bargaining after summary conviction.

Most Americans who have visited the Philippines after 1945 confirm this dependency: Filipino society is a nearly successful replica of the United States—except that its citizens are mostly dark skinned, poor, ostensibly "Roman Catholic" in faith, and also speak a mixed variety of American English. On this last difference, Arjun Appadurai, a postcolonial expert, thinks that it is negligible on the testimony of world traveler Pico Iyer, who swears that Filipinos can sing American songs better than Americans themselves. How is this feat possible? Can we believe that a mimicry or facsimile is better than the original—unless the original itself has lost its foundational, originary virtue and becomes a mere simulacra?

Are we now, by that token, postcolonized and cast into what Aijaz Ahmad (1995) calls "the infinite regress of heterogeneity"? Is the Filipino experience of subjugation by and resistance to U.S. imperialism then a case of postcoloniality analogous to the experience of the Canadians and Australians, the Indians and Jamaicans, as the authors of *The Empire Writes Back* claim?

By grace of over 400 years of colonial and neocolonial domination, the inhabitants of the islands called the "Philippines" have acquired an identity, a society and a culture, not totally of their own making. We share this fate with millions of other "third world" peoples. We Filipino(a)s have been constructed by Others (Spaniards, Japanese, the *Amerikanos*); recognition of "our" utterances and deeds have not been fully given. We are still misrecognized. What is ours and what has been imposed is still a burning issue, reflecting divisions across class, gender, ethnicity, religion, and so on.

Four hundred years of servitude to Spanish feudal suzerainty preceded our famous American "tutelage," a racialized experience that made us almost fortuitous *tabula rasa* for the doctrine of market liberalism and meritocracy; at the turn of the twentieth century, the metropolis wrote its signature in our psyches in the form of U.S. "manifest destiny," the "White Men's Burden" of civilizing the barbarian natives into well-behaved, English-speaking, forever-adolescent consumers. The traumatic fixations began in those 40 years of "compadre colonialism" and patronage. When formal independence was granted in 1946, after the harrowing years of Japanese imperial occupation, U.S. "tutelage"—to use this academic euphemism—assumed the form of a perpetual high- and low-intensity warfare of "free world" democracy led by the United States over our souls and bodies threatened by the evil forces of communism. Recently the U.S. government's gospel of salvation redeemed us from the banal corruption of Ferdinand and Imelda Marcos. You can read this version of contemporary events in Stanley Karnow's *In Our Image: American Empire in the Philippines* (1989), an inflated apologia for imperial plunder and neocolonial hypocrisy. And you can read an oblique commentary of Karnow's narrative (which Peter Tarr [1989] calls the "Immaculate Conception" view of U.S. imperial history) in Jessica Hagedorn's *Dogeaters* (1989), acclaimed by American novelist Robert Stone as "the definitive novel of the encounter between the Philippines and America and their history of mutual illusion, antagonism and ambiguous affection." "Definitive" may be premature, to say the least; but the epithet "mutual" presumes a topsy-turvy make-believe world where the players begin with clean hands, all cards face up on the gaming table. In this chapter, I want to explore the themes of U.S. imperial hegemony and the construction of a historically specific, gendered, national identity by a leading Filipina–American writer, Jessica Hagedorn, in her two novels *Dogeaters* and *The Gangster of Love* (1996).

Who are these Filipinos(as)? The largest segment of the Asian Pacific American category in the U.S. population, the culture and ethos of the Filipino community (now close to three million) have not received the scrupulous and sympathetic attention it deserves. This is due not only to racial discrimination of citizens of Asian ancestry in the United States but mainly to the relentless neocolonial domination of the Philippines, the effects of which still defy inventory by orthodox postcolonial casuistry.

Postcolonial criticism today seeks to compensate for the subalternity of people of color by eulogizing their "hybrid," "in-between," decentered situation. In other words, we need not grieve over the predicament of exploitation, underdevelopment, and marginality. We need to celebrate our Otherness, our *differance*. Now it is easy to resolve one's problematic situation of being situated on the borders or on no man's land, deterritorialized by powers whose operations seem mysterious, by making a virtue of necessity, so to speak. It is easy to perform the unilateral trick of reversing the negative and valorizing our plight as immanently positive (e.g., "Black is beautiful") or else taking pride in the fact that we are beneficiaries of both cultures, North and South, and that our multicultural awareness, our putative cosmopolitanism, enables us to partake of the feast of humanity's accomplishments—from Egyptian funerary art and Plato's ideas to the latest IBM computer. This is in fact the fashionable axiom of postmodernist theorizing, which has also overtaken the academic and cultural elite of the periphery.

Before probing the web of geopolitical intertextuality underlying Hagedorn's fictions, I want to interpose here a brief historical background of the Filipino presence in the United States, a continuous transplanting of a people that unsettles the orthodox immigrant paradigm of misrecognizing the colonized subject as pioneering entrepreneur. This sketch of a duplicitous strategy of settling or finding habitat can give us a cartography of Filipino worldliness that undercuts the taxonomy of any Orientalist stereotyping implicit in the rubric "dogeaters" or their patronizing equivalents. The following metanarrative is of course designed to unravel Filipino duplicity and Hagedorn's rhetorical subterfuges.

Claims that "Luzon *Indios*" from the Spanish possessions of *Las Islas Filipinas* first landed in Morro Bay, California, in the sixteenth century and "Manillamen" settled near what is now New Orleans, Louisiana, in the eighteenth century are made to preempt or mimic the Puritan settlement of the United States. But they cannot overshadow the historical fact that Filipinos, unevenly Hispanized Malays with dark brown skin, first entered the American consciousness with their colonial subjugation as a result of the Spanish–American War at the turn of the twentieth century.

After the defeat of the first Philippine Republic in the Filipino–American War of 1898–1902, this Southeast Asian archipelago became a source of raw materials and reservoir of human capital. Peasants were recruited by the Hawaiian Sugar Planters Association as cheap contract labor when the Gentlemen's Agreement of 1908 cut off the Japanese supply. Feudal oppression and colonial brutality drove rural Filipinos from their homes, while the lure of adventure and easy wealth blurred the hardships formerly endured by Mexican farmhands now restricted by the Immigration Act of 1924.

About 400 students (called *pensionados*) on U.S. government scholarship are often cited as the first "wave" of immigrants (1903–1924). In reality, the new rulers invested in their education so that they could return to serve as the middle stratum of loyal natives who, subordinated to landlords and compradors, would legitimize U.S. domination. From this segment would come the bureaucrat capitalists of the Commonwealth and the postwar Republic. An ironic sequel to this initial moment of the Filipino diaspora is the influx of "brain drain" professionals (doctors, nurses, and technicians) in the 1960s and 1970s who now function as part of the "buffer race" displacing tensions between whites and blacks. Meanwhile, the political exiles and economic refugees during the Marcos dictatorship (1972–1986), such as president Corazon Aquino, returned home to further reinforce Filipino subalternity and promote the massive export of Filipino "Overseas Contract Workers."

Over 100,000 "Pinoys/Pinays" and "Manongs" (affectionate terms of address) helped build the infrastructure of U.S. industrial capitalism as the major labor force in agribusiness in Hawaii and the West Coast. From 1907 to 1933, Filipino "nationals," neither citizens nor aliens, numbered 118, 436—7 out of 10 percent of plantation workers in Hawaii. Severely exploited and confined to squalid barracks, Filipinos joined with Japanese, Chinese, Korean, and other nationalities in a series of militant strikes in 1920 and 1924. One of these agitators, Pedro Calosa, was forced to return to the islands where he figured prominently in the Sakdal insurrection in 1935 against feudal exploitation and U.S. imperial rule.

As late as 1949, 600 workers from the independent Republic of the Philippines were imported by the sugar planters to break up strikes led by the International

Longshoremen's and Warehousemen's Union. The 1990 census indicates that 168,682 Filipinos reside in Hawaii, most of them employed in the service industries (restaurants, hotels, tourist agencies, and entertainment) as low-paid semi-skilled labor. The election of Benjamin Cayetano as governor of Hawaii offers a signal lesson: His success depends more on Japanese and white support than on the political mobilization of his own fractious ethnic constituency.

The theory of "migration waves" breaks down when sizable numbers of Filipinos moved from Hawaii to California, Oregon, and Washington according to the business cycle and local contingencies. Predominantly male (only 1 out of 14 Filipinos were women), a majority of 30,000 Filipinos in bachelor communities circulated from farm to farm in seasonal rhythm. Others worked in the Alaskan canneries, as Pullman porters in Chicago, volunteers in the U.S. Navy, and more frequently as domestic help—janitors, kitchen helpers, cooks, house cleaners, and hospital attendants. Stoop labor generally received $2.50 a day for six days, half of what factory workers got in the late 1920s. Without benevolent associations or credit cooperatives like other Asians, Filipinos participated with other groups in union organizing and other progressive, multicultural initiatives in the 1930s and 1940s.

The Depression aggravated the racism toward Filipinos, already victimized by previous anti-"Oriental" legislation. Up to 1942, longtime residents were denied the right to own land, marry whites, or apply for welfare. Citizenship was still reserved for "white persons," as stipulated by a 1934 court ruling that upheld the 1790 naturalization law. Racist violence culminated in the 1930 riots at Exeter, Watsonville, and Stockton, California and elsewhere. These attacks were motivated by the belief that Filipinos lowered the standard of living while also enjoying "the society of white girls." Carlos Bulosan, the radical writer–activist, captured the saga of Filipino resistance from the 1930s to the outbreak of World War II in his testimony *America Is in the Heart* (1948). Displacing the fixation on taxi/dance hall, bar, poolroom, and Manilatown, union organizer Philip Vera Cruz memorialized the evolution of the indeterminate sojourner to the pioneer militant of the United Farm Workers of America in the 1960s.

Immigration was virtually halted by the Philippine Independence Act of 1934. Enormous Filipino sacrifices in Bataan and Corregidor fighting with their American comrades had a positive effect on public opinion. In 1942, Filipinos became eligible for naturalization. Thousands volunteered for military service. Because of unequal power relations between the two countries, however, about 70,000 veterans of World War II are still awaiting full benefits. The liberation of the Philippines from Japanese Occupation (1942–1945) restored the unjust social structure on top of the incalculable physical and spiritual damage wrought by the war. Neocolonial "Americanization," plus a continuation of "free trade" and privileges for a minority elite, intensified the impoverishment of the peasantry, women, petite-bourgeois entrepreneurs, government employees, and urban workers—hence the push to search for jobs in the United States and elsewhere.

From 1946 to 1965, 35,700 Filipinos entered as immigrants. Most of these families, residing in the big cities of Hawaii and California, Washington, New York, and Chicago, earned their livelihood from industrial occupations and blue-collar work. The post-1965 contingent of Filipinos decisively altered the character of the Filipino community: 85 percent were high school graduates, and most were professionals and highly skilled personnel who fitted the demands of the U.S. economy. But because of race-biased licensing and hiring practices, they found themselves underemployed or marginalized. Family reunification fostered by new legislation contributed to the leap from a total of 343,000 in 1970 to more than a million in the early 1990s. Today Filipinos number nearly three million, with over 70,000 coming every year—the largest of the Asian Pacific Islander category.

The Filipino American community at present occupies a peculiar position in the socioeconomic landscape. Although highly educated, with professional, military, or technical backgrounds; fluent in English; and nestled in large relatively stable families (average households include 5.4 persons, of which two at least are employed), Filipinos in general earn less than whites and all other Asian groups, except the Vietnamese. With women workers in the majority, Filipinos are invisible or absent in the prestigious managerial positions. Erroneously considered part of the mythical "model minority," they are denied benefits under Affirmative Action and "equal opportunity" state laws. Labor market segmentation, cultural assimilation under U.S. neocolonial hegemony, and persistent institutional racism explain the inferiorized status of Filipinos.

Owing to the rise of anti-imperialist mass movements in the Philippines since the 1960s and the recent outburst of nationalist insurgency, the Filipino community has undergone profound changes. While the "politics of identity" born in the civil rights struggles finds resonance among the informed middle sector, Filipino Americans as a whole tend to identify with mainstream society. Meanwhile, despite antagonisms arising from linguistic and regional diversity, Filipino youth are wrestling with the limitations of patriarchal authority, family togetherness, kinship, and residual filial piety. They are beginning to problematize and explore their commonality with other racialized communities (African Americans, Latinos, American Indians, Arab Americans, and others).

A reciprocal interaction, a fluid dialectic, between ethnic consciousness and historical determination characterizes the subjectivity or social behavior of Filipino Americans. Generalizations can only be haphazardly ventured here. While intermarriage continues, particularly worsened by the mail-order bride business, and while ethnic enclaves are being eroded amid residential segregation, Filipinos—both U.S. born and "foreign born"—are acquiring a more sophisticated sense of themselves as a historically specific nationality. In the last two decades, Filipino American intellectuals have begun to articulate a unique dissident sensibility based not on nostalgia, nativism, or ethnocentrism but on the long, durable revolutionary tradition of the Filipino masses and the emancipatory projects of grassroots movements in the Philippines, where their parents and relatives came from.

Claims that Filipino uniqueness spring from a cooperative family structure and egalitarian gender relation need to be questioned on the face of internal class conflicts, sexism, individualist competition, and color prejudice. It is impossible to divorce Filipinos from the problems of the larger class-divided society and from the effects of the global power conflicts configuring U.S.–Philippine relations. What needs more critical inquiry is not the supposed easy adaptation or integration of Filipinos in U.S. society but rather the received consensus that Filipinos remain unassimilable if not recalcitrant elements. That is, they are not quite "Oriental" or Hispanic; at best they appear as hybrid diasporic subjects (more than 7 million of 70 million Filipinos are now scattered around the planet) with suspect loyalties. Filipinos, however, cannot be called the fashionable "transnationals" because of racialized, ascribed markers (physical appearance, accent, and singularly marked folkways) that are needed to sustain and reproduce Eurocentric white supremacy. Ultimately, Filipino agency in the era of global capitalism depends not only on the vicissitudes of social transformation in the United States but, more crucially, on the fate of the struggle for social justice and popular-democratic sovereignty in the homeland.

Clearly, any attempt to describe or narrate the inscription of Filipino identity in the American palimpsest requires grappling with the historical contradictions binding the Philippines and the United States: two peoples, two nation-states. *Dogeaters* is, to my mind, an audacious if somewhat flawed attempt to engage that challenge. It is a work that confronts the multilayered contradictions of Philippine society, an uneven terrain alluded to by one of the characters as "a nation of cynics . . . betrayed and then united only by our hunger for glamour and our Hollywood dreams." It is a product not so much of American pop culture and archaic primitivism (epitomized, e.g., by Imelda Marcos in a Manhattan courtroom) as of a deracinated, diasporic sensibility torn apart by the crisis of late capitalism in the 1960s and 1970s.

Hagedorn's novel seeks to render in a unique postmodernist idiom a century of vexed U.S.–Philippine interactions: The novel can be conceived as a swift montage of phantasmagoric images, flotsam of banalities, jetsam of clichés, fragments of quotes and confessions, shifting kaleidoscopic voices, trivia, libidinal tremors and orgasms, hallucinations flashed on film and television screens— virtually a cinema text of a Third World scenario that might be the Philippines or any other contemporary neocolonial milieu processed in the transnational laboratories of Los Angeles or New York.

The feminist literary critic Catherine Stimpson compares Hagedorn to Salman Rushdie: Both deal with the collision of cultures, "the saga of immigration, cultural meltdown and renewal" (Talbot 1991, 17). In the introduction to her collection *Danger and Beauty* (1993), Hagedorn herself damns borders and describes her work as "a love letter to my motherland: a fact and a fiction borne of rage, shame, pride" (xi). Is this mimesis of Philippine history and the ambivalent attitudes that it arouses the "message" or signifying import of the form of the novel?

The novel is less a resolution of conflicts and ambivalences than a symptom of aestheticist resignation to them. Less feminist than feminine, its oppositional impulse dissolves in exhibitionist and stylized gestures of self-transcendence. The postmodernist technique of pastiche, aleatory juxtaposition, and virtuoso bricolage carried to its logical culmination is what presides in the first part of *Dogeaters*—a flattening of heterogeneous elements approximating Las Vegas simultaneity—until the introduction of Joey Sands, symbol of what is actually meant by "special Filipino American relations," forces the text to generate a semblance of a plot (cause–effect sequence, plausible motivation, and so on) whereby the scenario of sacrifice—Joey's slaughter of Taruk, iconic sign for the surrogate father who also functions as castrator/betrayer and for all the other patriarchs upholding the code of filial piety—is able to take place and the discourse to end in a prayer to the Virgin "mother of revenge." But that vestige of the traditional art of storytelling, in which irreconcilable victims of a neocolonial regime end up in a revolutionary guerrilla camp plotting retribution, finds itself embedded and even neutralized by a rich, multilayered discourse (exotic to a Western audience) empowered by what Henri Lefebvre (1971, 1976) calls the capitalist principle of repetition. This culture of repetition (pleonasm, tautology, and recycled simulations, in effect Baudrillard's world of pure mediations) of which the telltale index is the Hollywood star system (and its counterpart in the commercial mass culture of the Philippines: the regurgitated routine of cliches, stereotypes, and debased sexual rituals) conditions most postmodernist art, reducing even parody, satire, and irony to aspects of a relativistic and redundant cosmos against which the "Kundiman" concluding *Dogeaters* can only be a stylized gesture of protest. In sum, this narrative machine converts the concluding prayer of exorcism and *ressentiment* into a gesture of stylized refusal.

Conflating heresy and orthodoxy, Hagedorn's *Dogeaters* possesses the qualities of a canonical text in the making—for the floating multiculturati. It unfolds the crisis of U.S. hegemony in the Philippines through a collage of character types embodying the corruption of the Americanizing oligarchic elite (San Juan 1991a). In trying to extract some intelligible meaning out of the fragmentation of the comprador–patriarchal order that sacrifices everything to acquisitive lust, Hagedorn resorts to pastiche, aleatory montage of diverse styles, clichés, *ersatz* rituals, and hyperreal hallucinations—a parodic bricolage of Western high postmodernism—whose cumulative force blunts whatever satire or criticism is embedded in her character portrayals and authorial intrusions.

Addressed mainly to a cosmopolitan audience, Hagedorn's trendy work is undermined by a holier-than-thou irony: It lends itself easily to consumer liberalism's drive to sublimate everything (dreams, eros, New People's Army, feminism, and anarchist dissent) into an ensemble of self-gratifying spectacles. At best, *Do-*

geaters measures the distance between the partisanship of Bulosan's peasants-be-come-organic-intellectuals and the pseudo-yuppie lifestyles of recent arrivals. As a safe substitute for *GABRIELA* pronouncements and as one of the few prac-titioners of Third World/feminine "magic realism," Hagedorn may easily be the next season's pick for the Establishment celebration of its multicultural canon.

From another perspective, this time from an Italian feminist, Hagedorn's fic-tion cannot be coopted by an omnivorous U.S. multiculturalism because it is a cyborg's manifesto. Giovanna Covi (1996) argues that the main protagonist's movie–novel is not just stereotypical representation; its rhetoric aims for "a se-miotics capable of producing a discourse on the neo-colonial condition of the Philippines in the context of the Americanization of world culture" (74). So far, it is Covi who, to my knowledge, is the only critic who enunciates most cogently the internationalist horizon of *Dogeaters* for a cosmopolitan audience:

> Hagedorn expresses the Gramscian version of nationalism as the national-popular: she articulates the sense of her own country as the sense of her own *place,* of herself as occupying a given position whose social meaning derives from belonging to a historically-defined tradition. She rejects the nationalism of the nation-state which is supported by the identification with a specific ideology. . . . Precisely because the Philippines [is] an American colony—and this is not an invention—*Dogeaters* is not only a realistic portrayal of the cultural, social, and moral fragmentation derived from centuries of dependence on first the Spanish and later the Americans, but also—in Gramscian terms—the expression of a sociality which is historical and eth-ico-political and which is the condition for the artistic rendering of a genuine and fundamental humanity. (1996, 65–66)

Covi's perspective is salutary and prompts the contextualization of my previous remarks on *Dogeaters* in the allegory of the historical contingencies and ambigu-ities that subtend Hagedorn's *The Gangster of Love.*

In contrast to the quasi-surrealistic montage of her first novel, Hagedorn's sec-ond work centers on the adventures of a young Filipina in the United States growing up against the background of the obsolescence of the rock/hippie/youth counterculture of the 1960s, the decline of civil rights struggles and "Third World" revolutions, and the resurgence of reactionary ideology and practices. Can nostalgia replace the shock of living through alienation and commodity fe-tishism, racial bigotry and sexism, in the imperial metropolis? What is the fate of the post-1965 Filipino immigrant generation? Rocky Rivera's search for a viable community (the rock band functions as temporary surrogate and compensatory device) dramatizes the predicament of the adolescent Filipina stranded in the milieu of neoconservative America. Rocky decides to be a mother and replace patriarchal culture (signified by her aging mother still fixated on the absent phi-landering father) with the shifting positionality of a nomadic subject—Covi's cy-borg—who somehow survives the predatory disasters of her "flower-power" companions. She deploys tactics of mimicry, satire and burlesque, comic ruses, and happenstance stratagems. Her situation can be read as an allegorical rendering of the post-1965 cohort of Filipino immigrants whose neocolonial roots can only prompt a clinging to fragments of indigenous, damaged culture while aping the suburban lifestyle of conspicuous consumerism. The narrative stages Rocky's return after her mother's death to face the dying father in the Philippines and what he comes to symbolize: the decadent world of the Marcoses (a return of the past sacrificed in *Dogeaters*) and the moribund oligarchy. A politics of memory emerges whose libidinal figuration captures the uneven, unsynchronized social formation of the neocolony.

In the final analysis, one can say that Hagedorn's production of a "postcolonial" minoritarian discourse depends for its condition of possibility on what it denies or represses: the culture of resistance symbolized by the Manongs and, by extension, the revolt of the Filipino masses erased by Jimi Hendrix and Hollywood. On the other hand, one can argue that impulses of resistance are not completely extinguished but manifest themselves here in the form of grotesque characters, melodramatic juxtapositions, breaks and discontinuities in style and idiom, and above all in the absurd and fantastic incidents whose bizarre texture reflects precisely the profound crisis of late global capitalism registered in the bodies and performances of Hagedorn's "gangsters of love," temporarily disbanded and/or routed, in quest of laws and authorities they need to defy.

Here I interject the phenomenal explosion of the Filipino diaspora in the historical conjuncture of the 1980s and 1990s in the wake of the collapse of the Soviet Union and the decline of *Pax Americana*.

Given the unprecedented fact of seven million Filipinos scattered around the world as "contract workers" (including "hospitality" women in Japan and elsewhere), the neocolonial (not postcolonial) impasse of Filipino society has not suffered attenuation. On the contrary: The whole country has been refeudalized as a Western enclave in the cartography of global, transnational capitalism. This change demands a new historically grounded analysis, properly a collective and open-ended enterprise, one that would ideally be informed by an emancipatory and counterhegemonic praxis.

Within this horizon of exploring the terrain of the possible, adjacent to the embattled zone of subaltern metanarratives, I would like to examine more closely the thematic motivation and ethicopolitical agency implied in *The Gangster of Love*. One might remember that Hagedorn's first novel, *Dogeaters*, enjoyed a brief notoriety as an afterimage of the Marcos-dictatorship interlude in our history. This is the pretext to pose questions that have now occupied center stage in the debate on multiculturalism, identity politics, the existence of a "common culture," nationalism, racialized ethnicities, and globalized borderlands—themes and motifs rehearsed in the resurgent maelstrom of "political correctness."

The commentator Russell Jacoby (1995) censures postcolonial discourse for its obscure and solipsist grandiosity, its banal politics, its jargonized language, its tiresome and infantile self-obsession. Lest someone mistake me for Jacoby's target—he is actually referring to Gayatri Spivak, Homi Bhabha, and their epigones—I hasten to assure the reader that I do not consider myself a postcolonial critic if by that is meant someone from the Commonwealth countries that formed part of the nearly all-encompassing British Empire—a diasporic writer such as Salman Rushdie or a successful "third world" intellectual in a first-world institution of higher learning. But certain questions raised by Edward Said and others about the Orientalized construction of the Other by Western knowledge/power (to use Foucault's term), about the legitimacy of representations of indigenous and subaltern subjects and their capacity to speak for themselves, about the nature of agency and the possibilities of critique and transformation of world-historical inequalities—these questions, rather than purely formal questions of aesthetic form, will serve as the framework around which I offer the following brief observation on *The Gangster of Love.*

The story is simple: Brought by her mother to the United States in the year Jimi Hendrix died, Raquel Rivera (together with her brother Voltaire who eventually returns to the Philippines) grows up in the milieu of the 1960s; meets a felicitously named partner, Elvis Chang; and forms a band with him called "The Gangster of Love." She then befriends a versatile woman, Keiko Van Heller, and plunges into a series of somewhat *déjà vu* adventures with her as well as with a host of other idiosyncratic characters, such as her uncle Marlon Rivera. She then moves to New York City from California and teams up with Jake Montano, with whom she has a child and goes through grotesque and tragicomic scenes of her mother's death—a turning point in her life. She then returns to Manila to visit her dying father (the concluding episode is named after him), whose philandering—an index of the patriarchal regime that she is revolting against but also eulogizing—led to the dissolution of the family. Does the ending imply a return of the "prodigal" daughter, a reconciliation? Or does it prefigure a bridging of the gap between the homeland that had just witnessed the turmoil of the February 1986 uprising against the U.S.-backed Marcos dictatorship and the imperial power that offered a refuge to the despot in its Pacific outpost, Hawaii? Even if that is so, the dead Jimi Hendrix cannot be resurrected so easily, and the "Gangster of Love" remains defunct.

Part 4 indeed carries the heading "To Return." But that rubric is a gambit, a disingenuous alibi. It is undermined by the duplicitous connotation of the yoyo, the toy that serves here as an icon of Filipino ethnicity, which (Hagedorn instructs us) means not just "to return" but also "to cast out." At the beginning of part 1, Hagedorn provides the slang definition of the yo-yo—a person regarded not only as stupid and ineffectual but also as eccentric. More apropos of the narrative design of the novel—a bricolage interweaving of scenes using interior monologue, stream of consciousness, parody, lyric transcripts of memories and dreams, a thesaurus of trendy code words, and so on—is the colloquial sense of yo-yo: fluctuating, variable, but also automatic. If the postcolonial text is usually categorized as a pastiche of styles and idiom, a montage of heterogeneous materials that syncopate linear plot with a polyphony of voices, tones, and rhythms, then Hagedorn's invention fits the bill.

We are in the presence of a classic postmodern artifice: The causal narrative of the modern realistic novel inherited from nineteenth-century bourgeois Europe is here articulated with a picaresque mode reminiscent of feudal times, recurrent snapshots of grotesque characters symptomatic of an atomized industrial society, scenes of ribald festivity, sexual encounters, tableaux of recollections, and quotations from the mass confections of Hollywood and the pop music industry, all interwoven with introspective diary-like notations. This highly stylized fabrication tries not only to dovetail the past and present in a meaningful configuration but also to intimate the emergence of the new, of future forms of life that escape the fatal cycle of the yo-yo and the reproduction of the seemingly eternal round of the "return of the repressed." What I am trying to get at is that this work attempts to render the experience of transition, of what it means to live in and through the collision of contradictory modes of production in a historically determinate social formation defined by the colonial nexus between the Philippines and the United States. What is privileged here is the process of transition, not the terminals of origin and destination. That experience of uprooting, the subsequent struggle for survival translated here as the reconstitution of "family" or some analogue of traditional consanguinity in an alien environment, and with it the construction of a new identity, is usually designated as the archetype of the postcolonial experience.

My own argument, however, is that this is not postcolonial but anticolonial or, if you like, counterhegemonic and oppositional in motive and telos. This is not the surface intent of the novel, of course. I call it the "political unconscious" (after Jameson 1981) of the text, which goes beyond the exposure of the spurious "civilizing mission" of Anglo-Saxon white supremacy. I suggest a reconstructive reading here. What makes Hagedorn's text transgressive is its supersession of the countercultural cult of the superstars of the 1960s and its alignment with the social memory of the Filipinos in California crystallized by her mother's illness and death. In this itinerary of exile, the narrative begins to shape a modality of resistance to the commodifying power of late-capitalist culture and ideology. One may even suggest that its "unconscious" project, sublated in the variegated texture of the prose and its melange of genres, is to mobilize the submerged and hidden resources of indigenous forms of life for the goal of popular-national liberation. This paramount objective is indivisible with sexual and gender emancipation.

To illustrate my thesis, let me point to the fundamental contradiction expressed on the level of thematic detail. Rocky Rivera, a Filipina woman of mixed ancestry, seeks to chart her life in a society dominated by the instrumentalizing rigor of business and individualist competition. What is her point of departure? Two things are insinuated in terms of native resources: food and language. While the temper of postmodernist art is to refuse universals and exalt particulars, we discern here a fascination with spatial ordering that becomes a surrogate means of cognitive reconnaissance. There seems to be a fetishism of place (a metaphoric geography of culture, moods, and enigmatic personalities) that tries to compensate for the secular uniformities of industrialized society. Hagedorn knows that a rupture has taken place—her body and psyche have been transported in time and space—but pretends that it has not happened: Her mother and relatives cook and eat the native foods, talk the same language (now exoticized or defamiliarized), and carry on their customary ways, with some minor adjustments. But all the same, this pretense is grounded on the recognition of the truth of separation, of unequivocal distance: The brother's return confirms this. I locate this fetishism in the "Prologue," a testimony that celebrates the sheer incongruities, absurd juxtapositions, and seemingly gratuitous coexistence of idioms, lifestyles, artifacts, and tastes whose semiosis dramatizes the variegated temporal/spatial stratification of Philippine social life:

> There are rumors. Surrealities. Malacañang Palace slowly sinking into the fetid Pasig River, haunted by unhappy ghosts. Female ghosts. Infant ghosts. What is love? A young girl asks.
> Rumors. Malicious gossip, treacherous tsimis. Blah blah blah. Dire predictions, arbitrary lust. The city hums with sinister music. Scandal, innuendo, half-truths, bald-faced lies. Adulterous love affairs hatched, coups d'etat plotted. A man shoots another man for no apparent reason. A jealous husband beats his wife for the umpteenth time. The Black Nazarene collapses in a rice paddy, weeping.
> I love you, someone sings on the omnipresent radio. Soldiers in disguise patrol the countryside.
> Love, love, love. Love is in the air.
> Background, foreground, all around.
> But what is love? A young girl asks.
> A fatal mosquito bite, the nuns warn her.
> Rumors. Eternal summers, impending typhoons. The stink of fear unmistakable in the relentless, sweltering heat. (1996, 1)

At first glance, this opening landscape strikes us as a multimedia composite of elements with dissonant matrices and contexts. Location is not random or contingent but deliberate. Organized around a metonymic axis are the seat of government (the mention of Malacañang Palace fixes the historic determinateness of the narrative); the Pasig River that treads through Manila, the urban center; news of domestic violence carried by newspapers and radio; the religious icon of the Black Nazarene suffering an accident; the presence of the military in the countryside; and so on. This collage is cut through by a refrain, a deflated query about love. What sutures this series is the metaphoric cluster of "rumors" and the extremities of the climate. How to make sense of this seemingly unintelligible conjuncture of features of the natural and artifactual surroundings, of ubiquitous rumors whose reverberation is punctuated with violence, and of religious codes trying to put a lid on the explosive mixture—this crux, this bundle of contradictions, is what the novel will try to resolve on an imaginary plane. In other words, Hagedorn will attempt to grasp the deformed, uneven, fractured social landscape of the Philippines with the apparatus of a self-reflexive aestheticizing consciousness, one that is itself a product of the phenomenon of imperial violence that it is trying to grapple with and master.

In my opinion, this attempt fails—and that may be the underlying intent of the "political unconscious." In the section "Tropical Depression" toward the end of the novel, Hagedorn restages the landscape with a revealing dramatic variation: The appearance of a mythical Black Virgin functions to sublimate all the incongruities and discordances, permitting the force of Nature to normalize the phenomena of crisis. This occurs at the time of her return after her mother's death, an event signifying the loss of the pre-Oedipal anchor or center for her self-identifying explorations. On the terrain of chaos and unpredictability emerges a unifying and centralizing image. After the August typhoon subsides, the city is ravaged by epidemics:

> Strange scenes of violence and grieving occur without warning. Grown men weep uncontrollably. Women run amok, hacking at everyone in their path with any weapon they can find—bolo knives, scissors. Infants are born with webbed feet. The general mood of despair is alleviated by frequent sightings of the Black Virgin. She wanders the countryside, seeking to comfort those who cannot be comforted. A young woman wearing a blond wig has herself crucified in a public ceremony. Her spectacle of sacrifice draws thousands of believers, showy penitents flogging their own mildewed flesh with dainty, custom-made whips. Blood flows, the only vibrant color in this black sea of waterlogged depression. In Manila, phosphorescent crocodiles and moray eels lurk in the aquatic ruins of a submerged mega-shopping mall on Epifanio de los Santos. (1996, 290)

The sight of the flooded megamall on the highway where the February 1986 revolution took place may suggest either the inchoate level of industrialization, symptom of the inadequacy of the Filipino comprador bourgeoisie, or the irresistible power of the past, the archaic, what escapes rational and systematic control. In any case, the presence of the Black Virgin may be interpreted as symbolic of the enduring hold of mythical and magical thinking in the neocolony amidst a rationalizing, secularized business environment. Ironically, this ruse is available precisely because Weberian disenchantment and commodity fetishism have not completely saturated the public sphere, something that escapes the narrator's avant-garde sensibility and secretly assists its desire to ground the self (the imagination) in the field of mutual and reciprocal recognition. The author wants to have it both ways: affirm both primordial ethnicity and its antithesis, bureaucratized individualism. This anarchist politics of representation can also be read as a pretext for vindicating the status quo, business as usual. I think that is the point of the meeting of father and estranged daughter, a revealing encounter of self and other, at the end of the novel.

On the level of political significance, this staging of hybridity and "in-between" confluence of signs, objects, and happenings signifies the most fundamental characteristic of the kind of experience shared by subjects in most colonial formations: uneven and combined development. While a preponderant number of characters here may be viewed as walking cyborgs or amphibians, there are two characters that function as microcosms of unevenness: Keiko and Marlon. This mode of disarticulation prevails in the sociocultural level as an effect of the diverse modes of production (and its social relations) coexisting together. Underlying the complex social formation of a peripheral, dependent region, we find the juxtaposition of various precapitalist or archaic modes of production, the tributary or feudal and artisanal ones spliced together with assorted capitalist modes, the most visible of which are mercantile or trading and comprador business. Absent of course is an industrial fraction—that is, the space preempted by the transnational corporations as well as the World Bank and the International Monetary Fund. What is dominant, however, is a combination of bureaucratic and comprador capitalisms to which everything else—semifeudal and petite-bourgeois operations and class fractions—is subordinate. This nonsynchronic combination produces specific effects on the diachronic plane that explain the concrete, quotidian forms of behavior assumed by the juridicopolitical institutions and the dynamic interaction of ideological–cultural practices of all classes.

I think that it is within this perspective of geopolitical unevenness and overdetermination that we can grasp the singularity of the literary/aesthetic mode of production epitomized by Hagedorn's work. Despite the fact that Hagedorn produces chiefly for a first-world audience and more narrowly for a limited multicultural audience in urban zones, the practice that she exemplifies is defined by the uneven social formation that is precisely the condition of possibility for her kind of writing. What do I mean by this?

Postcolonial orthodoxy mandates that essentialism or any quest for roots be proscribed in the same breath as syncretism and hybridity are valorized and made obligatory. Gayatri Spivak (1991), for example, congratulates herself for reopening the "epistemic fracture of imperialism without succumbing to a nostalgia for lost origins" (272) and urges us to attend to the "archives of imperialist governance." Refusing to perform such a hermeneutic task, Hagedorn instead presents an anatomy of the Filipino colonized formation. Her style of cognitive mapping delivers an archaeology of multifarious signs alluding to several periods or stages of the development of the capitalist world system. I do not mean here a recapitulation of the evolutionary phases of the transition from feudal or precapitalist structures to modern industrial capitalism. What seems to transcend the binary opposites of the politics of blame and the politics of compassion—for Sara Suleri (1995) the "commonality of loss" that masks colonizer and colonized as complicitous binary opposites—is precisely the novel's drive to curb the vertiginous excess of heterogeneity by putting into question its feasibility for the Filipino subject on trial. That would mean perpetuating uneven development, even glorifying the hybrid and syncretic wretchedness produced and sustained by global capitalism and its local agencies.

The route of egocentric delirium finally arrives at a cul-de-sac. I have already noted the text's offering of postmodernist options addressed to Rocky Rivera's search for a community that would substitute for the neocolonial extended family her mother's departure repudiated: The first is Keiko with her chameleonic masks—"one day she's Japanese and black, the next day she's Dutch and Hawaiian" (44). She mimics the role of the performative self, as in some kind of unintended parody that harbors a half-serious and half-mocking resonance: "Yesterday I was Josephine Baker. . . . Tonight I'm Edith Sitwell, and Rocky's Marpessa Dawn. We can be them forever. Anytime we want" (117). The second option is Marlon Rivera, a Filipino gay who claims to have played Elvis Presley's happy-go-lucky sidekick in *Blue Hawaii* and also as a nonspeaking waiter in a Chinese restaurant in Samuel Fuller's *Pickup on South Street.* In the section "Film Noir," Marlon Rivera, who rechristened himself after seeing the film *The Wild One,* proves to be the only character who grasps his niece's implacable obsession: "She was reinventing herself moment to moment, day by day" (87). Rocky Rivera can make sense of the craziness of Isabel L'Ange and oddities like her only by juxtaposing them with movie stars and celebrity films of the past: Marlene Dietrich, Greta Garbo, Dorothy Dandridge, and Anna May Wong. This is self-identification achieved by metonymy and metaphor, the effect of linguistic mechanisms working on commercial, mass-produced culture in the United States and substituting for the refuge of kinship and community now slowly devalued in the periphery.

We are in the realm of simulations and mass-mediated images, a space like New York, which, aside from being a real place, is for Rocky "a source of intense inspiration, a daily barrage of worthy movie moments" (98). The move from San Francisco to New York signals a shift from the mother/kin-centered milieu that mediates between the semifeudal periphery and the core metropolis to the arena of anomic individualism, between the locus of ascription and the site of performance and social action. Before the second migration eastward, the breakup of Rocky's relation with Elvis Chang prompts Rocky's rejection of the two options as incapable of dealing with pain: "Maybe I'd rather fuck in my imagination. I allow myself to run wild and wallow in my own private kitsch. I dream of hermaphrodite angels with bronze skin floating alongside the naked, bleeding perfection of my tormented Saint Sebastian. . . . My mother's right. I am just like everyone else in my family. I believe in heaven and hell, the pleasures of denial, and the rewards of sin. . . . I enjoy this only because it's forbidden" (1996, 129–130).

Whatever the seductions of border crossings and other boundary violations, the protean pleasures of the cyborg, and the free-floating hubris of indeterminacy afforded by consumerism and the liberal marketplace, Rocky Rivera knows that it will be an ordeal to shed the markers of subordination and dependency. The stigma of Otherness persists. She cannot put aside "unbearable questions," such as "What's Filipino? What's authentic? What's in the blood?" Before she moves east and separates from her mother, Rocky meditates on this reprise of the first uprooting. The interrogative mood is displaced by the subjunctive:

> I am unable to leave, overcome by helplessness in the face of family, blood, and the powerful force of my own reluctant love. Family sickness, homesickness. Manila, our dazzling tropical city of memory. The English language confuses me. What is at the core of that subtle difference between homesick and nostalgic, for example? . . . "Ties to the spirit world, fierce pride, wounded pride, thirst for revenge, melodrama, fatalism, weeping and wailing at the graveside. We're blessed with macabre humor and dancing feet—a floating nation of rhythm and blues," Voltaire answers, repeating what this old guy known as the Carabao Kid used to say: "We're our own worst enemy." (1996, 57–58)

This passage reveals both the allure of imperial exoticism and the impulse of critique, skepticism, and sentimentality—the presence of the Manichaean duality once described by Frantz Fanon (1968) in the period of the Algerian Revolution. Evocation of the neocolony as the archetypal locus of incongruities and dissonances, a microcosm of opposites like the sadomasochistic figure of St. Sebastian, may be a tactic of eliding the discrepancy between the homeland and the place of exile. This may be called for by the yo-yo trope that seeks to define the method and architectonics of the whole narrative. But the tactic is not an endorsement of postcolonial multiplicity or "interactive mutuality" between master and servant. It is, on the contrary, an attempt to transcend the symbolic economy of fetishism that denies what is absent and by that token affirms it.

A telling instance of the novel's allegorical rendering of conflated modes of production may be found in the treatment of the Carabao Kid, a figure as legendary as the grandfather who invented the yo-yo. The section describing Rocky's encounter with the Carabao Kid is a recollection that occurs after the birth of Venus, Rocky's child. The Carabao Kid serves here as the character that links the first generation of Filipino farmworkers, the Manongs (whom Carlos Bulosan wrote about in *America Is in the Heart* [1948]), and the post-1965 influx of professionals. He was then considered the "unofficial spiritual leader" of the Pilipino arts movement in San Francisco whose emblem was the water buffalo. Even though the Carabao Kid was leading civil rights demonstrations and rallies against the Vietnam War, he was still a migrant worker (he dies before the start of a shrimping expedition in Louisiana); his residence, Watsonville, evokes the anti-Filipino riots of the 1930s. Rocky asserts at the end that she does not need him anymore—for her, he symbolizes the mawkish sentimentalism, humility, and need to suffer that afflicts the Filipino sensibility—so that the snapshot of the community at the end of part 2 turns out to be the sacrifice of the father at the altar of the pre-Oedipal mother. We confront here the petite-bourgeois Filipino of the 1960s and 1970s (still mired in the philistine barbarity of Cold War anticommunism) using a pretext for dissociating themselves from the working-class struggles of Bulosan, Chris Mensalvas, Philip Vera Cruz, and nameless thousands. Hagedorn's tribute to this generation is instructive as a gesture of solidarity and of demarcation:

> Ah, the Carabao Kid and what he taught us. How to be a F(P)ilipino. Voltaire's idealized father figure. And mine too, I suppose. He was this Pinoy poet from Watsonville with the sleepy, wise face of a water buffalo, a man totally obsessed with the Philippines who'd never been there. In hushed tones, he'd describe the fiery sunsets, swaying coconut trees, and white sand beaches, sounding like some romantic tourist brochure. Kinda ironic and laughable, except the Kid thought it was funny too. "Oh yeah, sister, I forgot—I've never been there. " America was here: vast, inhospitable, and harsh. The Philippines was there: distant, lush, soulful, and sexy. He made constant jokes out of what he called his "carabao dreaming" and wrote a series of self-deprecating haikus called "Existential Pinoy Paralysis," questioning his fears about returning to the homeland. "Maybe I just don't want to be disappointed," went one of the more quotable lines of his poem "Maybe." Another ditty was called "EXpat vs. EXile." The fact that Voltaire and I had actually been born in the Philippines had earned us his lasting admiration. (1996, 199)

This portrait explodes the model of postcolonial "sly civility" as one based on a fabric of fetishes, half-truths, and fraudulent mystifications. The dreaming carabao cannot distance itself from the illusion that the Philippines and the United States are on equal footing, autonomous, geopolitically independent from each other. References to the colonial situation abound (one example is the scene with the Puerto Rican taxi driver Eduardo Zuniga). The sections titled "Lost in Translation" seem like satiric spoofs on the postcolonial idea of translation as a way of negotiating the distance between oppressed and oppressor, a gap acerbically brought home by the "Joke Not So Lost in Translation": "Why did the Filipino cross the road? Because he thought America was on the other side" (70).

One hypothesis may be introduced here. The enunciation of apparent similarities and affinities as deceptive may be Hagedorn's warning that postcolonial erasure of conflict may be a disservice to people of color, not praise for their adaptive resourcefulness. Crossing the "road" from the Philippines to the United States is an act of cognitive mapping of present-day neocolonialism, euphemistically labeled "globalization." For Hagedorn, the symbolic yo-yo enacts this orientation in terms of an easy compromise between exile and return: She visits the Philippines in 1992 to say good-bye to her father, whose terminal cancer he has endured for at least 10 years. The yo-yo as "jungle weapon" also reaffirms a certain native ingenuity and resilience that distinguish his life under Western surveillance and *diktat*. This implicit nationalism, however, finds itself sublimated in the themes of youth revolt, the vicissitudes of the artist's education, and her endeavor to forge an identity outside the ethnic/racial and class determinations of her origin.

The figure of Jimi Hendrix finally offers us the key to specify the project of this anti-postcolonial text—if one may so categorize it in its generic impulse. Hendrix (together with Janis Joplin and later Jim Morrison) may be construed as emblems for the rock festival of the 1960s, the occasion providing the experience of community that the music expressed aesthetically. This experience is a renewal if not re-creation of trust, of the sense of possibility, the harmony between public and private life, the sense of honesty and authenticity—what Pilipino Cultural Night adumbrates via parody, excess, and commodification. Simon Frith (1984) comments on the value of this event for its audience: "Rock performance . . . came to mean not pleasing an audience (pop style) nor representing it (folk style) but, rather, displaying desires and feelings rawly, as if to a lover or friend. The appeal . . . of Jimi Hendrix rested on the sense that his apparently uninhibited pursuit of pleasures was on show, for all of us to see and share" (66). Hendrix was one of the cult stars who proclaimed a utopia without struggle, founded on the immediacy of pleasure and solidarity. In this context, Rocky Rivera's band "The Gangster of Love" seeks to imitate that politics of aestheticism, though now informed with a somewhat cynical toughness and punk's psychedelic playfulness: "Congo today, money tomorrow" (245).

In "Our Music Lesson #1" in part 1, Hendrix is worshiped as a historical charismatic figure. Rocky salutes him with "flames bursting out your skull. Salvation funky. Redemption funky." But here Rocky also confesses a certain distance. When Hendrix begs her to "Fuck me, then. Save my soul," Rocky retorts, "I know all about you. I was fourteen when you died, but I'm not stupid" (77). She would not —as she puts it—"suck King Kong's dick" to get to him. In "Our Music Lesson #2," Hendrix's ironic pathos is "appropriated and dissolved in 'Pilipino blood'," so that his "LSD-laced, corny cosmi-comic mythology" becomes indigenized, so to speak. For Hagedorn's generation, Hendrix represents the young martyr dying young, the doomed outsider who performs the ritual sacrifice to propitiate the gods of order. After Hendrix's death (at which point Hagedorn's narration begins), Todd Gitlin (1987) observes the decline of youth counterculture into the monadic narcissism of John Lennon: "Woodstock Nation's symbols peeled away from their Aquarian meanings and became banal with popularity" (429). In a sense, Hagedorn's novel is one long elegy to the demise of rock culture's internationalism as a strategy for overthrowing U.S./Western imperial hegemony over the oppressed and exploited masses of the planet.

After fifteen years, Rocky Rivera dismantles her band and bids farewell to the illusions of the 1960s. "We F(P)ilipinos can imitate, but this audience [in Zamboanga, a city in the southern Philippines] prefers the real thing" (245). Consid-

ered "postmodern, postcolonial punks," Rocky's band had to flee the irate natives, "condemned to exile as second-rate, Western imperialist, so-called artists,"
seeking refuge in the "safety of Motown memory" (246). Deprived of that ersatz
community, Rocky Rivera, now a mother, recuperates the memory of her mother's life before her move to the United States—a labor of unfolding the genealogy
of her deracination so as to derive meaning from that process. It is an act of
constituting experience that is coeval with the narrative (for Hagedorn's reflection on the substance of this experience, see Aguilar-San Juan 1992).

When she returns to the Philippines, Rocky Rivera is no longer just an isolated
individual. She becomes a collective presence, holding in a synthesizing trope the
dispersed and fragmented lives of generations of Filipinos whose chief claim to
distinction is (to paraphrase the Carabao Kid) their unrelenting pursuit of happi-
ness and their equally inexhaustible capacity to suffer. We are already beyond
the postcolonial economy of complicity and guilt, of narcissism and paranoia, of
Manichaean dualism and the metaphysics of difference and ambivalent identity
that Hagedorn syncopated in the adventures of her group, "The Gangster of
Love." There is no nostalgia for the return of an idyllic and innocent past. There
is no easy route to Arcadia or a remote classless utopia. We are in the zone of
accounting for difference as a symptom of unequal power relations between the
hegemonic imperial center and the colonized periphery, this time transcoded
into the decline of patriarchal authority (emblematized here by the dying Francisco Rivera) and the anticipated empowerment of the "mothers." This eventuality takes place in the "weak links" of uneven development, precisely where the
layers of temporalities do not coincide, where ruptures and breaks and discontinuities persist in reproducing conflicts that open up the space for grassroots intervention. This novel presents us with an allegory of how such a space can materialize in the interstices of alienation, displacement, and defeats. The carnival of
the dispossessed and the conquered is just beginning.

In the introduction to her collection *Danger and Beauty*, Hagedorn outlines
the genealogy of her vocation in the 1960s, citing not only Hendrix but also
George Jackson and Angela Davis aside from "water buffalo shamans" such as
Al Robles. She recalls their anxiety to celebrate "our individual histories, our rich
and complicated ethnicities . . . borders be damned" (ix). At about the time the
socialist Salvador Allende was overthrown by the CIA-backed junta in Chile,
Hagedorn marks a turning point in her life: "The year 1973 is when I begin discovering myself as a Filipino-American writer. What does this newfound identity
mean? The longing for what was precious and left behind in the Philippines begins to creep in and take over my work" (x). In the year when she formed her
band "The West Coast Gangster Choir" and Ho Chi Minh's guerrillas finally
drove the Americans out of Vietnam, she returned to the Philippines after an
absence of many years. Apart from her musical experimentation, it was her journey back home that inspired much of her later work. In the process, she believes
that her volatile voice "has hardened, become more dissonant and fierce." It was

during the precipitous decline of the Marcos dictatorship, the 1986 February insurrection, and the return of the oligarchs and warlords in the Aquino regime that she composed this novel, her "love letter to my motherland: a fact and a fiction borne of rage, shame, pride . . . and most certainly, desire" (xi). It is the politics of this ludic "desire," the "playful and deadly serious" trajectory of Hagedorn's performance, that I have tried to assay here, searching for clues to that permanent cultural revolution that Jose Rizal, Apolinario Mabini, Angel Baking, Felipe Culala, Rolando Olalia, and Maria Lorena Barros spoke of beyond the vigil of Pilipino Cultural Night and the elegiac farewells of *balikbayans* and other peregrine exiles.

At the dawn of the twenty-first century, we confront the ruins of U.S. military bases (but being resurrected, alas, in the revanchist enactment of the Visiting Forces Agreement between the Estrada administration and the U.S. government), symbol of neocolonial occupation and imperial bankruptcy. We need to salvage from the consumerist holocaust our indigenous heritage of resistance, 400 years of revolt against tyranny. In this emancipatory project to rebuild the scaffolding of our cultural tradition, we can learn how to safeguard ourselves from the danger of reclamation by a strategy of retrospective mapping and anticipatory critique, twin objectives that are approximated, elaborated, and irresistibly acted out in Hagedorn's fabulations.

6

Kidlat Tahimik's Cinema
of the Naïve Subaltern

Pigafetta mentions the slave about five or six times. . . . Possibly the first
man to circumnavigate the world was a slave . . . a Filipino.
—Kidlat Tahimik/Eric de Guia

Always in film, there were both frames and flows. How either was to be used
was always technically open. . . . It was usual to say that montage and the
dialectic were closely related forms of the same revolutionary movement of
thought.
—Raymond Williams

The controversy over the bells of Balangiga, Samar, during the centenary celebration of the first Philippine Republic (1898–1901) may yield more than a
journalistic and diplomatic side entertainment for students of an emergent
"transnational" cultural studies. It offers an unsolicited pretext to explore the
implication of certain appraisals of Kidlat Tahimik's film art, in particular, *The
Perfumed Nightmare*, and its alleged postmodern resonance. This somewhat gratuitous timeliness may in turn open the closure of ludic Eurocentric postality
(not to be decoded simplistically as a cosmic Americanizing modernity) to the
interrogation and critique of its victims. If only as an exercise in *conscientization*
(to use Paulo Freire's term), this effort will counter the postcolonial abjection to
the persisting legacy of U.S. imperialism. It may be salutary to revitalize popular
memory by inducing here a "return of the repressed." Shortly after General Emi-
lio Aguinaldo's revolutionary forces inaugurated the Republic in 1898, the Filipino–American War broke out, resulting in the death of about a million Filipinos, the brutal destruction of the nationalist forces, and the U.S. colonial

143

subjugation of the Filipino people and its collective psyche for over half a century (Francisco 1976).

One of the few incidents in which the Filipino revolutionary army inflicted a devastating defeat on the U.S. expeditionary forces was the attack at Balangiga, a town in Samar province, on 28 September 1901. Of the 74 soldiers in the Ninth Infantry Regiment of the U.S. Army stationed at the town, 45 were killed and 22 wounded—almost the entire regiment. In retaliation, General Jacob Smith, who commanded the Marine battalion sent to reinforce the U.S. occupation troops, ordered a mass slaughter: "The interior of Samar must be made a howling wilderness" (Vizmanos 1989, 14). This unofficial U.S. policy of indiscriminate pacification made the war (merely an "insurrection" to the invaders) an unpremeditated rehearsal of Vietnam and a template for the colonial and neocolonial subjugation of Filipinos for the entire century. We have not yet fully recovered from the effects of that "howling wilderness," some of which have been converted into pretexts for "pleasurable bricolage" and playful fantasies within the policed precincts of an academic metadiscourse called "postcolonial theory" (San Juan 1998a).

When the American veterans of the Indian Wars in the U.S. West and the Philippine pacification campaign returned, they brought with them three bells confiscated from the Catholic church in Balangiga, two of which are kept at Francis Warren Air Force Base in Cheyenne, Wyoming. On the occasion of the centenary, the Philippine government has requested Washington to return one of the bells and a copy of the other; the military has so far refused. A retired general who is a civilian adviser to the base justifies the refusal: "We don't have to rewrite history and give back the bells because, yeah, our men were involved in atrocities too. . . . Those bells were used to make the attack against our troops" (Brooke 1997, A10). Thus, those "souvenirs" are made to sublimate the single episode of defeat into a memorial of continuing supremacy over the enemy by possession of these captured part-objects invested with nostalgic wish fulfillment. For whom the bells toll? This is a question that has already been answered by the resistance of Macario Sakay, Pedro Abad Santos, Salud Algabre, Juan Feleo, Rolando Olalia, and thousands of victims–martyrs of U.S. imperialist domination of the Philippines. It is a question Kidlat Tahimik revived in 1975–1977 when he was composing *Mababangong Bangungot.* The title is a burlesque pun, a kind of *gestus* akin to Chaplinesque ironic twists; my literal translation, which does not capture the "shock of recognition" from *"bango"* to *"bangungot,"* is "Fragrant Asphyxiations."

The circumstantial background to its making is significant. It was the period of the Marcos dictatorship, characterized by the wanton violation of human rights and the plunder of the economy by foreign corporations aided by comprador oligarchs and semifeudal landlords. It was a regime of violence sanctioned by the U.S. government, which subsidized Marcos and his Pentagon-advised generals with an average of $100 million in foreign aid from 1972 to 1986. After the February 1986 urban insurrection, the old ruling elite (led by President Corazon Aquino and her faction of comprador oligarchs) has returned with schemes that revitalized the neocolonial stranglehold by transnational capital. This has led to the unprecedented immiseration of 70 million Filipinos, with a diaspora of over seven million Overseas Contract Workers, mostly female domestic help (Tadiar 1997). All these changes resituate *The Perfumed Nightmare* as less a retro, nostalgic film than an example of "third cinema" (Pines and Willemen 1989)—a reminder of what we have missed, forgotten, or repressed. In the introduction to *Questions of Third Cinema*, Paul Willemen posited the singular quality of this cinema to inhere in its "rhetoric of becoming," summoning in the place of the viewer "social-historical knowledges rather than art-historical, narrowly aesthetic ones" (1989, 28).

In what way is Tahimik's practice of an alternative/oppositional cinema distinguished from the canonical type? This sketch of a thematic and social semiotic analysis may give us a clue to an answer.

At the center of the film is the image of the bridge—passageway of life in motion, a metaphor of stasis amid mutations—connecting past and future, reality and dream, countryside and city, tradition and modernity. Like the travel/voyage motif, it splices the discontinuous and fragmentary with the recurrent, animating fixities and organizing flux. It also symbolizes for Kidlat, the narrator–protagonist, the ever-present possibility of self-fulfillment: "I chose my vehicle and I can cross all bridges." Werner von Braun and space travel (from the underdeveloped "periphery" where cannibalizing artisans still thrive to the imperial metropolitan centers; from the Philippines to Europe, in this case) form part of the cluster of themes expressing the drive to modernity or, in general, the impulse to transcendence. Space–time compression, the assertion of the national right to self-determination, and the affirmation of community intersect in Kidlat's dream of journeying to the United States, the site of Cape Canaveral and the Statue of Liberty. Commodifying ideologemes conveyed through mass media (e.g., rock music counterpointing the Igorot chant) and jet travel fixate the native consciousness on the promise of mobility and power suggested by rocket launching and American aggression in Vietnam and Africa. Kidlat becomes a willing captive of the American businessman whose chewing-gum machines evoke the myth of entrepreneurial individualism.

But the discrepancy is clearly revealed: Corporate capitalism thrives on such illusion. Abstract universality (exchange value measured in money) needs the sensory particulars of useful objects and places for circulation. Soon the dream of traveling to the United States turns into a *bangungot;* the image of the bridge metamorphoses into enclosed spaces of escalators, fortress interiors, and narrow urban streets. One sequence captures Kidlat transporting a carcass from truck to butcher shop in Paris, in direct contrast to an earlier scene where his passengers coddled pigs and goats as they traveled from Balian, Laguna, to Manila. Claustrophobia impels Kidlat to fantasize: His jeepney becomes a winged horse traversing boundaries and flying above the asphyxiating labyrinths of a late-modern Europe still pluralized or stratified by vestiges and survivals of the feudal/imperial past.

In the uneven space of a neocolonial formation, the trope of the bridge links local and global, individual and society. It is a marker of continuity amidst change. Associated with it are the image and voice of Kidlat's father, veteran of the revolution against Spanish colonial tyranny, whose absence marks the substitution of authority figures in the film. Kaya, the hut builder, evokes the father's independence and creativity. His father's revelry at managing a horse-drawn vehicle anticipates Kidlat's gusto as jeepney driver around whom secular and sacred activities gravitate. After the father is killed on the San Juan bridge in February 1898, the incident that sparked the Filipino–American War, the mother gives Kidlat the figure of a wooden horse carved from the butt of his father's rifle. This symbol of revolt then appears perched on the front of his jeepney, occupying center stage at the last sequence when Kidlat returns to the supermarket after "blowing away" leaders of the industrialized West at the farewell party of his American patron; it appears in the last shot when the mother closes the window of the nipa hut and foregrounds the wooden horse atop the toy jeepney Kidlat gave to his sister. We note here a postmodern spatialization of time superimposed on the usual temporalization of space in film (Stephenson and Debrix 1969).

I call attention to this miniature icon. It is both metonymic and metaphoric, a syntagmatic link to the father's horse-drawn carriage and his nature-inspired resistance. Paradigmatically, its size undercuts rocket imagery duplicated in ancient towers, bulbous chimney funnels, and other phalliclike figurations. Kidlat recalls his father's driving; this memory, mediated by Kaya and the mother, signifies the desire for autonomy and freedom, with his breath likened to the winds blowing from Amok mountain, an immanent force waiting to be released. We hear the refrain: "When the typhoon blows off its cocoon, the butterfly embraces the sun." Messenger from the domain of the rural "third world," the uprooted Kidlat blows life into a chimney of the Paris supermarket—a parodic image of Michelangelo's creator. He transforms the fragment into a rocketlike apparatus that dismantles the alienating technology of the modern world and guarantees the superiority of human willpower against machinery and business. After this, he declares his independence and resigns from the Werner von Braun Club. His discovery of his own native power, catalyzed through memory, reaffirms the value of kinship, communal affection, and political solidarity threatened by reified consumerism. The lesson occurs in his European sojourn but springs from a complex network of geopolitical experiences. The credits at the end, albeit internationalist in thrust, register the impact of Western technology around the world in the postcards celebrating Werner von Braun and space exploration.

Ostensibly crude and "home-made," Tahimik's film employs the trappings of a canny naïveté to instruct and inform his audience. This seemingly spontaneous pedagogy thematizes the "possibility of becoming," what Fernando Solanas and

Octavio Gettino (1976) consider the desideratum of a decolonizing, historicist and political cinema appropriate to a time when the masses have awakened as full participants in the making of history.

Placed in historical context, *The Perfumed Nightmare* can be read as an allegory of the Filipino artist's quest for agency, a testimonial claim to recognition. It tries to recuperate the suppressed energies of the revolutionary tradition through parodic mimicry, quotations, the "play of indexes and vectors," as well as the Herzogian figures of the Large and Small (Deleuze 1986). Consider, for example, the altered perspectives of jeepneys that Kidlat pulls across the bridge, the boy scout jamboree, the mock farewell ceremony, the Easter festival, and so on. Kidlat's quest, routed through a collective project of recovery, is sublimated in various ways: in folk religion, in the image of Kaya and the hut builders, in the circumcision and flagellation rituals, and most memorably in the long sequence on the Sarao jeepney factory. In the most famous commentary on this film, the preeminent American Marxist critic Fredric Jameson focuses on the "naïf" quality of Kidlat's cinematic technique—the use of an 8-millimeter color movie camera, nonsynchronized sound, characters from real life, and so on—and, above all, the postmodernist bricolage that evokes "the wonderment of sheer reproduction and recognition." Artisanal craftsmanship becomes highly prized over and above the Fordist mass-production regime and reified consumerism. While sympathetic to progressive trends in "third world" cultural practice, Jameson tends to overvalorize nonsynchronicity and postmodern spatiality at the expense of actual class conflicts and the praxis of "militant particularisms." In short, Jameson lacks an operative "spatiotemporal dialectic" that David Harvey (1996) sees as imperative for revolutionary action (for an updated take on postmodernism as a reflex of finance capital, see Jameson 1997).

The German philosopher of romanticism Friedrich Schiller once distinguished between naïve poets who create instinctually and depict reality as is and sentimental poets who try to embody an idealized nature in form. Neither naïve nor sentimental, or both at once, Kidlat Tahimik typifies the artist from an unevenly developed, neocolonized formation where capital operates in a way different from that in the metropolitan societies. For example, the demise of handicraft exemplified by the *Zwiebelturm* episode in Germany or the phasing out of street vendors in Paris is vestigial compared to the destruction of homes and whole forests to make room for a highway in Balian, Laguna. This proves only that capital's uneven development rules out for Tahimik the spontaneous acceptance of classic realism, the automatic suturing of the enunciation to the "enounced" (the represented object), hence a constant reflexive gesturing to the signifying practice itself reminiscent of Brecht's alienation-effect strategy or Augusto Boal's "theater of the oppressed."

I might add here that this stance of narrating performance, a means of canceling the dangers of interiorizing metaphysics and psychological subjectivism, recalls the Bolivian filmmaker Jorge Sanjines's (1989) call for an anti-individualist cinema and its dialectical subordination of "beauty" to the imperatives of "exposure, clarification, recovery and exaltation" (33).

Tahimik's art is determined chiefly by the logic of editing and montage under "third world" limited conditions. In terms of content, *The Perfumed Nightmare* registers the symptoms of a cultural production overdetermined by capitalist private property (the ice factory), communal modes of work (hut building, *bayanihan*), archaic ideology (flagellation, patriarchal standard of manhood), petty commodity business (jeepney transport), and feudal-bureaucratic arrangements (police, martial law). The film bears in its montage, cuts, shots, lighting, and other stylistic devices the signs of all these combined modes of production and reproduction. The ideology of this cinematic form thus repudiates the illusionism of classic Hollywood cinema, but it does not necessarily endorse the aleatory and gratuitous experimentalism of Godard, Antonioni, or David Lynch.

Consequently, I do not find Tahimik's populist return to "nature" necessarily negative, misleading, or counterproductive for an oppositional national-democratic program. Such populism is eventually absorbed in the "national-popular" framework of his thinking. The most seductive tendencies to fetishism (e.g., Nature as a restorative, purifying, and revitalizing power) are always undercut or neutralized by self-reflexive humor, naturalist texture, Bakhtinian heteroglossia, and intermittent historicizing references. In focusing on the work process and the routine of everyday life here and in *Turumba*, Tahimik educates our mimetic power by revealing "new structural formations of matter" necessary to transform it. Walter Benjamin describes this cinematic learning method thus: "Through closeups of what it inventories, . . . through exploration of banal milieus under the genial guide of the lens, film on the one hand increases our insight into the necessities that rule our lives, and on the other hand ensures for us an immense and unexpected field of action" (quoted in Buck-Morss 1989, 268). Tahimik's art is an attempt to restore the capacity for experience neutralized or damaged by alienated labor and the reification of social life under the reign of commodity exchange and the cash nexus. This implies that his intervention needs to be concretely inscribed in a conjuncture of a broad counterhegemonic movement united against transnational finance capital (United States, Europe, and Japan).

On this topic of contextualizing our responses to remedy our failure to obtain "experience," as Benjamin defined it, I want to make a detour here with a brief but relevant digression. While serving as a Fulbright lecturer at the University of the Philippines in 1987–1988, I was able to see the film *Balweg* (named after the controversial guerrilla leader of the New People's Army in northern Luzon, Philippines, recently slain by forces he had betrayed) and the commentary of Philippine News and Features published in the sophisticated magazine *Midweek* and circulated in the mass media. After consulting friends and colleagues who were fully informed of the circumstances surrounding the making of the film, I was struck by how the criticism of the film served as an uncanny if reversed mirror image of what it is addressing: the distortions and half-truths of the film as reported by five ex-comrades of Balweg (the real-life personality), all of them unnamed. It is an uncanny event because the report (or selections from it) poses as a news item. Actually, it is a summary of a statement "distributed to media"; hence, its source is conjectural and its countercharges close to artifice, virtually a mimesis of the film as an artifice, a contrived appearance or "semblance" (if we want to avoid the term "representation" and its assumption of an original reality that cannot be presented bodily but that can be re-presented in another mode).

The film in question, I take it, does not purport to be a documentary. It claims to be a fictional account centering on the figure of Father Conrado Balweg modeled after the legally credible or veridical personality who, in turn, owes his controversial public existence to the mass media. The real person named Father Balweg is nowhere to be found in the juxtaposition of film and "news release." Obviously, the film is parasitic on the discourse of the "real," as all illusions are. As a constructed illusion or appearance, it shares the conventions of film production and reception dominant in our neocolonized cultural milieu. This would explain the heroic aggrandizement of the Balweg simulacrum (not the "real" or literal Balweg, the referent, now uncannily and permanently expunged), the elaborate foregrounding of romantic episodes, blood and violence, and so on. The signifier Balweg is to be contradistinguished from the signified Balweg in the audience's mind/consciousness. Consider the film then as a commodified spectacle cashing in on the headlines of quotidian routine. In short, the whole film is made up, a contrivance or invention in the realm of a market economy where cultural products (images) are sold for profit, not for their use value.

Even assuming for argument's sake that all the claims of the unnamed critics of the film are true—the film, that is, has no real referents insofar as it purveys falsifications, deceits, lies, and so on—there is strikingly no mention at all of the crucial ethicopolitical problem posed by the film as an ideological phenomenon or as an expression of political struggle in the sphere of culture: the right or principle of self-determination of the Igorot people. Absent that, does the media event then become a site for unabashed dogmatism and its opposite: anarchic and ultimately treacherous revolt?

In their zeal to oppose a potential personality cult in the making (which the film itself at various points openly disavows, even as the critics themselves do not refute the Communist Party's erstwhile glamorizing of Balweg as a personality in the New People's Army), our critics have chosen to be silent on the central issue projected by the last portion of the film: the collision between the vanguard party of the proletariat and the claim by the Igorots (represented by the actant function of Balweg) that the indigenes' struggle for self-determination has overriding urgency for them and therefore that their interests cannot be subordinated to what the party claims should have priority. This theme was ignored or passed over in silence by critics of the film. It is a forceful if somewhat melodramatic critique of instrumentalism, of commandism in political action. Underlying this is the more serious error of economistic reductionism based on a mechanical and empiricist distortion of the historical materialism that presumably informs the ideology of national liberation: What happened to materialist dialectics and the ineluctable oscillation of contradictions? This critique awaits a serious response, not the dismissive *ad hominem* argument to which flunkies are addicted.

In my view, this critique of authoritarian and bureaucratic politics itself has been unfortunately subordinated to the prior commercial needs of the producers. It is utilitarian exigency that ultimately governs the aesthetics of the film, and so the critics insist on something with which the film never takes issue: that "history proves. . . ." Balweg himself, I feel sure, would agree that the Igorot struggle for self-determination would go on without him, and this becomes confirmed, it seems, with Balweg's eventual degeneration as an instrument of the Aquino regime's policy of cooptation and utilization of ethnic resistance. The verdict carried out by the NPA solicits no appeal. What this proves is a historic truism: The actant or functional role of "Balweg" is larger than the empirical and contingent personalities that may fill it at any one time. Balweg's death leaves the question of Igorot self-determination still unresolved.

If the film is indeed full of fraudulent images, distortions, lies, and so on, why should our critics worry? Won't the audience see through these deceptions? Are the spectators so naïve as to mistake the illusion for the reality? Moreover, don't these pro-people critics trust the political acumen and sensitivity of the masses whom they have always acclaimed as "the makers of history" to make the correct judgment? Perhaps they do not.

On the other hand, if the audience had been so deceived, I would like to know from the critics why people would enthusiastically clap when they see the banner with hammer and sickle unfurled or why they cheer when the brutal military troops are punished. Aren't we really faced here with a more complex experience that is incapable of being reduced to a few polemical allegations, a spectatorial effect whose message and force depend on whose critical/theoretical will articulates them? Could it be that the five critics (all ex-comrades of Balweg), for all their good intentions, have shortchanged themselves without their knowing it and fallen into a philistine sophism worse than the object they were denouncing? Indeed, what they have accomplished is a polemical trivializing of a complex and important topic for national discussion—the question of ethnic and popular self-determination—which cannot be addressed by simplifications demonstrated in the platitudinous terms of the controversy surrounding this film. For all the equivocations and ambiguities evoked, where then can we locate the obtuse "third meaning," the substance of what Roland Barthes (1977) labels the "filmic" as that "representation that cannot be represented," "the *transition* from language to *signifying*" (59)? It may be in the women or the female partisans, some of whom have been associated with Balweg and whose proximity have generated all these suspicions. I recall an image in Lino Brocka and Jose Lacaba's *Orapronobis* where the actor who played Balweg, Philip Salvador, embraces the dead body of his child and then stares at us: The pathos exceeds the semiotics of cinema in this reversal of the *pietas*, just as the collective struggle of millions of Igorots, Lumads, Negritos, and others exceeds the normative individualism typified by the film *Balweg*, now promptly consigned to oblivion. In a recent visit (1999), I viewed a startling film by Chito Rono and Ricardo Lee, *Curacha—Ang Babaeng Walang Pahinga*. Here we have the antithesis of *Balweg*: A *torera* becomes a secular saint whose melodramatic schizoid life literally conveys the impossibility of individualism. The "third meaning" or the essence of the filmic at last materializes here in this postmodern hybrid production via the analogy suturing the chugging of the superferry's engine and the spasmodic sounds and heartbeats of copulating bodies.

To return to our original subject: Instead of continuing to engage in the customary hermeneutic gloss on *The Perfumed Nightmare* (which simply replicates New Critical formalism in this area), I would like to comment on why the film text lends itself to a wide variety of interpretations. Can this film be considered a specimen of "third world" postmodernism? What kind of audience position does it offer, and what kind of reception does it enable? Can we make use of this film as a pedagogical agency for social enlightenment and transformation? In short, can Kidlat Tahimik be crudely judged on the basis of his class affiliation, or can his films be deployed for broader, nonsectarian, emancipatory purposes? What follows is a preliminary review of possible answers by way of returning to Jameson's metacommentary.

It seems that what has provoked the animus of Filipino intellectuals is the kind of gratuitous patronage instanced by Jameson's self-serving appropriation of elements of the film for his own discursive purposes. Obviously, Jameson is searching for art forms and cultural practices that have succeeded in resisting late-capitalist commodification and reification, hence his theoretical constructs of "national allegory," "art naïf," Soviet sci-fi films, and the American conspiracy film genre. His framework is the totalizing (but not absolutizing) mode of cognitive, geopolitical mapping by means of which he and other citizens in the West can find a position (even hypothetical or vicarious) to understand the global relations of forces and to grasp possibilities of social transformation in a time when presumably all spaces (nature, the unconscious, and even the "third world") seem to have been preempted by the enemy. I have no serious objection to this, provided that one does not replicate the hierarchizing drive of Western "civilization" (Patterson 1997).

From a diasporic vantage point, the British cultural studies expert Stuart Hall may regard an inquiry (such as Jameson's) as an engagement with the contemporary politics of ethnicity. This is a task premised on the axiom that "representations are possible because enunciation is always produced within codes which have a history, a position within the discursive formations of a particular space and time" (Hall 1996, 446). One may ask from this historicizing angle: Is Tahimik's film an oasis of indigenous collectivity quarantined safely from the incursions of the cash nexus, standardization, and exchange value?

Filipino film scholar Roland Tolentino has competently surveyed the objections to Jameson's approach and also expressed reservations about certain of Jameson's speculations. He mentions in particular those dealing with the conversion of the jeepney from parody to pastiche, Kidlat as clown, the utilization of body imagery, and so on. Tolentino, I believe, is correct in taking Jameson to task for proposing a literalist or vulgar empiricist reading instead of a properly historicizing one:

> When Jameson mentions that *Perfumed Nightmare* is not a direct intervention to Marcos' dictatorial regime because of its lack of connecting images to the regime, he is limited by his lack of a "native informant" position. In the film, the town's patron saint is St. Mark, known locally as San Marcos. The cultural regime of rituals can therefore be paralleled to the political culture of the Marcos dictatorship. (Tolentino 1996, 123)

In addition to the domesticated saint (his lion appears later in the decisive confrontation with the masquerade of Western rulers), I would cite other telltale signs—the posturing American "boy scout" who rides Kidlat's jeepney (eventually pushed out to the carabao sled at the back, a revealing change), the figure of the policeman, the reference to "discipline and uniformity" echoing a well-known slogan of the martial law regime, the Marlboro Country billboard in the barren landscape, the Voice of America propaganda, and others—all of which index the milieu of surveillance and control under the U.S.–Marcos dictatorship.

Such traces or indicators escape the hegemonic American intellectual unfamiliar with the historical specificity of U.S. racialized ideological, economic, and political domination of the Philippines (acutely diagnosed by, among others, Roxanne Lynn Doty [1996]) . The obsession with a totally administered and commodified society has characterized Jameson and Frankfurt Critical theory to the degree that within their frameworks only a negative dialectics (Adorno) or a messianic utopian break (Benjamin) can remedy this fatality. Despite his stress on utopian space, Jameson shares this flaw with Western Marxism. This time, instead of Kidlat Tahimik's film being read as a communal or populist allegory where the private dilemma resonates with public meaning (albeit burdened with "compensatory originarism" [Shohat 1995, 175]), it is selectively construed to reinforce a "first world/third world" binary, as already noted by many critics (Ahmad 1992; Homer 1997).

On the other hand, I am surprised by the blindness of some insightful critics obsessed (justifiably so, I think) and provoked by Western impositions. I agree with Stephen Heath (1981) that "no referent can guarantee a discourse; the represented a discourse produces is grasped, realized, exists as such in the particular discourse of representation" (191). A few details of the mode of representation can be highlighted here. No one has noticed the function of such constituent elements as the white carabao (beautiful outside but cold and aggressive inside), the speaking role of the Virgin Mary (a dialogic antithesis for the farewell party in Paris where masked westerners dwarf Kidlat), and above all the wooden Pegasus-like horse that becomes an icon at the prow of the voyaging jeepney. Kaya's tattooed butterfly is also charged with meaning. Such motifs of resistance against U.S. imperial domination and liberal market ideology become secondary or completely obscured when the focus on bodies, artisanal work, hybrid or syncretic overtones, and Foucauldian genealogy of exoticized details (circumcision) preoccupy the commentators.

Postmodernism focuses on pastiche and bricolage over against Bakhtinian multiaccentuality or Brechtian distanciation. In postmodernist video text, the random play of signifiers and image flows precludes the radical aim of diagnostic contextualizing and "exploring misdirection" (Williams 1989, 117) , concealment, and mystification. For his part, Jameson unreservedly celebrates the novelty of a refunctioned handicraft mode of work inscribed within a comprador/ tributary system of production, making him oblivious to unequal power relations. The sequence of individual shots of Sarao factory workers performing their specialized assignments on the assembly line (which turns out an average of 20,000 vehicles a year) stands out for Jameson as exemplary:

> . . . unlike the "natural" or mythic appearances of traditional agricultural society, but equally unlike the disembodied machinic forces of late capitalist high technology which seem equally innocent of any human agency or individual or collective praxis, the jeepney factory is a space of human labor which does not know the structural oppression of the assembly line or of Taylorization, which is permanently provisional, thereby liberating its subjects from the tyrannies of form and of the preprogrammed. In it aesthetics and production are again at one, and painting the product is an integral part of its manufacture. Nor finally is this space in any bourgeois sense humanist or a golden mean, since spiritual or material proprietorship is excluded, and inventiveness has taken the place of genius, collective cooperation the place of managerial or demiurgic dictatorship. (Jameson 1992, 210)

Filipina critic Felicidad C. Lim (1995) has pointed out that this not only is contrary to the factual situation but also vitiates Jameson's entire interpretation. The point is well taken, even if somewhat incognizant of Jameson's larger pragmatic horizon. Instead of being cooperative and pleasure filled, the Sarao factory is perhaps more alienating and dehumanized than firms in the notorious free-trade zones since here semifeudal patronage conceals exploitation, the violation of minimum-wage labor laws, sexism, and other excesses. What looks like bricolage is really systematic cannibalizing of "dead labor" in the interest of profit. On the surface, this refunctioning of waste materials can serve to emblematize Kidlat's theme of converting "vehicles of war" into "vehicles of life"—a reversal of the damage wrought by imperial modernization and market-driven progress. But a long time has elapsed since World War II, when U.S. army jeeps were first re-functioned as civilian passenger transport; in fact, such jeepneys are now produced from Pentagon surplus or smuggled in by criminal syndicates.

Yet, despite the commodification of bricolage, the Filipino jeepney with its bold designs and flamboyant decorations easily strikes the tourist or visitor as surreal, carnivalesque, and garishly extravagant. With over 50,000 of them plying the streets of Metro Manila, they appear, in the words of John Lent (1995), "more ostentatious, expressing not only the penchant of many Filipinos to over-decorate but also the individuality of the drivers. With an aesthetic canon that proclaims 'Nothing is too much,' jeepney owners attach plastic headdresses, chrome horses (as many as 16), stainless steel bars, up to ten side mirrors, antennas not connected to radios, and blinking lights on the hood"; with the jeepney's body displaying images of seascapes and landscapes, "rocketships in wild chase, jet formations, planets in orbit, bursts of flame" (175). Tahimik's jeepney may be a synecdochic device to evoke this indigenous craft of transforming the ordinary utilitarian object into a magical phenomenon without forfeiting its quotidian use value. In any case, the jeepney's indexical function historicizes the transition from artisanal to petty commodity production, problematizing the emergence of alienated labor and the cash/exchange nexus in an obsolescent tributary or feudal formation. In Paris, however, the entrepreneurial driver confronts a gigantic corporate mall, naïvely awestruck; he soon withdraws to a somewhat provincial German milieu where the celebration of handicraft and community ritual precedes his German wife's delivery of their child, with the versatile Filipino vehicle expediting the passage.

Aside from the ironical innuendo on Sarao's duplicitous handicraft setup, Kidlat, as painter of the miniature jeep given to his sister, performs a shift in discursive register. The jump cut from that sequence to the next disrupts any fetishizing of manual repetitive labor. It elides the process in which the machine changes from a utilitarian or commercial means to a symbolic one when it travels to Paris and Germany: Note that its last hilarious service was to ferry his pregnant wife to the hospital, recalling the block of ice loaded earlier as well as the statue of San Marcos. The jeepney thus becomes a "vehicle of life," enabling him to finally break off from the mystique of Werner von Braun as he leaves Germany. When Kidlat in Paris declares his independence from America and its hallucinatory icons (American beauty queen versus Virgin Mary), he resigns from the von Braun Club, the scenario where he "blows" away the Western leaders gazing down on him and immediately follows to evoke the old hoary ramparts of San Juan bridge, where his father, in 1898, confronted the U.S. aggressors and sacrificed his life. What needs underscoring is the running commentary that his father and millions of Filipinos refused to be bought for $12 million dollars—the price the United States paid to Spain for ceding the Philippines at the Treaty of Paris. When we see the Parisian vendor riding next to Kidlat in his jeep, the "weak link" is seized: An alliance with other oppressed subalterns across race and nationality, across space and generation, is established. In effect, the nuanced techniques of countercinema (Wollen 1982)—foregrounding, estrangement, multiple diegesis, and so on—generate a narrative intransitivity that combines nationalist impulses with a quasi-Herderian critique of capitalist civilization.

Fragments of classical illusionistic cinema—flagellants with bleeding flesh, the block of ice sliding out of the jeep, facial contortions, and so on—may be found aplenty here. But the whole construction of *The Perfumed Nightmare* may be described as modernist and avant-garde. Instead of psychological complexity tied to close-ups or smooth narrative causality, juxtaposition of pictorial surfaces and jump cuts predominate. Tahimik follows Brecht's rule of interrogating the rationality of the status quo by interrupting narrative continuity, stressing contradictions within an emerging unity by techniques of distanciation and displacement. The principle of montage and strategic cuts precisely serves to question the illusionistic or auratic power of representation found in classic realist cinema, which interpellates individuals into bourgeois subjects. Here, dreaming is literalized wish fulfillment reduced to static-filled reception of the Voice of America. In general, montage aims to overcome mimesis, introspective psychology, the hero as unified consciousness, and the need for identification (Heath 1992). What subversive cinema of this kind seeks is the ushering in of subjects into "permanent crisis" so that reality (the exploitative status quo) can be questioned and transformed. Aside from montage, the production of a "third meaning" through the friction between image and diegesis (following Barthes's [1977] semiotic analysis) can be explored. I am thinking here of the trope of fixed structures being set off into motion, the tremor rocking the camera itself, as well as the synthesizing figure of blasting rocket ships engendering "fragrant asphyxiations" of slumbering neocolonial subjects.

Problematizing in his own "naïve" way the bourgeois paradigm of intelligibility, Kidlat Tahimik deploys avant-garde methods not by choice but more by necessity. To be sure, he is neither Eisenstein, Godard, nor Kurosawa—Tahimik is inventing his own filmic signature. Addressing a "first world" audience, he finds resources in the generic constraints of ethnographic and documentary films (Nichols 1981), for example, the indexical function of animals, children, native habitats, and so on. In one interview, he described his method of composition:

> The way I make my films is like collecting images; it's like making a stained glass window. You collect colored pieces of glass over the years. Today I may find a broken beer bottle, tomorrow I may find a 7-UP bottle. I'll have all these in a box and maybe two years later, I start sorting them out and I may find a pattern: if I like a landscape or profile, I pursue that and I finish the film by shooting any holes that are still missing in that stained glass mosaic. . . . Maybe I'm just an accumulator of images and sounds and then I make *tagpi-tagpi* [patching up] and sew them together. . . . I just work with images and I put my sounds on and then I put a flow of thoughts and start juggling the sequences back and forth. I don't try to find surrealist images

even in the way it happened in *Perfumed Nightmare*. I was a madman when I was making that film and I still am. I sometimes wonder how certain elements enter the film. (quoted in Ladrido 1988, 38)

This craft of allowing "found" materials may be naïve at first glance, but the gathering and fabrication of images are framed by an intuitive process of organizing and synthesizing. Kidlat Tahimik holds that "it's better to just raise questions" instead of positing statements (Manlogon 1989), but of course we know that the process of formulating questions already implies a perspective for answering them. Tahimik exploits the objective richness of his materials, but this does not mean allowing the unconscious or instinctive tropisms to simply take over. In fact, the opposite is the case: The conscious investigation of experience forces attention to the modalities of representation, the signifying or enunciating practice. This becomes patent in the section depicting the Easter festivities, the passport picture-taking scene, the ceremony of Kidlat's leave-taking, and so on.

Stylization and self-referential techniques predominate. Thus, instead of a sustained action sequence—the longest ones are the flagellation and circumcision scenes—we get individual shots combined in a sometimes unpredictable imagistic duration. This structure also prevents the formation of aesthetic aura by risk-taking cuts, as in the shift from wide shots of landscapes to Kidlat's sleeping face, from shots of carabaos in mud pools to the Virgin Mary, even while continuity is provided by the element of sound: broadcasts of rocket-ship launchings, rock music, and the Igorot chant that sutures disparate scenes together. The montage seems jerky at times, especially in the sequence of urban traffic, where repetition of motifs is absent. But the overall impression is not the "polyphony of decontextualized voices" (Connor 1989, 176) characteristic of postmodern films, such as *Blue Velvet,* that seek to re-create the cultural experience of past eras. Ad hoc combinations may perhaps describe the sequence happening in Paris and Germany—here Kidlat ceases to have control over his vehicle (i.e., his body and its motions) since his journey is directed by the American entrepreneur who dangles before the von Braun admirer the bait of a visit to America, the center of space travel and moon exploration. Recall that Kidlat the driver has been dispossessed of his artisanal means, reduced to walking to the chewing-gum machines that he tends. Any incipient pastiche is foiled by the pressure of an underlying historicity that is interrupted: quotations of the death of Kidlat's revolutionary father and the loss of control of the "vehicle" of independence by Filipinos. One can extrapolate this unifying theme from the iterative motifs of breath, wind, and traffic—motion as such—that undercut the temporal discontinuity and generic heterogeneity of the whole artifice.

From this allegorizing stance, it may be instructive to compare *The Perfumed Nightmare* with Kidlat Tahimik's later film *Turumba* (1981–1983). Mike Feria (1988) considers this latter film technically the best mainly because of a clear narrative line punctuated with "disquieting humor" (36). On the surface, the theme of *Turumba* concerns the destructive and unstoppable power of modernization. It unfolds in the rapid erosion of the traditional way of life of a family in Pakil, Laguna, that makes papier-mâché dolls for a living; the livelihood also symbolizes the artisanal pride in one's craft and the persistence of a residual communal tradition. The family's dream of wealth is nearly fulfilled at the cost of disrupting their organic solidarity: The father assumes the part of a bureaucratic manager who abandons his role in the annual "turumba" festival, and the grandmother becomes a quality control officer. American critic Pat Aufderheide (1986) comments, "Like *Perfumed Nightmare*, Turumba makes canny use of the accidental and the available, turning junk-littered reality into art in the same way that the Filipinos turn the detritus of industrialism into handicrafts" (22).

Kidlat Tahimik believes that *Turumba* is "my smoothest film to date," more like canvas instead of collage, with "color elements and the sound and everything blending." He also testifies that, except for his nephew Kadu, all the characters are real people who played themselves in their actual work as blacksmith; *cantore;* Aling Bernarda, who fixed the clothes of the Virgin; and so on. He confessed that he "was always fascinated with the blacksmith because of the way he made Mercedez Benz shock absorbers into real beautiful bolos" (quoted in Ladrido 1988, 42). Mang Pati, the blacksmith, functions as the bricoleur, the free spirit, who converts the scrap iron of rusting Japanese war vehicles left in the jungle into useful tools. He stands for the independent artisan resisting the encroachment of the alienating capitalist division of labor that seizes hold of one family and destroys the enchantment of life nourished by religious ceremony and its organic liaison with nature's rhythms. A "third meaning" often insinuates itself when various forms of signs and sounds—the family playing together, the father conducting the band, cable wires transmitting radio and television signals, the sounds of nature and traffic—intrude into the unfolding of the business routine and demystifies its rationality. We are then led to reflect on the film's mode of representation as images, characters, and actions are distanced, then displaced from their natural environment, and finally sutured into a composite artifice that barely sustains the illusion of narrative continuity.

Despite the ingenious and witty cuts, the film follows an implicit logic of causality based on the presence of the market and media of communication (radio, television, highway traffic, exchange of goods). The "march of progress" is communicated by the sudden appearance of the German buyer/trader, antagonist of the Virgin mother, source of the money that allows electricity and technology to penetrate the family *habitus*. Over against this, the libidinal investment in the future never finds a presentable image. The film ends with the townfolk saying good-bye to the father and son as they leave for Germany, the heavy downpour of rain shrouding the whole scene. That possibility of enjoyment in the fabled metropolis is foiled by the cathexis of traditionally made artifacts. For example, the grandmother and children perform a mock race with the toy animals accompanied by Rossini's *Wilhelm Tell Overture*, a pleasure-filled game absorbing

Western influence in indigenous make-believe. This scene, among others, problematizes the instrumental value of production for exchange, the market itself.
Spectacle never displaces narrative since the annual *turumba* festival and its year-
long preparation draws into it all the libidinal energies of the populace into a
social event whose value is dispersed and shared by the whole community.

Meanwhile, the spectator of the film cannot help but identify with the boy as
the community's "naïve" intelligence. The curious and dutiful son of the *cantore*
provides the point of gravity, a locus that allows a degree of empathy; his curios-
ity and sensitivity lead us to decipher the enigmatic code—what will happen
next?—without much anxiety. And so, in the midst of the accelerated pace of the
"assembly line" production, the shots are dragged on to suggest a moment of
introspection. A voyeuristic element insinuates itself in certain scenes when sus-
pense develops: Will the family meet the production deadline? What will happen
to the *turumba* festival in the absence of the father? But despite this tendency
to classic expressive-realist cinema, the invocation of a disruptive nature—the
typhoon winds—distracts us from the failure of the film to present the unrepre-
sentable, the Munich Olympic festival: scene of wealth and prodigious energies
but also of international carnage.

We are then brought back to the immemorial present at the end of the film:
the festival procession of the Virgin Mary winding back into the cavernous womb
of the church, surrounded by the chanting and dancing of the people, the undy-
ing matrix (in Bakhtin's dialogic thought) of vitality, resourcefulness, and creativity. Kidlat Tahimik overcomes the seduction of technology and speed by a
suggestion that what is complete is really uncomplete and unfinished. In this,
Turumba rejoins the pioneering first work in asserting the *auteur's* control. The
film director/editor is the shaper of a critical dialectic based on the transforming
movement between production and representation, the disclosure of social relations as historical and changeable. Kidlat Tahimik should then be judged as an
adequate or a deficient makeshift artist on the basis of the oppositional and
transgressive inducement of his films. As interrogator of Western power, he tries
to mediate between the containment strategy of a nativist, sometimes idealizing
populism proud of one's ethnic heritage and a radical critique of colonial mentalities and neocolonized sensibilities that block change and liberation of individual potential. In this context, nature (winds, rain, animals) serves as surrogate
for the emancipatory energies repressed by iniquitous property/power relations
and the entire reifying system of transnational capital.

Lacking a full assessment of Kidlat Tahimik's other works and those in progress, I can only provisionally conclude here by speculating on what audience position and effects the films may have. So far, the consensus is that Tahimik's films
are viewed and appreciated mainly by a Western metropolitan audience, objects
of cinema spectating as an institutional mode and performance of classical cinema (Ellis 1981). Commercial Filipino films damaged by populist melodrama
and formulaic repetitions continue to overshadow quality productions, such as

those by Lino Brocka, Ishmael Bernal, and others (Armes 1987). Tahimik's works have never been commercially shown in the Philippines; only the government's Cultural Center of the Philippines has exhibited them at certain times. A Filipino mass audience, still narcotized by Western illusionism via American television and videocassettes, waits in the wings, still fascinated by imported performance artists, such as Australian Mike Parr, whose *Daybreak* unwittingly fetishized the Other while claiming to explode our fear of Otherness underlying Western racism (Stoler 1996). If Bienvenido Lumbera is right in contending that only the logic of irony can save local cinema from clichés, anachronisms, and lapses of taste, the reservoir of irony and self-reflexive enunciations in Tahimik's art may still exert a redemptive influence if the current populist indulgence of the anomic crowd subsides.

My engagement here with Tahimik's film art exceeds the connoisseur's interest in mere aesthetic properties—after all, form cannot be divorced from the logic of a concretely determinate content. I am interested more in the functional ideology or practical resonance of their "truth-effects." What is the political significance of Tahimik's cultural practice in the context of the Philippine struggle for popular democracy and genuine independence? What kind of "third world" cinema do they exemplify? Teshome Gabriel (1994) once speculated on the possibility of a distinctive "third world cinema" patterned after the three stages of the national-liberation struggle theorized by Frantz Fanon. I do not think that Kidlat Tahimik is concerned with indigenization or "chromatically literal self-representation," aiming to combat the "world cinematic language" of, say, Spielberg, Lynch, or Coppola (Coppola is his North American distributor) or vindicating the folk/oral art of the Igorots and other ethnic groups in which spirit and magic predominate. There is, indeed, spatial concentration in both films, demonstrated in wide and panning shots, long takes, graphic repetition of images with few intercuttings between simultaneous actions, rare close-ups (except for comic touches), and an abundance of witty juxtapositions and humorous parodies. But Tahimik precisely questions even the terms of Western art-historical discourse, which frames the intelligibility of this chapter, a problem of which I am fully aware. But does this then imply the need for a "new cosmopolitanism" whose advent is hailed by Wimal Dissanayake (1994) as one that will pluralize the fabled monolithic East and unfold its diverse historicities and temporalities against an essentializing Western gaze?

Despite such affinities with a universally defined "third cinema," Tahimik's filmic practice, however, cannot be categorized as "third world" throughout. Overall, it is a mixed and unevenly developed practice that, for the most part, stimulates critical reflection by techniques of displacement and distanciation (Tahimik 1989). Stanley Aronowitz (1979) regards film as the "art form of late capitalism" insofar as the montage permits the viewer to "experience the emergence and assemblage of the image" (110). Consonant with the principle of montage, the capitalist logic of infinite mechanical reproducibility of all objects "not only demolishes the bourgeois hero, the introspective subjective consciousness, but separates form from content, lets processes dominate things" (115).This is also what to some degree Tahimik's films afford, but their message is oppositional. More important, the relation of form and content in each film is dialectical, not dualistic. In what other conceptual language or theoretical analytic (ideally non-Western) should we describe this filmic practice?

On the whole, Tahimik's vernacular cinema aims to arouse critical scrutiny of our assumptions and frames of reference. Only rarely does it summon hypnotic identification with heroic protagonists because invariably the illusionistic power of image movement is always undercut or decentered by the devices we have noted. Its realism is intermittent, purposefully contingent, and qualified by stylized self-reflexive gestures and idioms. The audience position that it allows, I think, will be chiefly skeptical, inquisitive, and partisan—even wrongheadedly utopian as Jameson's. After all, Tahimik himself consciously utilizes a whole repertoire of Western techniques, adapting and modifying them to suit his sensibility and also to induce a critical, transformative political self-awareness in the metropolitan audience. (Joel David [1995] has amply inventoried the influences and effects of Western "New" cinema on local production, except Tahimik's, a telltale lacuna; see also Tiongson [1983].) Given their formal limitations and lack of a mass native audience due to the previously mentioned historical and political circumstances, the pedagogical impact of Tahimik's films can at best contribute to catalyzing or forging an agency that can raise oppositional consciousness and ultimately mobilize a critical mass for the collective task of radical social transformation.

POSTSCRIPT

Crossing the Pacific, I would like to recall here an occasion in the early 1970s in New York City when I participated in what proved to be an aborted undertaking dedicated to one aspect of that previously mentioned task of radical social transformation: a project of the Visual Communications of California to film Carlos Bulosan's quasi-autobiography *America Is in the Heart,* directed by Linda Mabalot. Before the funding ran out, I had the opportunity to review the script titled *Quiet Thunder* (by Norman Jayo and A. Valdez) and the completed sequence.

The film project concentrates on the initial struggles of a group of Filipino farmworkers in the 1930s to assemble a printing press and set up a newspaper to support the strike of Filipino and Mexican workers. Except for one or two characters, the film seeks to present a collective hero: the conscious elements of the community organized to articulate the demands and will of their members. What the film endeavors to translate in cinematic language, in the mode of visual practice, is the truth of alienated labor in the process of dialectical metamorphosis. It strives to render the truth of exploited migrant workers, their labor power converted into commodities for sale, becoming historical subjects as they question the cash nexus, the logic of the profit-centered market and exchange value, which provides the rationale of everyday life in capitalist society. Such a truth acquires visual immediacy in the form of a dramatic situation: a political meeting of workers disrupted by white racist violence, a meeting held for the purpose of organizing the physical and spiritual resources of the members to give a symbolic coherence and reflexive meaning to the reality of socialized labor as the creator of wealth and the ultimate foundation of national self-determination. The characters of the film are conceived as functions of the dramatic situation.

Allow me to quote an excerpt of a review I wrote for a socialist newspaper in generalizing the lessons of the project: The central task to which progressive Asian American filmmakers should address themselves is that of discovering the appropriate cinematic practice, the specific mode of film production, that would effectively *historicize* and *problematize* the experience of each nationality or community. We have to assert this dimension of nationality against the ghettoizing strategy of white chauvinism—it is our only hope of preventing genocide. "Experience" may be the origin or genesis, but action is the goal or objective. We don't really need a full-blown aesthetics in free play; what we need is praxis, planned and organized action, a program of reasoned conduct. Of course, ideally theory and practice should be integrated and should coalesce, but because of the law of uneven development in history and social formations, a nonsynchrony between theory and practice results. Often consciousness lags behind spontaneous mass revolts. Could Eisenstein have made *October* or *Potemkin* without the popular insurrections?

Given the raw materials of experience, we have to situate events, individual thoughts and feelings, in the thickness and density of the concrete process of historical development. We need to enact or perform the manifold possibilities of the specific historical conjuncture. This alternative mode of communication as production and reproduction of ideology may be obvious to a few, unavoidable for some, but certainly ignored by many. This is understandable because of the powerful influence of business metaphysics, positivist thinking, and vulgar empiricism; hence, our artists in general continue to produce on the basis of commercial formulas either sentimentalized melodrama or fashionable avant-garde experiments. Curtis Choy, the maker of the classic *The Fall of the International Hotel,* warns us that "[t]he commercial is the ultimate propaganda of a capitalist society. . . . You can penetrate the market and never find any AA [Asian American] consciousness. I do my bit by explaining the "Chonk Moonhunter" labels stuck to my gear" (1991, 183). A difficult piece of advice but well worth heeding. Let's refine and educate further our critical sensibilities for a survey of achievements in Filipino/a American media arts since the 1970s. While we are all products of everyday experience and social movements occurring around us, we hope to comprehend our situation and reshape ourselves in our collective activities so as to re-create the Other, the negation, of U.S. monopoly racism. We hope to construct the Other of imperialist hegemony—this time not the exoticized and subjugated Other but the self-conscious and critical subject of a liberated and joyous future in the making.

The task of rendering the Filipino experience into cinematic language confronts those twin perils of liberal individualism and of mechanical empiricism. Should we focus on one heroic individual, say Bulosan, and condense in this romanticized image the entire tortuous odyssey of generations of Filipino immigrants from 1900 to the present? Or should we choose the documentary path, raiding chronicles such as Sam Kushner's *Long Road to Delano* and other accounts, in order to represent the Filipino struggle as "news," "that's the way it was," and so on. The first way leads to reducing the complex dialectic of social and personal forces to abstract psychology, while the second, for all its attractiveness, leads to superficial mechanical splicing of images and empiricist opportunism. What we should strive for is to capture what Brecht calls the social *gestus,* or the pregnant moment of the sociohistorical process that synthesizes multilayered contradictions in a memorable dramatic scene or episode evoking the catalyzing epiphany, the "shock of recognition," and eventually the revolutionary rupture.

We glimpse how this can be accomplished in the problematizing and historicizing effect that media activists should aim for. One exemplification of this end can be found in one scene in *Quiet Thunder.* I am referring to the scene where Pasqual, a Filipino migrant worker, says to Miguel (a young man trying to learn English) that the eucalyptus trees of the forest, which have afforded the strikers a haven to plan strategy and tactics safe from fascist encroachments, were planted years ago by the Chinese, who built the transcontinental railroad so that they could make masts for ships to take them back to their homeland. That is indeed an inspiring vision: Those trees planted by comrades of legendary times await our harvest.

7

⁓

Prospects and Problems of Revolutionary Transformation

We did what we ourselves [peasant masses] had decided upon—as free people, and power resides in the people. What we did was our heritage. . . . We
decided to rebel, to rise up and strike down the sources of power. I said "We
are Sakdals! We want immediate, complete, and absolute independence." No
uprising fails. Each one is a step in the right direction.

—Salud Algabre

The coincidence of the changing circumstances and of human activity can
be conceived and rationally understood only as revolutionary practice.

—Karl Marx

The revolution is inevitable. . . . We will fight alongside the men. We should
take up arms, if necessary. We are working for a better society for men and
women alike, so why should men always bear the brunt of the struggle?

—Maria Lorena Barros

In a magisterial survey, the "Problems of Socialism in Southeast Asia," Malcolm Caldwell (1970) summed up the central political problem besetting societies like the Philippines, namely, "the evolution of appropriate institutions, with
viable indigenous roots, which will afford the peasants and other classes an opportunity to voice and right their grievances" (376–377). While other societies
in the region have suffered from local despotism and vastly unequal division of
property, the Philippines is afflicted with authoritarian abuses and social inequalities that centuries of Western colonialism have worsened and deepened. While
the nationalist movement in the Philippines is the oldest in Southeast Asia, Caldwell reminds us, U.S. colonialism suppressed it by rescuing and reinforcing "the

wealth and power of the landowning classes" and enlarging that oligarchy with a middle strata (businessmen, bureaucrats, professionals) subservient to its interests. One testimony to the efficacy of this tutelage is provided by Colonel Edward Lansdale, CIA adviser to President Ramon Magsaysay, who tested brutal counterinsurgency measures against the Huks that were later applied against the Indo-Chinese in the 1960s and 1970s. Lansdale offers the rationale for neocolonialism: "We tutored the Philippine people and encouraged them in self-government in the same brotherly spirit which elsewhere today could make all the difference in struggles between freedom and Communism" (Ahmad 1971, 189). The "brotherly spirit" translated into millions of Filipinos killed in the pacification of 1899–1903 and millions more in the extirpation of numerous peasant–worker insurrections that have enriched the historical archive of national-democratic revolutions, of "people's war," uniting "third world" countries (Selden 1971).

The passage of the Visiting Forces Agreement (VFA; noted in chapter 3) at the end of the twentieth century signifies not a "return of the repressed" but a symptom of the loss of memory, a historical amnesia that disavows the unspeakable barbarism and carnage that masked itself in "brotherly spirit." For Filipinos, however, it is a ritual of trying to remember. One may venture the opinion that the Philippines is unique among "third world" countries not for the pollution, number of Overseas Contract Workers (OCWs), corruption, and so on but as one of the few ex-colonized formations that continue to celebrate the sacrosanct foundation date of the former colonial master: July 4. This is not just a neocolonial phenomenon but exactly, I think, a reflection of prevailing power relations: not just the increase of U.S. investments exceeding that of Japan, the multiple access to military installations, the Filipino military's nostalgia for West Point (ex-President Ramos is an alumnus), but also the continued immigration of Filipinos to the United States, the presence of over three million Filipinos in the United States, and the profound penetration of U.S. media and mass consumer culture in the Philippine terrain. Here I do not mean McDonald's, Coca-Cola, and so on but the entire ethos of consumerism, what philosopher Henri Lefebvre calls "the bureaucratic society of controlled consumption."[1] The chief enemy of any socialist agenda here is not perhaps the oligarchy and the comprador elite. It may be the mass *habitus* of consumerism, mass hypnosis by the commodity fetish, the sacramentalization of the mall/megamall spectacles—in short, the acquisitive/possessive drive, which for some can be realized by installment and credit cards; for others, by persevering work plus fantasies, hallucinations, dreams; or by going abroad, preferably to the United States.

In a *Sunday Inquirer Magazine* article from 14 January 1996, the British novelist James Hamilton-Paterson replied to a question that his novel *Ghosts of Manila* presented a grim portrait of the country that would scare tourists:

> I react by saying that it's not me painting the grim portrait. The portrait is painted by Filipinos themselves everyday in the newspaper. It's priests, editors, and journal-

ists, teachers and mayors and other people who actually reveal these appalling stories of what goes on. They're not the inventions of a foreigner at all. . . . But to the best of my knowledge, although I did use some novelist's license in "Ghosts of Manila," there's nothing there that's actually false. Nearly all the details come straight out of journalistic stories which I checked as well.

Indeed, Hamilton-Paterson is not malicious nor stupid, only spontaneously if not naively acting out the "white man's burden" of advising the "poor" brown natives what they already know. Except that in the global stratification of power, the white British novelist exercises power not just of mirroring what people of color say about themselves but charging this repetition with an ethical value: it is not me, the superior Western artist who is responsible for the novel; it is only yourselves speaking. So do not blame me, please. This also explains why so much time and energies were wasted in responding to pundits such as James Fallows, whose notion of the Filipinos' "damaged culture" reflects more the legacy of American "racist corporatism" (Aguilar 1998, 191) than the internal class warfare between the propertied minority and the exploited citizenry.

Unfortunately, Filipinos give more attention than they merit to their victimizers, whose exoticizing impressions are journalistic fare ladled without criticism. Hamilton-Paterson is fascinated by the Philippines in general—not individual Filipinos who scarcely exist for him: "It's exasperating, horrible, the country's all those things, but I like it here and I still don't know what it is and that's why." Aside from supplying raw material to this fictional machine, Filipinos provide strokes and attention. And of course any white trash, rich or poor, from the Western affluent countries occupies a niche and status higher than any person of color around. Enough compensation, surely, for all the exasperation and sycophancy the well-paid fictionist has to put up with.

Instead of the potboiler *Ghosts of Manila*, I recommend an alternative by another multiawarded novelist, William Boyd, and his novel *The Blue Afternoon*. I am not aware of Boyd having lived in the Philippines or given interviews and lectures to our local literati, but his novel weaves a love story and a detective/mystery fable around a surgeon who is half British and half Filipino and an American woman married to a Yankee officer. The second and major section of the novel is set in the Manila of 1902, with the reprisals of the U.S. military against the natives before and after the Balangiga massacre in Samar. While on the surface the Philippines serves only as a temporal/spatial background, in the symbolic scheme of motives and accidences, the Filipino resistance to American occupation acquires flesh-and-blood reality in the actions of the protagonists and in the unfolding of erotic-cum-gore events. In retrospect, I have not read any recent novel written by a westerner that treats seriously the brutalization of Filipinos during the Filipino–American War except for this 1993 novel. So I recommend it as an example of how the inescapable exoticizing of the Philippine historical landscape can yield a surplus of insights into the political economy of racial/ethnic conflicts.

The lesson here is obvious: Exchange relations in culture cannot be equal when political, economic, and social relations between peoples, nations, states, and groups are not equal. Who is speaking? To whom? For what reason? We have not yet fully transcended the normalizing asymmetry of nation-states, the hegemony of the industrialized states over dependent and subordinate peoples (Gill 1993; Wood 1999). Racist and chauvinist practices, underpinned by corresponding ideologies, characterize the general economy of exchange of intellectual and other kinds of property around the world between North and South, between the West and "the Rest," mainly people of color, in this epoch of globalized, late or transnational capitalism.

When the United States seized the Philippines at the turn of the twentieth century under the aegis of what Mark Twain then called the "skull and crossbones" of international piracy, scarcely did imperial wisdom foresee that a century hence the islands would harbor a Communist insurgency committed to extirpating U.S. imperialism and the corrupt system its policy of "Benevolent Assimilation" (adapted in various ways from McKinley to Bush and Clinton) has foisted on millions of Filipinos. The "New World Order" marked by the collapse of bureaucratic/statist regimes may have overlooked what is going on in the Philippines. Is the past of the Soviet Union/Eastern Europe the future for the Philippines? Or is the horizon of socialist revolution, far richer than the five-year blueprints of official Marxism–Leninism, still to be discovered and assayed by 70 million Filipinos?

In 1992, after several decades of militant organizing by nationalist forces, the United States yielded to the Philippine government control of territory occupied by its military bases; over a dozen bases were used for military intervention in China, Korea, Indonesia, Vietnam, and the Middle East. Such affirmation of sovereignty (to be reversed in 1999 with the VFA) is an index of a popular mandate for national self-determination, an unprecedented event in the annals of Third World struggles against colonial domination. The intensity of popular mobilization for this and other liberatory agendas is a prophetic sign of the times indeed. It is not a stage but an event in a permanent revolution distinguished by what I would call the rebirth of the Filipino imagination, the conquest of a space for imagining ourselves as an authentically free nation for the first time. But this achievement of no mean proportion has been ignored or dismissed by Filipinos and Americans who claim that what demands immediate attention today is a crisis in a whole progressive movement, particularly manifested in the post-1986 weakening of the National Democratic Front (NDF), the Communist Party of the Philippines (CPP) and its guerrilla army, the New People's Army (NPA), by consensus acknowledged as the spearheads of the national democratic revolution since 1969. What is this crisis all about?

A leading spokesman of this current tendency subsumed in the U.S.-based Forum for Philippine Alternatives (FOPA), Walden Bello (1992) argues that the crisis is evidenced by the 40 percent decline of "organized forces" and "a similar 40 percent reduction in territories controlled by the NPA in the last few years." In 1987, the NPA (numbering at most 30,000 fighters) controlled 40 percent of the rural areas—69 fronts embracing 20 million people (Davis 1989, 50). What caused these losses? From his survey of opinion given by cadres and partisans in the underground, Bello found both objective and subjective factors: effective government counterguerrilla operations, war weariness in the peasant base, and the "militarization" of the Left's strategy (see the response of the CPP 1992). This last factor bulks large in the explanation. It entails a failure to adjust insurgent strategy from 1983 (when Senator Aquino was assassinated) to the 1986 urban uprising against the Marcos dictatorship when the middle forces became politically active and thus the consequent neglect of "creative forms of intervention in the legal and electoral arenas" whose "continuing vitality" functions up to now as sources of political legitimacy for the landlord/comprador elite. This programmatic militarism—privileging revolutionary violence as the means for seizing state power—is compounded with economism, whose testimony is the failure of CPP analysis to attend to "culture, consciousness, and values," especially to the influence of traditional values (e.g., the peasantry's "split-level consciousness") on everyday behavior. In addition, Bello notes one other factor that precipitated the crisis for middle-level cadres: "the collapse of socialism in Eastern Europe and the Soviet Union."

The thrust of the accusation centers on economism and mechanical reductionism committed by the CPP/NPA. But what I think functions as the burden of Bello's argument is the shocking discovery of "self-inflicted wounds" (5–6). These refer to the "Anti-DPA (deep penetration agents) Campaigns" in 1985, 1986, and 1988–1989 launched by elements of the CPP leadership to counter government agents in its ranks, leading to the alleged execution of at least 700 cadres and NPA fighters. While Bello cites abuses of authority by leadership cadres because of the "insurrectionary line" as well as the "absence of an institutionalized system of justice and scientific assessment," the chief interpretive concepts that Bello deploys are themselves reductive and mystifying: a "collective paranoia," lack of "common sense," "a crime against humanity." Others who later echoed Bello (together with those who denounced the party of which they were former high-ranking officials) remind me of the Yogi as Commissar portrayed by Maurice Merleau-Ponty in his powerful critique of draconian anticommunism, *Humanism and Terror* (1969).

Obviously, history cannot be understood by means of the constricted lexicon and method of bourgeois psychology. If the facts invoked were indeed accurate, then we need a rounded scientific explanation that would clarify these "tragic" circumstances and calculate responsibility. A psychoanalytic ontology of paranoia (such as the CPP's notion of "anti-informer hysteria") would only foster obscurantism and be self-defeating. Instead of a dialectical approach (as would befit the putative politics of the participants in this fraught affair), Bello and associates attack Marxism–Leninism and claim the prerogative to pronounce judgment. Bello agrees with those who impute to Marxism a lack of "a developed concept of individual rights" so that individuals have rights "only by virtue of their membership in the right classes or, failing that, in their holding the right politics." A class enemy, therefore, "has no innate right to life, liberty, and respect." He concludes then that the key problem is "an instrumental view of people . . . making [Marxist–Leninists] vulnerable, during moments of paranoia at the height of the revolutionary struggle, to expedient solutions involving the physical elimination of real or imagined enemies" (1992, 6). Any serious student of Marxist ethics can discern here the parroting of a Cold War schematism that reduces the principle of what Cornel West (1991) calls Marx's "radical historicism" into a caricature of police state tactics. Nor does it evince any awareness of the ambiguities of the tradition, its power and subversive resilience, expounded by non-Marxist scholars such as Steven Lukes, Andrew Collier, Andrew Levine, and others. Do the victims deserve the sacrifice of scapegoats named Marx and Lenin?

Such questioning of perceived/received doctrine, however, is salutary. But my purpose here is not to engage in academic casuistry. Nor do I intend to apologize for confirmed inadequacies and immaturity of CPP/NPA cadres, which, I hope, the second rectification movement of the 1990s has remedied to some extent. It is clear that Bello focuses on this "shameful episode" because it caused the Left's impotence "during the critical period from September 1985 to March 1986, when the Marcos regime fell and the Aquino administration consolidated itself" (Bello 1992, 5). If so, then the reinvention of the movement and the drafting of "a comprehensive vision and strategy for change" (toward what seems to be a more perspectival or nontotalizing direction) indeed hinge on learning lessons from this mistake and rectifying the situation that brought it about.

What is at issue is the critical analysis of the present conjuncture, its political economy and laws of motion. A whole volume of functionalist and empiricist essays attacking Marxism applied to the Philippines titled *The Revolution Falters: The Left in Philippine Politics after 1986* (Abinales 1996) argues that the only lesson to be learned from three decades of struggle is to return to liberal, market-centered electoral democracy and acquiescence to U.S. *diktat*. In fact, the ascription of U.S.-style liberal democracy (with patrimonial excrescences) to the Philippines is one of the cardinal mistakes indulged by Filipino pundits trained in the U.S. academies. Joining the chorus of disabused intellectuals is P. N. Abinales (1996), who accuses the organized Left (i.e., the Communist Party of the Philippines and its military arm, the NPA) of "authoritarian paranoia," "dogmatism," and terrorist purges of its ranks (157–158). Anticommunist clichés are repeated from the self-righteous platform of metaphysical hindsight and entrepreneurial moralism.

Any tactful concern for discrimination or more precise calculation of effect is then abandoned in formulating blanket political–ethical judgments. Is the philosophy of Marxism–Leninism, that is, the dialectical method of analyzing and transforming class society, the reason for the militarist adventurism and other errors that have vitiated the struggle for participatory democracy and genuine independence? Or is it ignorance if not rejection of the Marxist mode of analysis—"the concrete analysis" of multifaceted and overdetermined conditions, the synthesizing grasp of the internal contradictions in any social process, the self-critical assessment of hypotheses, and so on—that has occasioned the subjectivist excesses of administrative/commandist politics? Is not class reductionism a violation of the unity of theory and practice that constitutes precisely the enabling genius of Marxism as a revolutionary politics that reveals and opposes commodified society's fragmentation of fact and value, the bifurcation of consciousness and social existence? Is not the one-sided, static, and empiricist orientation of Bello's analysis (his pronouncements should be taken as epitomizing a trend in Filipino Left revisionism) a reflex symptom of the malaise among activists impatient for quick victories? Since 1969, the movement was doing fine. Suddenly, in 1985–1986, something erupts: "a crime against humanity"! A Reign of Terror!

In an analogous tenor, Omar Tupaz (1991; in an article in the trend's organ *Debate: Philippine Left Review*) denounces what he conceives as the CPP's dogmatic scripture: Mao's theory of protracted people's war. Tupaz advocates an insurrectionist strategy focusing on urban mass uprising modeled after the 1986 EDSA revolt, repudiating what he deems the outmoded militarist, rural, stagist approach of the CPP/NDF. While he correctly points out neglected spheres for oppositional agitation (elections, peace negotiations, the Filipino diaspora), Tupaz's obsession with "armed insurrection" in Manila betrays a putschist love of the operatic grand finale that is only the mirror image of the militarism that he decries in vague generalities.[2] Marshaling citations from assorted Vietnamese and Central American authorities, Tupaz displays neither an acquaintance with the rudiments of dialectical materialism nor any comprehension of the historical specificities of the Philippine formation that distinguish it from the Vietnamese, Nicaraguan, and El Salvadoran contexts. His scholastic cataloging of data leads to overestimating the role of technological innovations (37) over against organized and coordinated mass struggles. There is indeed a need for change in strategy—but not a revival of eclectic and opportunist pragmatism!

Of late, Filipino leftists have become fascinated with a postmodern neoromantic tendency in *Ideologiekritik,* which proposes a logic of contingency, identity politics, postutopian heteroglossia, and the aestheticization of agency/subject position as a substitute for dialectics.[3] Foucauldian deconstruction substitutes for historical specification and totalizing hypothesis, individualist cultural politics for mass political struggle (Larrain 1995; Mulhern 1995). This might be considered catalyzing, and heuristic at best, if the whole enterprise is negotiated in dialogue with the indigenous tradition, the counterhegemonic narrative of Filipino self-recovery from colonial victimization and the reconstitution of the people's historical memory that is the foundation of communal self-directed life for an emergent nation.

As Lenin never ceased to remind us, reality/praxis is richer than our thoughts. However, the postmodern critique of necessitarian, deterministic "Marxism," turns out to be a pretext for celebrating the virtues of market liberalism and such formal freedoms that have inflicted so much violence, torture, protracted misery, and painful death to millions of Filipinos and other people of color.[4] The irony is that the anti-Marxists in the Philippines who pay homage to the value of open-mindedness and dissent do so in order to foreclose any dialogue with radicals who address the centrality of property relations, state power, and "delinking" from the injustice of a polarized center/periphery world system. Consequently, "history repeats itself" when all the symptoms of neocolonial underdevelopment (mechanical thinking, ahistorical essentialism, and so on) are reproduced—in the name of an advance from Left orthodoxy.

One of the virtues of Marxism as a scientific worldview and guide to action lies in its principle of comprehending the problem of any given society through a model of system interaction, a conceptual mapping of the ensemble of interconnections and the laws of motion that render social phenomena intelligible and open to alteration. What it foregrounds is the totality of the dynamic contradictions animating class society, not only the major contradictions between the productive forces and social relations (including reproductive relations in the broad sense) and so on but also the tension between the system of needs of any social formation and the objective circumstances subtending it that underlie class conflict and its myriad sublimations. It is only within this synthesizing framework, complicated by layered mediations, that agency can acquire its measured effectivity. In contrast to dualistic or idealist thinking, Marxism conceives agency in its complex historically defined differential embedding, intertwined with the future it is trying to create. Thus, Georg Lukács (1972) emphasizes the human ideal of the realm of freedom for which Communists strive. Not only is the Communist Party the "organizational expression of the revolutionary will of the proletariat," it is "the primary incarnation of the realm of freedom; above all, the spirit of comradeliness, of true solidarity, and of self-sacrifice" (66, 69).

Materialist dialectics concerns not just opposites conceived separately but also their coalescence and interpenetration (Bhaskar 1993; Ollman 1993). Any view valorizing either one side of the dialectic between, say, mutable forms of consciousness and their structural conditions of possibility leads to either a voluntarist deviation ("political will" as primary) or a fatalist surrender to the operations of supposed irrational forces (Weber's iron law of bureaucracy, immutable peasant mentality, geographic/demographic flux, and so on). Given the changes in the objective conditions of social life (technological innovations, complexification of needs, flexible division of labor, and political upheavals) in the contemporary world, Marxist theory strives to integrate these changes to the one fundamental truth in our epoch of history, namely, the contradiction between capital and labor as lived and suffered in the vicissitudes of the periphery/center polarization (Amin 1998, 4). It is not anachronistic to say that we still inhabit a planet dominated largely by the logic of capital accumulation, of the private appropriation of natural resources and social wealth whose form changes in time and place. As the Mexican theologian Enrique Dussel (1992) suggests, for 80 percent of the world's population under capitalist dispensations, the analytical categories they seek do not center on the "free play" of signifiers in an ideal game of communicative action (Habermas) or polite conversation (Rorty); rather, they spring from "the pertinent originating moment of human existence: the economic base (in an anthropological, ethical, and even ontological sense)" (122). Everything else then finds its appropriate valence within this materialist horizon. The contradiction of center–periphery and its local realizations engender and reproduce all the problems of alienation, human rights violations, starvation and disease, war, ecological disasters, as well as illusions of pluralist freedom and individualist self-fulfillment that have now—except in beleaguered sites of resistance, such as Cuba, North Korea, Colombia, and other enclaves—become the universal fate of everyone in the actually existing world system of capital.

But this has of course been the fate of millions of Filipinos ever since the Philippines became a direct colony in 1898, and after 1946 a neocolonial appendage, of the United States (Alavi 1964) . We have suffered the exploitation of monopoly capital for almost a century now, this time increasingly by multi-/transnational corporations through the "conditionalities" of the International Monetary Fund/World Bank. Appropriation of immense surplus value (superprofits) created by the labor of Filipino workers and peasants, surveilled by a collaborationist dependent state, remains the purpose and goal of foreign investment and U.S. diplomacy. Any talk about sustainable development, populist "democratic space," ecological harmony, pluralism of "new social movements," and attenuation of armed resistance by beleaguered communities divorced from class exploitation and national oppression will only promote the neocolonial-racist subjugation of the Filipino people and their continuing subservience to the dictates of the affluent nation-states. It will do so if it does not confront the rock-bottom condition of possibility for inequality, injustice, and class–race–gender oppression: the rule of capital in its various (tributary, bureaucratic patronage, "free trade zones") modalities of extracting surplus value. Those who refuse this axiom have indeed shifted paradigms beyond historical verification. This does not mean that everything is subordinated to economics in its crude meaning or to the law of value. On the contrary. As a synthesizing analytic of praxis, the discipline of historical materialism counsels us to focus on the axis of social relations and discriminate the manifold mediations between political, ideological, and economic levels and their mutual overdetermination (Miliband 1977; Sayer 1987).

Of paramount importance are the history and intensity of political consciousness of different sectors in an uneven and disaggregated terrain (Löwy 1981), the alignment of competing groups with their incommensurable scenarios of self-assertion, the weak link in the uneven field of forces, and the possibilities of co-alitions and alliances at any given instance. The revolutionary process encompasses both gradual accretions (reforms via existing channels) and sudden qualitative ruptures, with collective action grounded in a knowledge of the totality of institutional linkages and bodies in motion.

Marxism as theoretical guideline still demarcates the horizon of our everyday life (to quote Sartre). Whatever the historical specificities involved, given the domination of transnational capital over the state and civil society in the Philippines, one can say that the resources of the Marxist tradition, its efficacy as a theory/practice of radical social transformation and people's empowerment, still remain to be fully understood, mastered, and creatively applied by millions of Filipinos, notwithstanding haphazard attempts in the past to do so. We can certainly do better. We persevere in blazing a world-historical path in uncharted and dangerous territory. We have no choice. What is at stake is the survival and renewal of a whole people whose daily degradation is carried out in the interests of the capitalist world system and an exclusive minority.

Reality changes at varying tempos, requiring adjustments in our consciousness. Because the Philippine social formation (in the Althusserian sense) is an uneven terrain constituted by coalesced modes of production (petty commodity, semifeudal, comprador, transnational, and so on), there has been a long debate among Filipino intellectuals about the kind of transitional system that we inhabit and the alignment of class and sectoral forces.[5] This has led to differences in the formulation of revolutionary strategy and tactics and the forms of mass mobilization. Much energy has been expended on disputing whether the formula introduced by Jose Maria Sison in *Philippine Society and Revolution* (Guerrero 1971)—the Philippines as a semifeudal and semicolonial society requires a protracted people's war based in the countryside (see Sison 1989; Sison and de Lima 1998)—remains valid, given the changes since the fall of Marcos and the demise of Soviet-style communism and the setbacks alluded to earlier. In a recent modification of his views, Sison, collaborating with Julieta de Lima (1998), has elaborated with more nuanced descriptions the Philippine "mode of production," clarifying the linkages between the Marcos land reform scheme, export manufacturing, and neocolonial industrialization. While Sison's productivist notion of "feudalism as a social base of imperialism" is clearly inadequate in the light of such detailed investigations of regional political processes found in the volume *From Marcos to Aquino: Local Perspectives on Political Transition in the Philippines* (Kerkvliet and Mojares 1991), the attention to the plight of the rural masses within the social totality evinces what I think is the only efficacious method of understanding the concrete dynamics of uneven development by grasping the nodes of the various contradictions of the modes of production and their interaction that constitute the social formation.

At this point, I think the observer needs to draw a boundary between the neo-liberals cited earlier and those articulating a socialist practice grounded in Philippine reality. Refusing the call to discard Marxist principles, Francisco Nemenzo (1992a), a founding member of BISIG (Union for the Development of Socialist Ideas), represents a tendency that seeks an *Aufhebung* (cancellation, preservation, and upgrading) of the Filipino anti-imperialist tradition. He bewails the lack of creativity and inventiveness in the Left that has authorized such negative representations I have summarized. He believes that the rise of "politically conscious sectoral and community organizations" (not nongovernmental organizations [NGOs]) has brought significant achievements in the building of popular democracy. He deplores any vanguard party's manipulation of such organizations as reinforcing the "culture of servility" propagated by, and reproduced in, schools, churches, mass media, families, and kinship networks (1992b, 26–28). But if (as Nemenzo contends) the cultural spheres of struggle have been neglected, this is not because the characterization of the social formation was wrong. I think it is because the rigor of dialectical thought applied to understanding contradictory forms of social motion has not been properly pursued (see Lukács 1991; Alavi and Shanin 1982). Hence, phenomena such as ideological divisions in the Pentagon-managed military, the susceptibility of the masses to Christian fundamentalism, and mutations in the realm of the "superstructural" (e.g., "the revenge of civil society") have been discounted or repressed—only to return in the shape of tortured victims of the government, or victims of "paranoid" verdicts. Other progressive movements have of course been guilty of "Marxisms" that Marx himself was the first to disavow.

Part of the reason for the misapprehension if not distortion of Marxism in the Philippines derives from the intervention of citizens of the metropolitan power and the vulnerability of subalterns, the fabled "little brown brothers," to imported advice. One can mention here the role played by U.S. Communists in such groups as the Trade Union Unity League and the Communist Party USA (CPUSA). In 1929, for example, the League advised Crisanto Evangelista's group KAP (Proletarian Labor Congress of the Philippines) that the alliance of workers and peasants at the head of the struggle for economic improvement and independence must be subordinated to "the city proletariat [which] must play the guiding role" (Pomeroy 1992, 69). The model here is of course U.S. society. What this urban vanguard consists of may be gleaned from William Pomeroy's account of how, when the Communist Party of the Philippines (PKP) was founded on 25 August 1930, it was distinguished in all of Asia for having a central committee with a "wholly working class composition," namely, four printers, seven tobacco workers, four woodworkers, four peasants, two cooks, two slipper makers, two seamen, two electricians, a plumber, two journalists, a clerk, a railroad worker, and three worker representatives of the Chinese Labor Federation of the Philippines" (71). Do we need more enlightening Anglo-Saxon tutelage? The other occasion is the intervention of James Allen, representative of the CPUSA, who counseled the adoption of a Comintern "popular front" policy without first thoroughly appraising the internal alignment of local forces in the

Philippines (Historical Commission, PKP 1996). I am not imputing any malign motive to these well-intentioned "missionaries." Just as the party (led by the Lava brothers) in the 1950s made fatal mistakes in confusing its subjective wishes for the revolutionary maturity of the masses, here Pomeroy could not distinguish between class-in-itself and class-for-itself. This is an elementary distinction emphasized by Georg Lukács as crucial for ascertaining the degree of class consciousness, for implementing effective policies for united-front activities, and for consolidating the mass base—two key problematic areas unresolved by current party doxa.

An ironic replication of colonial aggression occurred. What is more unforgivably destructive for the embryonic indigenous Left is the ignorance of Pomeroy and his party to heed Lenin's theory of imperialism and its dialectical lesson. This lesson inheres in the two-sided analysis of imperialism as an economic reality engendering uneven development and as a political conjuncture producing a new revolutionary subject: the national liberation movement of oppressed peoples. Lenin writes,

> The social revolution can come only in the form of an epoch in which are combined civil war by the proletariat against the bourgeoisie in the advanced countries and a whole series of democratic and revolutionary movements, including the national liberation movement in the undeveloped, backward and oppressed nations. Why? Because capitalism develops unevenly, and objective reality gives us highly developed capitalist nations side by side with a number of economically slightly developed or totally undeveloped nations. . . . The dialectics of history are such that small nations, powerless as an *independent* factor in the struggle against imperialism, play a part as one of the ferments, one of the bacilli, which help the real anti-imperialist force, the socialist proletariat, to make its appearance on the scene. (1968, 162; K. Anderson 1995)

Because of this ignorance or failure to grasp the revolutionary essence of the struggle for national self-determination, Pomeroy, Allen, and their well-meaning comrades imposed a mechanical and crude class analysis that dismissed the burden of the colonial reality that Filipinos (the majority of whom were peasants) were grappling with. The turn to the peasantry as a revolutionary force, and the reaffirmation of the national-democratic stage of the socialist revolution, had to wait for the nationalist resurgence in the 1960s (catalyzed by the Cultural Revolution in China and the worldwide antiwar movement) culminating in the reestablishment of the Communist Party of the Philippines and the founding of the NPA, with all the vicissitudes inseparable from any experiment with the rebirth of the popular imagination.

Apart from Pomeroy's own rationalization of the PKP's inability to use the theoretical weapons of historical materialism, it might have been another American initiative in 1936 that induced the PKP leaders to concede to the United States and the native compradors leadership in the antifascist movement in the

1930s. What this illustrates is something not broached by the renewers, namely, the Filipino Left's insensitivity to the problem of racism and symbolic rituals of cooptation. To what extent is a legitimate critique of what passes for "Marxism" complicitous with the oppressor? It might be instructive to examine the process by which military fetishism, vanguardism, and verticalism have been selected and then rejected by Latin American activists (Robinson 1992) relative to other agendas.[6] But, one might ask, why at this stage in the anti-imperialist struggle is there a drive to shift the main arena to bourgeois "civil society," where pluralism supposedly reigns, while the machinery of state power continues to be wielded by the propertied elite? It would be naive to think that all these discourses and exchanges are occurring in a vacuum or in a milieu where all participants are equal, decorous, and free.

It is to Francisco Nemenzo's credit that he still accords primacy in the renewal of a socialist vision to nationalism and equality, while the neoliberals concentrate on "Paradigm Crisis"—that is, doing away chiefly with the Marxist or socialist paradigm that is equated with the notion of "vanguard party," "democratic centralism," and so on. Issues such as ethnicity or "national identity" are considered "peripheral," while Japan's ascending power has replaced the declining United States as the principal concern. But nothing much is said about the nature of Philippine civil society and its stratified interaction with state ideological apparatuses or to what extent the authoritarian *habitus* and hierarchical phallocratic attitudes and behavior originate from tributary social codes/norms and are reproduced in the neocolonized public sphere. In short, disingenuous polemics on behalf of pragmatic relativism seem to have preempted the space that should have been devoted to a vibrant historical-materialist analysis of the Philippine formation.[7]

As a gesture of response to this "crisis of socialism" ascribed by the FOPA Initiative (February 1992) to "lack of moral courage" and "the failure of radical imagination," Sison himself issued a "Statement on the Future of Socialism" (November 7, 1992), a prelude to the second rectification movement launched nationwide. In a sociological mode, Sison points to "the petty bourgeoisie" who infiltrated the Communist Parties of the Soviet Union and Eastern Europe as "the class basis for the betrayal of socialism." This proposition essentially distills the Chinese criticism of Soviet revisionism made during the vicissitudes of the Cultural Revolution of the 1960s. Its precarious validity rests on the more elaborate cogent criticisms made by Charles Bettelheim, C. L. R. James, Ernest Mandel, and others (see Corrigan, Ramsay, and Sayers 1978) of the centralized, statist design of various socialist experiments carried out under determinate global constraints.

A more dialectical critique is offered by Hans Heinz Holz (1992) in "The Downfall and Future of Socialism," which I would endorse with a few qualifications: "Consequently, a bureaucratic Party apparatus arose not as a 'deformation,' but rather as a social form required by the organization of socialist production relations under conditions of economic and social immaturity" (104). In view of the configuration of the modes of production and social relations in the Philippines today, one can speculate that the moment of Yenan may be over (we have learned what we can from Mao), but those of Marx and Lenin are still on the horizon. Conceived within a relational whole in motion, any phenomenon (e.g., degeneration of parties, obsolescence of strategy) thus becomes an intelligible moment in the unfolding of what Hegel calls "the cunning of Reason" in history. .

It remains for revolutionary thinkers to materialize this "Reason" and identify the agents of humanity's liberation from capital and historical necessity. The future of the socialist project, of the collective praxis of Marxism, is bound up with the destiny of the Enlightenment ideals distilled in the *Communist Manifesto*'s key principle: "the free development of each is the condition for the free development of all." Such ideals, however, have been imprisoned within the limits of the instrumental and alienating form of the rationality integral to capitalism. That same rationality underwrites the anti-Marxist discourse of disillusioned activists. The fate of the socialist project is, however, not mortgaged to the plight of individual careers or party formations. It inheres in the center–periphery contradiction shaping the world system of capital today. It is possible that the Philippines may prove to be the "weak link" in this chain. Sison rightly points to the sharpening "crisis of the world capitalist system," a reality erased or occluded by the FOPA Initiative (now defunct). However, one should insist that such a crisis does not spell the system's automatic dissolution and that, from a Marxist perspective, "crisis is a form of motion of capitalism, in which internal contradictions form a unity of opposites and that the contradictions had by no means reached the limits of tearing that unity apart" (Holz 1992, 83). That insight demands careful appraisal. Because of the mechanical way in which such a notion was interpreted before, serious errors were made by the Soviet leadership in intermediate and long-term planning as well as in the exercise of state authority. In the same way, I think that the syllogistic and deductive use of notions such as "strategic defensive" and "primary versus secondary" in the CPP discourse, plus the empiricist quantification of logistics and territory, muddles the dialectic of mediation between general and particular, between class-in-itself and class-for-itself, between subjective agencies and objective determinants. Proceeding along this line, such discursive practice subordinates Marxism to the imperatives of wish fulfillment, unrealistic goals, and triumphalist rhetoric. This becomes painfully evident in the way the Lava brothers (Vicente, Jose, and Jesus, who occupied leadership positions in the PKP) defined "analysis" as a matter of survival skill, of "imbibing and respecting centuries of *barangay* tradition, understanding how relationships were forged and kept at the village and family level" (Dalisay 1999, 12). In effect, the Huk movement that they led was patterned on the extended family and the semifeudal tenancy system, regardless of what social scientists have said about the nature of peasant guerrilla wars with a long-range anti-imperialist program (Hobsbawm 1973; Shanin 1976; Wolf 1976). What then results is, aside from defects and personal tragedies, general stagnation in the vocation of refining the theory/practice of the national-popular project—that is, Filipinizing Marx, Lenin, and Mao against the grain of atrophied Eurocentric orthodoxy.

Granted that deviations from revolutionary principles occurred, is the solution then a return to the basic texts and a talmudic hermeneutics of what Marx, Engels, and Lenin really said?[8] I want to register here my view that Marxism is definitely not a Foucauldian diagnosis of textual knowledge/power nor Nietzschean postmodernist genealogy of one sort or another. In the first place, were the basics ever studied? Yes, by rote, as doctrinal catechism. Proof of this is my personal encounter with cadres who without second thought dismiss Lukács, Luxemburg, and Althusser as irrelevant Western thinkers (because they did not lead successful revolutions, the party belittles or ignores their contributions to the Marxist tradition). These functionaries take offense when you suggest that Gramsci's concept of hegemony is not identical with party leadership of the united front. Such dogmatism has roots not only in petite-bourgeois elitist syndrome but also in the metaphysics of patriarchal absolutism pervading family life, sanctioned by religion and by quotidian business routine. At any rate, I think that this failure to appreciate hegemony as not merely cultural ascendancy but in fact the whole process of the revolutionary transformation of society—the winning of consensus by a bloc of national-popular forces so that a way of life, norms of behavior, life goals, and horizons of expectations, in short, a socialist worldview, become organically integrated into the everyday life of every person—and the corollary failure to grasp what striving to attain hegemonic position implies have undermined the progressive movement as a whole. (On the other hand, the practice of hegemony has never been securely mastered or sustained by the native elite.) To what can this be attributed?

Unequal and combined development of the Philippine social formation implies that the concrete needs of the masses are historically conditioned by diverse and even antagonistic modes of production that are sometimes synchronized but often disarticulated from each other. The dominant ideology is not necessarily that of a homogeneous oligarchy; the historicity of the social forms of consciousness reflect overlayered strata of feelings and ideas symptomatic of uneven development, characterized by displacements and condensations of every kind. Notwithstanding my reservations, I believe that, on the whole, the national democratic movement has made a difference. While the comprador–landlord oligarchy may control the ideological state apparatuses and key institutions of civil society, it can be said that given the nationalist gains in the last three decades since the resistance against U.S. imperialism was revitalized in the late 1960s, the elite does not exercise complete dominance. One can even say that with the splits and rivalries in the ruling circles, the Ramos regime (and its successor, the lumpen-populist Estrada government) represents a very unstable equilibrium of the client state in a volatile conjuncture. Democratic advances in the field of gender relations, liberation theology, anti-imperialist *conscientization* of peasants/workers and middle strata, and noncorporative trade unionism cannot be so easily reversed despite U.S-motivated fundamentalism and, let us not forget, the enormously profitable escape valve of immigration to the United States and contract labor in the Middle East, Europe, and Asia (the country's biggest dollar earnings comes from the remittances of millions of Filipino workers abroad). We have surely not returned to the pre–martial law days when the CIA stooge Magsaysay recuperated the glory of "Benevolent Assimilation" from the mutilated bodies of Huk insurgents. But given the regrouping of landlord private armies, persisting vigilante violence, rampant criminality, and the raw neo–Social Darwinists struggle for survival, emancipated zones have been eroded, and much remains to be done. At least we need to strive for a modestly balanced accounting of what thousands have sacrificed their lives for—not in vain, we hope.

Theory, to be intelligibly valid, cannot exceed the limits of reality. Given the intense immiseration of the people and their level of resistance, despite setbacks underscored by the enemies of Maoism, the "material conditions [the rudiments perhaps for the birth of more just and equitable social relations] have matured in the womb of the old society," to echo Marx (Fischer 1996, 173). In this context, hegemony is not merely wrestling over ideological meanings and symbols in civil society, although that is certainly part of it. Collective education and persuasion are important, geared to the demands of circumstances and local acts of transgression but always one step ahead of traditional habits and thinking; otherwise, we lapse into nativist pathology and other archaic self-defenses. Hence, one cannot dispense with political parties and organizations serving the multiethnic populace. That is why a mass revolutionary party operating on genuinely democratic rules is needed whose vanguard role is earned and deserved by concrete deeds of solidarity and the material improvement of lives as the basis for personal self-realization, an exemplary leading role not simply proclaimed in self-congratulatory slogans. As the Comintern proposed to the Filipino communists in 1928, they were duty bound to "transform gradually the Labor Party into a party of the masses" (Pomeroy 1992, 70). This does not rule out the construction of multiple complementary strategies and tactics, programs with diverse flanks geared to satisfy the widest range of communities and sectors, provided that there is political unity on the fundamental problems that the majority of Filipinos face in long- and short-range periods.

What is key to the rectification of the national-democratic strategy, I submit, is the application of a Leninist principle in unifying theory and practice (Fischer 1996). Within the framework of world revolution demanded by imperialism as a global system (on the United States as a superimperialism, see Jalee 1972; Poulantzas 1974), it is necessary to locate and grasp the "weak link" in which the popular forces can be concentrated at the precise point where bourgeois ideology has been disrupted or displaced. Lenin reminds us, "It is not enough to be a revolutionary and an advocate of socialism in general; it is also necessary to know

He talks about Lenin's *Imperialism* as explaining potential revolution, but then also seems to state that it may come from the countryside, but he has previously discounted Mao.

at every moment how to find the particular link in the chain which must be grasped with all one's strength in order to keep the whole chain in place and prepare to move on resolutely to the next link" (Corrigan et al. 1978, 59). In the global geography of transnational economic processes, the "weak link" may be discerned in the grid of strategic concentrations of material infrastructure and the multiple linkages of finance capital—the "global cities" whose fragile anatomy Saskia Sassen (1998) has acutely described. In the Philippines, not only Metro Manila but also the grids that connect the major population centers may prove to be the "weak link" of the archipelagic chain of neocolonial command, depending on the alignment of political forces. Protracted encircling people's war can then be advanced more efficaciously (to extrapolate from the 1975 Shanghai textbook *Fundamentals of Political Economy*) by giving "full scope to the active and initiatory role of the superstructure" (Lotta 1994, 33).

Overthrowing neocolonial hegemony entails a radical politicization of civil society. We envisage in this process the fusion of a tactics of insurrection with the socialist governance of a democratic polity (Lukács 1991). In both, political education embraces collective praxis, self-criticism, and learning-by-transformation. So long as the oppressed and exploited masses do not recognize their common interests as dictated by their subaltern position in a commodified society, so long as they are not educated, disciplined, and impelled to action by a revolutionary theory "as critique of the present and a design for the future," hegemony of the national democratic forces cannot be attained. Such a theory practiced by committed nationalists is provided by Marxism, still (to paraphrase Sartre) the unsurpassable philosophy of everyone suffering under capital. It is also the guide for subjugated peoples of color fighting for liberation from the terror of racism and reification, from the hell of commodity fetishism and barbarisms galore, sustained by a really existing world system whose citadels are Washington, Tokyo, Berlin, Paris, and London.

[margin note: consciousness needed for revolution.]

As a comment on the much ballyhooed "democratic space" granted by President Aquino in the short time before she declared "total war" on the Left, it might be useful to quote what William Hinton (the renowned author of *Fanshen*) wrote in a letter to his sister. In part he reported about how some East Germans who recently visited Manila said that "they thought socialism was bad, a deadend, until they saw the end result of capitalism" in the Philippines. But this is not the moral fable that will redeem us from peripheral stagnation. Here is Hinton's impression of the situation in Manila in 1992:

> Behind all these phenomena [of NGOs sprouting all over the place, funded by foreign governments interested in business stability] lies an unusual balance of forces because state power currently is not exercised in a form preferred by the ruling class but in a form shaped by a revolutionary storm that overthrew the Marcos regime and created a kind of compromise interregnum wherein the old establishment clings uncertainly to power by making, or at least promising, concessions on many fronts,

freeing many political prisoners, and allowing considerable rope to various people's movements and people's leaders while at the same time organizing a large scale military campaign to crush the guerilla forces in the hills. On the one hand the army is trying to kill guerilla fighters, and on the other it allows people sympathetic to and even allied with these same guerillas to function openly in civil society. This creates a bizarre Catch 22 situation, a sort of political paralysis and social stalemate, perpetuated, in the last analysis, on the one side by the weakness of an army whose high command might wish to rule with a mailed fist but can't count on the loyalty of an officer corps below and can't rely on the rank and file to obey orders as was demonstrated on the EDSA (Manila's main street) during the [September 1986] upheaval. On the other side the popular forces are also too weak to tip the balance. Now and then they win a few concessions but they are by no means strong enough to overthrow the system and so this curious see-saw battle continues with militants moving in and out of the guerrilla movement, in and out of jail, and in and out of the government, sort of a revolutionary musical chairs game that is really hard to fathom. (1993, 4)

This rich and overdetermined cross section of an ongoing social drama that Hinton delineates with modulated precision speaks volumes about the crisis of elite democracy—what Robert Stauffer (1990) calls "a form of intraelite competition for office via elections" established by U.S. imperialism—the crisis of the old dispensation unable to rule in the old way. Meanwhile, the Filipino masses are still unable to totally unite to overthrow their moribund oppressors and build a society that will prevent their restoration.

In this sense, one can say that the national democratic movement is caught in a temporary impasse. But this predicament entangles its enemy too, both protagonists locked in a scene of contradictory coherence. When will the rupture occur? Change of the balance of forces cannot be accomplished in any way one desires; the objective limits of the possible modes of action by the oppressed (self-defense or active resistance), the weight of the past, and the power of media-purveyed fantasies to recuperate ground wasted by economic privations require a more sophisticated summing up of the complex totality of the situation. And it is not a situation difficult to fathom by Marxists precisely because it is what Marxism is all about, the unity of manifold contradictions in a specific historical conjuncture, a moment of convergence inscribed with gaps and fissures and thus affording opportunities for timely intervention.

To rehearse an old witticism: Reality is Marxist without knowing it. The challenge is for us to know it while changing it, thus to be Marxists. The task of elucidating this inhuman and mystified condition that implicates all of us, an effect produced by the logic of capital accumulation, is being confronted by Filipino progressives in a time of disarray in the international Left. Of course, we have no alternative if we claim to desire a humane, just, egalitarian, and autonomous nation. But it is not just a question of correct interpretation and more astute explanations of what self-determination and popular empowerment are all about; the desideratum is to bring about the social condition of possibility for their emergence. It is at this turning point of the movement that the role of the organic intellectuals of the nation-people becomes urgently crucial and decisive. And Marxism, insofar as it has not been "Filipinized" or really given the chance to open up the space for initiating the socialist adventure in the Philippines amid U.S. "low-intensity warfare," the seductions of laissez-faire pluralism and spectacles of consumerist jouissance, is a resource that we can dare use, test, enrich, and appropriate for a future waiting to be born.

Nothing is foreclosed; everything has yet to be tried and tested. Within the framework of the historical-materialist analytic sketched in the preceding observations, I propose seven theses for discussion and reflection at the dawn of a new century. Seven only—not because, like Ferdinand Marcos, I believe in a magic number but as an acknowledgment that we should heed constraints of time, human attention span, limited quanta of energy because of practical necessities, age, objective situation, and so on. These propositions are intended to be the raw materials for dialogue and debate or to serve as "sparks" to light a "prairie fire" of intellectual exchanges and creative elaborations.

Thesis 1: Like all dependent/peripheral social formations, the Philippines is a living testimony to the law of "combined and uneven development" and its complex operations. Uneven because of colonial plunder and domination, plus the barbarism of the U.S. military suppression of the Filipino revolutionaries in 1898 and up to the 1920s, together with the destruction inflicted by the Japanese and American liberation forces in World War II and the neocolonial years from Roxas to the present—all these have distorted the economy, stagnated the politics, and on the whole damaged the capacities of the majority for the autonomous management and direction of their lives. Given ineluctable class divisions and disaggregation of the various spheres of the social formation (economic, political, ideological) by colonial subordination, we have a melange of such features: Makati-style computerized business, transnational styles of administration, feudal or artisanal production, precapitalist slavery of children and women, archaic superstitions and practices, and of course comprador and bureaucrat capitalism of all kinds. In addition, we have the unprecedented distinction of being presumably the number one supplier of cheap labor to the world (especially the patriarchal/capitalist Arab sheikdoms) in the form of domestic help, entertainment/hospitality workers, and so on.

Combined development because the state strives to establish equilibrium among discordant elements for profit accumulation of transnational corporations and the local bourgeoisie and because capitalism subsumes the other modes of production to maintain extraction of maximum surplus value (Hymer 1972). Uneven also implies nonsynchrony, temporal disharmony, syncopations of spatial signs, and juxtapositions of all sorts—in short, a pastiche or hybrid combination of life forms and social practices, some of which have survived from the past, some are dominating the present, and others foreshadowing and anticipating the future.

Uneven and combined development also spells leaps, catastrophic transitions, and skipping gradual stages because signs of the future—what is emerging—are also found implicit or embedded in current processes. Contradictions and disparities on all levels of the state, economy, and civil society produce a highly overdetermined system that is always in crisis, never stable as the state-centered "welfare" capitalism of the West (now in serious devolution). Everything solid melts into air, as the *Communist Manifesto* proclaims, with reference to Europe of the 1840s. The melting is much faster in the dependent localities, the peripheries of the world system, where "ideal" subjective phenomena (such as nationalism) grow out of the most brutal "machinery of world political economy" (Nairn 1982, 432). The consequence of spatial disjunction is even more serious than the previous temporal ruptures in that it becomes well-nigh impossible to grasp the way that the imperial system functions as a whole (Jameson 1990b) and within it the disposition of the parts, except by reading the symptoms in the form of catastrophic breakdowns, decay of cities, anarchy, holocaust, and of course revolutionary upheavals.

Thesis 2: In the disarticulated social formation of our society, "civil" society cannot be analytically separated from the state and the "national" or popular basis of this more militarized or coercive state. Of late, Western-trained pundits inspired by the melancholy Max Weber have argued that political effort in the democratizing countries should be focused on mobilizing institutions in civil society rather than the masses gearing up for seizing state power in direct frontal assaults. Privileging the war of position over that of maneuver, civil-society ideologues go crazy over NGOs. Funding bonanzas for NGOs partly explain this, but the source is ignorance of political-social theory.

In the classical theorizing of "civil society" by Rousseau, Hegel, and Marx, "civil society" is the site of individual and group antagonisms for private interests, assuming the state as a neutral mediating entity. Philippine "civil society," however, is not based on the premise of institutionalized individual rights and procedural review. Kinship, familial habits, and customary values predominate. Communicative reason (as envisaged by Habermas) is an emergent and sporadic event. Force exercises disproportionate influence over all. Religion exercises an inordinate influence on people's lives to the extent that, with the resurgence of fundamentalism and other forms of revitalization movements, reactionary and obscurantist ideologies blend and interact with technicist and instrumentalist–utilitarian programs to dictate lifestyles and institutional *modus operandi*. Neocolonial "civil society" in fact cannot be divorced from the state and other coercive apparatuses associated with parastate or extralegal forces (Noumoff 1999).

Exclusive focus on "civil society" guarantees that the state can function without much constraint in maintaining class division, unequal power based on asymmetrical property relations, and transnational capital accumulation. Focus on the private life, family values, individualist concerns, and corporate business leaves the state and the bureaucratic apparatus safe from critical accountability. Alienation and fragmentation are bound to intensify personal anxieties, leading to a thorough psychologizing of everything—in short, to a general mystification of life forms.

Cultural practice cannot be confined to the realm of civil society in modernity because the means of communication and cultural production are subject to state laws and bureaucratic regulation. Moreover, corporate control of media and publishing also actualizes state laws and international agreements. While uneven development allows modernizing tendencies in private life to express themselves, hence the "international style" and postcolonial "world literature in English," fetishism in mass consumption and religious fanaticism collide with such globalizing trends, with the state abetting one and suppressing the other. The fiction of a mythical "civil society" insulated from the state is one effective expression of a hegemonic neoconservatism—the argument and rhetoric of the free unregulated market, the genuine simulacrum if ever there was one.

Thesis 3: Hegemony, in the original Gramscian construal of moral intellectual leadership of a social bloc in dominance, is the chief target of revolutionary change in Third World formations. Instead of the formula of seizing state power by head-on confrontation in armed struggle, Gramsci advocated a nuanced combination of the war of position (institutional reforms to test the limits of the system) and war of maneuver (mass strikes, guerilla warfare, street fighting), depending of course on the balance of forces, the alignment of classes and groups in play, the position of organic and traditional intellectuals in the history of society, and so on (Mouffe 1979). Concrete analysis of the situation is the desideratum, "concrete" meaning here the convergence of as many determinations as one can account for.

In cultural politics, hegemony can be effectively personified by organic intellectuals of the progressive forces, in this case an alliance of workers, peasantry, and middle stratum or intelligentsia. It will also include ethnic communities, women, and so on. By stressing the pedagogical and educational side of the hegemonic process, we valorize in effect a cultural revolution that would be permanent—a revolution that would erode the residual, promote the emergent, and critique the dominant oligarchical elite or power bloc that mediates imperial ascendancy.

In hegemonic politics, assuming that the state allows the national-democratic forces the means and freedom to propagate socialist ideas, the leading role of cultural organs is to remind us that revolution is a political–ideological, not simply physical, struggle for consensus. Violence plays a role chiefly in self-defense and to protect the gains and claims of the democratic masses to exercise popular self-determination.

Not just the sphere of civil society but also its manifold linkages with the state therefore become the site of hegemonic contestation. Hegemony is thus not just discursive or mere application of violence but also institutional; it will continue even when the coercive apparatus of the state has been transferred to popular control. The goal is to release forces and human potential repressed by outmoded social relations. Its aim is the creation of a new personality, a new character, for a new dispensation.

A digression on culture and cultural studies is required here.

Thesis 4: Within the uneven development perspective, culture is segmented into residual, dominant, and emergent tendencies whose confluence and interaction vary according to the politics of the social formation in specific periods or epochs. Following Raymond Williams, each epoch manifests a "structure of feeling" that equals the variable hierarchy of those three segments, with the emergent showing either alternative and oppositional aspects (alternative, as the various nativist or ethnic communities demonstrate; oppositional, as exemplified by the NPA and other radical challenges to the neocolonial setup). Apprehending the determinate form of the structure-in-dominance is needed to calculate the political consequences of specific cultural practices that cannot be known in advance.

Culture is then not a catalog of artifacts or tabulation of indigenous folkways. It refers to forms of antagonistic signifying practices and discourses that represent conceptions of the world associated with distinct classes, groups, sectors, or communities. In England, for example, the ethos of service characterizes bourgeois culture, whereas the ethos of solidarity distinguishes working-class culture (Williams 1983). In the Philippines, it is not *bayanihan*, contrary to official dogma, that distinguishes Filipino oppositional culture but perhaps millenarian adventurism or personalistic loyalties symptomatic of the distrust of bureaucratic rules. What is dominant in the culture can only be the inventory of preferred values and norms of the ruling social bloc.

In reaction to Marxist orthodoxy, Western cultural studies arose via the influence at first of Gramsci and later of Althusser and semiotic/linguistic theories plus psychoanalysis. The rise of gender, feminist, and ethnic constituencies and their specific or specialized intellectuals (Foucault) have neutralized or displaced class, more exactly social relations, as a criterion or focus of analysis, hence the contingent, dispersed, narrow academic interests of its practitioners.

Philippine culture studies, I propose, needs to attend to both the uneven/combined development of its field and its complicity in the sharpening class war. What is at stake is the reconfiguration of the whole nation-state. To mimic Western postcolonial cultural studies and its opportunism would be to reinforce subalternity. It is death by incorporation or assimilation.

It goes without saying that culture is both structural and superstructural, one dominant over the other, depending on the stage of hegemonic struggle and the weakness/strength of the transnational power blocs supporting the local ruling coalition and its space for maneuver, calculation, sublimation, and so on.

Thesis 5: Language and textuality, together with discursive politics, are important. But they cannot be fetishized by themselves at the expense of the education and mo-

bilization of the collective subjects in practical politics. Agitation and mass mobilization are fundamental in cultural politics in the South, and so the movement needs to communicate in the vernacular speech of the masses.

Given the continued dominance of transnational corporate English, the need to develop a national language remains a priority. At the same time, however, we should not forget that the enemy can also speak in Filipino or the emerging national idiom. Form and content should therefore be dialectically adjusted lest proponents of regional languages quarrel over trivial rewards and sidetrack what is significantly at stake: control of resources (such as the means of communication), ecological space, and the future.

Again, to borrow the insight of Walter Benjamin, it is imperative that progressives take control of the means of articulation and communication in its various material ramifications (including clandestine broadcasting, collectivization of private intellectual property, and so on). Such campaigns intend to educate the public and also assist specific reforms that can be tied to all-encompassing national issues and community projects and agendas.

In this task of nationalizing modes of expression, the goal of articulating the "national-popular" involves reconstructing histories of the people as well as communities, narratives of heroes, mass leaders, and so on. The people as nation, the producing masses, is what needs translation. Who is authorized to represent whom? The struggle for legitimacy via language and other means of representation (multimedia, Internet, performance art) is an integral and crucial part of the process of hegemonic struggle.

Thesis 6: We need to grasp the basic principles of cultural revolution in our historically specific milieu. Bakhtin taught us that the sign is an arena of ideological and political struggle. In any class-riven formation, it is always an arena of war. But the fight for national self-determination cannot just be waged by "purifying the language of the tribe," as the aesthetes would have it, or, following the heroic efforts of the late Virgilio Enriquez, decolonizing colonial psychology by squeezing Pilipino phrases, words, and idioms in order to extract a Filipino essence (e.g., *pakikipagkapwa*). Such essentialism, however strategic or provisional, can only lead to new forms of reification. Contradictions in the historical process are erased or marginalized, in effect evacuated by trying to recuperate what is claimed to be authentically native, "Filipino," aboriginal.

In this hypothetical inventory, I hope that I have not forgotten the primacy of feminist principles and the importance of the struggle for gender equality. The unequal sexual division of labor lies at the heart of the uneven and combined development of our social formation, the antagonisms of worldviews and epistemes, so that while we may neglect it, it will not forget us. If repressed, it will haunt us and take revenge in various horrific ways.

In any "long march" to materialize the national-popular canon, it is imperative that we do not become sectarian and exclusive—withdrawing from the terrain of mass struggles (the fight for democratic rights, individual civil liberties, and specific demands of various sectors on the level of their consciousness) and choosing our own field of battle. We are free, but only under certain conditions determined by historical legacies, geography, environment, and so on. Just as the English bourgeoisie fought the landed aristocrats on the same ideological level of religious beliefs (Milton versus the royalists), the Filipino socialists will have to fight on the same field where the masses are: the milieu of popular beliefs, individual rights, and so on. However, the requirement of hegemony cautions us not to tail behind, to constantly provide advanced unifying ideas that would help humans take control of their social and physical environment—in short, to grasp the flow of history for emancipatory ends. We need leadership to inspire and direct the movement, not just to peacefully manage the order of the march.

Cultural revolution is the rubric we use to refer to the class struggle on the terrain of hegemonic discourse, with the aim of interrogating, discriminating, and sublating the discourse to a higher level of synthesis. Given uneven/combined development, the nature of cultural revolution in the Philippines, in the context of globalized late capitalism, involves adapting modern technology and secular modes of organization to raise the quality of life. In doing so, we are always mindful of the destructive effects of capitalist modernization on the environment and its resources, not to speak of the violence on women, children, and all the victims of scientific industrial progress.

Engaging in cultural revolution entails wrestling with canonical texts and standards. Because Nick Joaquin has been generally considered a paragon of English-speaking writers, I have had to conduct hemeneutic and semiotic maneuvers at the risk of appearing to be a formalist New Critic within the terrain of critical discourse on Joaquin in order to ascertain reusable utopian/subversive elements embedded in Joaquin's signifying practice. Opting out of this terrain and damning Joaquin's retrograde politics (see Lenin on Tolstoy, Marx and Engels on Balzac, Cardenal and Macdiarmid on Pound) automatically surrenders the "sign" called "Joaquin" to the enemy.

Cultural revolution also never forgets Benjamin's hard saying that every document of art or culture contains marks of both human refinement and barbarism.

Thesis 7: We touch the topic of globalization and the role of people of color in the "New World Order" decreed by capital. Homelessness and uprooting characterize the fate of millions today—political refugees, displaced persons, émigrés and exiles, stateless nationalities. Solidarity acquires a new temper. In the postmodern transnational restructuring of the globe after the demise of the Soviet Union, the Philippines has been compelled to experience a late-capitalist diaspora of its inhabitants. The OCWs, an unprecedented sociopolitical category of seven million Filipinos (mostly women as domestic help) scattered around the markets of various nation-states, in particular the Middle East, is the new arena of hegemonic contestation. Overseas Contract Workers remit billions of dollars, enough to keep the neocolonial system afloat and the elite in illusionary bliss. Most of these overseas female Filipinos are modern slaves, at best indentured servants

(Beltran and Rodriguez 1996). They can be seen congregating in front of Rome's railway station, London parks, city squares in Hong Kong and Taipei, and other stigmatized public quarters of peripheral and core capitalisms.

Marginality of racialized contractual labor (reconfigured as an "inscrutable" alterity) defines the identity of the master citizens while the metropole, the putative space of flows (aside from labor power, commodities as money, intellectual property, and so on), prohibits these foreigners from carving a locale for their sociality. For these deracinated populations, their nationality signifies their subalternity within the existing interstate hierarchy of nation-states (emasculated but not yet fungible or defunct), while money (yen, petrodollars) permits them the aura of cosmopolitan status. The semblance is reinforced by the whole ideological apparatus of consumerism, the ironically betrayed promise of enjoying appearances (Haug 1986). Meanwhile, the almost globalized city of Metro Manila exudes an illusion of consumerist affluence, sporting the postcolonial mirage of hybrid and syncretic spectacles in megamalls and quasi-Disneylands amid the ruin of fragmented families, criminality, and other degrading symptoms of anomie. Articulated with this transnational flux of labor, the urban experience of Filipinos replicates and also parodies that of residents in the global metropolis: segregation, fissured communities, ethnic tensions, and so on. Whether conceived as machine or text, Metro Manila becomes a carceral site for OCWs killing time while waiting for the next contract and also an inhospitable conduit for commodified bodies and other damaged goods of neocolonial production/reproduction.

In a cynical gesture, ex-President Cory Aquino paid homage to the OCWs as "new heroes" ("*mga bagong bayani*"). Their novelty cannot be sustained since the Philippines supplied contract laborers to the Hawaii sugar plantations as early as the 1920s. However, in their alienation and deprivation, these "slaves" of postmodern globalization constitute the negativity of the Other, the alterity of a permanent crisis of transnational capital. I do not mean a global or international proletarian vanguard but simply a potentially destabilizing force—they act as the dangerous alien, eliciting fear and *ressentiment*—situated at the core of the precarious racist order.

If the Other (of color) speaks, will the former "master" from the West listen? What needs urgent critical attention today is the racial politics of the transnational blocs to which we have been utterly blind, obsessed as we have been with class, gender, *amor propio*, and so on (on gender struggles, see Eviota 1992; Aguilar-San Juan 1992). We have been victims of Euro-American racializing ideology and politics, but characteristically we ignore it and speak of our racism toward Moros, Igorots, Chinese, and so on. Race and ethnicity have occupied center stage in the politics of nationalist struggles in this post–Cold War era. We need to inform ourselves of the complex workings of racism and chauvinism as practiced by the industrialized states. On this hinges the crucial issue of national autonomy, whether a dependent formation such as the Philippines can uncouple or delink from the world system in order to pursue a different, uniquely Filipino kind of socialist growth and a radically different kind of national project.

Perhaps the trigger for a new mass mobilization can be the awareness of racial politics as a way to restage the national-democratic struggle in the new framework of neoliberal market discourse—unless there is an oppositional systemic challenge to the corporate interests.

The prospect of radical social change beckons for further exploration, replete with detours, beguiling traps, and blind alleys.[9] Let us examine one of these traps, a Western view of these seductive islands now ready for commodification twice over, a view more blatantly patronizing than Hamilton–Paterson's but no less instructive on the need for our thorough education in the dynamics of racial politics around the world that takes a deliberate cognitive mapping of class, gender, race, and nationalitarian themes. Here is a passage by a British writer, Simon Winchester, published in the tourist magazine *Condé Nast Traveler*. Winchester visited the world-class Amanpulo resort on Pamalican Island in Palawan and muses on the fascinating intertextuality of signs (Baudrillard's simulacra and hyperreal simulations):

> The ending of island isolation has in general meant that the world's wealthiest travellers are now being set down willy-nilly among the world's poorest and most innocent people—a reality that seems likely to have a far more profound and lasting effect on the poor and innocent than on the wealthy and worldly. . . . I now receive regular letters from one of the girls who cleaned my room at Amanpulo. She says she wants, more than anything in the world, to find an American man, to marry him, and to come live in New York City. I write back to her: Mary-Jane, I say, you live in paradise but you just don't know it. Don't even dream of coming here. Stay in a place where there has never been a crime committed, where everyone shares everything, where everyone looks after everyone else, where the weather is perfect, the air is clean, the sea is crystal clear.

If this is true, I would have liked to have spent our two-month summer vacation in Amanpulo, Palawan, every year. However, the point here is that this is a white Western optic, a mercantile consciousness claiming the superior anthropological and prophylactic knowledge about our surroundings, telling us (via Mary-Jane) what we have been missing all these years. Is this all we deserve, a deceptive mock-utopian image straight from the glossy tourist brochure?

Revolutionaries are not enemies of utopia, as Ernst Bloch has so passionately argued. On the contrary, the drive for, and even libidinal fixation on, the utopian is one of the strongest motivating forces for the radical transformation of society. As Ernest Mandel (1995) put it, the categorical imperative for socialists is "to strive to overthrow all social conditions in which human beings are exploited, oppressed, humiliated, and alienated" (447). But cultural politics in the Philippines behooves us also to comprehend the dynamics of class power relations, including those between races and nations as conditioned by the history of colonialism and imperialism. With such knowledge of history and the relevant cultural praxis, we begin to be suspicious of business wisdom and yearn for a dissident and recalcitrant voice with its utopian resonance.

Let me then conclude by calling your attention to the prophetic passage from Rizal's prescient and memorable essay "The Philippines a Century Hence" (1961a), a text that ought to replace the hackneyed and rancid texts of Derrida, Lyotard, Foucault, and other poststructuralist gurus in our reading program. Listen to Rizal's invocation of what we all desire:

> With the new humans that will spring from their soil and with the recollection of their past, they will perhaps strive to enter freely upon the wide road of progress, and all will labor together to strengthen their fatherland, both internally and externally, with the same enthusiasm with which a youth falls again to tilling the land of his ancestors so long wasted and abandoned through the neglect of those who have withheld it from him. . . . Perhaps the country will revive the maritime and mercantile life for which the islanders are fitted by their nature, ability and instincts, and once more free, like the bird that leaves its cage, like the flower that unfolds to the air, will recover the pristine virtues that are gradually dying out and will again become addicted to peace—cheerful, happy, joyous, hospitable and daring. (1961a, 7)

NOTES

1. Leslie Sklair (1991) argues that the ideology of consumerism has legitimized the triumph of global capitalism, even to the extent of reviving a version of the "civilizing mission," as he attests: "It is possible that the Filipino hamburger is more efficiently and hygienically served (and perhaps made) than before" (153).

2. Not so long ago, everyone agreed with Mamerto Canlas's (1988, 77) view that the parameter of electoral politics was restrictive and also that U.S. power was preponderant, as substantiated by Villegas (1983) and others. The Aquino interregnum then really did wonders in convincing former "hardliners" to rehabilitate themselves for the contingencies of the "New World Order."

3. I cite two well-intentioned examples: Ruiz's (1991) postmodern speculations, to which I have indirectly responded (San Juan 1992b), and St. Hilaire (1992). A corrective to St. Hilaire's misapplied Foucauldian intervention may be the feminist standpoint theory (see Harding 1993) where the epistemic violence of phallocratic institutions is juxtaposed with the total vision of society ascribed to marginalized subjects, a vision without which no radical change in the periphery can even be imagined.

4. In *Crisis in the Philippines*, I called attention to the need to remap the terrain by underscoring "strategic interventions" by women, church people, and ethnic minorities; a whole chapter is devoted to the Moro People's struggle (San Juan 1986). In *From People to Nation: Essays in Cultural Politics*, I inquire into the hegemonic process of reconstituting the people as nation and the saliency of the national-popular project as a quest for articulating the Filipino "general will" (San Juan 1990).

5. For an example of this genre, see the contributions of Ricardo Ferrer (1984, 1987).

6. See the contrasting views of Carlos Vilas, Pablo Gonzalez Casanova, and Maria Helena Alves in Tabb (1990).

7. Most of those critical of the thesis of "protracted people's war" appear to be unreformed veterans of the KDP (Union of Democratic Filipinos)/Line of March's frustrated effort to found a U.S. Marxist–Leninist party in the 1970s. Since no autocritique of their sectarian-elitist past has been made, there is warrant for suspicions about the real motives and provenance of this demonstration of "bad faith." This concerns political consistency and ethics, not psychology.

8. Other incidents concerning the case of Father Conrado Balweg, once publicized as an internationally celebrated NPA commander and recently executed by the NPA; the NPA retreat from Agdao, Davao City; the breakaway of cadres in Negros; Victor Corpuz's return to the military as its foremost counterinsurgency expert; and many other controversial topics all await elucidation more nuanced and all-sided than those found in Chapman (1987) or Grossman (1986).

9. One example of counterrevolutionary propaganda disguised as sympathetic concern for progressive social movements is found in a book that documents the infiltration of the KMU (*Kilusang Mayo Uno*) by the CPP. Its theoretical scaffolding is easily exposed by statements such as the following: "A combination of military might, independence from the colonizer, and the opening of the political system defeated revolutionary movements in the Philippines during the 1940s and fifties" (West 1997, 188). This is surely not much of an improvement over Karnow and his ilk. Nor is it much more informed than this self-righteous and ridiculous pontification of a writer in the reactionary magazine *Filipinas* (November 1998, 25): "In terms of principles, the breakup in 1993 [of the leading ranks of the CPP] saw the anti-Sison factions adopting the purely Marxist-Leninist strategy of raising the consciousness of the working class, and dropping Sison's cherished Maoist tactic of a protracted armed struggle." Another Western "take" is the Trotskyite superimposition of the "correct line," instanced by Mark Johnson's opinion (*International Viewpoint*, no. 313, July 1999, p. 20) meant to herald a scandalous apocalyptic novelty: "Since 1992, large sections of the Philippine left have thrown off the Maoist straitjacket, and embraced a more dynamic—and democratic—revolutionary strategy, based on the self-organization of the oppressed."

Afterword

After the long Bonapartist interlude of martial law punctuated by the spurious "democratic space" of Corazon Aquino's presidency, the Philippines has now plunged into the swamp of theatrical, neofascist barbarism presided over by the alleged "poor man's president," Joseph Estrada, attended by the survivors of the Marcos era, foremost of which are Imelda Marcos and the paragon of comprador cronyism, Danding Cojuangco. Is this repetition (to echo Marx's *The Eighteenth Brumaire*) a tragedy or a farce? A novelist from Hong Kong, Timothy Mo, had no scruples hurling his barbs at Filipinos. In his notorious *Brownout on Breadfruit Boulevard* (1995), Mo targeted the "moral slightness of the Filipino" whose culture has "no honour, no depth," lacking commitment and showing only "poor moral accountancy." Aside from being a "born informer," a "Judas" or a criminal, the Pinoy seems to be the acme of degradation for Mo:

> Why was it Filipinos liked to crucify themselves on their own words? It was the intellectual's equivalent of the Holy Week flagellants who had themselves nailed to crosses. Shit, they'd still be pending in the Philippine courts when the Last Trumpet sounded. . . . If the country was to have a future it had to export something better than house-servants and whores. (1995, 31, 34)

Instead of mounting a direct refutation of Mo's self-righteous indictment of the wayward Filipino, I would like to explore here the possibilities of a multicultural democracy in the Philippines against the background of a persistent U.S. neocolonial apparatus of knowledge production preempting Filipino claims to national self-determination.

PROBLEMATIZING MULTICULTURALISM

The ideal of a multicultural democratic society is often celebrated today without a clear understanding of the difficulties or problems its realization entails, for the

191

articulation of plural cultures and democratic institutions can be envisaged as a practical project only within the complex and changing social formations that they inhabit. In the case of "third world" societies in Asia, Africa, and Latin America, colonialism introduced a politics of difference that multiplied boundaries within and without: The subjugated communities were polarized internally and against one another. Differences marked by race, class, gender, religion, nationality, and other ethnic particulars functioned as the instruments by which the hegemony of the colonial power was established and maintained. In effect, a policy of multiculturalism was devised and applied in order to disintegrate former cohesive groups, to foster antagonisms between and among their members, and to prevent any sense of national unity that would challenge colonial rule. With an apartheid regime of cultures that are plural but hierarchized, the antithesis of democracy—political and economic inequality—flourished. Racism reigned supreme.

I subscribe to David Harvey's (1996) belief that "it is hard to discuss the politics of identity, multiculturalism, 'otherness,' and 'difference' in abstraction from material circumstances and of political project" (334). We cannot do without concrete historical specification.

Colonized for over 300 years by mercantile Spain, the inhabitants of the Philippine islands acquired a sense of national unity after 350 years of peasant revolts culminating in the revolution of 1896–1898. That was forged by an alliance of classes and popular sectors that established the first Philippine Republic. This emerging nation-state was destroyed by the military and economic might of the United States in the Filipino–American War of 1899–1902. The Philippine Republic that was granted independence in 1946 reflected a half century of hegemonic multiculturalism instanced by the use of the English language as the medium of communication in business and government. The dominance of American commodified culture persists amid residual customs and archaic practices in various regions, with 20 major ethnolinguistic groups uttering their demands for recognition and for their share of the social goods.

Before illustrating how multiculturalism, the politics of difference, operates in the Philippines today, allow me to quote a capsule description of the country from an American geographer. The Philippines, writes George Demko (1992), is characterized by egregious and unconscionable class divisions:

A few landowners have acquired massive wealth, while almost three quarters of the population of 65 million live in direst poverty, unable to satisfy basic needs. Mestizos make up 2 percent of the population but garner 55 percent of the personal income. . . . [Demko then describes the dependence of thousands of Filipinos on the U.S. military bases, part of the U.S. Pacific Defense system, dismantled in 1992.] Communist guerrillas—the New People's Army—are spirited. Muslims have fought a secessionist war in Mindanao. Most of the people are Malay in origin, but there are more than 75 ethnolinguistic groups. All but 5 percent of the population live on the

11 largest islands. Some people like the Tasadays live so remotely, they have only recently been discovered, and disturbed, by the outside world. About 75 indigenous tongues, including eight major ones, are spoken. The official one is Tagalog. (295–296)

Aside from some factual errors, this geographer has drastically selected the classic markers of underdevelopment. What is striking here is the configuration of a social formation disintegrated by class, language, ideology, religion, and colonial depredations. The Philippines seems vibrant with differences—at the price of the suffering of the majority of citizens.

In most anthropological accounts, the two main unifying features of the Philippine formation are the racial type (Mongoloid) and the Austronesian, or Malayo-Polynesian, language family. In general, the majority is supposed to share the "lowland peasant culture," a Malay culture characterized by settlement patterns determined by geography and by the two major religions: Christianity and Islam. Such differences are said to come "from the specific ways ethnolinguistic groups adapted to their particular environment over long periods of time, the varying impact of outside influences . . . and the degree of their involvement in national affairs" (Roxas-Lim 1996, 617). In the 1960s, an American political scientist commented that despite the efforts of the government's "Commission on National Integration," "for all practical purposes, the non-christians are excluded from the designation 'Filipino' " (Grossholtz 1964, 53).

In this static tabulation of determining factors that supposedly explain cultural pluralism, the classic stress on objective conditions (settlement and subsistence patterns) is supplemented with the standard reference to kinship, sociopolitical institutions, and religion or belief systems. The status quo becomes reified when this ethnographic scheme erases the historical process contoured and complicated by group antagonisms: "Sociopolitical institutions were focused on kin and village groups until the establishment of the central government. However, contemporary national institutions are weak and splintered; thus greater reliance is placed on mutual support groups through extended kinship ties which are fundamental and are rarely, if ever, transcended even within the framework of governmental and national organizations" (Roxas-Lim 1996, 618). Why kinship becomes paramount in this setup is never really explained except as a consequence of weak governmental and national institutions, which in turn requires explanation. One concludes that in contrast to industrialized urban societies today, a dependent peripheral formation such as the Philippines manifests an extremely uneven, disintegrated surface where heterogeneous, shifting identities and affiliations thrive amid economic and political vortices of strife. Multiculturalism indeed abounds in an unstable, unequal, class-torn society.

One of the theoreticians of the concept of a multicultural society, John Rex (1997), posits a neo-Weberian paradigm centered on the split between public and private domains. This split is analogous to the distinction made by German sociologist Ferdinand Tonnies between *Gemeinschaft* (primary groups revolving around the family, kinship, and ethical relations) and *Gesellschaft* (impersonal bureaucratic and judicial processes in cities). My reservation about this paradigm concerns its occlusion of unequal power/property relations, of which more later.

Rex believes that the ideal of multiculturalism is consonant with equality of opportunity, a basic democratic principle, when a society is unified in the public domain (law, politics, economics) but at the same time encourages diversity in private or communal matters (domestic life, religion, morality). Obviously, this requires the separation of church and state and the nearly total secularization of a citizen's life. When, on the other hand, a society is unitary in the public realm and also enforces unity of cultural practices in the private realm, then we have an assimilationist polity such as France—but not Germany or Japan. Another setup alluded to by Rex, which strikes me as quite problematic, is the U.S. Deep South before the reforms of the civil rights era: Differential rights in the public sphere presumably coexist with homogeneous cultural practices shared by whites and blacks alike—"separate but equal." Finally, the opposite of the ideal multicultural society—almost a parody or ironic mirror image—is the South African apartheid system where differential rights of groups prevail in the public domain together with the law-governed disparate cultural practices of incommensurable nationalities. The *bantustan* phenomenon is the index of such segregation in both public and private domains.

In my view, Rex's argument hinges on the premise that the public domain, defined by the formal equality of individuals (as proclaimed in a republican constitution and Bill of Rights), can coexist with an unconstrained diversity of private/communal groups with their ethnic particularities (morality, religion, kinship network of diasporic cohorts tied to various homelands). But surely Western juridical regulations infringe on and delimit certain practices of marital arrangements and codes/mores of sexuality in ethnic communities. In the United States, for example, cases of Kampuchean ritual sacrifice of animals in church have been brought to court, and the mass media have condemned the beating of children by immigrant parents with a more authoritarian upbringing. Despite such incompatibilities in polities regulated by the welfare state, Rex insists that dialogue and tensions in the multicultural society are an integral part of the civic culture.

I believe that such dialogue and the ostensible equilibrium of everyday life hides the sharp internal contradictions in the multicultural society in which the public domain legitimizes the way that one group exercises hegemony—in both coercive and consensual senses—over others. In this hegemony, the control of land and labor power, its production and reproduction, is key. When we examine the existing conflicts in the Philippines between the Muslims (about six million in Mindanao and Sulu) and the central government, we find Rex's conceptual dualism inadequate. The sheer asymmetry of status and wealth in public life between Muslims and the Filipino elite renders the static distinction between individual and collective untenable.

THE MOROS STRUGGLE

The Muslim situation may be taken as exemplary of the problematic nature of the plural society as historically constituted in the Philippines. While the antagonism between Muslims and Christians dates back to Spanish colonization from 1565 to 1898 and U.S. colonial domination from 1898 to 1946, the present conflict is not religious but fundamentally economic and political. The Spaniards tried to establish theocratic rule over the islands but failed to subdue the Muslims, Igorots, and other aboriginal communities. They believed that the infidels can be pacified only by conquest and conversion.

In contrast, the United States, based not on a tributary but a capitalist mode of production, applied a dual policy of violence and diplomacy. Shaped by the experience of racialized wars against the American Indians, U.S. public opinion considered the Muslims as savages to be disciplined, even though the Bates Treaty of 1899 recognized the Sultan of Sulu as a "protected sovereignty." The Moros of Lanao and other areas mounted fierce resistance to U.S. invasion (witness the Bud Dajo massacre of 1906, in which more than 600 men, women, and children were slain by the U.S. military).

In June 1907, the United States devised the Organic Act for the Moro provinces, which provided for a measure of local autonomy except in the area of customs and forest revenues. Such autonomy, however, did not mean the toleration of practices such as slavery (the American anthropologist Dean Worcester wrote a sustained invective against non-Christian cultures in his report of 1913 titled *Slavery and Peonage in the Philippine Islands*). Religious practices remained untouched, but ethics and family life could not but be affected by universal mass education geared toward individualist competition in entrepreneurial careers and government service. Reflecting on the accomplishments of U.S. "compadre colonialism," Governor General W. Cameron Forbes praised the American forcible imposition of a legal system that dismantled the linkage between public and private in tributary systems. Two decades after the suppression of the Philippine Republic, Forbes (1945) described the feudal customs of the Moros in which we find attention focused on what became notorious typifying markers:

> Left to themselves, the Moros would unquestionably have maintained a system purely feudal in its essence. . . . When a Moro became tired of life he could go *juramentado*. Such a Moro would shave his eyebrows, get blessed by a priest, don a white garment, and rush in to kill as many Christians as he could before meeting his death. . . . The juramentado will steal up toward his intended victims, keeping as much as possible unobserved, until a chance arrived to rush in and start slashing with a cold steel. One Moro was seen to seize the rifle of his opponent and pull the bayonet through himself so as to get near enough to reach his adversary with his kris before dying. (280, 282–283)

Way back when a five-member Peace Commission was appointed by President McKinley to sign the Treaty of Paris, in which Spain ceded the Philippines to the

United States for $20 million, Whitelaw Reid, publisher of the *New York Tribune* and member of the Commission, wrote in his journal that the Philippines "embraced a great variety of races, pure and mixed, including many still in a stage of savagery. . . . A large section of the South was under the control of Mohammedans, who had never been conquered by Spain, and who were believed to be depraved, intractable and piratical" (quoted in A. Ocampo 1998, 236). There could only be one judgment on how to civilize this "depraved" and "intractable" hordes, as witnessed by a rare photo of carnage, the massacre of about 600 men, women, and children at Mt. Dajo in 1906 (reproduced in Zwick 1992, 169).

One would think that after independence, U.S. knowledge of the Filipino Muslims would have progressed far enough to correct if not cancel outright such misleading impressions. But positivist social theory evidently could not move away from the problem of immediacy. It could only set up what Georg Lukács calls a "formal typology of the manifestations of history," taking reified appearance as unmediated truth (Shaw 1975, 73). So we find U.S. structural functionalism deployed in identifying, for example, the idea of *maratabat,* or personal esteem, pride in one's honor or that of kin: "Injury to one's *maratabat* demands revenge, most appropriately in the form of killing" (Chaffee et al. 1969, 55).

We find this repeated in historian David Steinberg's (1986) invidious reference to "sporadic terrorist attacks" launched by the Moro National Liberation Front (MNLF) in the 1980s and in a recent essay by anthropologist Charles O. Frake (1998) titled "Abu Sayyaf: Displays of Violence and the Proliferation of Contested Identities among Philippine Muslims." Like the postmodernist analysis of Philippine violence by Jean-Paul Dumont (1995), in which the depoliticized peasants are blamed for their passivity and the unjust, exploitative social arrangement is acquitted because violence "is informed and constructed by a variety of factors that transcend the *hic et nunc* of its occurrence" (277), Frake locates the explanation for the violence of political groups such as the Abbu Sayyaf in the quest for affirming identity "in the face of deadly indifference" (1998, 51). While such phenomenological and ethnographic investigations yield some interesting insights, they generally tend to mystify, in a stereotypifying manner, the actual if complex historical situation of the Muslim peoples. One symptom of this mystification—a form of symbolic violence unleashed on this collectivity—is the failure of these accounts to include the canonical Islamic paradigm that valorizes the *ummah* or the religious community so necessary in a full and rounded understanding of the quite durable struggles of the Moro peoples for self-determination (Bauzon 1991). A Filipino Muslim scholar, Michael Mastura, asserts that "Muslim minority consciousness made the Filipino Muslims receptive to the argument that it was their obligation to protect and strengthen the *ummah*" (1983, 158).

As for the phenomena of indigenist and fundamentalist trends, we need to historicize and reinscribe these in the world system of uneven development to ascertain their import and full intelligibility. The translation of the Islamic moral universe, of Islam as political and ethical signifier, into intransigent populist discourse (immanent in Abbu Sayyaf's emergence) needs to be contextualized in the dislocation of cultural authenticity and tradition brought about by the operations of global capitalism and its instrumentality, the Philippine neocolonial state (Sayyid 1994). Absent this political economy of religious movements, we succumb to the easy pragmatism of postmodernists such as Frake, Dumont, and other knowledge fabricators of the Moro community.

There is no doubt that the U.S. colonial policy of integration through education, jurisprudence, and contractual business led to the gradual erosion of the datu monopoly on power. But it was the government-sponsored migration of Christian settlers—accelerated by President Ramon Magsaysay's resettlement of the Huks in the 1950s—that exacerbated the land disputes that raged during the entire period of U.S. ascendancy up to the Cold War epoch. The full-scale war between the MNLF and the Marcos dictatorship in the 1970s demonstrates the failure of a liberal-capitalist policy of tolerance via differential incorporation based on ascribed "primordial" lifeways. While Muslim religious rituals and familial customs were allowed, denial of economic opportunities to the majority continued precisely because the patronage system preserved the datu patriarchal regime while neocolonial oligarchic rule upheld predominantly Christian priorities framed within the Cold War strategy of the Western imperial powers.

With the historically oriented MNLF, the category of the Bangsa Moro nationality rather than class or race became the salient marker of contradiction between itself and the Manila-based central government. The MNLF leader Nur Misuari, who eventually accepted political accommodation if not subordination to the comprador–neocolonial oligarchy, at first espoused a militant separatist nationalism. His radical roots in left-wing student activism blended with a sense of an indigenous Moro identity that fused public and private, the personal and the collective. While the MNLF originally derived inspiration from a historical materialist philosophy based on class struggle, the group that splintered from it, the Moro Islamic Liberation Front (MILF), evinces more orthodox leanings; its supporters, according to some reports, are the mainstream World Islamic League and the World Islamic Conference (Noble 1987, 198). A recent Islamic fundamentalist group, the Abbu Sayyaf, is mounting a more formidable challenge to the near monopoly of symbolic and physical violence wielded by the Estrada administration (Frake 1998).

With the pressure from the Islamic Conference of foreign ministers and Libya, the MNLF was finally persuaded to accept a limited form of regional autonomy in September 1996. This agreement seriously compromised its original demand of independence for the Moro nation, a demand now taken up by the MILF. Misuari's Southern Philippines Council for Peace and Development has been transformed again into a battleground between forces defined by ethnic, class, and national allegiances. Multiculturalism's civic ethos of mobile subject positions flourishes in this part of the Philippines.

EPISTEMIC VIOLENCE

Before I move on to survey the situation of the indigenous peoples who at present comprise more than three million people, I want to enter a parenthesis here on the reactionary temper of the U.S. production of knowledge about Filipinos (myself included), Philippine society and culture, and even the future and destiny of the Filipino nation. This expands my critique of American anthropologists earlier and takes up the theme that I broached in chapter 3. The phrase "reactionary temper" would refer to the apologetic mode of recounting/explaining U.S. colonial domination of the Philippines and legitimating its aftermath in the wake of the nationalist resurgence in the 1960s to the 1980s up to the peace talks in the 1990s between the government and the National Democratic Front.

Ever since the advent of the Cold War, U.S. production of knowledge about Filipinos began revising American accountability for underdevelopment and social injustice in their former colony. As mentioned in chapter 3, George Taylor's historic intervention, *The Philippines and the United States* (1964), set the trend for ascribing backwardness and inequality to the Filipinos themselves. David Steinberg and Theodore Friend followed, with the eventual popularizing of such a retrograde neoconservative tendency in Karnow's *In Our Image: American Empire in the Philippines* (1989), which I discussed earlier. The numerous critiques of this book by Michael Salman, Peter Tarr, and others are devastating and, to my mind, incontrovertible: Salient among them is a pertinacious method of reification, positivism (accepting colonial ideology as fact and/or rationale), and a revindication of the imperial "civilizing mission." The term "Orientalism" sums up, for the postmodernist scholar, the inadequacy of this approach derived by Karnow, the vulgarizer of academic lore, from such teachers as Steinberg, Friend, Peter Stanley, and Glenn May. Salman (1991) comments on Karnow's epistemological apparatus:

> Unable to blink the violence [of U.S. military pacification], Karnow reduces its significance by perpetuating the myth of the conquest as inadvertent and adding his own myth of atonement. He contends the United States lacked a "colonial vocation," although the conquest of the Philippines was preceded by centuries of North American experience with conquest, enslavement, genocidal policies, and the general political and social subordination of non-European peoples. (230)

In short, U.S. history before 1898 already displays the *habitus* of hierarchy, subordination, and racializing domination and oppression of people of color, so that it is quite impossible to chronicle the U.S. adventure in the Philippines, including its "Benevolent Assimilation" policy and Taft's slogan of "Filipinos for the Philippines," divorced from that contextual ground or framework of "internal colonialism" tied to the rise of merchant capitalism and the emerging world system of core–periphery inequalities.

An example of U.S. Anglo-Saxon "manifest destiny" may be discerned in the selective application of the U.S. Constitution and statutes on the new subjugated peoples. In 1914, Justice Grant Trent of the Philippine Supreme Court explained this differential treatment:

> With the acquirement of the Philippine Islands a most important change in the territorial policy became necessary. The United States found here a monarchical form of government. The municipal law was for the most part that of Latin Europe. The "habits, traditions, and modes of life of the people were entirely dissimilar to those of continental America." A general and unqualified extension of the Constitution and laws of the United States to these Islands was considered impracticable and tending unnecessarily to disturb the existing order of things. For reasons which it is unnecessary to set forth in this opinion, Congress did not desire that the Philippine Islands should be admitted into the customs union; that the inhabitants of the Philippine Islands should be given the status of citizens of the United States. (quoted in Fernando 1998, 157–158)

Premised on the mission of tutelage announced by President McKinley in his decision to annex the islands, the selective or differential incorporation of the Philippines is symptomatic of that Orientalizing hubris that has, since the early reports of the Civil Commission to the canonical texts of Foreman, Worcester, Cameron Forbes, Hayden, and others, defined the epistemological parameters of scholarship on the Philippines. One genial illustration of this Orientalizing predisposition may be found in Victor Heiser's "knowledge" of Filipinos presented in his memoirs, *An American Doctor's Odyssey* (1936).

About 30 years ago, William Appleman Williams (1971) already explained the contradictory forces that converged in the 1898 Spanish–American War and the conquest of territories overseas. That "expansion for freedom" was implicated in the conception of the world marketplace as part of the frontier that gave the agricultural interests "freedom and prosperity." This domestic colonial majority, the populist farmers and rural producers, conflated economic nationalism with "the ideology of political freedom," articulating the need for "empire in terms of freedom." Williams analyzes the contradictory motivation of these agricultural blocs of interests: "They believed in the interrelationship between expansion and freedom because their conception of expansion and empire could be demonstrated to offer better conditions than European colonialism, as well as because it could be demonstrated that more markets improved their welfare at home" (1971, 126). Thus, the ideology of the capitalist marketplace informs the original thrust for empire, just as it does its belated exponents Karnow, May, and others. The more elaborate description of this "imperial anticolonialism" is found in the first chapter of Williams's classic work *The Tragedy of American Diplomacy* (1962).

The neoconservative ascendancy in the late 1970s and 1980s revitalized pragmatic and atomized empiricism as the normative paradigm of knowledge production. With the overthrow of the Marcos dictatorship in 1986 and a revanchist policy toward Central America and Vietnam, the outlook among academic intellectuals changed. Liberalism adopted a defeatist stance, retreating to empiricism and sociobiological metaphysics. A symptom of this regression, with respect to Philippine area studies, may be perceived in Benedict Anderson's highly influential 1988 article in *New Left Review*, "Cacique Democracy in the Philippines: Origins and Dreams" (reprinted in Anderson 1995).

Anderson's main thesis recapitulates an emergent trend in Philippine studies: The internal structures and institutions of Philippine society, scarcely altered by over half a century of U.S. rule, explains to a large extent the backwardness of Filipino democracy now classified as "cacique democracy." Anderson tries to apply a materialist analysis by locating the source of the distorted development of the country in the Spanish period. The lack of a "substantial criollo hacendado class," the absence of a *lingua franca* that would unite the population, the absence of an intelligentsia, and so on allowed the mestizos (with the help of British and American trading capital) to become the feudal dynastic family of caciques that would dominate society and make deals with the American colonizers. In fact, Anderson thanks McKinley for deciding to annex the islands, thus preventing the country from fragmenting into weak, caudillo-ridden states similar to Venezuela or Ecuador. Anderson also attributes the formation of the Filipino "national oligarchy" to the minuscule bureaucracy the United States set up in the Philippines:

> [T]he American authorities in Manila, once assured of the mestizos' self-interested loyalty to the motherland, created only a minimal civil service, and quickly turned over most of its component positions to the natives . . . up to the end of the American era the civilian machinery of state remained weak and divided. (1995, 12)

This is patently false. Up to the time of the so-called filipinizing governor Harrison, Filipino recalcitrance toward U.S. hegemony never abated. Note the sporadic peasant rebellions throughout the islands. The ferocity of Filipino guerrilla resistance after Aguinaldo retreated and the resolute nationalist temper of the intelligentsia required massive military campaigns of repression, seditious laws, and other coercive measures to ensure peace and order. Anderson admits that "American power depended on military dominance and the tariff," but surely the bureaucratic machinery involved in military campaigns and commercial taxation—not to mention the assiduous pedagogical and educational apparatus at the heart of U.S. ideological disciplining of "hearts and minds"—testifies to a dual policy of violence and manipulation of consent. Hegemonic authority or legitimacy of governance had to be established and sustained by violence and its lawmaking effects.

Anderson's thesis relies on a belief that cannot be sustained: The lack of an American autocratic territorial bureaucracy permitted the Filipino mestizo families to take over—from Quezon and Osmena to Aquino. Anderson even goes to the extreme of claiming that the United States could not succeed in reestablishing the prewar agrarian and political order because of the "severe weakening of the state's capacity for centralized deployment of violence." Omitted from this account is MacArthur's draconian suppression of the Huks and the democratic forces with the help of Roxas, the Magsaysay–Lansdale rehearsal of Vietnam War tactics in the total mobilization against the peasant uprising in the late 1940s and early 1950s, and the Cold War rearming of the Philippine military for over 20 years after the end of World War II and during the Korean War and the Vietnam War. The heyday of Philippine "cacique democracy," 1954 to 1972, witnessed the intensification of U.S. Cold War strategy played out in the Philippines as a springboard for aggression in Korea, Indonesia, Vietnam, and elsewhere.

Anderson's mode of analysis privileges primordial ties of kinship and family so entrenched in the culture-and-psychology school of Frank Lynch and others criticized by Virgilio Enriquez and the proponents of *sikolohiyang Pilipino*. (The absurd limits of psychological speculation applied to grasping the vicissitudes of the revolutionary movement may be illustrated by Benedict Kerkvliet's attack on Sison's personality in the lead essay in Patricio Abinales's volume *The Revolution Falters* [1996].) But this adaptation of Parsonian structural functionalism ignores power relations grounded on property and the political economy of the uneven formation. In particular, it obscures if not hides completely the profound extent of U.S. control of the economic, political, and military institutions that determine elections and the techniques of governance. American electoralism, which presumably disperses power horizontally, for Anderson partly conceals "Spanish caciquism in a geographically fragmented, ethnolinguistically divided, and economically bankrupt polity" (1995, 31). This caciquism signifies inequality and the unjust distribution of resources, rights, and obligations. But does the ritual of periodic elections, "politics in a well-run casino," explain by itself why Aquino, the Cojuangcos, and the entire oligarchy continue to exploit the majority of workers and peasants in the Philippines?

REVISING HISTORY

The resort to primordialism as instanced by the priority placed on kinship and the patrimonial estate—the status group—reflects the attenuation of class politics in the United States and the West in general after the end of the Indo-China War. It signals a return to a kind of fundamentalism both in ethics and social theory. Marx's guiding concepts of political economy and the articulation of the modes of production are replaced by Max Weber's hermeneutics of the meaning of action. Weber's stress on status and estates over against class gives legitimacy to the primacy of ethnicity, language, and religion in the sociological analysis of conflicts, while his stress on rationality, especially the instrumental organizing of means to ends, allows for the refunctioning of concepts of patronage and clientelism. The recourse to primordialism (family, ethnic bonds, and so on) leads to mystification of affects, a desocializing of bonding or identity formation. In this context, the use of primordialism betokens a bankrupt tendency toward metaphysics and obscurantism: "taking phenomena that are simply 'already existing' and 'persistent' and reifying and mystifying them into things that are 'natural,' 'spiritual,' and 'have always existed and always will' (Eller and Coughlan 1996, 50). Primordial factors suited a utilitarian and pragmatic ethos in a reductive simplification of complex social problems (see Kolakowski 1968).

The typology of "cacique democracy" offered by Anderson to explain the sameness and cyclic repetition in Philippine history clearly shifts the causal judgment to the Filipinos themselves, now that the country is nominally independent. Unlike Raymond Bonner's exposure of Washington's complicity with authoritarian excesses in *Waltzing with a Dictator* (1987), Anderson downplays U.S. interventionism in favor of the inertia of tradition and primordial sentiments. Weber's notion of patrimonialism in connection with the discretionary exercise of power, with prebendal domination and arbitrary will, serves as the framework of intelligibility for the peculiarities of Philippine "democracy." The term "cacique" evokes certainly a precapitalist, feudal, or what Samir Amin calls "tributary" social formation, but Anderson firmly locates it within the framework of modern global capitalism. Instead of being a neutral, value-free category, "cacique democracy" becomes a stigmatizing mark of the Philippine sociopolitical formation in which the heritage of Spanish colonialism outweighs the legacy of U.S. imperial rule.

One measures the distance between Anderson's neo-Weberian diagnosis and the potency of concrete historical materialist analysis by comparing his essay with Jonathan Fast's (1973) commentary "Imperialism and Bourgeois Dictatorship in the Philippines." The disparity may be explained by the altered political milieu of the late 1960s and early 1970s and that of the 1980s, from the renaissance of Marxism and its subsequent displacement by a seductive but compromised social democracy and the blandishments of outright neoconservatism.

Social contextualization of knowledge production does not elucidate everything, but I think it is a necessary initial point of departure for evaluation of research programs and results. The volume *Philippine Colonial Democracy*, edited by Ruby Paredes (1988), finds its condition of possibility in the years immediately before and after the collapse of Marcos's authoritarian rule. Unlike Anderson, the contributors to the volume (which include the avowed enemy of Filipino nationalist historians, Glenn May) have not completely erased U.S. complicity in the making of the Philippine state and its institutions. In fact, the editor points to the ambivalent attitude of the Filipino elite in its response to U.S. intentions during the 1986 crisis as part of a historical legacy of U.S. colonialism. Nonetheless, the theoretical framework here is the patron–client one supposedly given a novel twist, novel in the sense that the relation is reversible and not one-sided. In fact, the clientelist scheme is claimed to be reciprocal:

Denied equality with Americans under law, Filipino leaders adopted tactics of guile and manipulation to win from American patrons political concessions they needed to maintain the loyalty of their Filipino clients. Since American colonials were ambitious careerists, they needed Filipino cooperation to give them the aura of administrative success necessary for further advancement. This symbiosis of interests produced a complex pattern of patron-client interactions. A Filipino politician in Manila could be simultaneously patron and client to a variety of American colonials, just as an American official could find himself promoting Filipino inferiors and cultivating Filipino superiors. (Paredes 1988, 6)

This argument is disingenuous, to say the least. In the first place, the Filipino elite cannot be so simply defined as genuine representatives of the Filipino masses whose collective interests they were supposed to articulate. Second, concessions given by the American colonial administrators to these selected Filipinos who used "rhetorical militance" before their mass clientele and obsequiousness to their masters cannot be so one-dimensionally interpreted as a sign of equal treatment. And third, this historical account of Filipino shrewdness and American managerial cunning further confirms instead of neutralizes the asymmetrical relation between the colonial subject and the metropolitan master. It does not provide "the middle ground between the colonial chronicles of civilization's proconsuls and the nationalist epics of heroic resistance." On the contrary, it apologizes for the failure of the United States in conforming to its proclaimed vocation of civilizing the natives, a failure due not to American racist arrogance and commercial greed but to Filipino ineptitude and docility. This is basically a rehearsal of Karnow's program to rehabilitate the U.S. colonial record in the Philippines and, by implication, in Vietnam, Puerto Rico, and its "internal colonies."

There seems to be an ill-concealed attempt here to establish Filipino–American relations during the colonial period as one characterized by reciprocity and mutual exchange—the shadow of Marcel Mauss and his notion of the gift as the complex system of exchanges between groups by means of which undivided (prestate) societies functioned. The gift is "the primitive way of achieving the peace that in civil society is secured by the State." But in modern societies, under the fetishized social relations of capitalism, relations are no longer reciprocal, even though the ideology of reciprocity is celebrated, as in "a fair day's work for a fair day's pay" (Hulme 1992, 330). In a situation of colonialism, client–patron relationship denotes absence of reciprocity. It is not a middle ground or compromise between colonial tyranny and nationalist heroics. One of the best demonstrations of this thesis is found in Roxanne Lynn Doty's book *Imperial Encounters* (1996),where U.S. discourse on the Philippines, particularly at the height of the Cold War, is deconstructed as a new version of the imperial "civilizing mission" dating back to the Open Door Notes of 1899–1900 (see Patterson 1997).

Alfred McCoy, another expert on Filipino society and politics, is one of the contributors to the volume *Philippine Colonial Democracy*. In his contribution to a 1991 volume of essays, *From Marcos to Aquino: Local Perspectives on Political Transition in the Philippines* (Kerkvliet and Mojares 1991), McCoy rejects the model of localized social equilibrium used to produce knowledge of Philippine society. He criticizes Kerkvliet's reliance on the patron–client paradigm (used by Lynch, Lande, and many Filipinologists) that implies reciprocity, not compulsion, between the propertied classes and the propertyless. McCoy notes that "much of Western writing often describes Philippine politics in terms of patron–client ties, a pattern of reciprocal exchange between superiors and inferiors that maintains society in a state of equilibrium" (1991, 106). Here we encounter perhaps the beginning of a change in mainstream knowledge production about Filipinos/the Philippines, its methodology and epistemic foundations. But no luck. It turns out that McCoy is aiming for a reconciliation of conflict theory with clientelism since he cannot explain otherwise why the planters, who use a mix of coercion and patronage to stay in power, succeeded in restoring the status quo before Marcos during the Aquino regime. Crude empiricism takes over, displacing insight into structures and material determinants of power, abandoning any pretense to define the nexus of causal forces that condition the alternation of violence and acquiescence.

This empiricist pragmatism is inflected into an eclectic aggregation of data in the recent work of scholars studying the weakening of the revolutionary movement in the 1990s. If you examine Rosanne Rutten's contribution to the previously mentioned Abinales volume, you will confront a narrow empiricist obsession with microprocesses of political mobilization that conflates the "how" and "why," setting aside the whole history of agrarian/land agitation and U.S. colonial complicity with the preservation of the tenancy system detailed in numerous works, among them James Putzel's *A Captive Land* (1992) and James K. Boyce's *The Philippines: The Political Economy of Growth and Impoverishment in the Marcos Era* (1993). The crippling limitation of research confined to one hacienda for10 months of fieldwork in Negros Occidental is obvious in the uncritical acceptance by a white Western scholar of the statements by native informants, the indiscriminate lumping of evidence taken from various participants in the struggle, and the deliberate bracketing of U.S. intervention in Marcos's national security state throughout the period studied.

History disappears, displaced by snapshots of a tragicomic narrative that reaffirms a cyclic tendency in social life. What is striking is Rutten's claim to value-free neutral description of motives and reasons for the conduct of social actors and the reduction of the complex field of political forces to a matter of subalterns struggling for survival—the basic means–ends instrumentalist approach prized by positivist technocrats of the Huntington/Rostow school. In the massive catalog of Filipino leftist errors and mistakes presented by the commentators in Abinales's volume, the positivist innocence of ideology, in particular anticommunist liberal ideology that has grounded American scholarship on the Philippines, flourishes. Scarcely is there any analysis of the peculiar nature of the "postcolonial," or what Teodor Shanin (1982) calls "overdeveloped," state; the politics of global dependency; the class nature of "developing" societies; and the complex character of the state and its apparatus in an uneven, disarticulated social formation. Nor is the problematic of the overarching metanarrative of "modernization" ever addressed (see Luke 1990). This discursive tradition of empiricist positivism endures, as in recent works by Brian Linn, David Timberman, and Carl Lande. Its resonance vitiates even revisionist stances, manifest when a reflexive practitioner of postmodernist anthropology such as Raul Pertierra critiques classical anthropology but links racism and nationalism as reifications of the cultural and the social, devoid of historical contexts and the differentiated totality in which such discourses and practices are inscribed.

Recently, in the context of the centenary of the Philippine revolution of 1896–1898, the historian Glenn May (1996) issued his debunking of the revolutionary plebeian Andres Bonifacio together with his all-round condemnation of Filipino historians as "mythmakers," if not outright liars. In effect, May practically indicts all Filipino intellectuals as frauds and impostors. On the surface, the professor claims that he is not trying to attack the accomplishments of Bonifacio or his stature; rather, he is trying to expose the alleged shenanigans and fraud of scholars such as Epifanio de los Santos, Agoncillo, and others. True enough, except that his doubts and suspicions about the authenticity of certain documents ascribed to Bonifacio, his reservations about the honesty and competence of Filipino historians, and of course his view about the total gullibility of the Filipino public (not only the educated intelligentsia but also the ordinary folk) accumulate a suasive force that questions not only the hermeneutic skills of certain individuals but also the moral character and integrity of a whole people. If Filipinos like the esteemed historians whom May accuses are wanting in integrity and honesty, then Bonifacio turns out to be a product of liars and forgers and the whole society as accomplices and accessories to the fraud.

We thus owe May this unsolicited service of setting us marching along the straight course of historical veracity. But is the professor himself a neutral value-free agent of empirical value-free objectivity? Is his choice of investigating the whole affair a professional one, or is it a program motivated by more than personal reasons or professional interests? The conflicted and contentious relation between a neocolony and the imperial power can be dismissed by May, but it will not ignore him. So then we realize that the "special relation" of the Philippines and the United States that persisted smoothly through the Cold War period and survived the days of the February 1986 "people power" uprising is being critically examined again in the midst of a resurgent revolutionary development.

May's performance is symptomatic of a general outlook among American experts on the Philippines, whom I call "Filipinologists," that the Philippines needs to be reinscribed in a geopolitical post–Cold War cartography that divides the world into the civilized North and the barbaric South, following Samuel Huntington's notorious thesis on the "clash of civilizations." In this discourse, culture becomes the key to explaining social problems and nation-state subordination. In this culturalist axiomatic, history is rearticulated toward a racialized direction subtending a hierarchy of powers/civilizations. Overall, the anniversary of the defeat of the first Philippine Republic by the United States at the turn of the twentieth century affords a fortuitous if shameful venue for reviving a tarnished Orientalizing scholarship that testifies less to the contentious nexus of Philippine–American transactions than to the revanchist and hegemonic goals of U.S. imperial power.

Ideas are never innocent of practical consequences, if one may repeat a platitude. One may propose here that future researchers consign the patron–client cliché to the dustbin and deploy instead such theoretical concepts as "counter-revolution" proposed by Arno Mayer, the "authoritarian state in peripheral societies" suggested by Clive Thomas, and "tributary formation" elaborated by Samir Amin for a sharper and more historically specific analysis of developments in Philippine society.

We are already familiar with world-systems theory and the Gramscian adaptation of hegemony to international relations (Gill 1993). What is needed is the dialectical understanding of how current theories as well as traditional approaches to Filipino society and experience have a history and genealogy imbricated with the West's "civilizing mission," U.S. "exceptionalism" and its global crusade against communism, and the contemporary globalizing trend of transnational corporations, mediated by the International Monetary Fund/World Bank, the General Agreement on Tariffs and Trade (GATT), the World Trade Organization (WTO), and other agencies. And, most crucially, we need to demonstrate concretely how the practical consequences of such theories spell the fates not only of the scholars and researchers themselves but also of millions of peoples in both sides, past and future, of the geopolitical arena.

REMEMBERING THE FUTURE

I turn now to the situation of the indigenous communities, a heterogeneous category impossible to reduce to the textbook stereotype of "cultural minority," to use the bureaucratic and administrative rubric.

The Microsoft *Encarta Encyclopedia,* accessed by millions, propagates the textbook cliché of Christianized Malays as comprising the bulk of the population (approximately 75 million today), with mestizos (mixed Filipinos with white or Chinese descent) forming a small but economically and politically significant minority. I might interject here that the elevation of Corazon Cojuangco Aquino to the presidency (1986–1992) foregrounded the immense leap in status and prestige of Filipinos of Chinese descent since the colonial days, when they were treated as pariahs and outcasts (Corpuz 1965).

Obscured in the conventional description of the Filipino nationality are the indigenous or tribal Filipinos whom I referred to at the outset. They number more than four million, with over 40 ethnolinguistic groups, inhabiting mineral-rich lands all over the archipelago. While usually classified as uplanders engaged in slash-and-burn cultivation, the tribal communities are as variegated as the lowlander Christians whose form of life has been the model for Filipino national identity. Objects of exoticizing spectacle and prophylactic official investigation from the time that they were displayed in the St. Louis Exposition of 1904, these aboriginal peoples have been severely victimized by government agencies, among them the notorious Presidential Assistance on National Minorities (PANAMIN), whose administrator Manuel Elizalde invented the Tasaday hoax (for an example of reifying propaganda, see Reyes 1980). In the last 15 years, the term "Lumad" (meaning "grown from the place," autochthonous) has emerged to characterize the 18 ethnic groups native to Mindanao who have begun an organized campaign to oppose the capture and control of their resources by the expansive comprador state in the service of transnational corporations (Duhaylungsod and Hyndman 1997).

As with the Moros, the indigenous groups, such as the Igorots, Tingguians, Dumagats, T'Bolis, and others, have been differentially incorporated in the colonial polity under foreign rule and subsequently in the neocolonial republic. The historian William Henry Scott (1993) has pointed out that the Igorots became a "cultural minority" on account of 350 years of resistance against foreign aggression. Having resisted assimilation and preserved their ethnic distinctiveness, they were forced during the Marcos period to submit to a nation-building agenda couched in the fascist slogan "*Isang lahi, isang bansa, isang tadhana*—One race, one nation, one destiny" (Scott 1982, 28). Their armed guerrilla resistance, committed to preserving their cultural integrity and insuring the survival of the community, continues to this day.

United States colonial rule established the Bureau of Non-Christian Tribes in 1901 to integrate ethnic minorities into the polity (Chaffee 1969). In general, a tacit policy of assimilation through education and law to promote business defined the subaltern role of the indigenous peoples throughout the twentieth century. Decisive in this process is the institution of the market (chiefly of labor and natural resources), which originated from U.S. colonial law. The colonial administration "granted private land titles to large owners, placed all undeclared land under state ownership, opened such land to exploration, occupation and purchase by citizens of the United States and the Philippines" (Swenson 1987, 200). Indigenous groups were excluded from public parks, forest reserves, and other lands sold by the Philippine government to settlers, foreign investors, and crony capitalists. More flagrantly during the Marcos regime with its export-oriented development program, the tribal lands were opened to mining and logging concessions, development projects such as the World Bank–funded Chico River Basin Dam, as well as the plantation agriculture of foreign corporations attracted by tax incentives and the absence of environmental protection laws (Komite ng Sambayanang Pilipino 1980; Anti-Slavery Society 1983).

We should also add here the corollary attempt to enforce "primitivism" on the reservations where indigenous communities have been assigned. Such commodifying strategies of exploiting the glamor of multiculturalism for tourist/media consumption definitely intrude into the private, communal domain. They undermined the peoples' right to survival and promotion of their cultural integrity. Given their role as suppliers of cheap labor and of bodies destined for resettlement (a deliberate colonial/neocolonial policy to alienate the tribal lands), the struggles of this "fourth world" coincide with those of the masses of oppressed peasants, workers, women, youth, and middle strata, as well as seven million OCWs abroad, for social justice and popular democracy.

In the 1950s, social scientists located the problem of the "cultural minorities" as one of acculturation, a euphemism for assimilation or absorption into the majority culture. Of all the ethnic groups, the Chinese are held to have successfully acculturated to the point where they are losing their identity. Most academic experts criticize the Muslims, Igorots, and other indigenes as groups lacking sophistication in the manipulation of the legal–commercial culture, unlike the Chinese. Most Filipinos are urged to learn the rules of liberal democracy, stop criticizing the presence of U.S. airbases, and persevere in the general "loyalty to Marilyn Monroe" (Espiritu and Hunt 1964, 11). In essence, according to these experts, the problem inheres in the difference between a barter economy practiced by the indigenous groups and the monetary culture of the larger, "civilized" society. Clearly, the paradigm of modernization and developmentalism predicated on the superiority of Western political and economic institutions determined then, and continues to influence, the instrumentalizing technologies and policy implications offered by those who claim to be authorities on the cultural diversity of the Philippines.

Such fractious diversity of ethnolinguistic groups has led to the notion of a self-destructive Filipino nation that Karnow has propagated in his notorious apology for U.S. imperialism, *In Our Image: American Empire in the Philippines* (1989). Meanwhile, David Steinberg (1982) has taught the American public that the Philippines is "a plural society" not so much because of colonial divide-and-rule tactics or policies of resettlement and marginalization but because of the "reality of the centrifugal, noncohesive facts of life" (18). In fact, Steinberg adds, the pluralism of the Filipino oligarchy overshadows the class disparities in the general population.

In the midst of the centennial of the Philippine revolution against Spain in 1896–1898, we need to pose the question whether the unity of the Filipino nation originally postulated by the revolutionary Malolos Congress of 1898 has been achieved on the bodies of Muslims, Igorots, Chinese, and other ethnic communities. The legacy of Jose Rizal, the Filipino national hero, to the Asian renaissance, according to the Indonesian scholar Adriana Elisabeth (1998) is "cultural rebirth and empowerment" (5). Whatever its European derivation, nationhood, racially or ethnically diverse, was then conceived by the *ilustrado* nationalists as an organic unity with one soul (*kaluluwa*), one mind (*isip*), and one heart (*puso*), a oneness founded on the security of the nation (*bansa*) (Bauzon 1991). In the postindependence days, the Filipino nation was analyzed in terms of theoretical models, such as the minority/majority and rural/urban dichotomy, Tonnies's *Gemeinschaft* and *Gesellschaft*, and most frequently as a society governed by the patron–client relation, reciprocity, dyadic network, and so on. American experts have often deployed a structural-functionalist method that cloaks the ideological dicta of the dominant classes with scientist value-free aura, evident in statements such as that the Philippines is "a conservative, capitalist society in which the value of private property is cherished and the importance of wealth is stressed" (Steinberg 1986, 34). This functionalist approach has served invariably to legitimize the socioeconomic stratification of the status quo, with cultural difference utilized to explain the rationality of the unequal distribution of resources and exercise of power. Despite opposite trends, sociologists concur in ascribing to Filipinos the tendency to "stress tradition, authority, the importance of the group rather than the individual, shame rather than guilt, the particularistic rather than the universal, and the acceptance of fate rather than the demand to remake the world" (Hunt et al. 1963, 58).

What is missing in the conventional doctrine of functionalist and empiricist scholars is the historical context of social life. We miss the dynamics of conflict and the intentionality of contradictions across nationality, gender, race, class, sexuality, locations, and so on. There is no appreciation of the grounding in lived and remembered experience of various cultural styles or ethos, of the life forms and ensemble of practices in which the agency of the interacting collectives becomes paramount. Cultures cannot be isolated from the shaping of history and the conflicts of social classes and groups. When social inquiry privileges the axiom of acquisitive individualism and ignores the problem of hegemony—in Gramsci's sense, domination and intellectual–moral leadership of a historic social bloc—then multiculturalism degenerates into romantic hypostatization of cultures as flower gardens frozen in time. Postmodern relativism and neopragmatism may have fostered the version of multiculturalism that denies coevalness and reinforces the temporal distancing found in all Eurocentric "civilizing missions"(Fabian 1983). This may explain the recurrent resort to the fetishizing of national character and the allochronic taxonomy of traits that accompany it in the disciplinary research into non-Western societies. We can diagnose this research strategy as a symptom of the profound alienation that afflicts the observer/expert.

On the question of hegemony, we need to be reminded of the lesson of World War II and the attempt to impose the "Oriental traditions of humanity and morals" by bayonet. In 1942, the Marquis Yorisada Tokugawa, adviser to the Japanese Military Administration in the Philippines, came to Manila to launch a "cultural campaign" to replace Anglo-American materialism and individualism with a "Co-Prosperity Sphere. . . . founded on cultural ties and affinities" (Gosiengfiao 1983, 238). The attempt ended in unprecedented barbarism, the destruction of cities and entire communities, and incommensurable suffering for millions.

"Divide and rule" remains the unbeatable strategy for the party of civilization. A native of the Marianas Islands, Chailang Palacios describes "the colonization of our Pacific Islands": "When white nations [Spaniards, Germans] come to conquer us, to colonize us, they divide us. . . . Right after the war, the Americans came, like the missionaries, in the name of God, saying, 'We are here to Christianize you, to help you love one another, be in peace.' We still have the Bible while the missionaries and their white governments have all the land" (1993, 400). At the turn of the twentieth century, Mark Twain expressed that eloquent sentiment of outrage that I quoted in chapter 3 and that would be shared by victims of the Holocaust; the carnage in Vietnam, Guatemala, and El Salvador; and other horrendous scenes of conquest. What alternative future awaits their descendants? If the peoples of the Pacific Rim, 70 million Filipinos included, decide finally to do away with the myth of Manifest Destiny, what normative standards and goals will they have to forge in order to construct an egalitarian and just society rid of ethnic and racial hatreds?

We return to the vexed and complicated interaction of political economy and culture. In a famous exchange of views on multiculturalism, Charles Taylor, Jurgen Habermas, and others rehearsed the pros and cons of the politics of recognition of group identities vis-à-vis the primacy of individual autonomy that informs the "common culture" of most Western nation-states. The editor of this book of exchanges on multiculturalism concluded that despite differences, all the views converged on the belief that "some form of constitutional democracy may offer such a politics, based not on class, race, ethnicity, gender, or nationality, but rather on a democratic citizenship of equal liberties, opportunities, and responsibilities for individuals" (Gutmann 1994, xi–xii). What is deeply problematic here is not the polarity of public and private domains that I discussed at the start; rather, it is the use of the individual citizen as an optic or a measure of value, the valorization of the individual detached from the web of social relations that enable any subject to exercise transformative agency. It is here that we should heed this warning concerning the danger of Establishment multiculturalism: "Multiculturalism is based on a construction of community through a celebration and fossilization of differences" (Castles et al. 1996, 365). With the intensifying commodification of ethnic particularisms, the multicultural spectacle now operates as the authentic "cultural logic of multinational or global capitalism" (Zizek 1997, 44).

What is ultimately at stake in this debate? When we talk of the ideal of multiculturalism in enabling social change, the question of leadership—of hegemony as a directive force uniting individuals as groups or collectivities—cannot be shirked, particularly if we assume that civil society in liberal democracies is the site where the power of capital is articulated with conscious effectivity, where cultural action or the production of meanings and affects takes place. In this context, the government or state can act as the organizer of consensus and the site where ideological struggle transpires. Bourgeois hegemony in civil society (i.e., the ideological subordination of the masses to the bourgeoisie instead of simple coercive domination) enables the propertied class to control the state; "it is the cultural ascendancy of the ruling class that essentially ensures the stability of the capitalist order" (Anderson 1976/1977, 26), such cultural–ideological supremacy mediated by various compromises being equivalent to the consent of the ruled. Only when we factor in this historic process of the struggle for hegemony (and, by extension, for state power) among groups can we really begin a substantive discussion on the cognitive and pedagogical value of multiculturalism for "third world" societies where, in most cases, the violence of the neocolonial state often supervenes over a polymorphous civil society characterized by ceaseless antagonisms across class, gender, nationality, religion, locality, kinship, and so on. There is no substitute for political choices and resolutions. Only within the totality of sociohistorical determinations does culture then acquire its proper valence and efficacy in the complex plots of historical transformation. It is also within the framework of this complex and constantly changing totality that a just and accurate reappraisal of the actual historical relations between the Philippines and the United States can be initiated for the first time.

Appendix: Writing and the Asian Diaspora

Interview with E. San Juan, Jr.

Joon Park

1. How do we go about classifying Asian American literature? Are there issues or themes that the literature must focus upon. For example, Ishiguro (a Japanese native) wrote Remains of the Day. *Should that be classified as Japanese–English literature?*

For all "minority" writers, language is a political question. While the linguistic base for Asian American writers remains American English, the literary mode is constantly being modified. Ishiguro's work is, in my view, legitimately part of a literature written in an "english" that is undergoing global changes. It's part of a diasporic literature written in English by a writer of Japanese ancestry domiciled in the U.K., dealing with experiences in the U.K. Salman Rushdie's work, although it focuses on the histories of India or Pakistan, is also part of this diasporic literature which links times, spaces, and so on.

Neither subject matter nor medium alone can dictate the criteria for classification. But why classify? We need to ask the reasons for this impulse to "divide and master."

2. What type of things do you discern when you merit "good" Asian American literature? (Perhaps I'm making too many structuralist assumptions here.)

"Good" is a term that postmodernists (and I am not one) have prohibited as not "politically correct." However, I think writing that reflects—of course in highly mediated ways—the histories of various Asian communities, their complex interaction with the dominant society, their individual predicaments and prospects, would be useful for students of color who need to understand where they're coming from, what kind of alliances they need, and especially where they want to go.

This is one way of exploring its pedagogical function in terms of reconfiguring "identity politics." This recurrent "identity" crisis is a product of a system that enunciates differences into hierarchies of race, gender, class, and so on.

I think Asian American writing needs to contribute to the radical transformation of consciousness and, by implication, social practices in a racist patriarchal system. There's no particular subject, theme, or style that can be privileged for this purpose because the situations of readers and writers are contingent and infinitely diverse. What's important is to historicize both the reading and the writing situation.

3. What types of approaches should a reader take when reading Asian American literature, if there is one. For example, Asian American literature often focuses on the issue of ethnic identity, and the internal contestation of the author usually becomes apparent. Should we pay closer attention to authorial intention?

I would propose a historical-materialist approach. The parameters of the act of communication should be taken into account: author, reader, circumstance, various subtending forces, and so on. Authorial intention is only one of the aspects that can serve as a stimulating point of departure, although, as D. H. Lawrence warned us, trust the tale, not the teller.

The reason why the question of ethnic identity comes up in "ethnic" writing is, I think, a function of the exclusion, marginalization, segregation, and segmentation of these nonwhite communities enforced by the racializing state and its cultural apparatuses—including all kinds of communicative action.

Of course, today, with the emergence of white studies, Norman Mailer can claim to be an ethnic writer, and the entire hegemonic corpus of American literature can be presented as multicultural and ethnically diverse. But then one begins to be suspicious of this free-market notion of multiculturalism.

4. Who are the great Asian American writers, and what can we learn from them? What Asian American writers do you believe should be in the canon but are not?

I am not in the business of setting up canons, like Henry Louis Gates and company. This is necessarily a collective enterprise, whatever the individual preferences of the canon-makers. It's a dialectic between tradition and the "others" that it excludes.

Canons are formed by institutional practices of reading and writing usually determined by the nature of the struggle between the hegemonic power and the forces resisting it. No single individual makes up the canon of legitimate and authorized texts. Often it is a compromise between residual, dominant, and emergent social forces contesting the ideological–cultural terrain in any historical period.

In my teaching practice I usually choose texts that can address the historical issues and problems of the different communities, in particular how the U.S. racial and gendered system acted on them, their variegated responses, and so on. I have no problem teaching the "canonical" writers Maxine Hong Kingston, Toshio Mori, Joy Kogawa, Carlos Bulosan, Hisaye Yamamoto, Bharati Mukherjee—I particularly like Kim Ronyoung's *Clay Walls*, a major text now displaced by the favorite of postmodernists, Theresa Cha's *Dictee*. I find Frank Chin's plays and novels extremely useful side by side with Fae Ng's *Bone* or even Amy Tan's bestsellers.

Critical voices are just emerging from the Filipino community, younger contemporaries of Jessica Hagedorn like R. Zamora Linmark, Nick Carbo, and Eileen Tabios. I also find *M Butterfly* by David Henry Hwang useful in introducing the "orientalizing" of Asian bodies, especially when juxtaposed with *Miss Saigon*, the recent reincarnation of the Puccini archetype.

But again this has to be placed within a historical field—such as the one outlined skillfully by Glenn Omatsu in *The State of Asian America*. Omatsu's "historical field" refers to the 1980–1990 period when Asian American neoconservatives, primarily in California but also elsewhere, changed the hitherto defensive or marginalized position of Asian Americans and began to be political players or actors while maintaining the old traditional patriarchal order, the "orientalist" logic of Western power, in the community. Omatsu's essay is rich in describing these complex changes in which white supremacy continues to exoticize Asian bodies while allowing multiculturalism or ethnic difference within policed, safe limits—in particular, within the "model minority" framework of utilitarian individualism.

With the post-1965 contingent of U.S.-based Filipinos, a new generation of Filipino scholars and critics are emerging (I can only mention a few like Theo Gonsalves, Neferti Tadiar, Melinda de Jesus, and Jorshinelle Sonza) who will participate in the revision of a multitude of reading lists that will eventually constitute the canon. It's time Filipinos are heard and paid attention to. Their innovativeness resides not in their diverse personal idioms and styles; rather, it inheres in their critical vision of the global material conditions that link the Philippine crisis with the vicissitudes of U.S. transnational capitalism and the alienation/ reification that characterizes all cultural practices in this society.

Having had the "privilege" of being the most violently subjugated group of Asians in the Pacific Rim by U.S. power, Filipinos may also have some unique insights into the nature of this experience. They may be able to register the new changes going on in U.S.–Philippine relations and in the Pacific Rim that may contradict the neoconservative wisdom expressed, say, in Samuel Huntington's thesis of the war of civilizations and the need to preserve U.S. Western purity. And this has profound implications not only for Asian Pacific Americans but for the entire society.

6. What makes Asian American literature distinct from other "minority" literature?

Asian American literature is distinctive, say, from African American and Chicano literature only in the way U.S. imperial power impinged on the homelands of the various groups and in the way each group was incorporated into the U.S. racial formation. That is why one cannot homogenize all of the texts as "Asian American" in much the same way you can more or less take black literature from the slave narratives and Frederick Douglass to Richard Wright and Toni Morrison as one distinct continuous body. Not Asian American writing. For one, the experiences of colonization of Filipinos and, in another way, of Vietnamese, Kampucheans, and Laotians would set them apart from the Chinese, Japanese, and Koreans.

No doubt there are similarities, affinities, and commonalities that these cultures have in responding to the racial state; we can point them out and learn from them lessons in organizing coalitions, alliances, and so on. Much more instructive and catalyzing are the differences due to specific historical conditions.

7. What do you remember about the Philippines when you were there? Are there certain books that recapitulate this experience?

The Philippines in the 1950s, when I was in the university, was a neocolony of the United States, dependent economically, politically, and culturally. Cold War McCarthyism in its local version suppressed dissent and critical thinking throughout the society.

The centennial of the Philippine Revolution and the Filipino–American War (1899–1902) that began with the annexation of the Philippines by the United States in 1898 should remind everyone that of all the Asian countries, the Philippines was the only one subjected to enormous violence and ideological pacification by the entire state machinery of the United States. One can probably say the same thing about Indo-China—metaphorically speaking, we Filipinos share the existential predicament of the "boat people"—but, as I say this, over seven million Filipino "Overseas Contract Workers" are now virtually refugees so that our diaspora, an unprecedented historic development, rearticulates the "immigrant" paradigm in a way that reveals the nature of globalized, flexible capitalism in late modernity.

The Cold War defined my education: We learned New Criticism, idolized Ernest Hemingway and Robert Penn Warren, rejected socialist or even realist writing, shunned vulgar politics and social problems, and so on.

Meanwhile, the U.S.-supported Filipino ruling elite suppressed the majority of Filipinos who were unlettered peasants and workers; corruption continued and worsened, class inequalities sharpened, and poverty and oppression were deemed "natural" and eternal, thanks to the indoctrination of the Church, Hollywood, and U.S. mass media. But the resistance shown by the Huk uprising in the 1940s and 1950s smoldered and caught fire in the late 1960s and early 1970s with student youth revolts and the rise of the New People's Army. When I was a student at the University of the Philippines, I participated in the nationalist movement led by Claro Recto and Lorenzo Tañada.

With this background, when I came to this country in 1960, the writings of Bulosan (which I discovered late in 1965 when I began teaching at the University of California, Davis) affected me in a powerful way. I had read Villa, Bienvenido Santos, and others, but only Bulosan was able to address those experiences and conditions that linked the Philippines and the United States. Filipinos subsisted in what Paulo Freire called the "culture of silence" until the anti–martial law movement in the 1960s afforded space for Filipinos born here to participate in acts of transgression and rebellion.

Let me interpolate something about Freire here. Freire, the Brazilian revolutionary educator, described the culture of the impoverished peasants in Brazil—and by implication of the Third World—as one that is distinguished by "silence." That doesn't mean that unlettered peasants couldn't speak, are passive, mute, and so on.

The plight of the "silent" victims stems from historical, man-made circumstances. The "hewers of wood and drawers of water," to use a cliché, have been deprived of the weapon of words, the "print capitalism" Benedict Anderson considered as essential to the birth of nationalist consciousness, so that no matter how versatile and sharp their oral communication might be, the Western imperial system, or the knowledge/production of instrumental rationality, consigned them to "silence."

Through his method of generative themes in literacy education, Freire was able to make that "silence" speak in a language that accompanies the conscious practice of subalterns attempting to transform life conditions. Freire was challenged by the fact that the resources of peasants and workers in the Third World were being channeled to reinforce their oppression rather than mobilized for their own good.

So the "silence" of the "wretched of the earth," to use Frantz Fanon's phrase, is perhaps louder and more articulate than the tired gibberish of consumerism and the fashionable avant-gardism of academics and media pundits. I think Freire continues to inspire many Filipino educators, particularly nuns and priests active in fashioning a Filipino "theology of liberation."

To return to the Filipino experience: The first "waves" of Filipinos in the United States have not produced much in terms of written texts; their oral culture supported them in their daily lives, especially the first generation of "Manongs." This is a problem of class domination and the silencing of the labor-segmented nationalities in late capitalism.

Only in the 1960s and 1970s do you find a new group—in particular Al Robles and Jessica Hagedorn—beginning to connect the Manongs and the Philippine neocolonial plight in their own singular voices. But then, after the 1965 change in immigration, you have a new generation of Filipino professionals and middle strata who have life forms and orientations quite distinct from the migrant farmworkers of Philip Vera Cruz's time. Vera Cruz's biography (reconstituted by Craig Scharlin and Lilia Villanueva in the collaborative work titled *Philip Vera Cruz: A Personal History of Filipino Immigrants and the Farmworkers Movement*) is "must" reading for all Filipino Americans and people of color.

8. Observing the effect of English-based language on writers in the Philippines, do you believe writing in the vernacular really addresses the masses' concerns because the English-based speakers are coincidentally the elite?

The enemy can also speak in the vernacular. In this context, language should be viewed as one potentially efficacious instrument in political mobilization. It depends on what is conveyed through it and what situations embody the act of communication. I use English because I want to address a specific audience familiar with the ideas and issues I discuss. I also write in Pilipino to communicate with the larger segment of the population interested in general questions of freedom, exploitation, and the radical transformation of social structures.

We have had decades of controversy over which language to use: This was partly solved in the 1970s when the New People's Army began using the vernacular in various regions to raise consciousness and organize people. Filipino (the evolving national language) has now developed tremendously to the point of intellectuals producing works in philosophy and social theory and scientific treatises in Filipino that are accessible to millions.

English continues to be a "prestige" language used in Congress, business, and so on not because the most educated and elite Filipinos are the only ones engaged in serious conversation but because we are still a peripheral society dependent on global capitalist business and media whose language is English. Ideally, we need to use all languages to reach the widest audience that can be mobilized for emancipatory ends. And those who can use two or three languages would be much more effective; we shouldn't refuse versatility. Isn't the emerging global culture of the Internet multilingual?

9. As regards the Filipino diasporic experience, what do you perceive as challenges for the next one hundred years?

Prophecy is not my business, it's a hazardous undertaking. Still, for pedagogical purposes, I'll hazard this. If we have not yet been strangulated by the smog and effluvium of a degraded environment in the next millennium and the deluge of consumer goods, fungible trivia, the challenge for Filipino intellectuals— "intellectual" in the Gramscian sense refers to anyone who has some critical judgment, however miniscule, and exercises civic responsibility—is how to re-constitute the Filipino "nation" from the dispersal of men and women who iden-tify themselves as "Filipino," whether they are in Australia, Saudi Arabia, Alaska, Italy, Hong Kong, New York, or Makati. In other words, are we resigned to just being "domestic servants" of the world, which is our current reputation?

We won't be a "chosen" people, to be sure, but we can all cooperate to gener-ate that solidarity and intelligence required to destroy an exploitative system based on profit and alienated labor. This is not just mere "leftist" rhetoric be-cause the everyday experience of domestic helpers and "entertainment" workers confirms this. Yes, despite all the postmodernist chic about globalization and the advent of the "netizen" (the emergent cyborg citizen of the Internet), the oppres-sion of peripheral or subaltern nations by the sovereign powers of the West, the United States and Japan, with their own "white supremacist" agendas, continues to determine the life chances of peoples in the Philippines, Sri Lanka, Indonesia, the Caribbean, African countries, and many countries in South America.

Filipinos will either resist the transnational Leviathan of technoconsumerism and assert their own national will and dignity, or they will continue the servility of the last four hundred years. Hopefully, we can continue the socialist experi-ment that suffered disfigurement in the Soviet Union, China, and elsewhere in more creative and original ways. We have great potential as Filipinos, but that is being denied or suppressed by globalized capitalism.

10. You said that you write poetry primarily in Filipino now? Why and how does that affect the substance and form of your own poetry?

Ah, yes, I mined the lyrical inspiration in English up to the bitter end, from the halcyon days in high school reading Villa up to the 1960s and the explosion of the Cultural Revolution in China, in the Philippines, and elsewhere. That partic-ular mother lode was long exhausted, figuratively and literally. The limits of T. S. Eliot's "The Waste Land" or of Allen Ginsberg's "Howl" could not be tran-scended by mere poetic technique; only revolution can save the poet in English from solipsism, selling his soul to politicians and business, and suicide—this has been the real future for certain contemporaries in my lifetime.

Why choose Pilipino or "Filipino"? Primarily because the poet who writes in English in the Philippines has no real responsive audience and will have none, as the trend goes. The writers in English today write to a coterie or to their admirers and patrons if not to their own pathetic selves. There's a lesson here for writers in other societies plagued with multiple languages based on class inequalities.

What I mean by audience is not just readers but people whose experiences and life forms provide the materials, intonation, rhythm, imagery, and body language for the poet and who are the potential (if not actual) receivers of the emotional and intellectual charge in poetry and other verbal/linguistic performances.

English has no future in the Philippines—unless it is artificially supported by the neocolonial clientele of transnational power—as the living speech of the masses. I don't mean here that it is, by some intrinsic virtue, the language of the colonizer—after all, the Communist Party of the Philippines conducts its propaganda and education in English and in various vernaculars, even in French and Japanese.

It may be argued that English of a sort is now the speech of the Overseas Contract Workers, but Japanese and Arabic are really more useful for many of them. And of course, one should not forget the universal language of dollars. . . .

Let me cite an example from my activist inventory. During the 1960s and 1970s, when we were active in the anti–martial law movement, the most popular poems read in most meetings and conferences were Amado V. Hernandez's poem in Pilipino, "Lumuha ka, aking bayan . . ." and Jose Corazon de Jesus's lyrics for the song "Bayan Ko." It's not just a question of historical exigency. There's also the human collective hunger and desire for the renewal of memory, dreams, solidarities, and the imagination of the future. It's a question of discovering your humanity, your collective agency together, seemingly trapped in a racist and sexist and brutalizing system.

Ultimately, it's a matter of resurrection (please don't confuse this with "born-again" fundamentalism) in a milieu of vulgar egotism and mindless consumerism. We, writers in English, were petite-bourgeois intellectuals reborn in the campaign to "serve the people!" (to use the Maoist slogan).

Thanks to the U.S. civil rights movement, George Jackson, the Red Book, Che Guevara, and the antiwar movement, I discovered the rich praxis and tradition of Western Marxism—Georg Lukács, Antonio Gramsci, Walter Benjamin, Wilhelm Reich, and so on. But thanks more to the ordinary folk who died in Mendiola and in many parts of the Philippines, we (privileged children of the middle strata) realized that we had to commit "class suicide" and integrate with what Benedict Spinoza calls the "multitude."

Back to belle lettres: When you are writing for a living audience in an emergency—and for people of color, every day is an emergency (we don't have to read Frankfurt Critical Theory on this)—you write "in situation," as Sartre would say. Your speech becomes more integrally a part of an ongoing process of communication, dramatic or dialogical in a genuine sense, than if you were writing in English usually addressing your self or versions of your own poetic persona.

Today, of course, postmodernists would claim that you can't tell now which is genuine and which is fake—everything is a simulacrum! Nonetheless, there is the alternative route for artists of color. Self-fetishism may be replaced with the kind of poems Bertolt Brecht called teaching/learning poems, not utilitarian or simply pragmatic but tested and feasible equipment for the survival and strengthening of the spirit. "Arm the spirit" was one of the slogans of the 1960s youth movement. Brecht's achievement, just as those of Pablo Neruda and Cesar Vallejo, has become something of a model for many writers, young and old, in the Philippines today.

We are open to knowing and appreciating all cultures from anywhere in the world that may be useful in the national liberation struggle. We of course also have indigenous sources and local inspiration from our own history and tradition.

This has been said before, but let me repeat it for this occasion. I believe that only in meeting the challenge of freeing society from the alienation and exploitation endemic to a market system based on profit can the artists and writers recover the humanistic (in a materialist sense) and truly revolutionizing power of art. In short, we shall be reconstructing a society in which art and literature are organic parts of the life forms we invent for ourselves in the process of objectifying our possibilities together with our fellow humans and with nature.

We need to reinscribe art and literature in the concretely determinate sociohistorical contexts from which they derive their blood and flesh, their reason for existence. Only in this perspective can we also understand the logic of the aesthetic revolt (Charles Baudelaire, Ruben Dario, Jorge Luis Borges) against bourgeois society: art for art's sake!

11. Please share any other reflections you may have, given the Philippines' centennial commemoration.

A hundred years of suffering and resistance are over; now let us welcome another hundred years of struggle, of defeats and victories!

This may sound like an old Faustian theme from the Western canon or a sick repetition of Don Quixote's song from the kitsch musical. Our struggle is not nationalist in the narrow sense; it's a worldwide struggle for social emancipation from a global systemic enemy: capital accumulation and its ideology of white patriarchal supremacy.

Let's consider the fact that the Malaysians and other countries in the Pacific Rim continue to regard the Philippine Revolution of 1896, with Rizal and the propagandists, as one powerful harbinger of the days of national liberation movements in the 1950s and 1960s for Malaysia, Indonesia, Indo-China, even India. Remember that Mariano Ponce and other Aguinaldo survivors had good relations with Sun Yat-sen and other Asian progressives.

And the resistance against U.S. aggression in 1899–1902 in the Filipino–American War had enduring resonance in Cuba and many Latin American countries reacting against years of U.S. intervention since the Monroe Doctrine. We're a small country in those tiny islands out there, but geopolitics operates in geometric ways.

The Philippine Revolution of 1896 may have been defeated—that's why comrades of the First Quarter Storm in 1970 call it "unfinished—but its example lives on. Revolutions proceed through defeats and setbacks, as they say.

We Filipinos in "the belly of the beast," as the Cuban hero Jose Marti called the United States at the turn of the century, need to reconnect not only with the

1896 revolution the sacrifices of Mabini, Sakay, Crisanto Evangelista, the Huks, and the New People's Army but also with current struggles today in order to recover sources of hope and energy for the task of reconstituting the deracinated Filipino community in the United States.

It's not just the delirium of the other within you that needs to be released, as deconstructionists would say; it's the actual others around you where you find your possibilities, your future. Your integrity also. You can only find the meaning of your life in solidarity with others as you build a future in which possibilities repressed today can be given a chance to flourish in a just, egalitarian order. That commitment is not a matter of postponement or deferral but an actual endeavor to live dangerously every moment of the day. It's actually the project you try to realize in a whole lifetime.

Lest I sound existentialist in the dilettantish sense, I end with a tribute to Salud Algabre, the woman who led the Sakdal rebellion in the 1930s and who was inspired by Pedro Calosa, a Colorum leader who learned the art of the mass strike in the Hawaiian plantations of the 1920s.

Algabre's words need to be remembered: "No uprising fails. Each one is a step in the right direction." And I might add, quoting the Chinese writer Lu Hsun, if each one walks along that path, then we shall have built a road where none existed before.

[First published in *The Asian Pacific American Journal* 7(spring–summer 1998): 100–109. Revised for this book.]

References

Abaya, Hernando J. 1967. *The Untold Philippine Story*. Quezon City: Malaya Books.

———. 1984. *The Making of a Subversive*. Quezon City: New Day Publishers.

Abinales, Patricio N., ed. 1996. *The Revolution Falters: The Left in Philippine Politics after 1986*. Ithaca, N.Y.: Cornell University Southeast Asia Program.

Ablemann, Nancy, and John Lie. 1995. *Blue Dreams*. Cambridge, Mass.: Harvard University Press.

Adamkiewicz, Andrei. 1994. "Cultures and Tests: Representation of Philippine Society." In *Cultures and Texts: Representation of Philippine Society*. Quezon City: University of the Philippines Press.

Agoncillo, Teodoro A. 1974. *Filipino Nationalism 1872–1970*. Quezon City: R. P. Garcia Publishing.

Agoncillo, Teodoro A., and Oscar Alfonso. 1967. *History of the Filipino People*. Quezon City: Malaya Books.

Aguilar, Delia. 1988. *The Feminist Challenge*. Manila: Asian Social Institute.

———. 1998. *Toward a Nationalist Feminism*. Quezon City: Giraffe Press.

Aguilar, Filomeno, Jr. 1998. *Clash of Spirits*. Quezon City: Ateneo de Manila University Press.

Aguilar-San Juan, Karin, ed. 1992. *The State of Asian America*. Boston: South End Press.

Aguirre, Adalberto, and Jonathan Turner. 1998. *American Ethnicity*. Boston: McGraw-Hill.

Ahmad, Aijaz. 1992. *Classes, Nations, Literatures*. London: Verso.

Ahmad, Eqbal. 1971. "Revolutionary Warfare and Counterinsurgency." In *National Liberation*, edited by Norman Miller and Roderick Aya. New York: The Free Press.

———. 1982. *Political Culture and Foreign Policy: Notes on American Interventions in the Third World*. Washington, D.C.: Institute for Policy Studies.

———. 1995. "The Politics of Literary Postcoloniality." *Race and Class* 36, no. 3: 1–20.

Alavi, Hamza. 1964. "Imperialism, Old and New." In *Socialist Register 1964*. New York: Monthly Review Press.

Alavi, Hamza, and Teodor Shanin. 1982. *Introduction to the Sociology of "Developing Societies."* New York: Monthly Review Press.

Amin, Samir. 1977. *Imperialism and Unequal Development*. New York: Monthly Review Press.

———. 1980. *Class and Nation*. New York: Monthly Review Press.

———. 1989. *Eurocentrism*. New York: Monthly Review Press.

———. 1994. *Re-Reading the Postwar Period*. New York: Monthly Review Press.

———. 1998. *Spectres of Capitalism*. New York: Monthly Review Press.

Amott, Teresa L., and Julie Matthaei. 1991. *Race, Gender and Work*. Boston: South End Press.

Anderson, Benedict. 1995. "Cacique Democracy in the Philippines: Origins and Dreams." In *Discrepant Histories*, edited by Vicente Rafael. Philadelphia: Temple University Press.

Anderson, Kevin. 1995. *Lenin, Hegel and Western Marxism*. Urbana: University of Illinois Press.

Anderson, Perry. 1976/1977. "The Antinomies of Antonio Gramsci." *New Left Review* 100: 20–56.

Anderson, Warwick. 1995. " 'Where Every Prospect Pleases and Only Man Is Vile': Laboratory Medicine as Colonial Discourse." In *Discrepant Histories*, edited by Vicente Rafael. Philadelphia: Temple University Press.

Andrews, Chris. 1946. "American Imperialism in the Philippines." *Fourth International* 24 (February): 41–44.

Anti-Slavery Society. 1983. *The Philippines: Authoritarian Government, Multinationals and Ancestral Lands*. London: Anti-Slavery Society.

Appadurai, Arjun. 1994. "Disjuncture and Difference in the Global Culture Economy." In *Colonial Discourse and Post-Colonial Theory*, edited by Patrick Williams and Laura Chrisman. New York: Columbia University Press.

Appel, Benjamin. 1941. *Fortress in the Rice*. New York: Bobbs-Merrill.

Appelbaum, Richard P. 1996. "Multiculturalism and Flexibility: Some New Directions in Global Capitalism." In *Mapping Multiculturalism*, edited by Avery Gordon and Christopher Newfield (pp. 297–316). Minneapolis: University of Minnesota Press.

Armes, Roy. 1987. *Third World Film Making and the West*. Berkeley and Los Angeles: University of California Press.

Aronowitz, Stanley. 1979. "Film—the Art Form of Late Capitalism." *Social Text* 1: 110–129.

Arrighi, Giovanni. 1993. "The Three Hegemonies of Historical Capitalism." In *Gramsci, Historical Materialism and International Relations*, edited by Stephen Gill. New York: Cambridge University Press.

Asad, Talal, ed. 1973. *Anthropology and the Global Encounter*. London: Ithaca Press.

Ashcroft, Bill, Gareth Griffiths, and Helen Tiffin. 1989. *The Empire Writes Back*. London: Routledge.

Atienza, Glecy, et al., eds. 1998. *Bangon: Antolohiya ng mga Dulang Mapanghimagsik*. Diliman, Quezon City: Office of Research Coordination, University of the Philippines.

Aufderheide, Pat. 1986. "Kidlat Tahimik." In *The Challenge of Third World Culture*. Mimeographed program of the Duke University Conference, September 25–27, Duke University, Durham, North Carolina.

Augelli, Enrico, and Craig N. Murphy. 1993. "Gramsci and International Relations: A General Perspective with Examples from Recent US Policy toward the Third World." In *Gramsci, Historical Materialism and International Relations*, edited by Stephen Gill. New York: Cambridge University Press.

Bakhtin, Mikhail. 1968. *Rabelais and His World.* Cambridge: MIT Press.

————. 1981. *The Dialogic Imagination.* Austin: University of Texas Press.

Balibar, Etienne. 1990. "Paradoxes of Universality." In *Anatomy of Racism,* edited by David Goldberg. Minneapolis: University of Minnesota Press.

————. 1999. "Class Racism." In *Racism,* edited by Leonard Harris. New York: Humanity Books.

Balibar, Etienne, and Pierre Macherey. 1992. "On Literature as an Ideological Form." In *Contemporary Marxist Literary Criticism,* edited by Francis Mulhern. New York: Longman.

Balibar, Etienne, and Immanuel Wallerstein. 1991. *Race, Nation, Class: Ambiguous Identities.* London: Verso.

Barraclough, Geoffrey. 1967. *An Introduction to Contemporary History.* New York: Penguin Books.

Barratt-Brown, Michael. 1982. "Developing Societies as Part of an International Political Economy." In *Introduction to the Sociology of "Developing Societies."* New York: Monthly Review Press.

Barthes, Roland. 1972. *Critical Essays.* Evanston, Ill.: Northwestern University Press.

————. 1977. *Image-Music-Text.* New York: Hill & Wang.

————. 1981. *Camera Lucida.* New York: Hill and Wang.

————. 1985. *The Responsibility of Forms.* New York: Hill and Wang.

Baudrillard, Jean. 1984. "The Precession of Simulacra." In *Art after Modernism,* edited by Brian Wallis. New York: Museum of Contemporary Art.

Bautista, Lualhati. 1988. *Gapo.* Manila: Carmelo and Bauermann.

Bauzon, Kenneth. 1991. *Liberalism and the Quest for Islamic Identity in the Philippines.* Durham, N.C.: The Acorn Press.

————. 1992. "Social Knowledge and the Legitimation of the State: The Philippine Experience in Historical Perspective." *Political Communication* 9 (1992): 173–189.

Baxandall, Lee, and Stefan Morawski, eds. 1973. *Marx and Engels on Literature and Art.* St. Louis: Telos Press.

BAYAN. 1998. "Philippines: A Brief Situationer on the Political and Economic Landscape of the Philippines." Available at http://www.geocities.com/CapitolHill/Lobby/4677.

BAYAN International. 1994. *The Truth about the Ramos Regime.* Los Angeles: Bayan International.

Beard, Charles, and Mary Beard. 1968. *New Basic History of the United States.* Garden City, N.Y.: Doubleday.

Bello, Walden. 1992. "The Philippine Progressive Movement Today." *Philippine Alternatives* 1 (September): 3–6, 12–14.

Beltran, Ruby Palma, and Aurora Javate de Dios, eds. 1992. *Filipino Women Overseas Contract Workers . . . At What Cost?* Manila: Goodwill Trading Company.

Beltran, Ruby Palma, and Gloria Rodriguez. 1996. *Filipino Women Migrant Workers: At the Crossroads and Beyond Beijing.* Quezon City: Giraffe Press.

Benjamin, Walter. 1968. *Illuminations.* New York: Schocken Books.

————. 1978. *Reflections.* New York: Harcourt Brace Jovanovich.

Bennis, Phyllis, and Michael Moushabeck, eds. 1993. *Altered States: A Reader in the New World Order.* New York: Olive Branch Press.

Berger, John. 1984. *And Our Faces, My Heart, Brief as Photos.* New York: Pantheon.

Berlow, Alan. 1996. *Dead Season*. New York: Pantheon.

Berreman, Gerald. 1990. "The Incredible 'Tasaday': Deconstructing the Myth of the 'Stone-Age' People." *Cultural Survival Quarterly* 15: 3–25.

Beveridge, Albert. 1987. "Our Philippine Policy." In *The Philippines Reader*, edited by Daniel Schirmer and S. Shalom. Boston: South End Press.

Bhaskar, Roy. 1993. *Dialectic: The Pulse of Freedom*. London: Verso.

Blauner, Robert. 1972. *Racial Oppression in America*. New York: Harper and Row.

Blount, James H. 1973. *The American Occupation of the Philippines, 1898–1912*. 1912. Reprint, New York: Oriole Editions.

Bock, Deborah, ed. 1979. *Pearls*. Springfield, Va.: Educational Film Center.

Bodley, John. 1990. *Victims of Progress*. Mountain View, Calif.: Mayfield Publishing.

Boggs, Grace Lee. 1998. *Living for Change: An Autobiography*. Minneapolis: University of Minnesota Press.

Bonacich, Edna. 1996. "The Class Question in Global Capitalism." In *Mapping Multiculturalism*, edited by Avery Gordon and Christopher Newfield. Minneapolis: University of Minnesota Press.

———. 1998. "Inequality in America: The Failure of the American System for People of Color." In *Sources: Notable Selections in Race and Ethnicity*, edited by Adalberto Aguirre and David Baker. Guilford, Conn.: Dushkin/McGraw-Hill.

Bonner, Raymond. 1987. *Waltzing with a Dictator*. Quezon City: Ken Incorporated.

Bourdieu, Pierre. 1998. *Acts of Resistance*. New York: The New Press.

Bouvier, Leon, and Robert Gardner. 1986. *Immigration to the U.S.: The Unfinished Story*. Washington, D.C.: Population Reference Bureau.

Boyce, James K. 1993. *The Philippines: The Political Economy of Growth and Impoverishment in the Marcos Era*. Honolulu: University of Hawaii Press.

Brecht, Bertolt. 1977. "Against Georg Lukács." In *Aesthetics and Politics*, translated by Ronald Taylor. London: New Left Books.

———. 1996. "A Short Organum for the Theater." In *Marxist Literary Theory*, edited by Terry Eagleton and Drew Milne. Oxford: Blackwell Publishers.

Bresnan, John. 1986. *Crisis in the Philippines: The Marcos Era and Beyond*. Princeton, N.J.: Princeton University Press.

Brewer, Anthony. 1990. *Marxist Theories of Imperialism*. New York: Routledge.

Brooke, James. 1997. "U.S.-Philippines History Entwined in War Booty." *New York Times*, December 1, A6.

Bruin, Janet. 1996. *Root Causes of the Global Crisis*. Manila: Institute of Political Economy.

Buck-Morss, Susan. 1989. *The Dialectics of Seeing*. Cambridge, Mass: MIT Press.

Bulosan, Carlos. 1973. *America Is in the Heart*. 1948. Reprint, Seattle: University of Washington Press.

———. 1995. *The Cry and the Dedication*. Edited by E. San Juan. Philadelphia: Temple University Press. Previously published as *The Power of the People*, Manila: National Book Store, 1986.

———. 1995. *On Becoming Filipino: Selected Writings*. Edited by E. San Juan. Philadelphia: Temple University Press.

Burton, Sandra. 1989. *Impossible Dream*. New York: Warner Books.

Buss, Claude. 1987. *Cory Aquino and the People of the Philippines*. Stanford, Calif.: Stanford Alumni Association.

Cabezas, Amado, and Gary Kawaguchi. 1989. "Race, Gender, and Class for Filipino Americans." In *A Look beyond the Model Minority Image*, edited by Grace Yun. New York: Minority Rights Group.

Caldwell, Malcolm. 1970. "Problems of Socialism in Southeast Asia." In *Imperialism and Underdevelopment: A Reader*, edited by Robert I. Rhodes. New York: Monthly Review Press.

Callinicos, Alex. 1989. *Against Postmodernism*. New York: St. Martin's Press.

Canlas, Mamerto. 1988. "The Political Context." In *Land, Poverty and Politics in the Philippines*, edited Mamerto Canlas et al. London: Catholic Institute for International Relations.

Capulong, Romeo. 1986. "U.S. Intervention Still the Main Problem of the Filipino People after Marcos." Paper presented to the National Lawyers Guild National Convention, Denver, Colorado, June 11–16. New York: PHILCIR Educational Services Program.

Cariño, Benjamin. 1996. "Filipino Americans: Many and Varied." In *Origins and Destinies*, edited by Silvia Pedraza and Ruben Rumbaut. Belmont, Calif.: Wadsworth Publishing.

Cashmore, E. Ellis. 1998. *Dictionary of Race and Ethnic Relations*. London: Routledge.

Castles, Steven, et al. 1996. "Australia: Multi-Ethnic Community without Nationalism?" In *Ethnicity*, edited by John Hutchinson and Anthony D. Smith. New York: Oxford University Press.

Catholic Institute for International Relations. 1987. *The Labour Trade: Filipino Migrant Workers around the World*. London: Author.

Caudwell, Christopher. 1937. *Illusion and Reality*. New York: International Publishers.

Center for Women's Resources. 1996. *Philippines 2000 in the Year 1995*. Quezon City: Catholic Women's Resources.

Chaffee, Frederic, et al. 1969. *Area Handbook for the Philippines*. Washington, D.C.: U.S. Government Printing Office.

Chan, Jeffery. 1997. "The Chinese in Haifa." In *Aiiieeeee! An Anthology of Asian American Writers*, edited by Frank Chin et al. New York: A Monitor Book.

Chan, Sucheng. 1991. *Asian Americans: An Interpretive History*. Boston: Twayne.

Chang, Robert S. 1995. "Toward an Asian American Legal Scholarship: Critical Race Theory, Post-Structuralism, and Narrative Space." In *Critical Race Theory: The Cutting Edge*, edited by Richard Delgado. Philadelphia: Temple University Press.

Chapman, William. 1987. *Inside the Philippine Revolution*. New York: W. W. Norton and Quezon City: Ken Incorporated.

Chatterjee, Partha. 1986. *Nationalist Thought and the Colonial World*. London: Zed Books.

Chilcote, Ronald. 1984. *Theories of Development and Underdevelopment*. Boulder, Colo.: Westview Press.

Chin, Frank. 1981. *The Chickencoop Chinaman/The Year of the Dragon*. Seattle: University of Washington Press.

———. 1994. *Gunga Din Highway*. Minneapolis: Coffee House Press.

———. 1998. *Bulletproof Buddhists and Other Essays*. Honolulu: University of Hawaii Press.

Chomsky, Noam. 1982. *Towards a New Cold War*. New York: Pantheon Books.

———. 1986–1992. *What Uncle Sam Really Wants*. Berkeley, Calif.: Odonian Press.

———. 1992. *Deterring Democracy*. New York: Hill and Wang.

Chow, Esther Ngan-Ling. 1994. "The Feminist Movement: Where Are All the Asian American Women?" In *From Different Shores*, edited by Ronald Takaki. New York: Oxford University Press.

Choy, Curtis. 1991. "Suckcess above the Line: From Here to Obscurity." In *Moving the Image: Independent Asian Pacific American Media Arts*, edited by Russell Leong. Los Angeles: UCLA Asian American Studies Center and Visual Communications.

Churchill, Thomas. 1995. *Triumph over Marcos: A Story Based on the Lives of Gene Viernes and Silme Domingo, Filipino American Cannery Union Organizers, Their Assassination, and the Trial That Followed.* Seattle: Open Hand.

Clifford, James. 1988. *The Predicament of Culture.* Cambridge, Mass: Harvard University Press.

Collier, Andrew. 1990. *Socialist Reasoning.* London: Pluto Press.

Communist Party of the Philippines, Central Committee. 1992. "Reaffirm Our Basic Principles and Carry the Revolution Forward." *Rebolusyon* (January–March): 1–36.

Connor, Steven. 1989. *Postmodernist Culture.* New York: Basil Blackwell.

Constantino, Renato. 1970. *Dissent and Counterconsciousness.* Quezon City: Malaya Books.

——. 1975. *A History of the Philippines.* New York: Monthly Review Press.

——. 1978. *Neocolonial Identity and Counter-Consciousness.* New York: M. E. Sharpe.

Cordova, Fred. 1983. *Filipinos: Forgotten Asian Americans.* Dubuque, Iowa: Kendall/Hunt Publishing.

Corpuz, Onofre D. 1965. *The Philippines.* Englewood Cliffs, N.J.: Prentice Hall.

Corrigan, Philip, Harvie Ramsay, and Derek Sayers. 1978. *Socialist Construction and Marxist Theory.* New York: Monthly Review Press.

Covi, Giovanna. 1996. "Jessica Hagedorn's Decolonialization of Subjectivity: Historical Agency beyond Gender and Nation." In *Nationalism and Sexuality: Crises of Identity*, edited by Yiorgos Kalogeras and Domna Pastourmatzi. Thessaloniki: Aristotle University.

Crenshaw, Kimberle, et al., eds. 1995. *Critical Race Theory.* New York: The New Press.

Dalisay, Jose Y., Jr. 1999. *The Lavas: A Filipino Family.* Pasig City, Philippines: Anvil.

Daniels, Roger. 1993. "United States Policy towards Asian Immigrants: Contemporary Developments in Historical Perspective." *International Journal* 48: 310–334.

Davenport, Kiana. 1998. *Shark Dialogues.* New York: Plume Books.

David, Joel. 1995. *Fields of Vision.* Quezon City: Ateneo de Manila University Press.

Davis, Leonard. 1989. *Revolutionary Struggle in the Philippines.* London: Macmillan.

Dean, Vera Micheles. 1966. *The Nature of the Non-Western World.* New York: New American Library.

Debray, Regis. 1977. "Marxism and the National Question." *New Left Review* 105 (September–October): 25–41.

De Dios, Aurora Javate, Petronilo Daroy, and Lorna Kalaw-Tirol, eds. 1988. *Dictatorship and Revolution.* Manila: Conspectus.

De la Cruz, Enrique, and Pearlie Baluyut, eds. 1998. *Confrontations, Crossings, and Convergence.* Los Angeles: UCLA Asian American Studies Center and UCLA Southeast Asia Program.

De la Torre, ed. 1986a. *The Philippines: Christians and the Politics of Liberation.* London: Catholic Institute for International Relations.

————. 1986b. *Touching Ground, Taking Root.* London: British Council of Churches.

Deleuze, Gilles. 1986. *Cinema 1: The Movement Image.* Minneapolis: University of Minnesota Press.

Deleuze, Gilles, and Felix Guattari. 1982. *Anti-Oedipus: Capitalism and Schizophrenia.* Minneapolis: University of Minnesota Press.

————. 1986. *Kafka: Toward a Minor Literature.* Minneapolis: University of Minnesota Press.

————. 1987. *A Thousand Plateaus.* Minneapolis: University of Minnesota Press.

Delgado, Richard, ed. 1995. *Critical Race Theory.* Philadelphia: Temple University Press.

Delgado, Richard, and Jean Stefancic. 1997. "Images of the Outsider in American Law and Culture." In *Critical White Studies.* Philadelphia: Temple University Press.

Della Volpe, Galvano. 1978. *Critique of Taste.* London: New Left Books.

Demko, George. 1992. *Why in the World: Adventures in Geography.* New York: Anchor Books.

Dews, Peter. 1987. *Logics of Disintegration.* New York: Verso.

Diokno, Jose. 1987. *A Nation for Our Children.* Quezon City: Claretian Publications.

Dirlik, Arif. 1996. "Asians on the Rim: Transnational Capital and Local Community in the Making of Contemporary Asian America." *Amerasia Journal* 22, no. 3: 1–24.

————. 1997. *The Postcolonial Aura.* Boulder, Colo.: Westview Press.

Dissanayake, Wimal. 1994. "Epilogue: Asian Cultural Texts and Western Theory." In *Gender and Culture in Literature and Film East and West: Issues of Perception and Interpretation,* edited by Nitaya Masavisut, George Simson, and Larry Smith. Honolulu: University of Hawaii and the East-West Center.

Doronila, Amado. 1992. *The State, Economic Transformation, and Political Change in the Philippines, 1946–1972.* Singapore: Oxford University Press.

Doty, Roxanne Lynn. 1996. *Imperial Encounters.* Minneapolis: University of Minnesota Press.

Dudley, William, ed. 1997. *Asian Americans: Opposing Viewpoints.* San Diego: Greenhaven Press.

Duhaylungsod, Levita, and David Hyndman. 1997. *Where T'Boli Bells Toll: Political Ecology Voices behind the Tasaday Hoax.* Document 73. Copenhagen: IWGIA.

Dumont, Jean-Paul. 1995. "Ideas on Philippine Violence: Assertions, Negations and Narrations." In *Discrepant Histories,* edited by Vicente Rafael. Philadelphia: Temple University Press.

Dussel, Enrique. 1992. "Theology and Economy: The Theological Paradigm of Communicative Action and the Paradigm of the Community of Life as a Theology of Liberation." In *Development and Democratization in the Third World,* edited by K. Bauzon. Washington, D.C.: Crane Russak.

Eagleton, Terry. 1990. *The Ideology of the Aesthetic.* Oxford: Basil Blackwell.

————. 1996. *The Illusions of Postmodernism.* Oxford: Blackwell Publishers.

Eggan, Fred. 1991. "The Philippines in the Twentieth Century: A Study in Contrasts." *Review in Anthropology* 21: 13–23.

Elisabeth, Adriana. 1998. "The Philippine Revolution and Nation Formation in Southeast Asia." In *Toward the First Asian Republic,* edited by Elmer Ordonez. Manila: Philippine Centennial Commission.

Eller, Jack, and Reed Coughlan. 1996. "The Poverty of Primordialism." In *Ethnicity,* edited by John Hutchinson and Anthony Smith. New York: Oxford University Press.

Ellis, John. 1981. "Notes on the Obvious." In *Literary Theory Today,* edited by M. A. Abbas and Tak-kai Wong. Hong Kong: Hong Kong University Press.

Encarta Encyclopedia. 1993–1997. "Philippines, Republic of the." Seattle: Microsoft Corporation.

Engels, Friedrich. 1935. *Anti-Duhring.* Translated by Emile Burns. New York: International Publishers.

Enriquez, Virgilio. 1992. *From Colonial to Liberation Psychology: The Philippine Experience.* Quezon City: University of the Philippines.

Escobar, Arturo. 1995. *Encountering Development: The Making and Unmaking of the Third World.* Princeton, N.J.: Princeton University Press.

Espiritu, Socorro, and Chester L. Hunt, eds. 1964. *Social Foundations of Community Development.* Manila: R. P. Garcia Publishing.

Espiritu, Yen Le. 1994. "The Intersection of Race, Ethnicity, and Class: The Multiple Identities of Second-Generation Filipinos." *Identities* 1, nos. 2–3: 249–273.

———. 1995. *Filipino American Lives.* Philadelphia: Temple University Press.

———. 1996. "Asian American Panethnicity." In *The Meaning of Difference,* edited by Karen Rosenblum and Toni-Michelle Travis. New York: McGraw-Hill.

Eviota, Elizabeth Uy. 1992. *The Political Economy of Gender.* London: Zed Books.

Fabian, Johannes. 1983. *Time and the Other.* New York: Columbia University Press.

Falk, Richard. 1993. "Prospects for Korea after the Cold War." In *Altered States,* edited by Phyllis Bennis and Michel Moushabeck. New York: Olive Branch Press.

Fallow, James. 1987. "A Damaged Culture." *The Atlantic Monthly* November: 49–58.

Famighetti, Robert, ed. 1995. *The World Almanac and Book of Facts.* New York: World Almanac.

Fann, K. T., and Donald C. Hodges, eds. 1971. *Readings in U.S. Imperialism.* Boston: F. Porter Sargent.

Fanon, Frantz. 1968. *The Wretched of the Earth.* New York: Grove Press.

Fast, Jonathan. 1973. "Imperialism and Bourgeois Dictatorship in the Philippines." *New Left Review* 78 (March–April): 69–96.

Feria, Mike. 1988. "A Kidlat Tahimik Retrospective." *Kultura* 1, no. 1: 33–36.

Fernandez, Doreen G. 1996. *Palabas: Essays on Philippine Theater History.* Quezon City: Ateneo de Manila University Press.

Fernando, Enrique M. 1998. "A Regime of Constitutionalism and the Comparative Law Approach." In *Toward the First Asian Republic,* edited by Elmer Ordonez. Manila: Philippine Centennial Commission.

Ferrer, Ricardo. 1984. "On the Mode of Production in the Philippines: Some Old-Fashioned Questions on Marxism." In *Marxism in the Philippines,* edited by Third World Studies. Quezon City: University of the Philippines.

———. 1987. "The Political Economy of the Aquino Regime." *Diliman Review* 35: 89–103.

Fischer, Ernst. 1996. *How to Read Karl Marx.* New York: Monthly Review Press.

Forbes, W. Cameron. 1945. *The Philippine Islands.* 1928. Reprint, Cambridge, Mass: Harvard University Press.

Foucault, Michel. 1984. *The Foucault Reader.* New York: Pantheon.

Frake, Charles O. 1998. "Abu Sayyaf: Displays of Violence and the Proliferation of Contested Identities among Philippine Muslims." *American Anthropologist* 100, no. 1: 41–54.

Francisco, Luzviminda. 1976. "The First Vietnam—the Philippine-American War of 1899–1902." In *Letters in Exile*, edited by Jesse Quinsaat et al. Los Angeles: UCLA Asian American Studies Center.

Franklin, H. Bruce. 1988. *War Stars.* New York: Oxford University Press.

Franklin, John Hope. 1989. *Race and History.* Baton Rouge: Louisiana State University Press.

Fraser, Nancy. 1995. "From Redistribution to Recognition? Dilemmas of Justice in a 'Post-Socialist' Age." *New Left Review* 212 (July–August 1995): 68–93.

———. 1997. *Justice Interruptus.* New York: Routledge.

Freire, Paulo. 1972. *Pedagogy of the Oppressed.* New York: Herder and Herder.

Friend, Theodore. 1965. *Between Two Empires: The Ordeal of the Philippines 1929–1946.* New Haven, Conn.: Yale University Press.

———. 1989. "Latin Ghosts Haunt an Asian Nation." *Heritage,* December, 4.

Frith, Simon. 1984. "Rock and the Politics of Memory." In *The 60s: Without Apology,* edited by Sohnya Sayres, Stanley Aronowitz, and Fredric Jameson. Minneapolis: University of Minnesota Press.

Gabriel, Teshome. 1994. "Towards a Critical Theory of Third World Films." In *Colonial Discourse and Postcolonial Theory,* edited by Patrick Williams and Laura Chrisman. New York: Columbia University Press.

Giddens, Anthony. 1984. *The Constitution of Society.* Berkeley and Los Angeles: University of California Press.

Gill, Stephen. 1993. *Gramsci, Historical Materialism and International Relations.* Cambridge: Cambridge University Press.

Gills, Barry. 1993. "The Hegemonic Transition in East Asia: A Historical Perspective." In *Gramsci, Historical Materialism and International Relations,* edited by Stephen Gill. New York: Cambridge University Press.

Gitlin, Todd. 1987. *The Sixties: Years of Hope/Days of Rage.* New York: Bantam Books.

Glazer, Nathan, and Daniel P. Moynihan, eds. 1975. *Ethnicity: Theory and Experience.* Cambridge, Mass.: Harvard University Press.

Goldfield, Michael. 1997. *The Color of Politics.* New York: The New Press.

Gonzales, Juan L., Jr. 1993. *Racial and Ethnic Groups in America.* Dubuque, Iowa: Kendall/Hunt Publishing.

Gonzalez, N. V. M. 1992. "Even as a Mountain Speaks." *Amerasia Journal* 18, no. 2: 55–68.

Gonzalves, Theo. 1995. " 'The Show Must Go On': Production Notes on the Filipino Cultural Night." *Critical Mass* 2, no. 2 (spring): 129–144.

Gosiengfiao, Victor. 1983. "Orientalizing the Filipino." In *Rediscovery,* edited by Cynthia Nograles Lumbera and Teresita Gimenez Maceda. Manila: National Book Store.

Gotanda, Neil. 1995. "Critical Legal Studies, Critical Race Theory and Asian American Studies." *Amerasia Journal* 21, nos. 1–2 (1995): 127–136.

———. 1996. "Multiculturalism and Racial Stratification." In *Mapping Multiculturalism,* edited by Avery Gordon and Christopher Newfield. Minneapolis: University of Minnesota Press.

Gramsci, Antonio. 1971. *Selection from the Prison Notebooks.* New York: International Publishers.

Gran, Peter. 1996. *Beyond Eurocentrism: A New View of Modern World History.* Syracuse, N.Y.: Syracuse University Press.

Grossholtz, Jean. 1964. *Politics in the Philippines.* Boston: Little, Brown.

Grossman, Zoltan. 1986. "Inside the Philippine Resistance." *Race and Class* 28: 1–29.

Guerrero, Amado [Jose Maria Sison]. 1971. *Philippine Society and Revolution.* Manila: Pulang Tala.

Guillaumin, Colette. 1995. *Racism, Sexism, Power and Ideology.* London: Routledge.

Gurr, Ted Robert. 1993. *Minorities at Risk.* Washington, D.C.: United States Institute of Peace Press.

Gutmann, Amy, ed. 1994. *Multiculturalism: Examining the Politics of Recognition.* Princeton, N.J.: Princeton University Press.

Habermas, Jurgen. 1987. *The Philosophical Discourse of Modernity.* Cambridge: MIT Press.

Hagedorn, Jessica. 1989. *Dogeaters.* New York: Pantheon Books.

——, ed. 1993. *Charlie Chan Is Dead.* New York: Penguin Books.

——. 1993. *Danger and Beauty.* New York: Penguin Books.

——. 1996. *The Gangster of Love.* Boston: Houghton Mifflin.

Hall, Stuart. 1996. *Stuart Hall: Critical Dialogue in Cultural Studies.* Edited by David Morley and Kuan-Hsing Chen. New York: Routledge.

——. 1998. "Subjects in History: Making Diasporic Identities." In *The House That Race Built,* edited by Wahneema Lubiano. New York: Vintage Books.

Hamamoto, Darrell Y. 1994. *Monitored Peril: Asian Americans and the Politics of TV Representation.* Minneapolis: University of Minnesota Press.

Harding, Sandra. 1993. "Rethinking Standpoint Epistemology: What Is Strong Objectivity?" In *Feminist Epistemologies,* edited by L. Alcoff and E. Potter. New York: Routledge.

Harvey, David. 1989. *The Condition of Postmodernity.* Cambridge, Mass.: Blackwell.

——. 1996. *Justice, Nature and the Geography of Difference.* Cambridge, Mass.: Blackwell.

Haug, W. F. 1986. *Critique of Commodity Aesthetics.* Minneapolis: University of Minnesota Press.

——. 1987. *Commodity Aesthetics, Ideology, and Culture.* New York: International General.

Hayden, Joseph Ralston. 1942. *The Philippines: A Study in National Development.* New York: Macmillan.

Heath, Stephen. 1981. *Questions of Cinema.* Bloomington: Indiana University Press.

——. 1992. "Lessons from Brecht." In *Contemporary Marxist Literary Criticism.* London: Longman.

Heiser, Victor. 1936. *An American Doctor's Odyssey.* New York: W. W. Norton.

Hing, Bill Ong, and Ronald Lee, eds. 1996. *Reframing the Immigration Debate.* Los Angeles: UCLA Asian American Studies Center.

Hinton, William. 1993. "A Visit to Manila." *FFP Bulletin* (winter): 1, 4–7.

Historical Commission, Partido Komunista ng Pilipinas. 1996. *Communism in the Philippines: The P.K.P. Book 1.* Manila: Partido Komunista ng Pilipinas.

Hobsbawm, E. J. 1973. *Revolutionaries.* New York: New American Library.

Hoefer, Hans Johannes, ed. 1980. *Philippines.* Hong Kong: Apa Productions.

Hofstadter, Richard. 1967. *The Paranoid Style in American Politics and Other Essays.* New York: Vintage Books.

Holz, Hans Heinz. 1992. "The Downfall and Future of Socialism." *Nature, Society, and Thought* 5 (special issue): 17–128.

Homer, Sean. 1997. "Fredric Jameson and the Limits of Postmodern Theory." Available at http://www.shef.ac.uk/uni/academic.

Hongo, Garrett, ed. 1995. *Under Western Eyes*. New York: Anchor Books.

Hoogvelt, Ankie. 1987. "The New International Division of Labor." In *The World Order: Socialist Perspectives*, edited by Ray Bush et al. Cambridge: Polity Press.

Houston, Velina Hasu, ed. 1993. *The Politics of Life*. Philadelphia: Temple University Press.

Hu-DeHart, Evelyn. 1999. "Introduction: Asian American Formations in the Age of Globalization." In *Across the Pacific*. New York: The Asia Society.

Hulme, Peter. 1992. "Reciprocity and Exchange." In *Formations of Modernity*, edited by Stuart Hall and Bram Gieben. Cambridge: Polity Press.

Hunt, Chester, et al. 1963. *Sociology in the Philippine Setting*. Quezon City: Phoenix Publishing.

Hunt, Michael. 1987. *Ideology and U.S. Foreign Policy*. New Haven, Conn.: Yale University Press.

Hunter, Allen. 1988. "Post-Marxism and the New Social Movements." *Theory and Society* 17: 885–900.

Hutchcroft, Paul D. 1995. "Unraveling the Past in the Philippines." *Current History* (December): 430–434.

Hutchinson, John, and Anthony Smith, eds. 1996. *Ethnicity*. Oxford: Oxford University Press.

Hymer, S. 1972. "The Multinational Corporation and the Law of Uneven Development." In *International Firms and Modern Imperialism*. New York: Penguin Books.

Ichiyo, Muto. 1993. "For an Alliance of Hope." In *Global Visions: Beyond the New World Order*. Boston: South End Press.

Ileto, Reynaldo. 1997. "Outlines of a Nonlinear Emplotment of Philippine History." In *The Politics of Culture in the Shadow of Capital*, edited by David Lloyd and Lisa Lowe. Durham, N.C.: Duke University Press.

———. 1998. *Filipinos and Their Revolution*. Quezon City: Ateneo University Press.

Instituto del Tercer Mundo. 1999. *The World Guide 1999/2000*. Oxford: New Internationalist Publications.

Jacinto, Jaime Antonio, and Luis Malay Syquia. 1995. *Lakbay: Journey of the People of the Philippines*. San Francisco: Zellerbach Family Fund.

Jacoby, Russell. 1995. "Marginal Returns." *Lingua Franca* (September/October): 30–37.

Jalee, Pierre. 1968. *The Pillage of the Third World*. New York: Monthly Review Press.

———. 1972. *Imperialism in the Seventies*. New York: The Third Press.

James, C. L. R. 1993. *American Civilization*. Cambridge, Mass.: Blackwell.

Jameson, Fredric. 1981. *The Political Unconscious*. Ithaca, N.Y.: Cornell University Press.

———. 1986. "Third World Literature in the Era of Multinational Capitalism." *Social Text* 15 (fall): 69–80.

———. 1988. *The Ideologies of Theory*. Minneapolis: University of Minnesota Press.

———. 1990a. *Late Marxism*. London: Verso.

———. 1990b. "Modernism and Imperialism." In *Nationalism, Colonialism and Literature*, edited by Seamus Deane. Minneapolis: University of Minnesota Press.

———. 1991. *Postmodernism, or, The Cultural Logic of Late Capitalism*. Durham, N.C.: Duke University Press.

———. 1992. *The Geopolitical Aesthetic: Cinema and Space in the World System.* Bloomington: Indiana University Press.

———. 1997. "Culture and Finance Capital." *Critical Inquiry* 24, no. 1 (autumn): 246–265.

———. 1998. "Culture and Finance Capital." In *The Cultural Turn.* London: Verso.

Janiewski, Dolores. 1995. "Gendering, Racializing and Classifying: Settler Colonization in the United States, 1590–1990." In *Unsettling Settler Societies,* edited by Daiva Stasiulis and Nira Yuval-Davis. London: Sage Publications.

Jenkins, Richard. 1986. "Social-Anthropological Models of Inter-Ethnic Relations." In *Theories of Race and Ethnic Relations,* edited by John Rex and David Mason. New York: Cambridge University Press.

Jessop, Bob. 1982. *The Capitalist State.* New York: New York University Press.

Joaquin, Nick. 1987. "The Way We Were." In *Writers and Their Milieu,* edited by Edilberto Alegre and Doreen Fernandez. Manila: De La Salle Press.

———. 1982. "The Filipino as English Fictionist." In *Literature and Social Justice,* edited by L. Yabes. Manila: Philippine Center of PEN.

Johnson, Bryan. 1987. *The Four Days of Courage.* New York: The Free Press.

Johnson, Lawrence. 1989. "The Migration Waves of Filipinos." *Philippine-American Journal* 1, no. 2 (winter): 13–15.

Johnson, Mark. 1999. "Philippines: Liberating the Left." *International Viewpoint* 313 (July): col. 20.

Jones, Gareth Stedman. 1973. "The History of U.S. Imperialism." In *Ideology in Social Science,* edited by Robin Blackburn. New York: Vintage Books.

Kagan, Leigh, and Richard Kagan. 1971. "Oh Say Can You See? American Cultural Blinders on China." In *America's Asia,* edited by Edward Friedman and Mark Selden. New York: Vintage Books.

Kang, Younghill. 1974. "From East Goes West." In *Asian-American Heritage,* edited by David Hsin-Fu Wand. New York: Washington Square Press.

Kaplan, Amy, and Donald Pease, eds. 1993. *Cultures of United States Imperialism.* Durham, N.C.: Duke University Press.

Karapatan (Alliance for the Advancement of People's Rights). 1997. *The Ramos Presidency and Human Rights.* Quezon City: Karapatan.

Karnow, Stanley. 1989. *In Our Image: America's Empire in the Philippines.* New York: Random House.

Karnow, Stanley, and Nancy Yoshihara. 1992. *Asian Americans in Transition.* New York: The Asia Society.

Keen, Sam. 1986. *Faces of the Enemy.* San Francisco: Harper and Row.

Keene, Donald. 1962. "Native Voice in Foreign Tongue." *Saturday Review of Literature,* October 6, 44.

Keith, Agnes Newton. 1955. *Bare Feet in the Palace.* Boston: Little, Brown.

Kerkvliet, Benedict J. 1990. *Everyday Politics in the Philippines.* Berkeley and Los Angeles: University of California Press.

Kerkvliet, Benedict J., and Resil B. Mojares, eds. 1991. *From Marcos to Aquino: Local Perspectives on Political Transition in the Philippines.* Quezon City: Ateneo de Manila University Press.

Kessler, Richard J. 1989. *Rebellion and Repression in the Philippines.* New Haven, Conn.: Yale University Press.

Kim, Elaine. 1993. "Preface." In *Charlie Chan Is Dead*, edited by Jessica Hagedorn. New York: Penguin Books.

Kingston, Maxine Hong. 1976. *The Woman Warrior*. New York: Alfred Knopf.

———. 1989. *China Men*. New York: Vintage Books.

Kirk, Donald. 1988. *Looted: The Philippines after the Bases*. New York: St. Martin's Press.

Kitano, Harry. 1997. *Race Relations*. Englewood Cliffs, N.J.: Prentice Hall.

Kitano, Harry, and Roger Daniels. 1995. *Asian Americans: Emerging Minorities*. Englewood Cliffs, N.J.: Prentice Hall.

Klare, Michael, and Peter Kornbluh. 1989. *Low Intensity Warfare*. Quezon City: Ken Incorporated.

KMU International Department. 1999. "News from the Philippines." *Correspondence* (January–February): 1–6.

Kochiyama, Yuri. 1989. "A Quick Reflection." *Amerasia Journal* 15, no. 1 (1989): 99–102.

Kolakowski, Leszek. 1968. *The Alienation of Reason*. New York: Anchor Books.

Kolko, Gabriel. 1976. *Main Currents in Modern American History*. New York: Pantheon Books.

Komite ng Sambayanang Pilipino. 1980. *Philippines: Repression and Resistance*. Permanent Peoples' Tribunal Session on the Philippines. London: Komite ng Sambayanang Pilipino.

Korsch, Karl. 1990. "Independence Comes to the Philippines." *Midweek,* June 6, 40–42.

Kristeva, Julia. 1991. *Strangers to Ourselves*. New York: Columbia University Press.

Labor Research Association. 1958. *U.S. and the Philippines*. New York: International Publishers.

Laclau, Ernesto, and Chantal Mouffe. 1985. *Hegemony and Socialist Strategy*. London: Verso.

Ladrido, R. C. 1988. "On Being Kidlat Tahimik." *Kultura* 1, no. 1: 37–42.

Lande, Carl. 1996. *Post-Marcos Politics*. New York: St. Martin's Press.

Larrain, Jorge. 1995. "Identity, the Other, and Postmodernism." In *Post-Ality, Marxism, and Postmodernism,* edited by Mas'ud Zavarzadeh, Teresa Ebert, and Donald Morton. Washington, D.C.: Maisonneuve Press.

Larsen, Neil. 1995. *Reading North by South*. Minneapolis: University of Minnesota Press.

Leech, Margaret. 1959. *In the Days of McKinley*. New York: Harper and Brothers.

Lefebvre, Henri. 1968. *Dialectical Materialism*. London: Jonathan Cape.

———. 1971. *Everyday Life in the Modern World*. New York: Harper.

———. 1976. *The Survival of Capitalism*. London: Allison and Busby.

Lenin, V. I. 1968. *National Liberation, Socialism and Imperialism*. New York: International Publishers.

Lent, John. 1995. "The Moving Art Galleries of South and Southeast Asia." In *Asian Popular Culture,* edited by John Lent. Boulder, Colo.: Westview Press.

LeRoy, James A. 1905. *Philippine Life in Town and Country*. New York: Putnam.

Levine, Andrew. 1984. *Arguing for Socialism*. New York: Routledge and Kegan Paul.

Leys, Colin. 1982. "Samuel Huntington and the End of Classical Modernization Theory." In *Introduction to the Sociology of "Developing Societies,"* edited by Hamza Alavi and Teodor Shanin. New York: Monthly Review Press.

Lim, Felicidad. 1995. "Perfumed Nightmare and the Perils of Jameson's "New Political Culture." *Philippine Critical Forum* 1, no. 1: 24–37.

Lindio-McGovern, Ligaya. 1997. *Filipino Peasant Women.* Philadelphia: University of Pennsylvania Press.

Linmark, R. Zamora. 1995. *Rolling the R's.* New York: Kaya Productions.

Linn, Brian McAllister. 1989. *The U.S. Army and Counterinsurgency in the Philippine War, 1899–1902.* Chapel Hill: University of North Carolina Press.

Lipsitz, George. 1998. *The Possessive Investment in Whiteness.* Philadelphia: Temple University Press.

Loewen, James. 1999. *Lies across America.* New York: The New Press.

Lopez, Salvador P. 1940. *Literature and Society.* Manila: University Publishing.

———. 1976. "Literature and Society—a Literary Past Revisited." In *Literature and Society: Cross-Cultural Perspectives,* edited by Roger Bresnahan. Manila: U.S. Information Service.

Lopez, Sixto. 1900. *The "Tribes" in the Philippines.* Boston: New England Anti-Imperialist League. Available at http://web/syr/edu/~fjzwick/ailtexts/sl_tribe.html, August 1996.

Lotta, Raymond. 1994. *Fundamentals of Political Economy.* English version of the Chinese, *Marxist Economics and the Revolutionary Road to Communism: The Shanghai Textbook on Socialist Political Economy,* New York: Banner Press 1975.

Lowe, Lisa. 1995. "On Contemporary Asian American Projects." *Amerasia Journal* 21, nos. 1–2: 41–54.

Löwy, Michael. 1978. "Marxism and the National Question." In *Revolution and Class Struggle: A Reader in Marxist Politics,* edited by Robin Blackburn. Sussex: The Harvester Press.

———. 1981. *The Politics of Combined and Uneven Development.* London: New Left Books.

Lukács, Georg. 1971. *History and Class Consciousness.* London: Merlin Press.

———. 1972. *Tactics and Ethics.* New York: Harper Torchbooks.

———. 1973. "Approximation to Life in the Novel and the Play." In *Sociology of Literature and Drama,* edited by Elizabeth and Tom Burns. Baltimore: Penguin Books.

———. 1991. *The Process of Democratization.* Albany: State University of New York Press.

Luke, Timothy. 1990. *Social Theory and Modernity.* Newbury Park, Calif.: Sage Publications.

Lukes, Steven. 1985. *Marxism and Morality.* New York: Oxford University Press.

Lumbera, Bienvenido (with Cynthia N. Lumbera), ed. 1982. *Philippine Literature: A History and Anthology.* Manila: National Book Store.

———. 1997. *Revaluation 1997.* Manila: University of Santo Tomas Press.

MacDonell, Diane. 1986. *Theories of Discourse.* Oxford: Blackwell.

MacIntyre, Alasdair. 1984. *After Virtue.* Notre Dame, Ind.: University of Notre Dame Press.

McCord, William. 1991. *The Dawn of the Pacific Century.* New Brunswick, N.J.: Transaction Publishers.

McCoy, Alfred W. 1984. *Priests on Trial.* New York: Penguin.

McCoy, Alfred W. 1991. "The Restoration of Planter Power in La Carlota City." In *From Marcos to Aquino,* edited by Benedict Kerkvliet and Resil Mojares. Quezon City: Ateneo de Manila University Press.

McWilliams, Carey. 1964. *Brothers under the Skin.* Boston: Little, Brown.

Magdoff, Harry. 1969. *The Age of Imperialism.* New York: Monthly Review Press.

Mandel, Ernest. 1995. "The Relevance of Marxist Theory for Understanding the Present World Crisis." In *Marxism in the Postmodern Age*, edited by Antonio Callari et al. New York: The Guilford Press.

Manlogon, Melanie. 1989. "Illumination from Kidlat." *Midweek*, October 11, 7–12.

Mao Tse-tung. 1960. *On Literature and Art*. Peking: Foreign Languages Press.

Martin, Michael, and Terry Kandal, eds. 1989. *Studies of Development and Change in the Modern World*. New York: Oxford University Press.

Marx, Karl, and Friedrich Engels. 1959. *Basic Writings on Politics and Philosophy*. New York: Anchor Books.

Masters, Edgar Lee. 1981. "Filipinos, Remember Us." In *In Time of Hesitation*, edited by Roger Bresnahan. Quezon City: New Day Publishers.

Mastura, Datu Michael. 1983. "Filipino Muslims in Contemporary Society: Visions and Directions of Development." In *Filipino Muslims: Their Social Institutions and Cultural Achievements*, edited by F. Lanca Jocano. Quezon City: Asian Center.

May, Glenn. 1987. "The State of Philippine-American Studies." In *A Past Recovered*. Quezon City: New Day Publishers.

———. 1996. *Inventing a Hero: The Posthumous Re-Creation of Andres Bonifacio*. Quezon City: New Day Publishers.

Mayer, Arno. 1971. *Dynamics of Counterrevolution in Europe 1870–1956*. New York: Harper Torchbooks.

Mayuga, Sylvia, and Alfred Yuson. 1980. "In the Wrong Waters." In *Philippines*, edited by Hans Johannes Hoefer. Hong Kong: Apa Productions.

Melotti, Umberto. 1977. *Marx and the Third World*. London: Macmillan.

Mercado, Monina Allarey, ed. 1986. *People Power: An Eyewitness History*. Manila: James B. Reuter Foundation.

Merleau-Ponty, Maurice. 1969. *Humanism and Terror*. Boston: Beacon Press.

Merquior, J. G. 1986. *From Prague to Paris*. London: Verso.

Miles, Robert. 1986. "Labour Migration, Racism and Capital Accumulation in Western Europe since 1945: An Overview." *Capital and Class* 28 (spring): 49–86.

———. 1989. *Racism*. London: Routledge.

Miliband, Ralph. 1977. *Marxism and Politics*. New York: Oxford University Press.

Miller, Stuart Creighton. 1982. *"Benevolent Assimilation": The American Conquest of the Philippines, 1899–1903*. New Haven, Conn.: Yale University Press.

Min, Pyong Gap, ed. 1995. *Asian Americans: Contemporary Trends and Issues*. Thousand Oaks, Calif.: Sage Publications.

Miner, Earl. 1990. *Comparative Poetics*. Princeton, N.J.: Princeton University Press.

Mo, Timothy. 1995. *Brownout on Breadfruit Boulevard*. London: Paddlefeifer.

Mouffe, Chantal, ed. 1979. *Gramsci and Marxist Theory*. London: Routledge and Kegan Paul.

Mukherjee, Bharati. 1989. *Jasmine*. New York: Fawcett Crest.

———. 1990. "An Interview with Bharati Mukherjee." *The Iowa Review* 30l, no. 3 (fall): 7–32.

Mulhern, Francis. 1995. "The Politics of Cultural Studies." *Monthly Review* 47, no. 3 (July–August): 31–40.

Mura, David. 1993. "From *Turning Japanese*." In *On Prejudice*, edited by Daniela Gioseffi. New York: Anchor Books.

Nairn, Tom. 1977. *The Break-Up of Britain: Crisis and Neo-Nationalism.* London: New Left Books.

———. 1982. "Nationalism and Development." In *Introduction to the Sociology of "Developing Societies,"* edited by Hamza Alavi and Teodor Shanin. New York: Monthly Review Press.

National Asian Pacific American Legal Consortium. 1999. *1998 Audit of Violence against Asian Pacific Americans.* Sixth Annual Report. Washington, D.C. Author.

National Democratic Front. 1999. "Report from the Frontlines." *Liberation* 26, no. 1 (January–March): 3–39.

Nearing, Scott, and Joseph Freeman. 1969. *Dollar Diplomacy.* 1925. Reprint, New York: Monthly Review Press.

Nee, Victor, and J. Sanders. 1985. "The Road to Parity: Determinants of the Socio-Economic Achievements of Asian Americans." *Ethnic and Racial Studies* 9: 75–93.

Nelson, Raymond. 1968. *The Philippines.* New York: Walker and Company.

Nemenzo, Francisco. 1992a. "The Left Needs a New Vision." *Philippine Alternatives* 1 (September): 1–2, 10.

———. 1992b. "Questioning Marx, Critiquing Marxism." *Kasarinlan* 8: 7–28.

———. 1998. "What's Wrong with the Visiting Forces Agreement?" Paper presented at the National Defense College of the Philippines, Quezon City, September 18.

Nichols, Bill. 1981. *Ideology and the Image.* Bloomington: Indiana University Press.

Noble, Lela. 1987. "The Muslim Insurgency." In *The Philippines Reader,* edited by David B. Schirmer and Stephen R. Shalom. Boston: South End Press.

Noumoff, Sam. 1999. "Globalization and Culture." Working Paper 6 in Cultural Studies, Ethnicity and Race Relations. Pullman: Washington State University, Department of Comparative American Cultures.

Novack, George. 1966. *Uneven and Combined Development in History.* New York: Merit Publishers.

Ocampo, Ambeth R. 1998. *The Centennial Countdown.* Quezon City: Anvil Publishing.

Ocampo, Satur. 1998. "Militarization in the Context of Globalization under the Estrada Regime." Paper presented at the 19th Assembly of the Ecumenical Movement for Justice and Peace, United Church of Christ, Quezon City, August 1.

Ofreneo, Rene. 1995. *Globalization and the Filipino Working Masses.* Quezon City: Foundation for Nationalist Studies.

Ofreneo, Rosalinda Pineda, and Rene E. Ofreneo. 1995. "Globalization and Filipino Women Workers." *Philippine Labor Review* 19 (January–June): 1–34.

O'Hare, William P., and Judy Felt. 1991. *Asian Americans: America's Fastest Growing Minority Group.* Washington, D.C.: Population Reference Bureau.

Okada, John. 1974. "From *No-No Boy.*" In *Asian-American Heritage,* edited by David Wand. New York: Washington Square Press.

———. 1981. *No-No Boy.* 1957. Reprint, Seattle: University of Washington Press.

Okamura, Jonathan. 1997. "Filipino-Americans: The Marginalized Minority." In *Cultural Diversity in the U.S.* Westport, Conn.: Bergin and Garvey.

Okihiro, Gary. 1997. "Colonialism and Migrant Labour." *Nature, Society and Thought* 10, nos. 1–2: 203–228.

Ollman, Bertell. 1993. *Dialectical Investigations.* New York: Routledge.

Omatsu, Glenn. 1994. "The 'Four Prisons' and the Movements of Liberation: Asian

American Activism from the 1960s to the 1990s." In *The State of Asian America,* edited by Karin Aguilar-San Juan. Boston: South End Press.

Omi, Michael, and Howard Winant. 1986. *Racial Formation in the United States.* New York: Routledge and Kegan Paul.

Ong, Aihwa. 1999. "Cultural Citizenship as Subject Making: Immigrants Negotiate Racial and Cultural Boundaries in the United States." In *Race, Identity, and Citizenship,* edited by Rodolfo Torres et al. Oxford: Blackwell Publishers.

Ong, Paul, ed. 1994. *The State of Asian Pacific America: Economic Diversity, Issues and Policies.* Los Angeles: LEAP Asian Pacific American Public Policy Institute and UCLA Asian American Studies Center.

Ong, Paul, Edna Bonacich, and Lucie Cheng, eds. 1994. *The New Asian Immigration in Los Angeles and Global Restructuring.* Philadelphia: Temple University Press.

Ordoñez, Elmer, ed. 1998. *Toward the First Asian Republic.* Manila: Philippine Centennial Commission.

Osajima, Keith. 1995. "Postmodern Possibilities: Theoretical and Political Directions for Asian American Studies." *Amerasia Journal* 21: 79–88.

Palacios, Chailang. 1993. "The Colonisation of Our Pacific Islands." In *On Prejudice: A Global Perspective,* edited by Daniela Gioseffi. New York: Anchor Books.

Palmer, Bryan. 1990. *Descent into Discourse: The Reification of Language and the Writing of Social History.* Philadelphia: Temple University Press.

Palumbo-Liu, David, ed. 1995. *The Ethnic Canon.* Minneapolis: University of Minnesota Press.

———. 1999. *Asian/American: Historical Crossings of a Racial Frontier.* Stanford, Calif.: Stanford University Press.

Paredes, Ruby, ed. 1988. *Philippine Colonial Democracy.* New Haven, Conn.: Yale Center for International and Area Studies.

Parenti, Michael. 1989. *The Sword and the Dollar.* New York: St. Martin's Press.

———. 1995. *Against Empire.* San Francisco: City Lights Books.

Patel, Dinker. 1992. "Asian Americans: A Growing Force." *Race and Ethnic Relations 92/93,* edited by John Kromkowski. Guilford, Conn: Dushkin Publishing.

Patterson, Orlando. 1983. "The Nature, Causes, and Implications of Ethnic Identification." In *Minorities: Community and Identity,* edited by C. Fried. Berlin: Springer-Verlag.

Patterson, Thomas C. 1997. *Inventing Western Civilization.* New York: Monthly Review Press.

Paulson, Elisabeth, ed. 1999. *Philippines: Country Report.* London: The Economist Intelligence Unit.

Pertierra, Raul. 1994. "Philippine Studies and the New Ethnography." In *Cultures and Texts,* edited by R. Pertierra and Eduardo Ugarte. Quezon City: University of the Philippines.

Pines, Jim, and Paul Willemen. 1989. *Questions of Third Cinema.* London: British Film Institute.

Pomeroy, William. 1992. *The Philippines: Colonialism, Collaboration, and Resistance!* New York: International Publishers.

Poole, Fred, and Max Vanzi. 1984. *Revolution in the Philippines: The United States in a Hall of Cracked Mirrors.* New York: McGraw-Hill.

Potter, David, and Paul Knepper. 1998. "Comparing Official Definitions of Race in Japan and the United States." In *The Social Construction of Race and Ethnicity in the United States*, edited by Joan Ferrante and Prince Brown Jr. New York: Longman.

Poulantzas, Nicos. 1974. *Classes in Contemporary Capitalism*. New York: Verso.

———. 1978. *State, Power, Socialism*. London: Verso.

Pomeroy, William J. 1970. *American Neo-colonialism: Its Emergence in the Philippines and Asia*. New York: International Publishers.

Pratt, Mary Louise. 1989. "Linguistic Utopias." In *The Linguistics of Writing*. New York: Methuen.

Putzel, James. 1992. *A Captive Land*. New York: Monthly Review Press.

Quinsaat, Jesse, et al., eds. 1976. "Anti-Miscegenation Laws and the Filipino." In *Letters in Exile*. Los Angeles: UCLA Asian American Studies Center.

Rafael, Vicente. 1993. "White Love." In *Cultures of United States Imperialism*, edited by Donald Pease and Amy Kaplan. Durham, N.C.: Duke University Press.

Reimers, David M. 1992. *Still the Golden Door*. New York: Columbia Univrersity Press.

Rex, John. 1982. "Racism and the Structure of Colonial Societies." In *Racism and Colonialism: Essays on Ideology and Social Structure*, edited by Robert Ross. The Hague: Martinus Nijhoff.

———. 1997. "The Concept of a Multicultural Society." In *The Ethnicity Reader*, edited by Montserrat Guibernau and John Rex. Malden, Mass.: Blackwell.

Reyes, Elizabeth. 1980. "Once Forgotten Filipinos." In *Philippines*, edited by Hans Johannes Hoefer. Hong Kong: Apa Productions.

Rhodes, Robert I., ed. 1970. *Imperialism and Underdevelopment: A Reader*. New York: Monthly Review Press.

Richardson, Jim. 1993. "Review Article." *Journal of Contemporary Asia* 23: 382–395.

Ringer, Benjamin. 1983. *We the People and Others*. New York: Tavistock.

Rizal, Jose. 1961a. "The Philippines a Century Hence." In *Rizal*. 1890. Reprint, Manila: Comision Nacional del Centenario de Jose Rizal.

———. 1961b. *Noli Me Tangere*. Translated by Leon Ma. Guerrero. 1887. Reprint, London: Longman.

———. 1912. *The Reign of Greed* (El Filibusterismo). Translated by Charles Derbyshire. Manila: Philippine Education.

Robinson, William. 1992. "The Sao Paulo Forum and Post-Cold War Thinking in Latin America." *Monthly Review* 44 (December): 31–32. Reprinted in *Philippine Alternatives* 1 (February 1993): 7–8.

Rodney, Walter. 1982. *How Europe Underdeveloped Africa*. 1972. Reprint, Washington, D.C.: Howard University Press.

Root, Maria P. 1997. *Filipino Americans*. Thousand Oaks, Calif.: Sage Publications.

Rosaldo, Renato. 1994. "Social Justice and the Crisis of National Communities." In *Colonial Discourse/Postcolonial Theory*, edited by Francis Barker et al. New York: St. Martin's Press.

Rosenberg, David E., ed. 1979. *Marcos and Martial Law in the Philippines*. Ithaca, N.Y.: Cornell University Press.

Rotor, Arturo. 1973. "Our Literary Heritage." In *Literature under the Commonwealth*, edited by Manuel Quezon et al. 1940. Reprint, Manila: Alberto Florentino.

Roxas-Lim, Aurora. 1996. "Philippine Ethnolinguistic Groups." In *Cultural Dictionary for*

Filipinos, edited by Thelma B. Kintanar and Associates. Quezon City: University of the Philippines Press and Anvil Publishing.

Ruiz, Lester Edwin. 1991. "After National Democracy: Radical Democratic Politics at the Edge of Modernity." *Alternatives* 16: 161–200.

Safran, William. 1991. "Diasporas in Modern Societies: Myths of Homeland and Return." *Diaspora* (spring): 83–99.

Said, Edward. 1985. *After the Last Sky.* New York: Pantheon Books.

———. 1990. "Yeats and Decolonization." In *Nationalism, Colonialism and Literature,* edited by Terry Eagleton et al. Minneapolis: University of Minnesota Press.

———. 1994. *Culture and Imperialism.* New York: Alfred Knopf.

St. Hilaire, Colette. 1992. "Canadian Aid, Women and Development." *Philippine Development Briefing* 3 (December): 3–15.

Salman, Michael. 1991. "In Our Orientalist Imagination: Historiography and the Culture of Colonialism in the United States." *Radical History Review* 50: 221–232.

———. 1995. "Nothing without Labor: Penology, Discipline and Independence in the Philippines under United States Rule." In *Discrepant Histories,* edited by V. Rafael. Philadelphia: Temple University Press.

Sanjines, Jorge. 1989. *Theory and Practice of a Cinema with the People.* Willimantic, Conn.: Curbstone Press.

San Juan, E. 1986. *Crisis in the Philippines.* South Hadley, Mass.: Bergin & Garvey.

———. 1988. *Subversions of Desire.* Quezon City: Ateneo de Manila University Press.

———. 1990. *From People to Nation: Essays in Cultural Politics.* Manila: Asian Social Institute.

———. 1991a. "Beyond Identity Politics: The Predicament of the Asian American Writer in Late Capitalism." *American Literary History* (fall): 542–565.

———. 1991b. *Writing and National Liberation.* Quezon City: University of the Philippines Press.

———. 1992a. *Racial Formations/Critical Transformations.* Atlantic Highlands, N.J.: Humanities Press.

———. 1992b. *Reading the West/Writing the East.* New York: Peter Lang.

———. 1995. "Multiculturalism and the Challenge of World Cultural Studies." In *Hegemony and Strategies of Transgression.* Albany: State University of New York Press.

———. 1996a. "Configuring the Filipino Diaspora in the United States." In *Race and Ethnic Relations 96/97,* 6th ed., edited by John A. Kromkowski. Guilford, Conn.: Dushkin Publishing Group/Brown and Benchmark Publishers.

———. 1996b. *The Philippine Temptation: Dialectics of Philippines-United States Literary Relations.* Philadelphia: Temple University Press.

———. 1998a. *Beyond Postcolonial Theory.* New York: St. Martin's Press.

———. 1998b. *From Exile to Diaspora: Versions of the Filipino Experience in the United States.* Boulder Colo.: Westview Press.

Santos, Lope K. 1906. *Banaag at Sikat.* Manila: Limbagang E.C. McCullough.

Sassen, Saskia. 1998. *Globalization and Its Discontents.* New York: The New Press.

Sayer, Derek. 1987. *The Violence of Abstraction.* New York: Blackwell.

Sayyid, Bobby. 1994. "Sign O' Times: Kaffirs and Infidels Fighting the Ninth Crusade." In *The Making of Political Identities,* edited by Ernesto Laclau. London: Verso.

Schirmer, Daniel B. 1997. *Fidel Ramos—the Pentagon's Philippine Friend 1992–1997.* Cambridge, Mass: Friend of the Filipino People.

Schirmer, Daniel B., and Stephen R. Shalom, eds. 1987. *The Philippines Reader*. Boston: South End Press.

Scipes, Kim. 1999. "Global Economic Crisis, Neoliberal Solutions, and the Philippines." *Monthly Review* 51 (December): 1–14.

Scott, William Henry. 1982. *Cracks in the Parchment Curtain*. Quezon City: New Day Publishers.

———. 1993. *Of Igorots and Independence*. Baguio City: ERA.

Selden, Mark. 1971. "Revolution and Third World Development: People's War and the Transformation of Peasant Society." In *National Liberation*, edited by Norman Miller and Roderick Aya. New York: The Free Press.

Serrano, Isagani. 1994. *Civil Society in the Asia-Pacific Region*. Washington, D.C.: Civicus.

Shalom, Stephen. 1986. *The United States and the Philippines: A Study of Neocolonialism*. Quezon City: New Day Publishers.

Shanin, Teodor. 1976. "Peasantry as a Political Factor." In *Peasants and Peasant Societies*, edited by T. Shanin. New York: Penguin Books.

———. 1982. "Class, State and Revolution: Substitutes and Realities." In *Introduction to the Sociology of "Developing Societies,"* edited by Hamza Alavi and Teodor Shanin. New York: Monthly Review Press.

Shaw, Martin. 1975. *Marxism and Social Science*. London: Pluto Press.

Sheridan, Richard Brinsley. 1970. *The Filipino Martyrs*. 1900. Reprint, Quezon City: Malaya Books.

Shohat, Ella. 1995. "The Struggle over Representation: Casting, Coalitions, and the Politics of Identification." In *Late Imperial Culture*, edited by Roman de la Campa, E. Ann Kaplan, and Michael Sprinker. London: Verso.

Simmel, Georg. 1977. "The Stranger." In *Race, Ethnicity, and Social Change*. North Scituate, Mass.: Duxbury Press.

Sison, Jose Maria. 1986. *Philippine Crisis and Revolution: Ten Lectures*. Mimeographed edition. Lectures delivered at the Asian Center, University of the Philippines, Diliman, Quezon City, April–May.

———. 1989. *The Philippine Revolution: The Leader's View*. New York: Crane Russak.

Sison, Jose Maria, and Julieta de Lima. 1998. *Philippine Economy and Politics*. Manila: Aklat ng Bayan Publishing.

Sklair, Leslie. 1991. *Sociology of the Global System*. Baltimore: The Johns Hopkins University Press.

Smedley, Audrey. 1993. *Race in North America*. Boulder, Colo.: Westview Press.

Smith, Anthony. 1971. *Theories of Nationalism*. New York: Harper and Row.

———. 1979. *Nationalism in the Twentieth Century*. New York: New York University Press.

Smith, Joseph Burkholder. 1976. *Portrait of a Cold Warrior*. New York: Ballantine Books.

Smith, Neil. 1984. *Uneven Development*. New York: Blackwell.

Solanas, Fernando, and Octavio Gettino. 1976. "Towards a Third Cinema." In *Movies and Methods*, edited by Bill Nichols. Berkeley and Los Angeles: University of California Press.

Sollors, Werner. 1986. *Beyond Ethnicity: Consent and Descent in American Culture*. New York: Oxford University Press.

Solomos, John, and Les Back. 1996. *Racism and Society*. New York: St. Martin's Press.

Spivak, Gayatri. 1991. *The Post-Colonial Critic.* New York: Routledge.

Stabile, Carole. 1995. "Postmodernism, Feminism, and Marx: Notes from the Abyss." *Monthly Review* (July/August): 89–107.

Stanley, Peter. 1974. *A Nation in the Making: The Philippines and the United States 1899–1921.* Cambridge, Mass.: Harvard University Press.

———, ed. 1984. *Reappraising an Empire: New Perspectives on Philippine-American History.* Cambridge, Mass.: Harvard University Press.

Stasiulis, Daiva, and Nira Yuval-Davis, eds. 1995. *Unsettling Settler Societies.* London: Sage Publications.

Stauffer, Robert. 1985. *The Marcos Regime: Failure of Transnational Developmentalism and Hegemony Building from Above and Outside.* Research Monograph 23. Sydney: Transnational Corporations Research Project.

———. 1987. "Review of Peter Stanley: *Reappraising an Empire.*" *Journal of Asian Studies* 12: 103.

———. 1990. "Philippine Democracy: Contradictions of Third World Democratization." Paper presented at the Philippine Studies Colloqium, University of Hawaii, May 4.

Steinberg, David Joel. 1982. *The Philippines: A Singular and A Plural Place.* Boulder, Colo.: Westview Press.

———. 1986. "Tradition and Response." In *Crisis in the Philippines: The Marcos Era and Beyond,* edited by John Bresnan. Princeton, N.J.: Princeton University Press.

Steinberg, Stephen. 1995. *Turning Back.* Boston: Beacon Press.

Stephenson, Ralph, and Jean Debrix. 1969. *The Cinema as Art.* Baltimore: Penguin Books.

Stoler, Ann Laura. 1996. *Race and the Education of Desire.* Durham, N.J.: Duke University Press.

Suleri, Sara. 1995. "Woman Skin Deep: Feminism and the Postcolonial Condition." In *The Post-Colonial Studies Reader,* edited by Bill Ashcroft, Gareth Griffiths, and Helen Tiffin. London: Routledge.

Sullivan, William H. 1987. "The United States-Philippine Strategic Relationship." In *Rebuilding a Nation,* edited by Carl Lande. Washington, D.C.: Washington Institute Press Book.

Sussman, Gerald. 1992. "What 'Hearts of Darkness' Left Out." *Guardian,* April 29, 19.

Swenson, Sally. 1987. "National Minorities." In *The Philippines Reader,* edited by David B. Schirmer and Stephen R. Shalom. Boston: South End Press.

Tabb, William. 1990. *The Future of Socialism.* New York: Monthly Review Press.

Tadiar, Neferti Xina M. 1997. "Domestic Bodies of the Philippines." *Sojourn* 12: 153–191.

Tahimik, Kidlat. 1989. "Cups-of-Gas Filmmaking vs. Full-Tank-cum-Credit Cart Filmmaking." *Discourse* 11 (spring–summer): 81–86.

Tajima, Renee. 1991. "Moving the Image: Asian American Independent Filmmaking 1970–1990." In *Moving the Image: Independent Asian Pacific American Media Arts,* edited by Russell Leong. Los Angeles: UCLA Asian American Studies Center.

Takaki, Ronald. 1987. "Reflections on Racial Patterns in America." In *From Different Shores,* edited by Ronald Takaki. New York: Oxford University Press.

———. 1989. *Strangers from a Different Shore.* Boston: Little, Brown.

Talbot, Margaret. 1991. "Native Daughter." *San Francisco Examiner,* January 13, 11–17.

Tañada, Wigberto. 1994–1995. "Senator Tañada Addresses Security Issues." *Philippine Witness* 50: 5, 9.

Tapping, Craig. 1992. "South Asia Writes North America: Prose Fictions and Autobiographies from the Indian Diaspora." In *Reading the Literatures of Asian Americans,* edited by Shirley Lin and Amy Ling. Philadelphia: Temple University Press.

Tarr, Peter. 1989. "Learning to Love Imperialism." *The Nation,* June 5, 779–784.

Taruc, Luis. 1953. *Born of the People.* New York: International Publishers.

Taylor, Charles. 1992. *Multiculturalism and "The Politics of Recognition".* Princeton, N.J.: Princeton University Press.

Taylor, George. 1964. *The Philippines and the United States: Problems of Partnership.* New York: Praeger.

Tenbruck, Friedrich. 1990. "The Dream of a Secular Ecumene: The Meaning and Limits of Policies of Development." In *Global Culture,* edited by Mike Featherstone. London: Sage Publications.

Thomas, Clive Y. 1984. *The Rise of the Authoritarian State in Peripheral Societies.* New York: Monthly Review Press.

Thomson, George. 1945. *Marxism and Poetry.* London: Lawrence and Wishart.

Timberman, David G. 1991. *A Changeless Land.* New York: M. E. Sharpe.

Tinker, Hugh. 1993. "The Race Factor in International Politics." In *On Prejudice,* edited by Daniela Gioseffi. New York: Anchor Books.

Tiongson, Nicanor, ed. 1983. *The Urian Anthology 1970–1979.* Metro Manila: Morato.

———, ed. 1984. *The Politics of Culture: The Philippine Experience.* Quezon City: Philippine Educational Theater Association.

———. 1992. "Ang Paghuli sa Adarna: Tungo sa Isang Pamantayang Pangkultura." In *Kritisismo,* edited by Soledad Reyes. Pasig, Rizal: Anvil Publishing.

Tiongson, Nicanor, et al. 1986. "The Ideology and Culture of the New Society." In *Synthesis: Before and beyond February 1986.* Quezon City: The Interdisciplinary Forum.

Toffler, Alvin. 1990. *Powershift.* New York: Bantam Books.

Tolentino, Roland. 1996. "Jameson and Kidlat Tahimik." *Philippine Studies* 44 (first quarter): 113–125.

Torre, Ed de la. 1986. *Touching Ground, Taking Root.* London: Catholic Institute for International Relations.

Tujan, Antonio. 1998. "Globalization and Labor: The Philippine Case." Available at http://www.geocities.com/CapitolHill/Lobby/4677/index.html.

Tupaz, Omar. 1991. "Toward a Revolutionary Strategy of the 90s." *Debate: Philippine Left Review* 1 (September): 6–40.

Turner, Bryan S. 1994. *Orientalism, Postmodernism and Globalism.* New York: Routledge.

Twain, Mark. 1992. "Thirty Thousand Killed a Million." *Atlantic Monthly,* April, 52–56.

United States Census. 1991. *Statistical Abstract of the United States, 1991.* 111th ed. Washington, D.C.: U.S. Government Printing Office.

United States Commission on Civil Rights. 1992. *Civil Rights Issues Facing Asian Americans in the 1990s.* Washington, D.C.: United States Commission on Civil Rights.

Van Erven, Eugene. 1992. *The Playful Revolution.* Bloomington: Indiana University Press.

Vera Cruz, Philip. 1992. *Philip Vera Cruz: A Personal History of Filipino Immigrants and the Farmworkers Movement.* Los Angeles: UCLA Labor Center and Asian American Studies Center.

Vidal, Gore. 1986–1992. *The Decline and Fall of the American Empire.* Berkeley: Odonian Press.

Villegas, Edberto. 1983. *Studies in Philippine Political Economy.* Manila: Silangan Publishers.

Vizmanos, Danilo. 1989. "The Balangiga Incident." *Midweek,* September 27, 11–14.

Voloshinov, V. N., and Mikhail Bakhtin. 1973. *Marxism and the Philosophy of Language.* New York: Academic Press.

Vreeland, Nena, et al. 1976. *Area Handbook for the Philippines.* Washington, D.C.: U.S. Government Printing Office.

Wald, Alan. 1992. *The Responsibility of Intellectuals.* Atlantic Highlands, N.J.: Humanities Press.

Wallerstein, Immanuel. 1983. *Historical Capitalism.* New York: Verso.

———. 1991. "The Construction of Peoplehood." In *Race, Nation, Class: Ambiguous Identities.* London: Verso.

Wei, William. 1996. "Reclaiming the Past and Constructing a Collective Culture." In *Multicultural Experiences, Multicultural Theories,* edited by Mary F. Rogers. New York: McGraw-Hill.

Weightman, George. 1987. "Sociology in the Philippines." *International Review of Modern Sociology* 17 (spring): 35–62.

West, Cornel. 1991. *The Ethical Dimensions of Marxist Thought.* New York: Monthly Review Press.

West, Lois. 1997. *Militant Labor in the Philippines.* Philadelphia: Temple University Press.

Wilden, Anthony. 1987. *The Rules Are No Game.* London: Routledge and Kegan Paul.

Williams, Raymond. 1977. *Marxism and Literature.* New York: Oxford University Press.

———. 1983. *The Year 2000.* New York: Pantheon Books.

———. 1989. *The Politics of Modernism.* London: Verso.

Williams, Rhonda M. 1995. "Consenting to Whiteness: Reflections on Race and Marxian Theories of Discrimination." In *Marxism in the Postmodern Age,* edited by Antonio Callari, Stephen Cullenberg, and Carole Biewener. New York: The Guilford Press.

Williams, William Appleman. 1962. *The Tragedy of American Diplomacy.* New York: A Delta Book.

———. 1969. "The Large Corporation and American Foreign Policy." In *Corporations and the Cold War,* edited by David Horowitz. New York: Monthly Review Press.

———. 1971. "The Vicious Circle of American Imperialism." In *Readings in U.S. Imperialism,* edited by K. T. Fann and Donald C. Hodges. Boston: Porter Sargent.

Winant, Howard. 1994. *Racial Conditions: Politics, Theory, Comparisons.* Minneapolis: University of Minnesota Press.

Winchester, Simon. 1984. "The Philippines." In *Tourism's Ugly Face,* Rina Jimenez David, *Philippine News* May 2–8: 15.

Woddis, Jack. 1967. *An Introduction to Neo-Colonialism.* New York: International Publishers.

Wolf, Eric. 1976. "On Peasant Rebellions." In *Peasants and Peasant Societies,* edited by Teodor Shanin. New York: Penguin Books.

———. 1982. *Europe and the People without History.* Berkeley and Los Angeles: University of California Press.

Wolff, Leon. 1961. *Little Brown Brother: How the United States Purchased and Pacified the Philippine Islands at the Century's Turn.* New York: Doubleday.

Wollen, Peter. 1982. *Readings and Writings.* London: Verso.

Wong, Paul, ed. 1999. *Race, Ethnicity, and Nationality in the United States: Toward the Twenty-First Century.* Boulder, Colo.: Westview Press.

Wong, Paul, Meera Manvi, and Takeo Hirota Wong. "Asiacentrism and Asian American Studies?" *Amerasia Journal* 21, nos. 1–2 (1995): 137–148.

Woo, Deborah. 1989. "The Gap between Striving and Achieving: The Case of Asian American Women." In *Making Waves,* edited by Asian Women United of California. Boston: Beacon Press.

Wood, Ellen Meiksins. 1998. "Modernity, Postmodernity, or Capitalism?" In *Capitalism and the Information Age,* edited by Robert McChesney et al. New York: Monthly Review Press.

———. 1999. "Global Capitalism in a World of Nation-States." *Monthly Review* 51, no. 3 (July–August): 1–16.

Worcester, Dean. 1913. *Slavery and Peonage in the Philippine Islands.* [n.p.]

Worcester, Dean C. 1914. *The Philippines Past and Present.* New York: Macmillan.

Worcester, Dean C., and John Bellamy Forster, eds. 1995. *In Defense of History.* Special Issue of *Monthly Review* 47 (July–August).

Yamamoto, Hisaye. 1988. *Seventeen Syllables and Other Stories.* Latham, N.Y.: Kitchen Table Press.

Yamato, Alexander, et al., eds. 1993. *Asian Americans in the United States.* Vol. 1. Dubuque, Iowa: Kendall/Hunt Publishing.

Zinn, Howard. 1967. "History as Private Enterprise." In *The Critical Spirit.* Boston: Beacon Press.

———. 1984. *The Twentieth Century: A People's History.* New York: Harper and Row.

Zizek, Slavoj. 1997. "Multiculturalism, or, The Cultural Logic of Multinational Capitalism." *New Left Review* 225 (September–October): 28–51.

Zwick, Jim. 1995. "An Empire Is Not a Frontier: Mark Twain's Opposition to United States Imperialism." *Over Here: Review in American Studies* (summer–winter): 58–70.

———, ed. 1992. *Mark Twain's Weapons of Satire.* Syracuse, N.Y.: Syracuse University Press.

Index

Abaya, Hernando, 75
Adorno, Theodor, 107, 152
Agoncillo, Teodoro, 6, 82, 84, 106
Ahmad, Eqbal, 6
Algabre, Salud, 144, 163, 222
Allegory, 104–17, 132–35, 140, 147–62
Allen, James, 173
Allochronism, 26, 30–31, 36, 101, 209
Althusser, Louis, 172, 184
American Indians, 70–71, 101
Amin, Samir, 111, 113–14, 202, 206
Anderson, Benedict, 73, 93–94, 200–201, 217
Appelbaum, Richard, 57–58
Aquino, Corazon, 68, 124, 141, 145, 150, 167–68, 179, 187, 191, 204–06
Arguilla, Manuel, 107
Aronowitz, Stanley, 159
Arrighi, Giovanni, 80
Asian Americans, 18–41, 43–64; literature of, 213–22
Assad, Talal, 102

Bakhtin, Mikhail, 102, 104–06, 116–17, 148, 158, 169, 185
Baking, Angel, 107, 141
Balangiga, Samar, 82, 85, 143–44, 165
Balibar, Etienne, 21, 47, 109
Balweg, 148–151
Barraclough, Geoffrey, 69

Barrat-Brown, Michael, 65
Barros, Maria Lorena, 63
Barthes, Roland, 102, 150, 155
Baudrillard, Jean, 86–87, 128, 188
Bautista, Lualhati, 39, 115
Bello, Walden, 166, 169
"Benevolent Assimilation," 5, 77, 166, 198. See McKinley, William
Benjamin, Walter, 84, 105, 107, 152–53, 185–86, 220
Berger, John, 36
Berlow, Alan, 80
Bernal, Ishmael, 99, 159
Beveridge, Albert, 69, 99
Blauner, Robert, 25, 46
Bloch, Ernst, 188
Blue Dreams (Nancy Ableman and John Lie), 61
Boal, Augusto, 147
Boggs, Grace Lee, 43
Bonacich, Edna, 48, 58
Bonifacio, Andres, 4, 82–84, 205–06
Bonner, Raymond, 202
Bourdieu, Pierre, 71
Boyd, William, 165
Brecht, Bertolt, 115, 117, 147, 153–55, 162, 220
Brocka, Lino, 99, 113, 158–59
Bulosan, Carlos, 22–23, 27–29, 33–34, 55, 65, 107–08, 125, 129, 137, 161–62, 217
Buss, Claude, 75

247

Caldwell, Malcolm, 163–64

Capitalism, 2, 10, 17–18, 23, 26, 33, 39–40, 44, 48–49, 51, 54, 57–58, 61, 87, 102–03, 108–09, 112–14, 127, 130–32, 145, 153, 158, 162–89, 197, 210; booty, 31; flexible, 14, 29

Caribbean, 30, 50, 116

Caudwell, Christopher, 112

Césaire, Aimé, 116

Chan, Jeffery Paul, 20, 34, 36–38

Chan, Sucheng, 48

Chang, Robert, 52, 62–63

Chin, Frank, 19–21, 51, 60, 117

Chin, Vincent, 46

China, 2, 49, 59, 174, 219

Chinese Americans, 18–27. *See* Chin, Frank; Kingston, Maxine Hong

Chomsky, Noam, 65–66, 67, 80

Choy, Curtis, 161

Civil society, 7, 10, 53, 61, 84, 92, 96, 173–75, 178–79, 182–88, 211

Class struggle, 22–23, 47, 50, 58, 79, 83, 101, 163–65, 170–75, 181–89, 197, 213–22

Clifford, James, 102–03

Cold War, 5–7, 28, 39, 73–75, 79–80, 83–84, 88, 97, 107–09, 112, 138, 197, 200–202, 205, 216

Colonialism, 1, 26–28, 39, 43, 54–55, 65–96, 99–103, 163, 188–89, 191–212; internal, 3, 48–50, 52

Commodity fetishism, 13, 19, 31, 39, 44, 47, 85–87, 111, 129, 132–34, 145, 148, 164, 179, 187

"Common culture," 39, 45, 53, 78, 130

Communist Manifesto, 113, 176, 182

Communist Party of the Philippines (CPP), 2, 149, 166–70, 173–74

Community, 20–21, 29, 136, 139, 146, 158, 160–62

Conrad, Joseph, 85

Constantino, Renato, 6, 82, 97, 107, 109

Contemplacion, Flor, 57

Coppola, Francis Ford, 85, 159

Counterrevolution, 5, 77, 79, 88, 92, 181

Covi, Giovanna, 129

Critical Race Theory, 47, 52–53, 62–63

Cuba, 1, 30, 104, 221

Culture, 46, 61–62, 79–80, 184–86, 205–11

Cunanan, Andrew, 12

Daniels, Roger, 45

Debray, Regis, 114

Deleuze, Gilles, 26–28, 31, 33, 105, 112

Delgado Richard, 49

Demko, George, 192

Development, uneven and combined, 2, 25, 29, 33, 39, 43–44, 69, 72, 87, 95, 114, 135–36, 147, 177, 181–84, 196–97

Dewey, Admiral George, 14, 68–69, 87

Dialectic, 29, 34, 44, 70, 76, 84, 87, 93, 106–07, 117, 147, 150, 160, 167–69, 185, 214

Dialogism, 36, 116–17. *See also* Bakhtin, Mikhail

Diaspora, 4, 13, 15–19, 22, 26, 31–38, 56, 63, 91, 127, 130, 218–19

Difference, 26, 30–34, 59, 89, 98, 108, 115–16, 193

Diokno, Jose, 91

Dirlik, Arif, 2

Dissanayake, Wimal, 159

Doty, Roxanne Lynn, 79, 100, 152, 203

Eagleton, Terry, 118

Eisenstein, Sergei, 161

Emerson, Ralph Waldo, 119

Empire Writes Back, The, 109, 122

Engels, Friedrich, 60

Enriquez, Virgilio, 185, 201

Escobar, Arturo, 29

Espiritu, Yen Le, 47–48, 54–56

Essentialism, 2, 34, 170, 185

Estrada, Joseph, 9–10, 141, 177, 197

Ethnicity, 13, 23, 29, 36, 44, 46–49, 58–60, 98, 134, 175, 187, 194, 214

Ethnogenesis, 18, 26, 118

Exchange value, 29, 36, 53, 87, 114, 145, 148, 152

Fagan, David, 7

Falk, Richard, 8

Fallows, James, 165

Fanon, Frantz, 96, 114, 147, 159, 217
Fast, Jonathan, 202
Feminism, 33, 39, 52, 79, 185
Fernandez, Doreen Gamboa, 98
Feudalism, 172, 176
Filipino Americans, 3, 43–45, 50, 63–64, 90–93, 107–08, 123–41, 164. *See also* Bulosan, Carlos; Hagedorn, Jessica
Filipino–American War, 1–15, 22, 69, 82, 99, 104, 121, 124, 143–46, 154, 164–65, 192, 208, 216, 221–22
Filipinologists, 74, 78, 95, 205–06
Filipinos, 2, 43–44, 48–50, 59–60, 65–96, 121–41, 191–212
Forbes, William Cameron, 74–75, 195
Foucault, Michel, 53, 62, 81, 93–94, 109, 131, 153, 169, 177, 184
Francisco, Luzviminda, 82
Franklin, Bruce, 70
Franklin, John Hope, 49
Fraser, Nancy, 61
Freire, Paulo, 96, 143, 217
Friend, Theodore, 80, 83
Frith, Simon, 139
Functionalism, 7, 71–72, 75, 78, 80, 93, 162, 168, 196, 201, 204–05, 209–10

Gabriel, Teshome, 159
Giddens, Anthony, 78
Gitlin, Todd, 139
Globalization, 48, 66, 84–87, 98
Goethe, Johann Wolfgang, 113
Goldfield, Michael, 53
Gorki, Maxim, 119
Gotanda, Neil, 44, 62
Gramsci, Antonio, 15, 53, 89, 98, 110, 121, 129, 177, 183–84, 206, 218, 220
Grossholtz, Jean, 75
Guillaumin, Colette, 48
Guattari, Felix, 26–28, 33, 105

Habermas, Jurgen, 116, 182, 210
Hagedorn, Jessica, 13, 111–12, 121–41, 218
Hall, Stuart, 151
Hamilton-Paterson, James, 164–65
Harvey, David, 14, 58, 91, 147, 192
Hawaii, 48, 107, 117, 124, 131, 187

Hayden, Joseph, 74–75
Heath, Stephen, 152
Hegel, Friedrich, 36, 176, 182
Hegemony, 4, 26, 32, 38, 51, 56, 59, 64–66, 74, 79, 81, 84, 104–06, 152, 177–79, 183–84, 194, 201, 206, 209–10
Heiser, Victor, 199
Hendrix, Jimi, 131, 139–40
Hernandez, Amado V., 107, 109, 116, 220
Hinton, William, 179–80
Historicity, 20, 34, 37, 47, 156, 168. *See also* Development; Dialectic
Holz, Hans Heinz, 175–76
Huk uprising, 5, 108, 197, 201, 217
Huntington, Samuel, 205–06, 216

Ichiyo, Muto, 8
Identity, 12–13, 51–52, 57–58, 63, 98, 101, 112, 114, 117, 126, 140, 169, 214
Ideology, 51, 77, 98, 108–09
Igorots, 8, 101–03, 148–51, 159, 195, 207–08
Ileto, Reynaldo, 82–83, 93–94
Immigrants, 18, 27, 39–40, 49–50, 52, 55, 59–61, 125–27, 164
Imperialism, 1–18, 23, 28, 56–57, 65–69, 121–41, 143, 153, 162, 172, 180–81
Individualism, 15, 19, 21, 25, 33, 59, 61, 71, 89, 98, 132–36, 151, 162, 169
International Monetary Fund (IMF), 8–9, 66–68, 90–92, 109, 111, 135, 206–07
Iyer, Pico, 122

Jacoby, Russell, 130–31
James, C. L. R., 90, 114
Jameson, Fredric, 36, 40, 95, 107–09, 132, 147, 151–53, 160
Japan, 34–36, 46, 49, 59, 125, 164
Japanese Americans, 52, 64. *See also* Okada, John
Joaquin, Nick, 110–11, 186

Kafka, Franz, 24
Kang, Younghill, 32, 40, 43
Karnow, Stanley, 63–64, 72–80, 102, 123, 198, 203, 208
Keene, Donald, 110

Kingston, Maxine Hong, 21, 23–25, 29–30, 33–34, 51
Kipling, Rudyard, 69, 99
Kolko, Gabriel, 70–71
Korean Americans, 46 53, 61
Korsch, Karl, 88
Kristeva, Julia, 24, 38
Kushner, Sam, 162

Labor, 25–27, 39, 50, 56–58, 102, 107, 148, 152–53, 157–58, 160–62, 170
Laclau, Ernesto, 50, 52
Language, 103, 119, 184–85, 213, 217–18. *See also* Bakhtin, Mikhail; Dialogism
Lansdale, Edward, 77, 164
Larsen, Neil, 113
Lee, Ricardo, 99, 151
Lefebvre, Henri, 128, 164
Lenin, Vladimir, 170, 174
Lent, John, 154
Leroy, James, 7, 74
Liberalism, 10, 30, 38, 67, 108, 122, 128, 200
Lim, Felicidad, 153
Lim, Genny, 40
Linmark, R. Zamora, 117
Lipsitz, George, 61
Lopez, Salvador P., 97, 106–07
Lowe, Lisa, 52
Löwy, Michael, 72, 114
Lukács, Georg, 47, 170, 174, 196, 220
Lumbera, Bienvenido, 99, 159
Luxemburg, Rosa, 121

Mabini, Apolinario, 65, 109, 141, 222
MacArthur, Douglas, 72, 75
Macherey, Pierre, 109
Madame Butterfly, 33, 59
Magsaysay, Ramon, 73–77, 164, 178, 197, 201
Mandel, Ernest, 188
Manifest Destiny, 3, 55, 70, 80, 99, 101, 122–23, 198, 210
Mann, Thomas, 119
Mao Tse-tung, 25, 118, 169, 176, 220
Marcos, Ferdinand, 4, 67–68, 72, 79, 85–88, 110–13, 123–24, 127, 130–31, 141,

144–45, 152, 167–68, 170, 179–80, 197, 202–04, 207
Market, 25, 50, 53, 69, 79, 87, 102, 153, 157, 207. *See also* Commodity fetishism; Exchange value
Marx, Karl, 2, 17, 84, 98, 104, 113–14, 118, 166–68, 172–74, 176–80, 201
Mauss, Marcel, 203
May, Glenn, 4, 82–84, 94, 202, 205–06
Mayer, Arno, 77, 206
McCord, William, 43–44
McCoy, Alfred, 203–04
McKinley, William, 5, 70, 77, 99, 195, 199–200
McNutt, Paul, 75
Menchu, Rigoberta, 81, 83–84
Merleau-Ponty, Maurice, 167
Miles, Robert, 48
Min, Pyong Gap, 45–46
Miss Saigon, 33
Mo, Timothy, 191
Model minority, 11, 28–29, 38–41, 44, 48, 50–51, 63, 215
Modernization, 3, 36, 39, 44, 66–67, 78, 98, 100, 145, 205
Moros, 8, 195–97
Mukherjee, Bharati, 21–33
Multiculturalism, 9, 44–46, 57–60, 89, 91, 108, 117, 123, 129–30, 191–211, 214
Myrdal, Gunnar 47, 63

Nairn, Tom, 10, 114
Nation, 48–49, 54, 104, 107, 114, 181–89, 192, 219
National Democratic Front, 10, 113, 166–70, 179
Nationalism, 39, 49, 72, 75–78, 90, 98, 104–17, 126, 139, 161–62, 166, 169–70, 177, 184–86
National liberation, 8, 13, 55, 91, 108, 118, 132, 148–50, 164, 177–78, 188
Nemenzo, Francisco, 173–75
Neocolonialism, 9, 50, 56–58, 68–119, 121–41, 145–46, 155–57, 164, 179, 205–06
Neo–Social Darwinism, 14, 58, 178
Neruda, Pablo, 116, 220

New People's Army (NPA), 9–10, 85, 103, 128, 149, 166, 170, 174, 184, 192, 217–18

New World Order, 12, 28, 58, 68–69, 91

Nongovernmental organizations (NGOs), 10, 84

Okada, John, 34, 36

Omatsu, Glenn, 57

Orientalism, 2–3, 32, 39, 54, 63, 87, 131, 198–99, 206, 215

Overseas contract workers (OCWs), 3, 14, 39, 57–58, 85, 92, 124, 130, 181, 186–87, 208, 216, 220

Pacific Rim, 2–3, 210, 215, 221

Palumbo-Liu, David, 25, 56

Panethnicity, 45, 47–49, 53

Paredes, Ruby, 201–02

Philippine Commonwealth, 4, 105–06, 124

Philippine Educational Theater Association (PETA), 117

Philippine Studies, 74, 79–80, 87

Philippine Writers League, 107

Pluralism, 32–35, 47, 56, 59, 89, 111, 208

Pomeroy, William, 173–74

Postcolonialism, 2, 10, 21, 36, 59, 63, 67, 71–73, 81, 86–92, 97, 103, 108–10, 115–17, 121–23, 131, 137–38, 144, 184. *See also* Development; National liberation; Neocolonialism

Postmodernism, 19, 21, 29, 32–33, 39, 51–55, 67, 81–82, 86, 96, 102, 111, 123, 127, 143–56

Poststructuralism, 14, 40, 91

Pratt, Mary Louise, 116

Primordialism, 201–02

Puerto Rico, 48, 87, 121, 203

Racialization process, 48, 53, 79, 100, 165

Racism, 7–8, 11–15, 21–27, 35–37, 45–49, 52–56, 61, 72, 125, 129, 161, 165, 175, 187, 192–94, 205. *See also* Model minority; White supremacy

Ramos, Fidel, 68, 164, 177

Reification, 13, 19, 32, 37, 47, 58, 85, 151,

185, 196–98, 215. *See also* Commodity fetishism

Ressentiment, 38, 128, 187

Revolution, national-democratic, 1, 22–25, 28, 55, 58, 97–119, 107, 126, 141, 161–89, 221–22

Rex, John, 193

Reyes, Isabelo de los, 97, 104

Rizal, Jose, 103–04, 109–11, 141, 189, 208–09

Rodney, Walter, 77

Rorty, Richard, 61

Rotor, Arturo, 107, 119

Rushdie, Salman, 127, 213

Rutten, Rosanne, 204

Said, Edward, 38, 65, 116, 131

Saint Louis Exposition (1904), 11, 100–101, 207

Sanjines, Jorge, 147–48

Santos, Bienvenido, 15, 91, 117

Santos, Lope K., 104

Sartre, Jean-Paul, 172, 179, 220

Sassen, Saskia, 179

Schiller, Friedrich, 147

Scott, William Henry, 207

Serrano, Isagani, 10

Simmel, George, 40

Singapore, 59–60

Sison, Jose Maria, 6, 172, 175

Smedley, Audrey, 54

Smith, General Jacob, 82, 144

Smith, Joseph, 6

Smith, Neil, 26

Socialism, 163–64, 167, 174–75, 179, 181

Solanas, Fernando, 146

Sollors, Werner, 46

Space, 25–26, 38

Spanish–American War, 1, 22, 67–68, 103–04, 124, 199

"Special relations," 5, 7, 75–76, 128. *See also* Neocolonialism

Spectacle, 101–03, 128, 158, 181, 187

Spinoza, Benedict, 220

Spivak, Gayatri, 131, 135

Stanley, Peter, 76–77, 83

Stauffer, Robert, 7, 77, 94, 180

State, 53, 61, 204–05
Steinberg, David J., 7, 74, 83, 196–98, 208
Stimpson, Catherine, 127
Stone, Robert, 123
Suleri, Sara, 135

Taft, William Howard, 4, 85, 121
Tahimik, Kidlat, 9, 13, 95, 143–62
Tajima, Renee, 60
Tarr, Peter, 72–73, 123
Tasaday, 86, 102, 207
Taylor, Charles, 210
Taylor, George, 74–75, 198
Thailand, 43, 59, 85, 92
Theology of liberation, 115, 217
Third cinema, 143–62
Tiongson, Nicanor, 109, 112
Toffler, Alvin, 8
Tokugawa, Marquis Yorisada, 209–10
Tolentino, Roland, 152–53
Transmigrants, 11, 14, 91, 54–55
Tutelage, 74, 76, 88, 110, 122
Twain, Mark, 69, 99, 166, 210

Unamuno, Miguel de, 104
United Farm Workers Union, 56
U.S. exceptionalism, 4, 46, 50, 71, 77–78,
    106, 206
Utilitarianism, 19, 91, 108

Utopianism, 23, 160

Van Erven, Eugene, 95, 98
Vera Cruz, Philip, 55, 125, 138, 218
Vidal, Gore, 67
Vietnam War, 25, 30, 32, 70, 74, 85, 137,
    140, 144–45, 169, 203, 210
Villa, Jose Garcia, 105, 108, 111
Visiting Forces Agreement (VFA), 9, 12,
    66, 99, 141, 164, 166
Volpe, Galvano della, 116

Wallerstein, Immanuel, 48–49, 77, 170
Weber, Max, 170, 201–02
West, Cornel, 168
White supremacy, 12, 15, 20, 35, 48–52, 64,
    80, 91, 101, 127, 132, 219, 221. *See also*
    Racism; Racialization process
Willeman, Paul, 145
Williams, William Appleman, 5, 80, 199
Williams, Raymond, 184
Wolf, Eric, 17
Worcester, Dean, 74, 83, 99–100, 195
World Trade Organization (WTO), 66, 206

Yamamoto, Hisaye, 22, 36
Yamanaka, Lois, 48

Zinn, Howard, 7, 80

About the Author

E. San Juan, Jr. is professor and chair of the Department of Comparative American Cultures at Washington State University at Pullman. He received his Ph.D. in English and American literature from Harvard University. He has been a Fulbright lecturer in the Philippines; a fellow at the Institute of the Humanities, University of Edinburgh; and a visiting professor at the Universita degli studi di Trento. His recent books are *Hegemony and Strategies of Transgression, Beyond Postcolonial Theory,* and *From Exile to Diaspora. Racial Formations/Critical Transformations,* an early work, won several awards. He received the 1999 Award for Achievement in Literature from the Philippines Cultural Center, Republic of the Philippines.

sanjuan@wsu.edu .